UNIVERSITY OF MICHIGAN PUBLICATIONS
HISTORY AND POLITICAL SCIENCE
VOLUME XXIII

THE

ALLIED BLOCKADE

OF

GERMANY

1914–1916

The
ALLIED BLOCKADE
of
GERMANY
1914–1916

Marion C. Siney

ANN ARBOR

THE UNIVERSITY OF MICHIGAN PRESS

112375
D581

PRINTED IN THE UNITED STATES OF AMERICA

Preface

BOTH during and since World War I students of diplomacy and international law have discussed the legality of measures taken by the Allies to interfere with and stop the trade of their enemies. Little attempt has been made, however, to consider these measures as instruments of economic warfare, although the system of coercion was ultimately a decisive factor in the downfall of the Central Powers. The long-distance blockade of Germany was not based on the legal right of blockade; instead the Allies sought by other means to secure some of the results which would have accrued from stationing a naval force off German ports to prevent the entrance and exit of all ships. Some of these effects were gained by extending the traditional belligerent rights of visit and search and capture of contraband; some measures were undertaken as a reprisal against Germany's illegal actions. But the unusual factors in the system of trade controls were developed through exercises of certain sovereign rights over persons and property within the jurisdiction of the Allied states, and through other measures taken in pursuit of pure policy for which no legal justification could be given. Included within this latter category were the negotiations with neutral states and their citizens to restrict the rights of neutrals to trade with both belligerents. These four aspects of the blockade did not all begin to function at the same time. Each had its own development and they all affected the others.

The background of this vast operation is to be traced in large part in the development of belligerent practice and maritime law during the nineteenth and early twentieth centuries. This is obviously a very large subject and only those parts of it which are essential to an understanding of policies and practices of World War I will be surveyed in Chapter I. The major part of the study will be devoted to a consideration of the negotiations carried on by the Allies, principally the British, with the Netherlands, Denmark, Norway, and Sweden. A study of Allied relations with Switzerland, which was the meeting ground of the German and Allied systems of economic warfare, would involve many sources which have not been consulted, and this side of the blockade has, therefore, been omitted. The policy of the United States has been treated only insofar as it affected Allied policy; agreements made by American industries with the British have beeen included, since they had important repercussions on Dutch and Scandinavian trade. No particular attempt has been made to estimate the effects of the blockade on the Central Powers, although this in no way minimizes the importance of the Allied blockade on Germany's ultimate defeat. To include such an estimate would involve a complete consideration of German wartime economy, which is beyond the limits of this study. I have ended this volume with the year 1916 in the hope that I shall soon complete another on the period 1917–1919. So far as blockade policies were concerned, no innovations were made by the British before America's intervention, and since this event was so closely related to the German submarine campaign it seemed wise to omit the developments of the first months of 1917 from this volume.

In treating this whole period of World War I, one must be content with scattered and, often, fragmentary materials, since government archives are not yet generally open. During the war the British government published in the Parliamentary Papers important correspondence with the United States and Sweden. Although after the war the United States State Department published supplements to Papers Relating to the Foreign Relations of the United States for this period, which contain a great deal of valuable information, the British government made no similar revelation. During World War II, however, the Germans did in some, thus-far unexplained manner lay hands on a secret and confidential history of the blockade that was prepared by Commander Archibald C. Bell in the Historical Section of the Committee of Imperial Defence. The essential portions of the early part of this volume, down to the end of 1915, were published in 1943 under the editorship of Dr. Viktor Böhmert under the title Die englische Hungerblockade im Weltkrieg, 1914–1915.

An independent source of information is in the collection of papers of the French Comité de Restriction des Approvisionnements et du Commerce de l'Ennemi given at the end of the war by members of the Comité to the Bibliothèque et Musée de la Guerre de Vincennes, Paris. These documents are in mimeographed form just as they were circulated to members of the Comité for their official use; some of the papers have penciled annotations. Included in the collection are many British committee reports, opinions, and agreements, which were evidently communicated to the French government for its information. The Library of Congress, Washington, D.C., possesses a file of the weekly Bulletin published by this Comité.

From neutral sources much valuable information, not readily available to English and American readers, is in the official history of the Netherlands Oversea Trust written by Dr. Charlotte A. van Manen, as well as in monographs on the economic life of the Scandinavian countries during World War I. One of the purposes of this study is to integrate as much as possible these materials that show the neutrals' point of view with those coming from Allied sources.

There have been some rather general studies of the blockade, but none has attempted any detailed consideration of all the negotiations with the northern European neutrals. The best of these was written by Lieutenant Louis Guichard, who was attached to the Historical Section of the French Ministry of Marine. It appeared in English as *The Naval Blockade, 1914–1918*, and contains little that cannot be obtained in more detail from other sources. Maurice Parmelee, who was a member of the American delegation to the Allied Blockade Committee and chairman of the Allied Rationing and Statistical Committee, has written *Blockade and Sea Power, the Blockade, 1914–1919 and Its Significance for a World State*, in which the emphasis is placed on the last two years of the war. A third book has been published by Rear Admiral Montagu W. W. P. Consett, who was British commercial attaché in Stockholm during the war. In it, *The Triumph of Unarmed Forces, 1914–1918*, Consett gives particular attention to the excessive exportations from the United Kingdom to the border neutrals, and to the leakages in the system of guarantees required from neutral importers. I feel justified in presenting my study to give a much broader and more precise account of the whole blockade.

I wish to make grateful acknowledgment for the monetary aid I have received at various times in order to make this study: from the Social Science Research Council, from the Horace H. Rackham School of Graduate Studies, University of Michigan, and to Western Reserve University for a sabbatical leave. The librarians who aided in the search for material are too numerous to mention individually even if many of them had not remained nameless, but particular thanks ought to be given to the staffs at the Bibliothèque de la Guerre de Vincennes, the Peace Palace Library (The Hague), the Royal Libraries in Copenhagen, Stockholm, and Oslo, the British Museum, the Library of Congress, and the Hoover Library, Stanford University. The number of people who put me on the track of pertinent materials or tried to provide specific answers to my questions is great—officials and ex-officials of wartime governments, heads of neutral trade associations, and historians working on related subjects. The task of reading and criticizing the first version of this work, presented as a doctoral dissertation at the University of Michigan, was done by Howard M. Ehrmann; in its greatly expanded revision this was the role of Arvel B. Erickson, Western Reserve University— to both of them my deep appreciation. They cannot be held responsible for the defects, which would otherwise have been far greater.

Contents

Chapter

I. Belligerent Rights at Sea and Economic Warfare, 1856–1914   **1**

II. Early Allied Measures to Intercept Enemy Trade, August to December 1914   17

III. British Negotiations with the Northern European Neutrals in 1914   33

IV. The Reprisals Order in Council, March 11, 1915   61

V. Rationing Agreements, 1915   75

VI. Negotiations with Sweden and Norway for General Agreements in 1915   109

VII. The State of the Blockade at the End of 1915   123

VIII. Forcible Rationing, Navicerting, Black-Listing, and Interception of Neutral Mails   135

IX. British Controls over Goods Produced in the Empire, 1915–1916   157

X. Allied Co-operation in the Economic War: The Paris Economic Conference, June 1916, and the Abrogation of the Declaration of London   173

XI. Allied Purchasing Agreements   187

XII. Miscellaneous Negotiations with the Northern Neutrals in 1916   213

XIII. Accomplishments and Effects of the Blockade at the End
of 1916   245

Appendixes   259

Bibliography   277

Notes   289

Index   333

I

Belligerent Rights at Sea
and Economic Warfare, 1856–1914

AS A preliminary to consideration of the measures taken by the Allies to control trade with the enemy after the outbreak of war in 1914, it is proposed to show briefly the development of the law of maritime warfare since 1856—in particular, the limitations on the belligerent right to capture private property on the high seas and to blockade enemy ports, the dissatisfactions that arose with the law or its interpretations, and the attempts either to make new law or to codify that already in force.

Since it was chiefly the action of the British government that aroused neutral protests once war came, it is significant to see to what extent the plans for economic warfare had been laid by the Admiralty and Foreign Office in the prewar period. One cannot help but be struck by the great concern of the British government to maintain a broad interpretation of the right of blockade—a right which it never exercised in Europe in World War I, although it was willing to consider limitations on the right to capture contraband goods—a right which was widely extended by the end of 1914 and which

1

became one of the chief means of controlling enemy trade. Indeed, it was not until just a few years before the war that the British paid serious attention to the effect that new weapons, such as torpedoes, mines, and submarines, would have on the maintenance of a close blockade, after which new naval plans were made more in accord with the new conditions. It is only when one realizes the lack of foresight in planning for a realistic program of economic warfare that one can see why the Allied long-distance blockade of Germany developed so slowly. Yet, since neutrals continued to base their arguments on the international law that existed before the war began, it is particularly important to consider how far the codification of that law had proceeded.

THE CRIMEAN WAR AND THE DECLARATION OF PARIS

The practice of states has long recognized the right of belligerents to interfere with the commerce of their enemies by capturing both ships belonging to the enemy and goods on neutral ships destined to the enemy. A large number of treaties, most of them bilateral, had recognized that goods of a special military character, destined for the enemy, and known as contraband of war, were liable to capture regardless of the nationality of their owner. Likewise, the right of a belligerent to blockade the enemy's ports with a naval force and thus prevent the ingress and egress of ships of all nations had been well established. Since neutral states asserted their right to trade freely with both belligerents, however, the tendency was to restrict both of these rights.

At the end of the Napoleonic Wars the law on these points was still in a state of uncertainty, for the principles of the Armed Neutrality had not received general recognition, nor had belligerent practices regarding fictitious blockade and reprisals been regarded as representing the true Law of Nations. The first great war after 1815 that seriously involved maritime powers was the Crimean, and in it the Anglo-French allies were faced with the practical necessity of co-ordinating their naval operations against enemy commerce.[1] It had been the practice of British warships to intercept enemy cargoes on neutral ships; the French fleet did not trouble such cargoes. On the other hand, the French seized neutral goods on enemy ships, but the British returned such goods to their owners. Thus, with the British the nationality of the owner of the goods was decisive; with the French it was the flag which the vessel flew. Neutrals would quite rightfully have resented these variations in the law applied by the two allies, and Britain and France were quick to foresee this even before the declaration of war on Russia.

After several exchanges of views the British government, on March 28, 1854, and the French government, on March 29, issued identic declarations to neutrals as a result of which, without deciding the matter of law and only for the duration of the war, the British waived the right they had long exercised to seize enemy goods wherever found, agreeing to free enemy goods carried on neutral ships; and the French agreed not to seize neutral goods found on enemy vessels. As the war progressed, the attitude of the United States showed the British that what they had regarded as a temporary concession might well become a permanent one. The United States had already concluded several treaties that recognized the principle "free ships, free goods" and others that provided for "free ships, free goods and enemy ships, enemy goods." It was therefore quite in keeping with this policy that William Learned Marcy, the American secretary of state, should propose on April 28, 1854, that the rule of free ships, free goods, with the exception of contraband of war, be recognized by Great Britain and all powers unconditionally and for the future; and that all other powers (for Great Britain already recognized this rule) adopt the principle that noncontraband neutral goods on enemy ships be immune from capture. The proposal was accepted by the Russians, and a treaty was signed with the United States to this effect. The King of Prussia insisted that, in addition, privateering should be abolished; this, the United States was unwilling to accept.

As H. W. Malkin points out, Marcy's proposal was enough to indicate that the United States aimed to secure the suppression of the right to capture enemy goods under a neutral flag, while at the same time maintaining the right to issue letters of marque and to commission privateers—both antithetic to Britain's usual desires. It seemed so likely that the United States would continue to agitate the question after the war that Lord Clarendon, the foreign secretary, suggested to Prime Minister Palmerston on April 6, 1856, that Great Britain should make "a merit of necessity" and voluntarily proclaim the concession made in wartime as a permanent one, coupling it with the abolition of privateering. A draft resolution contained in this letter received the approval of the British cabinet.[2]

On April 8, 1856, toward the end of the peace conference meeting in Paris, Count Alexandre Walewski, president of the Congress, formally suggested that a declaration be made to provide a uniform maritime law in time of war insofar as neutrals were concerned. Walewski then proposed four principles, the acceptance of which he believed would attain this end: (1) privateering should be abolished, (2) the neutral flag covers enemy goods except contraband of war, (3) neutral goods, except contraband of war, are not subject to seizure even under an enemy flag, and (4) blockades are binding only so long as they are effective. In the discussion that followed the abolition of paper blockades does not seem to have been the subject of controversy, and marginal notes on the original draft of the declaration show that it was regarded merely as stating a generally accepted rule. Since the other principles had already been accepted by the allied states, Walewski's proposal, with some changes in wording, became the Declaration of Paris, a document which was immediately signed by the representatives of Russia, France, Great Britain, Prussia, Austria, Sardinia, and Turkey.[3]

The United States, however, believed that the sacrifice of privateering was too dear a price to pay for the recognition of the other principles of the Declaration and, therefore, refused to accede to it. In so doing, the United States believed it was espousing the cause of all nations not likely to be great naval powers which would only be able, when they became belligerents, to maintain their supplies by recourse to privateering. The United States soon went one step further and proposed to the British on February 24, 1857, that an addition be made to the Declaration of Paris that would exempt all non-contraband private property, even that of the enemy, from capture. The British were unwilling to go this far and negotiation on the subject was dropped in April 1857.

It should be noted that the Declaration was binding only on signatory states, but it had made permanent the temporary expedient adopted by two of the Great Powers during the Crimean War. Certainly it was a boon to neutrals whose goods, except contraband, could be carried safely on the ships of all nations and whose ships could now engage freely in noncontraband trade with both belligerents.

The American Civil War was the first occasion after the signature of the Declaration of Paris on which a blockade was declared, and questions immediately arose over what constituted proper notification of a blockade, when it actually began and ended, whether the temporary absence of the blockading fleet was sufficient to end it, and whether a cruising squadron was capable of maintaining an effective blockade. The fact that the United States was not a signatory to the Declaration of Paris did not affect the claims of neutrals under what they maintained was existing international law. The decisions of American prize courts aroused the distrust of neutral England, where many firms were notorious participants in a well-organized trade in contraband carried on with the Confederacy through intermediate ports in the Bahamas. These interests were particularly affected by the decision in the Springbok case in which the doctrine of continuous voyage, hitherto developed in the eighteenth century to cover the capture of goods ultimately destined to the enemy but consigned to a colonial port in neutral hands, was now extended to blockade. Here the ship with a cargo ultimately destined for a Confederate port was seized on the first stage of its journey from London to Nassau. Its cargo was condemned on the ground that the voyage was part of a longer one to a blockaded port, and therefore the goods were liable to confiscation at any time along the way. Up to this point British opposition to the Declaration of Paris had been on the ground that it limited Britain's rights as a belligerent, but now interest centered on the maintenance of Britain's rights as a neutral.[4]

The wars of the last half of the nineteenth century offered no occasion for a further definition of the law of blockade or of the law regulating trade with belligerents, for in 1866 the three states involved in the Austro-Prussian War decided not to interfere with commerce on the high seas in any way; and in the Franco-Prussian War of 1870–1871 the sole argument in this legal field arose from the Prussian demand that Great Britain should prevent the exportation of contraband, in particular coal, to France. This, Earl Granville, the foreign secretary, refused to do on the ground that the contraband nature of coal would depend solely on its destination to the enemy government, a question which could only be decided by a prize court.[5]

The chief opponent of the Declaration of Paris in the early twentieth century was Thomas Gibson Bowles, who carried on a literary campaign for regaining England's lost rights at sea; the most complete statement of his views appeared in his book on the Declaration of Paris published in 1900.[6] He was mainly concerned with Britain's rights as a belligerent. He believed that the security given to neutral ships to carry noncontraband goods unhindered arose from no *right* at all, and that any inconveniences caused to neutrals by a state of war were sanctioned "by universal consent and practice as well as by justice and reason." Moreover, he argued that a neutral, in carrying enemy property on its ships, was committing a flagrant violation of its own neutrality. He went on to assert that the right of blockade was made illusory by the Declaration when the enemy "is able to carry on his commerce and receive his supplies through the most adjacent neutral ports under the protection of the neutral flag." Strangely enough, Bowles did not consider the possibility of applying the doctrine of continuous voyage in such an instance.

Altogether, the complaint of the critics of the Declaration of Paris was not that it failed to define blockade carefully enough but that it defined too well and limited too much the right of capture. Concern was felt not only for this diminution of the right to prevent the supplying of goods to the enemy but also for the possibility that the British carrying trade would be taken over by rival neutral vessels. It is clear that commercial considerations ranked foremost here.

THE SECOND HAGUE CONFERENCE

The Russo-Japanese War, however, served to confirm the British government's belief that its true interests lay in maintaining neutral rights rather than in seeking to broaden its rights as a possible belligerent. A report made by Sir George Sydenham Clarke to the Committee of Imperial Defence in December 1904 indicated that it would be impossible in the existing state of international law for Great Britain as a belligerent to control neutral trade with its enemies.[7] Clarke, therefore, recommended that contraband should be defined as narrowly as possible so that Britain could derive every advantage from its neutrality during the wars of other states.

This question was given more careful consideration by a committee of experts for the Foreign Office when preparations were being made for the Second Hague Peace Conference where, it was assumed, the law of maritime warfare would be discussed.[8] The Admiralty had already given assurances that in a war with Germany, which was then regarded as the most likely one, German commerce could be driven from the high seas and the German fleet would be prevented from seriously interfering with British cargoes. The committee believed that it would be extremely difficult to apply the doctrine of continuous voyage to Germany's supplies from overseas and that, in any case, Germany would be able to secure large amounts of goods in European neutral markets. It, therefore, recommended that the right to capture contraband should be waived entirely, for Britain would thereby give up a dubious weapon and receive in return added assurances of the safety of its own overseas imports. Failing this waiver, Britain should secure a very rigid and restrictive definition of contraband, and also should cling tenaciously to the right of blockade, by whose exercise the British could, with superior sea power, attain all of their aims by preventing the direct supply of the enemy. Instructions in this sense were issued to the British delegation to the Hague Conference.[9]

When the conference began its sessions on June 15, 1907, problems involved in the law respecting contraband, blockade, and private property at sea were assigned to the Fourth Commission whose president was Martens, one of the Russian delegates. When the subject of contraband was first discussed, in the eighth meeting of this commission on July 24, Lord Reay, a British delegate, proposed the abolition of the right to capture contraband on the ground that only thus could neutral rights be adequately protected and the Declaration of Paris made more than an empty word.[10] Nowhere, however, did the British present a definition of the term contraband, a fact which makes their exact intention hard to determine. Ordinary definitions of contraband set up two criteria: the goods must be of a military character, and they must in fact have a military, or at least a governmental, destination. With this in mind, it might be said that the British aimed to remove the exceptions from the general rule of "free ships, free goods" and to make all neutral goods on enemy vessels free regardless of their military character. But that still leaves this question: What would be the fate of enemy-owned contraband goods found on enemy ships? In the law existing under the Declaration of Paris there was no need to define the effect of ownership of the vessel on goods adjudged to be contraband, for all such goods were subject to capture on both neutral and enemy vessels. That the British intended to free from capture military goods that were enemy-owned and carried on enemy ships is very doubtful. By 1908, on the eve of the London Naval Conference, the British government had arrived at the following definition which would exclude any such wide concession: "The term 'contraband' is applied to neutral property on board ship on the high seas or in the territorial waters of either belligerent which (1) is by nature capable of being used to assist in and (2) is on its way to assist in, the naval or military operations of the enemy."[11] But if, as it seems here, the term contraband was limited to *neutral* property, what then is the meaning of the second paragraph of the Declaration of Paris—"the neutral flag covers enemy goods except contraband of war"? To make the problem more confusing, the British opposed the suggestion put forward once more by the American delegation at the Hague Conference that the right to capture enemy merchant ships and their cargoes, except contraband of war, be abolished.[12] This, in itself, adds weight to the theory that the British intended only to give up the right to capture neutral-owned contraband; for otherwise they would be in the peculiar position of clinging to the right to capture enemy-owned noncontraband on enemy ships while letting contraband goods, under the same circumstances, go free. Lord Reay insisted, however, that he saw no connection "between the right to seize property and the seizure of articles of contraband, which are neutral property." Ruy Barbosa, Brazilian delegate, was the only one who challenged the compatibility of these two British views.[13]

All this shows that the British intentions were not understood by the other delegates at the Conference; one can even doubt that the British government had worked out the whole results of its own project! In any case, both the British and American proposals were voted down.[14] It was the French draft, introduced by Louis Renault, that was the subject of later discussions and which in a modified form was written into the Declaration of London in 1909. Renault proposed the establishment of three categories of goods: absolute contraband, conditional contraband (goods that were not per se military in character but which could be put to military uses, such as foodstuffs), and a third group of military goods which neutrals would automatically be forbidden to trade in during any war. The third list did not meet with favor; but the list of absolute contraband was discussed point by point and adopted with but few changes on August 15, this in spite of an objection by Rear Admiral Charles S. Sperry of the United States that it was impossible to formulate a list of contraband that would prove satisfactory over a long period of years. No agreement on conditional contraband was reached, nor was any attempt made to define the application of the doctrine of continuous voyage to such goods.[15]

In view of the British offer to abolish the right to capture contraband, it is interesting to note that when a discussion of blockade was taken up, the British made no special effort to maintain all their rights unimpaired. It is true that this proposal on contraband had already been rejected by the time blockade was under consideration. The speeches of the various delegates, their point of departure being an Italian draft proposal, showed such wide divergences between the Anglo-American and Continental interpretations of the law that Sir Ernest Satow found no opposition when he proposed that the whole discussion be suspended.[16] Thus, the British, as well as every other delegation, reserved its freedom to interpret the law of blockade, subject only to the principle laid down in the Declaration of Paris.

Probably the most important convention on maritime law made at the Hague Conference was that establishing an International Prize Court, which would be a court of appeal from national prize courts. Both the German and British delegations submitted projects to this effect; but they differed markedly on several fundamental points: the number of judges, whether the court should be a permanent one or merely constituted for each war, whether states alone or individuals and states might be parties before the court, and whether the court's jurisdiction applied only between belligerent and neutral or also between belligerent and belligerent.[17] A compromise was worked out and adopted on October 18, 1907, as the Twelfth Hague Convention.[18] It provided for a court of fifteen judges, eight to be designated by the Great Powers and seven by the smaller states. The court was to have jurisdiction over cases brought by (1) a neutral state, (2) a citizen of a neutral state if his government had no objection, and (3) a citizen of a belligerent state if his property rights in a cargo on a neutral ship had been adversely affected by a decision of a national prize court, or if he claimed that the seizure of his goods violated a convention in force between the belligerents or an enactment of the belligerent captor. The court was to apply treaties in force between the belligerent captor and the claimant state and, in their absence, the rules of international law. When no generally recognized rule applied, the court was to give judgment "in accordance with the general principles of justice and equity."

It seemed at the time that the Prize Court Convention would be the means of removing prize-court proceedings from the uncertainties of interpretation by belligerents who acted both as party and judge in the same dispute. However, the failure to define in more detail the law that this court was to apply marred the whole venture, a condition which the Great Powers soon tried to remedy in the Declaration of London.

THE DECLARATION OF LONDON

The divergence of views on the interpretation of maritime law was the reason Sir Edward Grey gave for calling a conference of naval powers to formulate the rules which the International Prize Court was to apply. He maintained that it would be difficult, if not impossible, for His Majesty's Government to carry through Parliament the legislation necessary to give effect to the convention unless some such definition was made. Invitations were extended on February 26, 1908, to the governments of Austria-Hungary, France, Germany, Italy, Japan, Russia, Spain, the United States, and later, to the Netherlands.[19] Each was asked to circulate to the others before the conference met a memorandum setting forth what it regarded as the correct rule of law on each of the points included on the agenda for the conference.[20]

This conference, which assembled in London on December 4, 1908, was much more restricted in its terms of reference than the Second Hague Conference had been; for although the delegations in 1907 had been given powers to bring about sweeping changes in the law of war and neutrality, the London Conference was limited to codifying existing rules. Of necessity, the document which resulted from this conference, the Declaration of London, was based on compromise.[21] For that reason, it could never have been wholly satisfactory to certain British circles that were convinced that Great Britain must maintain her rights at sea unimpaired.

For the most part, the Declaration regulated questions that might arise between belligerents and neutrals, and, in general, did not deal with belligerent action *inter se*. The statement of the law of blockade gave satisfaction to the British point of view except that capture was possible only in the blockaded area unless the ship had been actively pursued from the line of blockade. However, it was questionable, even at the time, whether the law of contraband, as stated in the Declaration, was favorable to British interests. Again, as in the Renault draft of 1907, lists of both absolute and conditional contraband were drawn up, and belligerents were given the right to add to them upon proper notification except in the instance of articles included on a free list which was now drafted. The list of absolute contraband almost reproduced that agreed upon at The Hague in 1907 and was generally acceptable. The conditional contraband list included foodstuffs, forage, military clothing, railway materials, and the like, whose contraband character depended on their having a military destination. Whether such a destination could be presumed would depend on the military and economic system of the belligerent state at a particular time, and it was for this reason that a rather vague definition of military destination was given. Article 34 of the Declaration laid down such a presumption when goods were consigned to enemy authorities or to a contractor established in the enemy country who, as a matter of common knowledge, supplied articles of that kind to the enemy government. Another such presumption was deduced from consignment to a fortified place belonging to the enemy or "other place serving as a base for the armed forces of the enemy." As a concession to neutrals, the doctrine of continuous voyage was excluded from application to conditional contraband. On the "free list" were articles which could never be declared contraband: raw cotton, wool, silk, jute, flax and hemp, oilseeds, rubber, raw hides, fertilizers, metallic ores, and so forth, many of which were of prime importance in manufacturing implements of war and in maintaining the civilian population. This provision obviously was a further guarantee of the freedom of neutral commerce from the hazards of war.

Most of the other provisions of the Declaration, although important in the general regulation of maritime warfare, have no immediate relevance to the question at hand, although in arriving at many of the regulations the old cleavage between those who had many overseas ports and those who had few or none was evident. In this respect, the Declaration further pushed aside the settled convictions of Great Britain when it recognized the right of a captor to sink neutral prizes should their nondestruction involve danger to the warship or to the success of the operations in which it was engaged; here was a question that would be raised anew with the use of the submarine.

All of the powers represented at the London Conference signed the Declaration and then apparently awaited its ratification by Great Britain. It became clear that there was great opposition to the Declaration in many British quarters and that there would be a real struggle before the legislation necessary to revise British naval prize law, and thus to implement the Declaration, would be passed by Parliament. Criticisms both good and bad, fair and unfair, were made against the Declaration, and it is sometimes difficult to know which were valid and which were not. With the experiences of World War I in mind, one may do injustice to some of the advocates, who could not have foreseen the scale and character of operations in a great modern war.

The greatest agitator against the Declaration, in terms of energy expended, was Thomas Gibson Bowles, who continued his crusade, begun first against the Declaration of Paris, for maintenance of all belligerent maritime rights against any neutral encroachments. Bowles saw in the Declaration a conspiracy among Continental military powers to reduce England's maritime strength; he accused Sir Edward Grey, the foreign secretary, of surrendering to these states without a struggle. Bowles objected to the blockade provisions which he thought made outward blockade-breaking easier, but in particular he found fault with the too restrictive definition of contraband and with the free list. These arguments, included in an article in the *Nineteenth Century* for May 1909, attracted official attention and Eyre A. Crowe answered them point by point in a minute written for the Foreign Office.[22]

The best indications of official opinion toward the Declaration are contained in the parliamentary debates on the Naval Prize Bill in 1911. This bill was intended to consolidate prize practice in order to allow for the establishment of the International Prize Court and, as a corollary, the ratification of the Declaration of London, which the Court was to apply. In the debate in the House of Commons, begun on June 28 and 29 and continued on July 3 and December 7, 1911, Thomas McKinnon Wood, undersecretary of state for foreign affairs, spoke first for the government.[23] The subject of chief concern seems to have been the safety of the British food imports in time of war; it was feared that since Article 34 of the Declaration failed to define a military base, almost any commercial port in the United Kingdom might be declared by the enemy to be a base of military supply. In that case all food imported by England would be treated as absolute contraband. However, McKinnon Wood showed that in time of peace British ships carried 90 per cent of this imported food, and regardless of whether food was conditional contraband or not, these cargoes would be subject to capture as enemy property on enemy ships. It was admitted that the Continental states were in a better position, since they could secure their foods through neutral territory without fear that the doctrine of continuous voyage, making them subject to capture on the first leg of their overseas journey, would be applied to them. But this immunity resulted from geographical factors which the Declaration could not equalize. The government maintained that the main point was that when Britain was a belligerent the Navy should keep the trade routes open for shipping to the United Kingdom, so that all ships, British and neutral alike, would enjoy the same safety. Arthur James Balfour, an opponent of the Declaration, admitted all this; but he insisted that in case of such a preponderant superiority of the British fleet, neither this Declaration nor any other would be likely to injure Great Britain when it was at war; he refused to admit the strength of the fleet as an argument for the Declaration of London. The government speakers had claimed great credit for securing the free list, but Balfour said that these articles had, for the most part, never been treated as absolute, or even as conditional contraband. With the advantage of hindsight, we must admit that neutrals at least had been given something of value when these important raw materials were put outside the contraband categories.

Grey, speaking with the question in mind of Britain's ability to carry on war against its adversaries, indicated that he thought all this argument over contraband rather beside the point, "because," he said, "we shall never bring a Continental enemy to his knees by dealing with contraband alone." He pointed with satisfaction to the regulations concerning blockade, a right which he placed second in importance to sinking the enemy's fleet.

Leslie Scott was one of the few members of Parliament who foresaw that under modern conditions of warfare blockade did not count for much. He cited the inventions of torpedoes and submarines as examples of new conditions that made the possibility of a close blockade of enemy ports very slight; just as important was the development of railway communications permitting the shipment across neutral territory of goods that had formerly come directly by sea. No one in the Commons took the trouble to challenge Scott's statements; in fact, Sir Rufus Isaacs, the attorney general, who followed Scott in the debate, said, "If there was ever any necessity of dealing with blockade, it was disposed of by the opening speech [of McKinnon Wood] . . . and, if there was anything left to be said, it would have been said long ago. . . ." Late in the debate on the second reading, July 3, Bonar Law restated with approval the argument set forth by Scott, and added, "I am strongly of the opinion that the reason why the Right Hon. Gentleman [Sir Edward Grey] so nearly got his way in regard to the matter is that those with whom he was dealing held it to be of little or no value."

The House of Commons accepted the Naval Prize Bill, but it was defeated in the House of Lords, where little was added in the way of argument.

Despite the failure of the bill, and the general supposition of the country that naval experts distrusted the Declaration of London, the Declaration was published as part of the *Prize Manual* in circulation at the outbreak of the war in 1914.

A more reasoned attack on the Declaration of London was made in a memorandum submitted to the Committee of Imperial Defence by Captain Maurice P. A. Hankey, its naval assistant secretary.[24] The memorandum foresaw so many of the conditions that came to exist in 1914 that it is important to consider it in some detail. Hankey based his argument on the assumption that in a war with Germany the British fleet would defeat the German fleet and then blockade the German coast. He foresaw that this operation would be of a new sort and would greatly increase the importance of economic warfare. He believed that the Declaration of London had hedged in blockade so much that it was an inefficient and easily evaded instrument. He then went on to consider what substitutes might be used for a close blockade of the German Baltic coast, provided Great Britain was not bound by the Declaration of London. He suggested that a blockade of the German coasts be declared and then be made effective at the entrance to the Baltic off the Skaw. Here the British warships would detain all merchantmen entering the Skagerrak. All those bound for German ports would be sent back, and those with cargoes for Copenhagen or Riga would be warned that if they did go to a German port they would be violating the blockade. Here, then, was the idea of the "long-distance blockade." Hankey foresaw the establishment of agents in the principal neutral ports to check on the fulfillment of promises given to the British fleet. The excellence of wireless and cable communications would make such a course quite easy, even though no precedents for it could be cited.

The next charge that Hankey brought against the Declaration was that it restricted too severely the articles which might be declared contraband, for those included on the conditional contraband and free lists comprised nearly the whole of Germany's seaborne trade. This trade could continue unhampered into German ports in neutral ships unless a blockade had been declared. Hankey's scheme for reducing Germany by economic means in the absence of the Declaration is worth quoting:

> In that case our obvious course, to be adopted as soon as the naval situation permitted, would be to declare a blockade of the North Sea ports, and simultaneously to make a sweeping declaration of what was contraband, including all the principal raw materials on which German manufacturers depend as well as her main articles of export. Neutral vessels would be rigorously held up and examined outside the Cattegat; the doctrine of continuous voyage would be rigorously applied; a system of agents in Swedish, Danish, and Russian ports would apprise us as to how trans-shipment was taking place and measures would be taken to deal with offenders . . . .

It is clear that there were great differences between the views expressed in the parliamentary debates and those in Hankey's memorandum. With one or two exceptions, members of Parliament understood very imperfectly the role that an ordinary blockade could play in modern war; other opponents of the Declaration, such as Bowles and some of the chambers of commerce, based their opinion on a simple dislike of any convention which regulated British sea power.[25] Hankey, however, foresaw the necessity of using a long-distance blockade that would inevitably affect neutral as well as enemy commerce; he also realized that no naval power could afford to limit itself to the capture of only a restricted list of absolute contraband. Unfortunately for the prestige of the British government, the men who negotiated the Declaration did not have such clear vision. It would have been better to fail at reaching an agreement than to try to maintain one that did not fit conditions of modern warfare.

BRITISH PREWAR NAVAL PLANS AND ECONOMIC WARFARE

Documents now available give only a very imperfect notion of the plans that the British Admiralty had made for dealing with a Continental enemy, and even less is known of the degree to which warfare against commerce was foreseen as one of the major operations of the fleet. What is certain is that consideration of this possibility came rather belatedly.[26]

The orders to the British fleet issued in 1905 directed the naval forces to be ready for (1) war with Germany, (2) war with France, and (3) war with both. No orders for particular operations were given, and there was no suggestion of economic coercion of the enemy. In 1906 the Admiralty informed the Committee of Imperial Defence that it intended to blockade the German coast if it could, but the Admiralty did not propose to do so as soon as war began.

July 1908 saw the completion of new naval plans which made the Admiralty and not the commander in chief responsible for the strategic conduct of the war and the distribution of the fleet. Provision was now made only for a war against Germany and therefore the preponderant force of the Navy was to be detailed to the North Sea and the Channel, with the fleet having specific orders to stop all enemy trade in the North Sea. It was also part of the plan of Sir Arthur Wilson, first sea lord, to take Helgoland to use as a base for the blockade flotillas.[27] This was the first time before the war that an economic objective was inserted in British naval plans, but even here it was a purely auxiliary operation, intended to bring out the enemy fleet to protect its commerce.

In May 1908 the first of several inquiries was made into Germany's dependence on overseas commerce in food and raw materials and the transportation facilities of the state for conveying these supplies, especially when they came through neutral ports. This inquiry was made through British consular officers upon the suggestion of Admiral Sir Edmond Slade. The replies from Sir William Ward, consul general at Hamburg; Sir Cecil Hertslet, consul general at Antwerp; W. A. Churchill, consul at Amsterdam; and Sir Francis Oppenheimer, consul general at Frankfurt-am-Main were received nearly a year later. In Ward's opinion, a blockade of German North Sea ports would only cause temporary shortages, for new channels for the importation of supplies would be developed. Antwerp and Rotterdam, he believed, would be temporarily choked by these extraordinary shipments. These opinions were confirmed by Churchill and Hertslet, and Oppenheimer added that he believed a blockade of Germany would be of little account unless neutrals were included in it. These reports were considered by Admiral Sir Alexander Bethell and Sir Graham Greene, both of whom were members of the Committee on Military Needs of the Empire. Sir Graham did not dispute the findings of the consuls, but Bethell thought that the case was made out too favorably toward Germany. He believed the dislocations of German commerce would be too great to be so easily overcome.

In November 1908, shortly before the London Naval Conference opened, the Committee of Imperial Defence ordered that an inquiry be made by the Admiralty to estimate the consequences of a purely naval war between Great Britain and Germany. The report indicated that the Admiralty placed great faith in the blockade of German North Sea ports, especially if the British government used its control of the marine insurance market to dissuade commerce from its regular routes. The Admiralty estimated that the blockade would be formidable in its secondary consequences, i.e., in weakening the resistance of the civilian population and ultimately that of the military forces, but nowhere did the Admiralty say that it would be decisive.

When new war plans were issued in August 1910, the blockade of the German coast was not included. However, the economic objectives were enlarged; the fleet commanders in the Orkneys and in the Channel were ordered to take whatever measures they thought necessary to protect British commerce and to destroy that of the enemy. Enemy traffic was to be watched by forces in the Dover Straits and by a cruiser squadron in the Atlantic. Reconnaissance forces off Germany were strengthened, but were given no specific orders to deal with enemy trade.

The Agadir crisis and the possibility that Great Britain might become involved in a Continental war brought the military and naval authorities together to consider plans for aiding France. On August 23, 1911, Herbert H. Asquith, the prime minister, convened a secret meeting of the Committee of Imperial Defence at which the principal officers of the Army and Navy outlined the strategy they believed should be adopted.[28] On many points the two departments most concerned were in complete discord. Sir Arthur Wilson, spokesman for the Admiralty, believed that Great Britain should confine its activities to the sea and maintain the threat of landing armed forces on German coasts. This, in his opinion, was preferable to the War Office plan for sending a British army to aid the French. However, the generals combated this idea and were supported by most of those present. Winston Churchill represents this serious conflict on such fundamental issues as the reason for his becoming first lord of the Admiralty in October, 1911, and in a letter to Grey on August 30 he indicated that he doubted the wisdom of the close blockade which the Admiralty evidently hoped to establish.

With Churchill's appointment was revived a scheme for the creation of a Naval War Staff to make a scientific study of, and detailed plans for, naval warfare. Sir Arthur Wilson had been opposed to this, but, with the aid of pressure exerted by Viscount Haldane, the secretary for war, a new Board of Admiralty was appointed by Churchill. It took over its duties on December 5, and in January 1912 established the Naval War Staff.[29] By May of that year, a first draft of new orders to the fleet was prepared; although many of its details were subsequently changed, the plans in principle were those that operated in August 1914. Under these orders, no watch was to be kept on the German Bight, and no coastal operations were to be undertaken until the German fleet had been fought and defeated. The old plan for a close blockade of German coasts was abandoned; instead, the fleet was ordered to close the exits from the North Sea into the Atlantic, the Grand Fleet being placed at Scapa Flow. All merchandise transported under the enemy flag was to be confiscated. Churchill describes this change in plan as a temporary abandonment of the fundamental principle of aggressive naval strategy in the face of unsolved practical difficulties: the lack of sufficient ships and the lack of North Sea bases.

Simultaneously, the Foreign Office, still uninformed of the impending change in naval plans, was inquiring about the possibility of exerting pressure on enemy trade. In a memorandum dated February 16, 1912, written by Cecil Hurst on the attitude to be adopted by Great Britain toward Belgium in the event that Germany violated Belgian neutrality during an Anglo-German war, the question of using economic weapons was discussed.[30] Hurst believed that if Belgium remained neutral there was little possibility that Great Britain could interfere directly with German trade passing through Antwerp, although such trade would be seriously handicapped by the lack of available shipping and the congestion of business. However, British military men regarded the violation of Belgian neutrality as a virtual certainty; and the question was whether, if Belgium was a cobelligerent with Great Britain, operations should then be undertaken against the Belgian coast. Hurst believed that any such action would hamper Belgian trade more than it would German trade, and that any attempt along this line would be useless unless Belgian "trading with the enemy" legislation was made comparable to that of the British. If, on the other hand, Belgium became an enemy,

Hurst believed the Schelde might be blockaded, although this might drive the Netherlands into belligerency, with very serious consequences for British trade.

Sir Eyre Crowe wrote a long minute concerning Hurst's memorandum on March 10, 1912, in which he agreed that from a purely strategical point of view there might be some justification for blockading at the outset of a war not only the Belgian but also the Dutch coasts.[31] Crowe believed that Britain would then take measures to hinder German trade passing through Belgium and would avoid treating Belgium as an enemy. The possibility that Germany might invade the Netherlands thus giving Britain an excuse for blockading the Dutch coast, he believed to be much less. Without such an excuse, any British action would bring down great odium on its head and the Dutch would probably declare war. However, if after a blockade of Germany's North Sea ports had been put in operation (recall that the new naval plans were not yet in force), it became clear that no real impression could be made on the enemy unless trade through the Netherlands was stopped, there would still be time to consider what action to take, and this action could be suited to circumstances.

From all the evidence now available, it seems that British plans for economic warfare were very imperfectly developed on the eve of 1914. It had remained for a new civil head of the Admiralty to force the career men to see that their plans for a close blockade of Germany were impractical. But even so, the Foreign Office had taken a very small part in preparing the ground for action against indirect trade to the enemy through neutrals. The British generally believed that short of blockading neutral coasts, it would be impossible to control this trade, and the diplomatic disadvantages of such action seemed so great that definite plans to that end were not seriously considered. Indeed, a policy of waiting was recommended.

II

Early Allied Measures to Intercept Enemy Trade, August to December 1914

THE outbreak of war in 1914 called into operation the naval plans that the British and French had arrived at, partly in co-operation, in the years immediately preceding. In order to understand the measures that were taken early in the war to intercept enemy trade, it is necessary first to consider the disposition of the Allied fleets, and then to investigate the changes made between August and the end of the year in the rules applied by these fleets in the search and capture of ships and goods.

MOBILIZATION AND DISTRIBUTION OF THE BRITISH AND FRENCH FLEETS

At the moment of the beginning of hostilities between Great Britain and Germany on August 4, 1914, the various departments of the British gov-

17

ernment were already carrying out the instructions laid down in the War Book. This document was the result of the labors of the subcommittee of the Committee of Imperial Defence that had been appointed in January 1911 to work out a plan of "co-ordination of Departmental action on the outbreak of war." The book contained minute instructions for each department during every stage of preparation for war—those taken in peacetime, those in the "Precautionary Stage," those in the period of "Strained Relations," and finally those in the period immediately following the decision to declare war.[1] Constant revision had gone on, and by June 1914, the work on the system was virtually completed.

The measures taken by the Admiralty were most important in protecting British and allied commerce and in carrying on warfare against enemy trade. The decision that the Grand Fleet should operate in Scottish waters commanding the approach to the North Sea made possible the protection of British coasts and trade in a war with Germany by the same measures that would prevent the free movement of a large part of German seaborne trade to and from its home terminals. The British fleet had another major task, that of keeping open the main trade routes on the high seas. To protect these routes from German warships coming out from their home ports, the control of the Channel by the Allied fleets was vital. The French not only had a great interest in this area but also in the Mediterranean, where they feared the combined action of Austro-Hungarian, German, and, possibly, Italian forces against these trade routes.

In the years 1911–1913 the French and British governments made certain arrangements respecting the distribution and use of their forces should the two states be allied in a war against Germany. On January 23, 1913, they agreed that the French Navy would be responsible for defending the part of the Channel west of a line drawn between the Cotentin peninsula in Normandy and the English coast, while the British were responsible for the area east of that line, although the French were to assist with flotillas of submarines based at Calais and Boulogne and with vessels of the "défense mobile." In the Mediterranean a similar division of spheres of operations was made in another accord dated February 10, 1913, the British to operate in the East from their base at Malta, and the French in the West.[2] These agreements in no way affected the concentration of Britain's main forces at the North Sea passage, and the burden of that defense was not increased, but a quasi obligation now existed for them to maintain certain forces in the Channel and the Mediterranean. As a result, the main Atlantic routes had to be left almost undefended.[3]

During mid-July 1914 the British fleet was holding a test mobilization that had been announced early in the spring; the exercises were over on July 23 and dispersal of the ships would have been accomplished by July 27.[4] On the afternoon of July 26, after it was known that Serbia had given an unsatisfactory answer to the Austrian ultimatum, that in Germany measures for the Precautionary Period had been put in force, and that the German High Seas Fleet had been ordered to concentrate on the Norwegian coast, orders were issued that the First Fleet was to remain in Portland and that ships of the Second Fleet were to remain at their home ports near their balance crews. Additional measures were taken: the Second and Third Fleets were to ship coal, stores, and ammunition as quietly as possible, certain ships were detailed for duty under the Admiral of Patrols, and the Mediterranean Fleet was ordered immediately to concentrate at Malta. After the Austro-Hungarian declaration of war on Serbia on July 28, the Admiralty ordered the Grand Fleet to proceed to Scapa Flow the next morning. That day, July 29, the action contemplated in the War Book was put in motion; the "warning telegram" was sent out authorizing everything short of full mobilization. From then on everything moved smoothly—all officers and men on leave were recalled, and on August 2 the Naval Reserves were mobilized, immediately after the German declaration of war on Russia became known. The Second Cruiser Squadron was sent to defend the Straits of Dover; and Sir Edward Grey, with the cabinet's approval, informed Paul Cambon, the French ambassador in London, that "if the German fleet comes into the Channel or through the North Sea to undertake hostile operations against French coasts or shipping, the British Fleet will give all the protection in its power."

In the meantime, French mobilization had been ordered on August 1, and by August 2 the second division of the fleet under Admiral Rouyer arrived at Cherbourg.[5] On August 3 (1:40 A.M.) he was ordered to prevent by force of arms the passage of the German fleet through the Channel; therefore, part of his small force was sent to the Dover Straits, while the first squadron of submarines formed a second line of defense midway of the Channel, between Le Havre and Portsmouth. At 3:30 A.M. on August 4, Rouyer received notice of the declaration of war between France and Germany, and an hour later he was ordered to conform to the plan established for operations in case of an alliance with Great Britain. Thus the French Ministry of Marine was taking for granted that war would be declared between England and Germany more than thirteen hours before the British ultimatum was sent to Germany. It is true that Grey had promised to aid France if the German fleet came into the Channel, but he had not promised to protect the Dover Straits in advance against such an entrance. In any case the order to Admiral Rouyer ended the role of French cruisers in the eastern part of the Channel, and the British became responsible for both military and economic warfare in that area. By 4:30 P.M. on August 5, Anglo-French dispositions in the western Channel were completed. Thus from the first days of the war co-operation between the British Second Fleet and the French squadron in the Channel was effective.

Equally important for the British people was the maintenance of traffic on the great trade routes. It fell mainly to the Third Fleet to protect the

Atlantic routes; part of this fleet, the Tenth Cruiser Squadron, was detailed to act with the Grand Fleet in controlling the north-about route into the North Sea.[6] From the point of view of the tonnage employed and volume of trade, the North Atlantic route was most important to England, combining as it did the trade from Canada and the United States to all northern and western Europe. The terminals of this trade lay in Irish waters and the Channel. To the protection of the former, the Eleventh Squadron was sent; while the Twelfth was to act with the French cruisers to protect the Channel approaches. The protection of the Mediterranean route fell, of course, to the regular force there; the Far Eastern, Northeastern Pacific, African, and South Atlantic routes were likewise the field of operations for the regular squadrons on duty in overseas stations.

There was, however, a great difference between the tasks of these squadrons and of those in home waters. The overseas forces were not intended to patrol the trade routes, but, instead, were to guard the focal areas where these routes converged. It was to these points that the enemy's commerce destroyers would be attracted; only there could the enemy hope to do appreciable damage to Britain's large overseas trade.[7] The British squadrons were intended to operate against whatever German cruisers might still be on the high seas and to give confidence to British shipping. By the end of 1914, the careers of most of the German warships had been ended; after that, the British had to concentrate on the new submarine menace. However, the forces stationed at the Channel approaches and the north-about passage had another major task—the inspection of a continuous stream of traffic in order to stop all contraband goods suspected of having an enemy destination.

At the beginning of the war German shipping was virtually paralyzed. Their orders to sail having been cancelled by all the German transatlantic lines on July 31, most of the merchantmen at sea took refuge in neutral ports.[8] Because of the close watch kept by the British both on the trade routes and in their home waters, it was impossible for German carrying trade to recover. The importance of that trade was great. During the years 1910–1913 the value of German imports for home consumption averaged some £510,000,000, while domestic exports from Germany averaged £445,000,000. Although no official German statistics on the point are available, probably nearly 70 per cent of the imports (by value) and 60 per cent of the exports were seaborne. Nearly half of the importations for German home consumption were raw materials for manufacture, and about 30 per cent were live animals and foodstuffs. Heavy importations of nitrates from Chile were necessary to keep up the yield of German fields; and the dairies were, to a great extent, dependent on imported forage.

When the distribution of the world's shipping in 1914 is considered, it can be seen that it was not very likely that a major belligerent who did not have command of the seas could depend upon neutrals to bring in the large amounts of goods usually carried by his own ships.[9] Not only would a large proportion of these cargoes be subject to capture as contraband, but there simply was not enough merchant tonnage under neutral flags to make up the deficiency. Of the steam tonnage existing in 1914, 58.8 per cent was under Allied flags, 14.7 per cent was owned by the Central Powers, and the remaining 26.5 per cent was so distributed as not to be easily available to Germany. In the years before the outbreak of war, British ships carried a considerable portion of that part of Germany's overseas trade that was not carried by German vessels. When the German merchant marine was disabled and Great Britain became an enemy, German seaborne commerce could continue only under great difficulties and by indirect means.

THE BRITISH ORDER IN COUNCIL OF
AUGUST 20, 1914

Next in importance to the distribution of the British and allied fleets as a factor in the prosecution of economic warfare were the orders given to those fleets as a basis on which to capture or release suspicious ships and cargoes. On August 5, 1914, Great Britain issued by royal proclamation, dated August 4, a list of contraband of war which corresponded to the lists in Articles 22 and 24 of the Declaration of London, except that aircraft and their component parts were transferred from the conditional to the absolute classification.[10] This change was made in accordance with Article 23 which allowed articles used exclusively for war to be added to the list of absolute contraband upon proper notification.

The United States government inquired of the belligerents in the first days of the war whether they intended to apply the Declaration of London in their maritime warfare.[11] The German government had already published on August 3, 1914, a Prize Code, dated September 30, 1909, which adopted substantially the rules of the Declaration. The German answer to the inquiry of the United States was that it would follow those rules on condition that its enemies did not disregard them.[12]

It was, of course, extremely expedient that British and French operations at sea against enemy commerce should have a common basis; and the French were quite as anxious as the United States that the Declaration should be observed. When the British Foreign Office staff came to consider the matter, it was pointed out that, although British trade had not thus far suffered adversely from enemy operations, there was a relative certainty that enemy trade through the Netherlands would greatly increase; and the rules of the Declaration of London would prevent effective measures being taken against that trade.[13] In the case of absolute contraband, the goods could be captured if it were proved that they were destined to Germany, but conditional contraband goods could not be touched even if their ultimate destination to the armed forces of the enemy was certain. The Admiralty believed that the German government controlled the distribution of all food in the country and that delivery of food to a German merchant had become the equivalent of delivery to the German government; such foodstuffs ought, therefore, to be treated as absolute contraband. The British government decided that it would be unable to maintain the compromise arrived at in 1909, which Germany had a special interest in upholding. Therefore, the Order in Council defining British rules of maritime war accepted the Declaration of London only with certain additions and modifications.

This Order in Council was issued on August 20, 1914;[14] a French Decree to the same effect was published on August 25,[15] and a Russian Ukase on August 26. The contraband lists contained in the proclamation of August 4 were kept, but important changes were made in other rules. Vessels carrying contraband under false papers were, by Article 2, made liable to capture up to the end of the ship's return voyage; the Declaration of London (Article 38) however, permitted capture only when the vessel was actually carrying the goods. Article 35 of the Declaration set up the rule that the ship's papers were conclusive proof concerning the voyage on which the vessel was engaged and the port of discharge, unless the vessel was clearly out of its course. The Order in Council now permitted enemy destination to be inferred "from any sufficient evidence," and further stated that such destination could be presumed if the goods were consigned to or for an agent of the enemy state or to a merchant or other person under the control of the authorities of the enemy state. The most far-reaching breach of the rules of the Declaration was the provision that conditional contraband destined to enemy armed forces, or to contractors known to be dealing with the enemy state, was liable to capture regardless of the port to which the vessel was bound. Thus the doctrine of continuous voyage became applicable to all contraband. The British, it is true, still maintained the two categories of contraband, and conditional contraband was still liable to capture only when proof—of a sort which neutral governments regarded as insufficient—was given of its *military* destination. Sir Cecil Spring Rice, British ambassador in Washington, admitted that the practical effect of the Order was to make foodstuffs absolute contraband.[16]

This extension of the application of the doctrine of continuous voyage raised new problems for the British government that had either not been foreseen in the prewar period or had been dismissed by saying that the pretension to such an extended right of capture would never be made. The difficulty of obtaining sufficient evidence to prove the military destination of conditional contraband was partially solved when any "sufficient evidence" from a reputable source, not merely the ship's papers, was admitted before the British prize courts. It had been too much to hope that, for example, American meat packers sending bacon to the German army through Rotterdam, would state their intention to do so in the bills of lading. This problem of gaining evidence that a continuous voyage was intended still persisted, and certainly in August 1914 the British and French governments were lacking the means of collecting and arranging such information for application in the case of a particular cargo. Indeed, the two governments had asserted a right without having the full means of exercising it.

Nonetheless, the overseas trade of the European border neutrals was now subjected to the closest scrutiny; cargoes were detained for long periods and perhaps not allowed to go forward at all if it was possible that the neutral consignee was dealing with enemy agents. It was soon clear that neutrals at both ends of the voyage were not above subterfuge, and drastic measures were necessary to discover the shipper's and consignee's real purpose. The British found, moreover, that the size of modern steamships and the complexity of their cargoes, in addition to the danger from submarines to any cruiser stopped in midocean, made the search of merchant vessels at sea impracticable. The practice was thus adopted of sending into port for examination all ships whose papers caused any suspicion.[17] The number of ships sent in was considerable; but, again, until detailed information about enemy trade in neutral territories was collected, the operation could have relatively little effect. The most that can be said is that neutral merchants found the delays and uncertainties as to Great Britain's intentions vexatious, and by the end of the year certain of them were willing to sacrifice something of their freedom and come to agreements with the British government.

Another source of trouble to the British government until well into 1915 was the popular demand at home that all materials used for munitions be declared contraband. The French government, which showed as early as September that it was concerned over German cotton imports, joined in the demonstration. British technical experts decided that too little cotton was being used by German ammunition factories for it to make any difference whether cotton was made contraband or not; and that, moreover, to declare it contraband would be certain to arouse a controversy with the United States.[18] The same political arguments might have applied equally well to hematite iron ore which Spain exported, and to magnetic iron ore produced in Sweden; but an interdepartmental conference recommended, nonetheless, that contraband lists be extended to include unwrought copper, lead, hematite iron ore, ferrochrome, glycerine, magnetic iron ore, rubber, hides, and skins. This advice was followed, and on September 21, 1914, a proclamation was issued which made these articles conditional contraband.[19]

THE UNITED STATES AND THE ORDER IN COUNCIL OF AUGUST 20

After due consideration of the Order in Council in the State Department, instructions were sent to Walter Hines Page, the American ambassador in London, on September 26, instructing him on the line he should take in his discussions with Grey.[20] The note made it clear that the United States had proposed the acceptance by the belligerents of the Declaration of London as a whole; it had not had in mind that a belligerent should accept only that part of the Declaration which it found convenient and disregard the rest. Specific objections were made to Article 3 of the Order in Council, which established the presumption of enemy destination of contraband goods consigned to enemy agents, and to Article 5, which applied continuous voyage to contraband. The note then continued:

> These articles strike at the very root of the indubitable right of neutrals to continue their industrial and commercial enterprises with the minimum inconvenience and confusion, which are inevitable consequences of maritime war. To concede the existence of such a right as is asserted by these articles of the Order in Council, would be to make neutral trade between neutral ports dependent upon the pleasure of belligerents, and give to the latter the advantages of an established blockade without the necessity of maintaining it with an adequate naval force. The effect of this asserted right suggests the result which was sought by the so-called "paper blockades" which have been discredited for a century, and were repudiated by the Declaration of Paris.

The United States further objected to the vagueness of the Order, especially the expression "any sufficient evidence," and coupled this with its fears concerning the seizure of goods consigned to neutral ports. The State Department professed to be in doubt whether the phrase "to or for an agent of the enemy state" was to be applied to agents in neutral as well as in enemy territory. It seems quite obvious that the British did intend to stop goods bound for enemy agents in neutral states, for their avowed purpose was to hinder indirect trade in contraband as much as possible.

Conversations were then carried on in London and Washington to arrive at some settlement that would placate the United States. It is easy to see why the British government should wish to keep in the good graces of the American government. Already the United States was becoming an important source of supply for munitions as well as for supplies of food and raw materials which the British could not afford to lose. The question was, what concessions *could* Great Britain make and still maintain her ability to deal with enemy trade? In September 1914 the British were by no means committed to unlimited economic warfare; they had made no attempt to stop German exports, or imports intended for the German civilian population. In order to arrive at some compromise with the United States it was necessary for the British government to consider carefully what its aims were and just what the results of its policy had been thus far. The Committee on Restriction of Enemy Supply, composed of representatives of the Admiralty, the Trade Division of the War Staff, the Foreign Office, the Board of Trade, and Parliament, was asked in mid-October to inquire what amount of supplies Germany was receiving through the border neutrals, and to what extent British measures had been successful in stopping this indirect trade. The Committee reported that the records regarding oil, copper, and other articles of conditional contraband that might be captured by applying the doctrine of continuous voyage were inconclusive as to the effect of the operation of the August Order in Council. The Committee believed that it would be better to forego any small advantage that had been gained by this extension of the Declaration of London in order to keep American good will.[21]

On the other hand, wherein did American interests really lie? There was never any doubt that the principal American statesmen were inclined to favor the Allied cause in the great conflict, and indeed at times it seemed that Page, at least, was more British than the British. Throughout these controversies that were to go on until the very eve of American intervention in the war, Robert Lansing and Page, President Wilson, and his personal representative, Colonel Edward M. House, showed every willingness to sit down with Grey or Spring Rice and arrive at some amicable settlement that would quiet the claims of American businessmen and leave the Allies a fair degree of freedom in their economic warfare. If one examines American policy in 1914 to 1917 solely from the point of view of its ability to maintain without limitation neutral rights of trade, then that policy was a failure and one must conclude that the American representatives at home and in London often acted like dolts. This is not the place to bring judgment either for or against these men in the broad scope of their actions; here interest lies only in the degree to which their complaints or their willingness to compromise altered the methods and aims of Allied economic policy.[22]

In the meantime Lansing, then the acting secretary of state, suggested to Spring Rice on September 28 that an answer to British difficulties might be found by procuring an agreement with the Dutch government whereby the latter would place an embargo on foodstuffs and other conditional contraband, or would agree at least to prevent the re-exportation of such articles.[23] Spring Rice told Lansing that his government was stopping and purchasing cargoes of copper, petroleum, and Swedish iron; but that it might be better to rescind the Order in Council and add these articles which were then used almost exclusively for war purposes to the absolute contraband list. Lansing did not object to this proposal, and Spring Rice therefore transmitted it to Grey.

Page was soon able to report that the British had received assurances from the Dutch government that the existing Dutch embargo would prevent the exportation of foodstuffs; he believed this would open the way to American cargoes and, in general, he viewed the situation with satisfaction. On September 30, in a British cabinet meeting, it was decided to issue a new proclamation regarding contraband along the lines Spring Rice had proposed and without mentioning the Declaration of London.[24]

Lansing was evidently dissatisfied with the course of negotiations in London, and on October 2 he again raised with Spring Rice the question of the acceptance of the Declaration of London. In his anxiety to persuade the British that this document gave them sufficient leeway, he gave it as his opinion that the definition of absolute contraband as goods used "exclusively for war" did not require a literal interpretation; and that the methods of warfare and the locality to which goods were destined should be considered. He emphasized that conditional contraband goods could be raised to the absolute category, and he doubted that the other provisions of the August Order in Council were important enough to justify sacrificing unanimity on maritime law. Lansing nowhere mentioned the free list, which apparently he still desired the British to regard as binding, all of which would tie in with his desire for assurances that raw cotton and other important raw materials would not be added to the contraband lists.

THE DRAFT ORDER IN COUNCIL OF
OCTOBER 9, 1914, AND LANSING'S PROPOSALS

The draft of a new order in council was transmitted by Page to the State Department on October 9, together with an offer of the British government to withhold its publication until the document had been discussed with the United States.[25] In Sections 1 and 2 of the draft Spring Rice's general suggestions in regard to contraband were carried out: hematite iron ore and pig iron, nickel ore and nickel, ferrochrome and chrome ore, unwrought copper, lead, motor vehicles, motor tires, rubber, mineral oils, and motor spirit [gasoline] were raised to the absolute contraband list; most of these articles had been declared conditional contraband only on September 21.

The third section repealed Article 5 of the August Order which had applied continuous voyage to conditional contraband; but the other articles, aside from those containing the contraband lists, remained unchanged. However, a new principle was introduced that made conditional contraband on a vessel bound for a neutral port and for which no consignee in neutral territory was named, liable to capture. In an accompanying memorandum the British explained that a large proportion of the cargoes shipped to Rotterdam was consigned "to order" of the shipper, who thus reserved the right to dispose of his goods after they arrived at their port of destination; and these goods might, in fact, be intended for shipment to the enemy. Therefore, they argued, they were justified in presuming the enemy destination of all contraband so consigned; and moreover, that it was actually destined to the armed forces of the enemy. To this extent, "to order" consignments of conditional contraband became assimilated to absolute contraband; the concession made in withdrawing conditional contraband from the operation of continuous voyage was, therefore, applicable only when goods were addressed to a named consignee.

Section 4 of the draft order was intended to cover cases where a neutral government laid no embargo, or failed to enforce it, so that the enemy government was able to draw supplies for its armed forces through that neutral territory. The draft provided that one of His Majesty's principal secretaries might declare and notify that Article 35 of the Declaration of London should not apply, and a vessel carrying conditional contraband to a port in that country would be liable to capture. Here then, continuous voyage could once more be applied to conditional contraband whenever the British knew of the existence of a brisk neutral trade with the enemy in these articles.

The precise attitude of the United States government to this draft order is difficult to ascertain in view of its attempt to pursue two conflicting lines simultaneously. In the first of two telegrams sent out over Lansing's signature on October 16, the United States continued to urge the acceptance of the Declaration of London and then suggested that Page propose unofficially to Grey that having done this, the British should extend their contraband lists and should, in addition, issue a proclamation declaring that certain neutral ports had acquired enemy character so far as trade in contraband was concerned.[26] The more official line of instruction was contained in a second telegram that day, in which protest was made against the provision in regard to "to order" consignments. Lansing made no complaint against the extension of contraband lists and said that the British could have made these changes under the Declaration of London. Here he appears to have been a bit befogged, for many of the goods recently declared contraband were on the free list of the Declaration. Even more confusing is the protest that Lansing made against the assimilation of a neutral country to enemy territory, whenever that state was serving as a base of enemy supply, in so far as conditional contraband was concerned. It seems likely that this was intended to be merely a formal protest; certainly it was far from forceful. But to return to the plan proposed earlier that day: it is hard to see any advantages in it from the American point of view. Indeed, whereas the British draft order intended its assimilation of neutral territory to enemy territory to affect only conditional contraband and therefore merely to be a continuation of the provisions of the August Order in Council, Lansing's proposal went even further and applied to all contraband. Thus absolute contraband going to that neutral's territory would be liable to capture without any necessity of proving that it was destined to real enemy territory. Certainly if Lansing's plan had been applied, all commerce to a neutral state declared to be a base of enemy supply would have been as closely watched as that sent directly to Germany. How then could "interference and loss" to neutral trade, as Richard W. Van Alstyne says, have been less than under the operation of the Order in Council?[27] In any case, the British government would still have been responsible for its execution, and neutrals would certainly have been irritated at having their territory declared a base of enemy operations.

The British reply to all this was that they could not accept the Declaration as it stood, nor could they accept it with the intention of immediately issuing a proclamation that contradicted it. Lansing, therefore, instructed Page on October 22, 1914, to withdraw the proposal to accept the Declaration on the understanding that in the future the United States would define its rights and duties in accordance with the existing rules of international law and treaties.[28] Thus ended the American attempt to secure a *modus vivendi* through the adoption of the Declaration of London by all the belligerents.

THE ORDER IN COUNCIL OF OCTOBER 29, 1914

The British government issued the new Order in Council on October 29, with only a few changes beyond those proposed in the October 9 draft. The contraband lists were more extensive, and a neutral ship guilty of carrying contraband to an enemy port under false papers was made liable to capture up to the end of its next voyage. The provision regarding goods consigned "to order" remained the same, but the presumption was stated to be rebuttable, i.e., the burden of proof was put upon the claimants in a prize court. Article 2 of the Order reproduced the much-debated Section 4 of the draft. The provisions of this Order were substantially adopted by the French and Russian governments, while the German Prize Code was amended with similar effect as a measure of retaliation.[29]

The October Order in Council was generally regarded in England as a concession to American opinion; by some it was regarded as a stupid blunder which gave away Britain's freedom to control neutral trade with its enemies. To allow shipments of contraband to go through to any named consignee was, to them, simply inviting collusive transactions between dummy neutral consignees and enemy agents. Actually the situation was much better in hand than these critics suspected. By November the military censors had collected a large mass of information about some three thousand firms in neutral countries, and all consignments of contraband made to any person who was known to be in the service of Germany would be captured and prize-courted. Britain's bare legal right to stop contraband going to the enemy remained unimpaired; the government had merely chosen to limit the exercise of that right in a manner that benefited and placated neutrals at a time when its administrative machinery did not allow anything more.[30]

However, the Order in Council, much to the disappointment of the British government, failed to allay the American controversy, for the State Department in response to telegrams, letters, and deputations from almost all the great commercial interests kept up a steady stream of inquiry and protest regarding British detentions and search in port. The United States was further disturbed by the Admiralty's announcement of November 3 that the North Sea was considered a military zone.[31] This had been prepared for by successive British protests against Germany's indiscriminate mine-laying in the North Sea in violation of the Hague Convention rules. The British even made the accusation, which they later admitted to be without foundation, that ships flying neutral flags had laid the mines. The announcement now warned neutrals that counter mine fields were being laid, and all ships proceeding to North Sea ports were advised to call in the United Kingdom for directions as to their course. This was admittedly a retaliatory measure against Germany, and the British tried to do what they could to protect neutral shipping from its effects.

Spring Rice realized that American furor against these measures might force the State Department into obstructing British negotiations with the border neutrals.[32] This fear synchronized with two invitations from other neutral states for co-operation against belligerent interference with neutral rights. One of these, coming from Venezuela in December, proposed that a League of Neutrals meet to define the rights and duties of neutrals. The State Department merely acknowledged the note and said it would receive the consideration of the government. In similar fashion the United States declined to join with the Scandinavian states in a protest against Britain's designating the North Sea as a military zone. So anxious was the United States to avoid the appearance of co-operation with any other neutral states that Page was rebuked rather sharply for discussing with the Scandinavian ministers in London a few technical questions about the seizure of contraband.[33]

Thus there was no evidence that the United States intended to challenge in common with other neutrals the foundations of the system of economic warfare then being set up. The British government still had to reckon with protests on particular matters, protests that might at any time be made effective by countermeasures.

MACHINERY FOR ADMINISTRATION OF THE ORDER IN COUNCIL

By the end of 1914 a beginning, at least, had been made in perfecting the administrative machinery in both Great Britain and France for carrying out their belligerent rights. From available documents it is difficult to ascertain the exact time that some of these organs were established, their relationship to the departments of government and to each other.

One of the earliest steps came in an order issued by Churchill on August 13, 1914, to establish a Committee on Restriction of Enemy Supply.[34] The terms of reference read in part as follows: "The duties of this Committee will be to examine and watch continually all means or routes by which supplies of food or raw material may reach Germany and Austria; to report weekly all importations or exportations to or from these countries coming to their knowledge; and to recommend by what methods, financial, commercial, diplomatic and military they may be hampered, restricted, and, if possible, stopped." The document went on to order the securing of information on all ships unloading in neutral ports cargoes that might go on to the enemy, with particular attention being called to the danger that Rotterdam might become a base of supply to the enemy. As a result, agents of the Committee were established in neutral countries, and the information they collected had a great influence on the demands that Great Britain made on neutrals. Sir Francis Hopwood was the chairman of this body.

The Trade Division of the Admiralty War Staff also performed important functions in determining what action should be taken in regard to contraband.[35] This division formed the nucleus of the Contraband Committee, made up of representatives of the Foreign Office, the Board of Trade, and of the procurator-general, whose first regular meetings began in November 1914 when a permanent secretariat was established. A separate organ, the Contraband Department, was set up by the Foreign Office sometime before November, with Alwyn Parker at its head, and Sir Eyre Crowe was made responsible for all negotiations with other states concerning contraband.

The Board of Trade appointed a Diverted Cargoes Committee in August 1914 to decide immediately on the disposal of ships and cargoes that were diverted to British ports because they were suspected of containing contraband. On this Committee were included representatives of Parliament and the Port of London Authority, as well as the various government departments. A Committee on Release of Prize Cargoes was established by the Board of Trade to deal with cargoes that were technically prize but which it was desirable, for reasons of policy, to release. The Board of Trade also appointed various committees to enforce trading with the enemy legislation. An interdepartmental organ, commonly known as the Licensing Committee, was appointed to deal with applications for import and export licenses and the movement of funds; Robert Vansittart was its Foreign Office representative. The work of all these committees changed continually, new ones were set up to supersede others, and always there was a certain amount of overlapping. So far as possible these shifts and changes will be traced from time to time.

The preparations made in France prior to 1914 for an economic war were even less than those in Great Britain, and once war came, the organization set up to cope with the problems that arose remained less complex.[36] During the Balkan War of 1912, when the general European peace seemed in danger, the French Ministry of Foreign Affairs drew up a rather schematic plan for a division of the services of state in case of war. Jean Gout, sous-directeur charged with questions of public law, has since written that this plan failed to take proper account of the importance the economic factor would have in a general European war. Under the plan Gout was placed in charge of all matters affecting public law: declaration of war and its consequences, public maritime law, and so forth. He was given one collaborator, Henri Fromagéot, who was one of the jurisconsuls in the Ministry. The French Ministry of Marine took no more elaborate steps: only Vice-Admiral Frédéric Paul Moreau was designated during the July crisis in 1914 to occupy himself with questions concerning contraband. In the Ministry of War the organization of controls over posts and telegraphs had been foreseen, but almost solely from the point of view of defense against enemy espionage. So far as is now known, no co-ordinating interdepartmental organs had been designated or even considered.

Both Great Britain and France, immediately upon the outbreak of war, had prohibited the exportation of many foods, raw materials, and manufactured articles; and it was in this field of economic action that the French government seems to have concentrated its efforts. These embargoes were laid by the Allied states in order to conserve domestic supplies of key materials, and sometimes to implement prohibitions against trading with the enemy. Both governments thought it desirable to permit the exportation of certain amounts of these prohibited articles when it could be shown conclusively that the goods would not go to the enemy, that they were not vitally needed domestically, and that the transaction was to the general commercial advantage of the state. By November the French customs authorities, and all the other ministries whose opinions had to be asked, were overburdened with requests for permission to export. It was at the suggestion of Millerand, minister of war, that Lieutenant Colonel Eduard Théry and a high functionary from the Ministry of Foreign Affairs were detailed to study these requests and decide upon them. However, long technical inquiries were sometimes necessary, and the task was too great for the two men. Therefore the Commission des Dérogations, an interministerial body, was created and attached to the Customs to deal with all questions of exportation to neutral countries of goods susceptible of military use.

The French government, as has been shown, followed the British example and made the same changes in maritime law, so that by the end of October the Allies had found a joint, and fairly satisfactory, basis for dealing with enemy trade. True, certain concessions had been made to neutral opinion—the neutrals often said they were no concessions at all—but more important was the fact that simultaneously the British undertook negotiations with neutral governments in order to gain some practical, nonlegal basis for hindering enemy commerce through border neutral states, with the aid of either these governments or their citizens. These negotiations, which at the same time offered the means of facilitating bona fide neutral trade, will be discussed in the next chapter.

III

British Negotiations with the Northern European Neutrals in 1914

T HE measures dealt with in the last chapter were undertaken by the British and French governments as a direct means of operation against seaborne trade destined for the Central Powers. But even though their effects on neutral trade were incidental to economic warfare, the repercussions on the political and economic situation in the states bordering on Germany were great.

The northern European neutrals realized at the outbreak of the war that they would play an important part in provisioning the belligerents, and in particular Germany. With little thought of coercing one belligerent or of aiding the other, these states almost at once began to regulate the exportation of goods from their territories simply to prevent undue depletion of supplies necessary for domestic consumption. It was, of course, to Allied interest that these embargoes should be rigorously executed. The British government had realized even before the war that its own regulation of German trade could not be in any way complete, or even very effective, unless indirect trade to the enemy through the border states was hindered. The British were unwilling to take such severe measures against this indirect trade that the neutral states would be forced to enter the war on the side of Germany. Certain long-standing commercial ties and political sympathies existed between England and the northern neutrals that made coercion undesirable. The obvious answer, therefore, was to seek by negotiation with neutral governments or their citizens limitations on their freedom of commerce, in return for relaxations of the Allied policies of detention and seizure that neutrals found most irksome. Such negotiations were begun with each of the northern neutral states toward the end of 1914, negotiations in which the French played a very minor part.

NEGOTIATIONS WITH THE DUTCH GOVERNMENT AND THE ESTABLISHMENT OF THE NETHERLANDS OVERSEA TRUST

The Netherlands has been called with good reason the keystone of world commerce between middle Europe and the North Sea.[1] Her position on the North Sea, her great rivers connecting with Germany and Switzerland as well as with France and Belgium made the Netherlands a great entrepôt for overseas goods destined to Central Europe, and offered easily accessible markets for native Dutch products.

Dutch commercial supremacy in Europe had long since been superseded; but Dutch carrying trade was by no means negligible, and the ports of Rotterdam and Amsterdam played an important part in European trade. Rotterdam received about one half of the Dutch imports brought in by sea, about one third of the importations of raw materials made by the Netherlands, and about one fifth of all Dutch imports—raw materials and merchandise together.[2] The transit trade through Rotterdam and thence up the Rhine to Germany was carried mainly for foreign account, and Dutch shipping had a comparatively modest place in it. The goods in the Rotterdam trade consisted mostly of raw materials: iron, grain, wood, metals, coal, copra, tobacco, petroleum, benzine, oils and fats, hides, and so forth, which were transshipped to Rhine vessels or were sent on over Dutch railways.

Amsterdam was just as firmly bound up with the colonial trade from the Dutch Indies. The city had developed into a great Dutch and even a world market for these goods with all the necessary warehouses. Regular supplies of cinchona, tobacco, tea, coffee, rubber, copra, rice, kapok, sugar, cocoa, spices, and tropical fruits came in. A large part of these goods was carried on Dutch ships and for Dutch merchants.[3]

The Netherlands had also developed industries which, although they were dependent on foreign countries for raw materials, were an important part of Dutch economic life. Thus large foundries and machine shops were established in South Holland, along with factories building ship motors, dredgers, locomotives, and bicycles. Copper, zinc, lead, enamel, and tin goods were manufactured, and a part of them were exported. Some of the industries, such as the oil refineries and textile mills, secured their raw materials abroad through branches or agents, while others such as the canning factories utilized the products of Dutch orchards, dairies, and fisheries. The purely agricultural activities of the country employed many people, and large amounts of dairy products, bulbs, and so forth were exported all over Europe.

The chief preoccupation of the Dutch government upon the outbreak of war was to insure its neutrality and preserve the economic well-being of the country. Declarations of neutrality were issued on July 30 and August 5.[4] In its zeal the Dutch government did even more than was required of a neutral under the Fifth and Thirteenth Hague Conventions of 1907 when it forbade the entrance of all belligerent warships or vessels assimilated thereto into Dutch ports and territorial waters. The transit trade through Rotterdam seemed to be assured by the Rhine Convention signed at Mannheim, October 17, 1868, which supplemented the convention of March 31, 1831. However, it was soon discovered that if the Netherlands was to receive any great advantage from the permission granted neutral tradesmen to continue commerce with both belligerents, and, above all, any benefit from the Rhine Convention, it was necessary to define precisely the meaning of "transit traffic." A declaration was issued by the Dutch government on August 21, 1914, that goods would be considered in transit if (a) they were sent with a "through bill of lading," (b) the goods, at the moment the ship entered a Dutch port, were recorded as being in transit, or (c) on arrival in port the transit-destination appeared from the documents on board the ship.[5] However, the Dutch government reserved the right to requisition, with compensation, foodstuffs, war necessities, raw materials, or anything else necessary for the defense of the state, regardless of to whom the goods were destined or to whom they belonged.

The Dutch, like other neutrals, found it very difficult to secure goods from overseas because of the general dislocations of commerce and shipping that followed the outbreak of war, and also to import goods from Great Britain and other allied states where embargoes had been imposed.[6] In addition, the Dutch foresaw that their markets would become very attractive places for German buyers seeking both agricultural and manufactured goods. No time was lost by the Dutch in imposing embargoes of their own. A certain amount of experimentation went on before satisfactory lists were drawn up; beginning on August 1, a new decree was published every few days in the Nederlandsche Staatscourant. In general, the lists soon included grains, oil-producing seeds, fuel, cotton, military clothing, packing materials, textiles, metals, and staple foodstuffs. At the end of the year the Dutch embargo list published in the British *Board of Trade Journal* contained 104 items.[7] These prohibitions were by no means absolute, and the pressure on the Dutch government to grant export licenses was great.

Prices in Germany were high, and the most honorable of merchants hated to let the opportunity to secure large profits slip by. German purchasing agents thronged the markets of all the northern states, eager to buy copper, rubber, iron, food, and forage. Sugar exports from the Netherlands were so great that the government became alarmed, and then reached an agreement on September 26, 1914, with Dutch sugar refiners that put an end to this uncontrolled trade with foreign customers.[8] But the very existence of neutral embargoes served to raise prices in Germany and consequently to increase the temptation to find a way around the prohibitions. When the embargo did not carefully define the articles, every evasion was used to continue trade in those not specifically named. When this kind of legal evasion was impossible, outright smuggling was resorted to. The Dutch government sent troops to protect the frontiers from hostile invasion and to control all traffic in goods, but even when the border areas were declared in state of siege the control was far from effective.[9]

In order to end all cause for British suspicions that cargoes of grain and other provisions bound for the Netherlands really had an ultimate enemy destination, and in the hope that detentions of such cargoes would cease, the Dutch government on August 21 closed all Dutch markets to certain grains and took over the buying and selling of them itself. Grain purchases were made on behalf of the Dutch government in London by A. G. Kröller, head of the firm of William Müller and Company, chief Dutch grain importers; the grain was consigned to the government and was carried on neutral ships. A royal bureau was established to regulate the distribution of this grain, with the co-operation of the municipalities and other administrative units.[10]

The British government found these steps insufficient. On August 26 it threatened to regard all foodstuffs bound for Dutch ports with extreme suspicion unless the Dutch government guaranteed that no equivalent amount would be sold to Germany. More precisely, Sir Edward Grey proposed to the Dutch minister in London, R. de Marees van Swinderen, that the Dutch government give a guarantee that the goods allowed by the British to proceed would remain in the Netherlands. The Dutch government refused the proposal and stated on September 27 that it had done as much as it could when it had undertaken the purchase and distribution of the most necessary goods.[11]

Although the Dutch government refused to negotiate with the British, it realized that a serious problem existed. The next step it took toward a solution was to reach a provisional agreement with the Holland-Amerika Line, under which the company agreed to accept only grain cargoes intended for importation in the Netherlands, so that any chance of capture of a ship because its cargo was "in transit" beyond the Dutch port was excluded. All

Dutch importers who desired to take advantage of the relative certainty that their goods would not be detained were required to conclude contracts with the Holland-Amerika Line guaranteeing consumption of the goods in the Netherlands.

Having failed to secure a guarantee from the Dutch government concerning all cargoes that might be permitted through the British control lines, the British soon tried to effect a similar agreement limited to goods capable of military use that were sent from England to the Netherlands. Since these goods were of British origin over which the British government might reasonably be expected to exercise some control, the Dutch government proved more amenable, and on October 5 it was agreed that such goods consigned to specified persons in the Netherlands would not be detained because of any existing British regulations. This accord temporarily calmed the situation and promised to make Dutch supply easier.

Perhaps of greater practical importance in the long run were the measures undertaken by Dutch merchants and shipping company officials to seek a solution for some of their problems. About the middle of September a group of them agreed to establish an organization known as the Dutch Commerce Commission (Commissie voor den Nederlandschen Handel), to disseminate information on commerce, and, in return for a small fee, to intercede with foreign governments on behalf of Dutch traders.[12] The Commission announced, at the beginning, its firm intention to maintain Dutch laws, decisions, and embargoes, to preserve Dutch neutrality from danger, to protect Dutch commerce from confusion, and, most significantly, not to intercede on behalf of Dutch merchants who attempted to act as middlemen in business that was forbidden between Englishmen and Germans. In both its functions and its membership the Commission foreshadowed the Netherlands Oversea Trust that was to be formed in late December. The moving spirits in the foundation of the Commission were Kröller, C. J. K. van Aalst, president of the Nederlandsche Handelsmaatschappij; L. P. D. op ten Noort, director of the Board of Governors of the Koninklijke Paketvaart Maatschappij; and Joost van Vollenhoven, member of the Second Chamber, ex-chairman of the Deli Maatschappij in the Dutch East Indies, who became chairman of the Commission. Cornelius van Vollenhoven, professor at the University of Leiden, became legal counselor; J. E. Claringbould headed the Secretariat.

The most immediate difficulty the Commission encountered was that of distinguishing between bona fide Dutch trade and that carried on in behalf of the Central Powers. It was found that many new corporations proved to be branches of German or Austrian companies, particularly those that dealt in food or wool, while other well-established firms that had suddenly changed their business also were open to suspicion. It should be added that the responsibility for trade with such firms, which the British government regarded as undesirable, was often shared by English exporters who made a declaration to the British Customs that the goods they were sending were only for internal consumption in the Netherlands, without having properly investigated the consignees' connections or intentions.[13] It was, of course, extremely difficult, even when the importer was a bona fide neutral trader, to trace the disposition of imported goods which might pass through several intermediate hands before reaching the consumer, particularly when the goods bore no distinguishing marks or were raw materials that were then manufactured in the Netherlands. Even though its information resources were limited, the Commission very soon threatened to make public the names of those who facilitated forbidden commerce between citizens of the opposing belligerent states.

The Dutch Commerce Commission also began to make agreements with shipping lines in order to continue and extend the arrangements made by the Dutch government. Acting in a fashion that was complementary to the negotiations carried on by the government with the Holland-Amerika Line, the Commission as early as October 2 pointed out that if the line was really going to transport grain cargoes consigned to the government, all other Dutch importers using its ships would have to give declarations that their goods would not go on to Germany.[14] The Commission insisted that while the government could not require such declarations, the Holland-Amerika Line, as a private company, could and must—as a condition for accepting goods for shipment. Here is the first clear evidence of a realization of the government's desire to escape from direct responsibility for all these arrangements. A week later another meeting was held with the representatives of all the large Dutch steamship companies, to discuss with the Commission details of sailing dates and cargoes. By this time two of the lines had, on their own initiative, sent representatives to London to impress on the British government the importance of the undisturbed passage of goods from the Dutch Indies to Amsterdam. The president of the British Board of Trade had given assurances, which were now transmitted to the general meeting on October 9, that the British would hinder Dutch shipping and trade no more than necessary, that tea, coffee, and tropical fruits would be allowed to go forward freely to the Netherlands, and that a revised list of foodstuffs that were considered conditional contraband would soon be issued. These assurances seemed sufficiently precise, and so the steamship lines then decided to carry no more goods for German account, although they refused to sign a contract to this effect with the Dutch government, as the British suggested, at least until the promised list of foodstuffs was forthcoming.

Actually the Dutch government was itself trying to work out some scheme along this very line. It was still unwilling to permit anything except the goods most urgently needed for feeding the population to be consigned to it. The Ministry of Commerce proposed a plan whereby declarations that the goods were for internal consumption would be given by the importer to the shipping company, which would send them to the Dutch government, which in turn would send the guarantee to the British legation. This failed, however, to meet the approval of the Dutch Ministry of Foreign Affairs

(October 2), for even though the Dutch government acted only as guarantor of a private scheme, such a plan would, in its opinion, be compromising to Dutch neutrality.[15] One concession was made by the government when it announced on October 21 its intention of becoming the sole consignee for all copper and petroleum imported into the Netherlands. It was hoped, of course, that such shipments would be permitted without question through the British contraband controls.[16]

The British government soon found that, in practice, consignment to a named Dutch firm was no real guarantee that foodstuffs imported from Great Britain under the October 5 agreement would not go on to Germany. Since, as we have seen, Britain lacked the machinery for more drastic action against indirect trade with the enemy, it undertook only limited measures in the October 29 Order in Council. When on November 2 Sir Alan Johnstone communicated the new contraband lists to J. Loudon, the Dutch foreign minister, he also informed him that the provisional arrangement of October 5, permitting foods consigned from Great Britain to a named firm to go forward freely to a Dutch port, could no longer be continued and that he understood it was his government's intention to reopen negotiations with the Dutch soon.[17] In the meantime all cargoes of cereals, rice, flour, meal, and meat that were not covered by guarantees of Dutch consumption and against transit or re-exportation to Germany would be "regarded as suspect and provisionally detained." The Dutch government on November 13 presented a strong protest against the Order in Council and this general detention policy.[18] The strongest exception was taken to Article 2 of the Order that opened the way to declaring neutral territory assimilated to enemy territory if it served as a base of enemy supply; but the Dutch also protested that the practice of detaining conditional contraband consigned to a named person on general suspicion and without evidence of an enemy destination even went beyond the provision set up in Article 3, where such enemy destination was presumed for "to order" consignments. Loudon renewed his earlier statements that the duties of neutrality, no less than the obligations resulting from the Rhine Convention, prevented the Dutch government from entering into any such negotiations as the British contemplated in regard to determining the ultimate destination of goods bound for Dutch ports.

Even while it was preparing this protest the Dutch government decided to increase its own obligations by permitting all goods on the Dutch embargo lists to be consigned to it provided the importer secured permission from the Trade Division of the Ministry of Agriculture, Industry, and Commerce. An announcement to this effect appeared in the *Nederlandsche Staatscourant* on November 7, and even though the government's task of determining what goods were intended for Dutch consumption was made somewhat easier by a more precise definition of "goods in transit," it nonetheless took on a tremendous moral obligation.[19]

At this point the British government addressed similar notes to the Dutch, Danish, Norwegian, and Swedish governments, making proposals concerning their trade. The memorandum with a *note explicative* to the Dutch government, presented on November 17, was intended to represent both British and French views and expressed the wish that neutral governments should hold within their frontiers all contraband goods by prohibiting export and transit trade in them and that certain goods that awakened "particular anxiety" should be consigned to the neutral governments or to a few approved firms. If these conditions were met, the right of search would be limited to the ships' papers, and detentions would therefore be short. The note renewed the invitation to the Dutch government to enter into negotiations for an "arrangement amical."[20]

In order to understand the reply made by the Dutch government to this proposal it is necessary to trace the arrangements that were made by Dutch businessmen in November and early December. Another meeting of the Dutch Commerce Commission with representatives of seven great steamship companies on November 10 showed with what alarm they had received the British threat to assimilate neutral territory to enemy territory.[21] From many sources the same idea was voiced: establish some general guarantee that goods imported into the Netherlands would not be sent on to the Central Powers. It was Kröller who proposed that a "Trust" be set up by Dutch importers and shipping companies to which goods would be consigned and which would give such a guarantee. The idea was at once accepted by those at the meeting and the work of organization began.

Conversations were held with Loudon and M. W. F. Treub, Dutch minister of finance, as well as with Sir Francis Oppenheimer, British commercial attaché, on November 14 in order to work out details of the organization, although the establishment of the Trust appears to have been entirely the work of Dutchmen. The Ministry of Foreign Affairs was quite decided in its opinion that no juridical ties should exist between the Trust and the government, so that Dutch neutrality would in no way be compromised. On the other hand, the Ministry of Commerce wanted Dutch consignees to enter into independent agreements with the Dutch government. In the end it was decided that this was unnecessary, and that, although the government should continue to be the consignee for certain essential articles, the Trust would become the means by which Dutch overseas commerce would be carried on. It was expected that the Dutch Commerce Commission would continue to give advice and defend Dutch trade.

The statutes of the new company were drafted and approved by the Ministry of Foreign Affairs on November 20, and royal consent to its establishment was given on November 23. The next day the document was witnessed before a notary and the Trust was thus duly established as the Netherlands Oversea Trust (Nederlandsche Overzee Trustmaatschappij— "N.O.T.").[22] The charter, which was to run until December 31, 1919, provided that capital stock be issued to the amount of 2,400,000 guilders in 2,400 shares, one half of which was to be subscribed by the merchants and shipping companies founding the Trust, while the remainder could be purchased only by other Dutch merchants or shipowners. The charter provided for a board of directors which in turn was to set up an executive committee to decide under what circumstances its intercession would be granted. In any case every person applying for such intercession was to give a declaration that the goods he wished to import, which were or might later be declared contraband by the belligerents, were either for internal consumption or for re-export to Dutch colonies or to the territory of another neutral state for consumption there. Fees in proportion to the value of the goods imported were to be charged by the Trust, and any profits remaining after its eventual liquidation were to be given to the Royal National Relief Committee.

The Board of Directors of the N.O.T. was made up of the founders of the company named in the charter and in addition Joost van Vollenhoven, Th. J. van Haren Noman, and F. S. van Nierop. C. J. K. van Aalst became president of the Trust, while he and op ten Noort, Adam Roelvink, G. H. Hintzen, van Haren Noman, and Joost van Vollenhoven were the Executive Committee, with A. Maclaine Pont as its secretary.[23] It is clear that there was a considerable overlapping in membership between the N.O.T. and the Dutch Commerce Commission, although the Trust was much broader in its scope. The British were on the whole sympathetic to the establishment of the Trust, although they had proposed that Sir Francis Oppenheimer should become a member of it.[24] The Dutch refused this suggestion, but the N.O.T. did promise to furnish Sir Francis with explanations if there seemed to be some disparity between the engagements entered into by Dutch importers and shipowners and the actual working of the whole arrangement. In due time a formal announcement of the existence of the Trust was made to foreign governments and its aims were explained.[25]

One of the first tasks of the N.O.T. was to devise contract forms to be signed by shipping companies and importers who used the Trust's facilities. To begin with, four "type contracts" were used.[26] One was signed by shipowners who thereby agreed to carry no contraband goods to Dutch ports unless they were consigned to the N.O.T. or to the Dutch government, to carry such contraband goods only to Dutch ports and to deliver them only if they were declared to be for internal consumption or for re-export to Dutch colonies or neutral states. Upon completion of the manifest of a cargo the shipowner was required to inform the Trust what part of the cargo was consigned to the N.O.T., what part to the government, and who the consignors were. The shipowner was subject to a fine up to 100,000 guilders for each nonperformance of the contract. It was intended to be a continuing agreement that would run until the N.O.T. was liquidated, or at least for as long as the shipowner lived up to its terms.

In contrast with this contract, those signed by importers covered only a particular kind of goods, and some of these only up to a specified amount. Other contracts made provision for importers who wished to maintain a continuing importation of a certain kind of goods. In either case the importer had to declare that the goods covered were destined exclusively for internal consumption in the Netherlands or for re-exportation to Dutch colonies, to the state of origin, or to other neutral states for consumption there. The importer was thereby made responsible for the use of the goods and for any products manufactured from them, either by himself or by anyone to whom they were sold. The goods imported were consigned to the N.O.T., which then endorsed and delivered the bill of lading to the importer, but any goods the Trust suspected of having a prohibited destination could be detained until after the war. To insure the performance of the contract, the importer was required to give a banker's guarantee or to post other security in proportion to the nature and value of the goods consigned; in addition, the importer paid an administrative fee of $\frac{1}{8}$ per cent of the value of the goods in order to help defray the expenses of the N.O.T. The fourth "type contract" was intended to cover goods imported on behalf of the Dutch government, which could not be re-exported to another neutral country, since presumably there was a pressing need for them in the Netherlands.

The most important shipowners and wholesale merchants in the country were already represented in the Trust, and time was to prove that all other importers and shipowners who wished to participate in overseas trade, reasonably free from Allied interference, would find the intercession of the N.O.T. a necessity.

It will be remembered that the British and French governments had, on November 17, expressed the hope that negotiations could be begun with the Dutch government for an agreement to regulate Dutch trade, with the Dutch government becoming the consignee for a long list of goods. This memorandum was followed on November 29 by another British note which attempted to justify Article 2 of the October 29 Order in Council, that permitted neutral territory to be assimilated to enemy territory.[27] The note called attention to the peculiar double character of Rotterdam which was in some respects a German port. The British intended to treat trade going to Rotterdam in its capacity as a German port "as trade going to enemy country which, as such, cannot in justice be considered covered by the provision of Article 35 of the Declaration of London." However, they held out the promise of safety to Dutch trade provided an agreement was made respecting goods passing into Holland for bona fide Dutch consumption or for transit to other neutral countries.

The answer of the Dutch government, sent by Loudon on December 4, was an absolute refusal to enter into any such agreement.[28] The Dutch government still insisted that such a course would be unneutral, and that while it had laid embargoes and permitted consignment of grain to itself for purely domestic reasons, it could not permit these exceptional measures to be made into a general rule, which would in practice bar the importation of contraband by individuals. Loudon then called attention to the formation of the N.O.T., vouched for the integrity of its members, and said that the interested parties had found in it the most simple and efficacious means of dealing with their difficulties. He therefore believed that any further intervention by the Dutch government in order to secure importations would be superfluous. Here then was almost an invitation to the British to take up negotiations with the Trust.

The British were not slow to follow the suggestion, and on December 16 Sir Francis Oppenheimer began more serious negotiations with the N.O.T. The first British proposals were apparently unsatisfactory and a new set was formulated that took into account the terms of the contracts already concluded by the Trust with Dutch shipowners and importers. On December 26, 1914, a note containing the terms of agreement between the British government and the N.O.T. was sent by Oppenheimer, and the Executive Committee of the Trust accepted it formally on December 29.[29]

In this accord the British agreed to accept consignment to the N.O.T. as sufficient evidence that the goods were intended for Dutch internal consumption, provided that the N.O.T. guaranteed that these contraband goods and any goods manufactured from them were only for home consumption. The definition of "home consumption" did permit re-exportation of goods that were not foodstuffs to the Dutch colonies or other neutral countries unless the goods were shipped across enemy territory before reaching their neutral destination; whenever this re-exportation took place the N.O.T. had to guarantee the consumption of the goods in the country to which they were sent. Special arrangements were made to facilitate imports of contraband articles sent in to Dutch manufacturers who then sold the finished goods to the Allies, and the Trust also agreed to consider fairly the applications of those who wished to have their consignments carried by Allied ships. If at any time the British commercial attaché suspected that the agreements between the Trust and the shipowners or importers had been disregarded, the Executive Committee agreed to furnish him a complete explanation, supported by documentary evidence. Finally, the contract forms drawn up by the Trust were attached to Sir Francis' letter, and they thus became an integral part of the guarantees made by the Trust to the British government.

On the same day, December 26, the British legation at The Hague sent a note to Loudon announcing that "with a view to the complete settlement of the questions relating to the trade in contraband, the British and French Legations at The Hague reserve the right to appoint Sir Francis Oppenheimer to make the necessary arrangements with the Netherlands Oversea Trust."[30] Loudon, who apparently knew of the contents of the note before it was officially presented, let van Vollenhoven know that he feared that reference to "complete settlement" of the contraband question might be construed as an undertaking given to a belligerent government and therefore compromising to Dutch neutrality. Indeed, Loudon was prepared to let the negotiations collapse entirely rather than permit this interpretation. Some slight alterations were made at the last moment and Loudon agreed to recognize the agreement between the British and the Trust as valid. The British then requested that the Dutch Commerce Commission be instructed by the Dutch government to supply the British commercial attaché with the necessary statistical information on Dutch imports and exports, and that the Dutch government should send information regarding each consignment addressed to the government to the commercial attaché as early as possible.

It seems quite clear that, although both parties to this agreement understood that changes would probably need to be made as faults in the system of control appeared, they were on the whole satisfied with these beginnings. Each had gained: the Dutch received a measure of safety for their domestic supplies that came in from overseas, and the British some measure of control over Dutch imports and the co-operation of neutral traders in distinguishing neutral trade from enemy trade. These negotiations were but one example of what experience showed time after time—that neutral traders were more willing to come to an agreement on commercial matters than a government, fearful lest it endanger its neutral status. Merchants, after all, cared less for legal arguments based on international law and more for a satisfactory settlement of their own immediate problems.

The Dutch government was far from sorry to be relieved of some of the troublesome negotiations that British action had forced upon it. Carrying out the guarantees given to the British was now the first responsibility of the tradesmen; the government's responsibility was of a secondary nature. It still maintained its embargoes, issued ostensibly for domestic reasons, and in fact they were complementary to the guarantees given by the N.O.T. The Dutch government continued to be very wary of British proposals, but by giving its assent to the formation of the Trust and by giving its moral guarantee of the good faith of the organization, it opened the door to what came to be a very far-reaching Allied control of Dutch commerce.

NEGOTIATIONS WITH DENMARK

Although Denmark had a small thriving textile industry, did work in hides and leather, had a fishing fleet and a merchant marine, there was no doubt that her chief economic interests lay in cattle and pig breeding and dairying. Although the country was in a slightly more favorable position with respect to the home production of bread grains and forage than the Netherlands, it was still necessary to import certain grains and feedstuffs if her dairy production was to be maintained at a high level. A large part of these importations came from Germany, especially rye, hay, corn, and barley. On the other hand the major part of Denmark's coal supply came from England, whereas England was the chief buyer of Danish butter, bacon, and eggs. It almost goes without saying that many of the raw materials for Danish industries such as cotton, tannin, heavy hides, oilseeds, hemp, cocoa beans, and so on, came in from overseas. Large quantities of these were not brought in directly from their source, but were purchased by the Danes at the great exchanges in Hamburg and Bremen, as well as in London. Thus the outbreak of war and the virtual cessation of imports in these German ports made it necessary for the Danes to make new trade contacts.[31]

The Danish government was anxious to remain outside the conflict that engaged its neighbors. On August 1 the first of several proclamations of neutrality was made in a royal message.[32] The next day an act was passed that forbade the provisioning of belligerent warships with stores and fuel in Danish ports.[33] In the hope that belligerent action could be avoided in Danish territorial waters, the Danish government on August 5 and 6 laid mines in the waters leading to the Baltic, even though it was realized, in view of the probable disapproval of Great Britain, this might have important consequences for the economic life of the country.[34] On the whole the Danish Court was sympathetic with the Allied cause, and King Christian sent H. N. Andersen as his personal representative to London in order to establish close ties with the British government. However much sympathy the King had with Great Britain, there was still considerable fear in Danish governmental circles that Germany might capture Esbjerg if Danish export policy operated too much in favor of the Allies.[35]

The Danish government immediately took a number of steps that were intended to protect the economic interests of the country. The near financial panic that accompanied the outbreak of war made it necessary to close the Borse in Copenhagen and to put a moratorium on the convertibility of bank notes into gold. On August 6 the exportation of a long list of goods was prohibited, which included fodder, corn, potatoes; gold and silver; coal, coke, petroleum; arms, ammunition, gunpowder and explosives intended for war purposes; electric cables and motor cars; instruments for the manufacture and repair of arms; raw materials for shipbuilding, and wood. At almost the same time an attempt was made in co-operation with the Industriraadet (the Danish Chamber of Manufacturers) to facilitate deliveries of goods by securing promises not to take advantage of the state of war and thus suspend contracts. The greatest concern was felt over coal deliveries, for the price of coal had doubled within a few days and no one knew whether more supplies could be obtained from England. It was with some relief that the Danes received British assurances that the export would continue as far as possible provided the Danish government guaranteed that coal would not be re-exported. On August 7 a law was passed giving the government power to control prices of food and other essential commodities, and on August 11 an ordinance was issued decreeing a reduction of 25 per cent in the price of coal. In order to encourage shipping companies and crews to risk their ships and their lives in the service of delivering coal, a War Risk Insurance scheme was arranged on August 11 with four Danish marine insurance firms whereby the shipping companies paid 25 per cent of the premiums and the Danish government the rest. A more permanent and more far-reaching plan was set up under laws passed on September 10 and September 14 that covered both vessels and goods, again with the government underwriting a considerable part of the cost.[36]

In spite of the fact that many articles on Allied contraband lists were embargoed by the Danes, the British government was not satisfied that contraband goods going to Denmark were not ultimately bound for Germany. By October the Restriction of Enemy Supply Committee had issued several warnings about a Danish transit trade in petroleum and other contraband. The Danish authorities always gave assurances that their export prohibitions were being enforced and would continue to be. On October 14 the British sent identic notes to the northern European neutral governments asking for assurances that cargoes, particularly oil, copper, and rubber, would be landed at the neutral port of destination and would not be re-exported.[37] The British also requested that all ships proceeding to Scandinavian ports stop at a British port, such as Falmouth, Lough Swilly or Kirkwall, in order to avoid the inconveniences of being stopped at sea. E. J. C. Scavenius, the Danish foreign minister, answered on October 22 only with assurances that no kind of cereal or forage would be permitted to be exported and that there was little chance that embargoes laid to prevent domestic scarcity would be lifted.[38] In the absence of more specific guarantees, the British ordered the detention late in October of several ships carrying oil from the United States to Denmark.[39]

The October Order in Council with its far-reaching contraband provisions was drastic enough to convince the Danish government that concessions were advisable. Just as the British order was issued the Danish government had secured the passage of a bill through the Rigsdag on October 29 that made it an offense to give a false declaration in a ship's papers concerning the destination of either the vessel or its cargo, a measure that was intended to make it possible for the foreign minister to guarantee that imported goods would remain in the country.[40] Additions to the original embargo list had been made from time to time and early in November a new list which more nearly approximated the British contraband lists was assembled.[41] Even so, important metals, mineral oils, and so on were not included, but for the moment the British accepted the list as an adequate assurance that the goods on it would not be exported or passed in transit to enemy territory. Orders were sent to the British fleet and to British customs authorities to restrict interference with neutral vessels carrying cargoes included on Scandinavian embargo lists to verification of the ship's papers and cargo.[42]

On November 19 the British and French ministers presented proposals to the Danish Foreign Office similar to those made two days earlier to the Dutch.[43] While the British realized that the existing Danish embargo list was less variable in its interpretation than that issued by the Dutch, they still wanted the Danes to regulate the exportation of Danish meat and dairy products. This Scavenius would not do, since freedom of trade in domestic products was something his government could not sacrifice. Nor would he agree to make the embargo list coincide with the British contraband list. To agree to this demand would be to discriminate between the two belligerent forces. What the British may not have known is that the Danes had received on August 1, 1914, a declaration from the German government that it would not lay hindrances in the way of Danish food exports to the English market and that in the interests of continued Danish agricultural production it would not interfere with overseas imports of grain and fodder, all on condition that deliveries of much-needed food to Germany would continue.[44] Certainly the Danes would not lightly sacrifice this gain.

It was toward the end of November that the British Restriction of Enemy Supply Committee became aware that Copenhagen had become a base of supply to Germany for tinned meat and lard on a very large scale. It was known that 1,005,000 pounds of lard had been imported into Denmark in October, that meat imports had trebled, and that Swift and Company and Armour and Company had both established new branch offices in Copenhagen.[45] Statistics gathered in Denmark showed similar increases in oil, rubber, and copper orders. The suspicion that these goods were intended for Germany was substantiated by information gathered by the British censors that traders in contraband were setting up regular business houses in Copenhagen; instructions for evading British confiscation by using dummy consignees were intercepted. It is true that Grey threatened, early in December, to take advantage of the authority conferred by the October Order in Council and formally declare Denmark a base of enemy supply; but there is no doubt that he much preferred to reach an agreement with the Danes to regulate this trade if possible, not only to establish better relations with Denmark but to avoid a worse controversy with the United States.[46]

The beginnings of a control over Danish shipping engaged in overseas trade were made in November 1914 when Captain C. M. T. Cold, director of the Forenede Dampskibsselskab (United Steamship Company), which had by far the greatest tonnage of any company under the Danish flag, agreed with the British that he would make inquiries about all Danish consignees of contraband and he would forbid his agents in the United States to accept any cargo until they had been informed by him that the purchasers were above suspicion. In return Cold was given assurance that his ships, mainly cargo steamers, would not be detained in large numbers under the October Order in Council.[47]

In mid-December J. C. T. Clan, director of the Trade Department in the Danish Ministry of Foreign Affairs, arrived in London to negotiate an agreement that would avert a general detention of all cargoes bound for Denmark.[48] The Danish minister in London, H. de Grevenkop-Castenskiold, had already admitted that Danish embargoes might become inoperative at any time simply from the pressure of an already overstocked market. The embargoes on food and forage might continue to be effective because the Danish market could absorb such large amounts of these articles, but no such assurance could be given in regard to copper or rubber. The British government proposed to Clan that a representative firm of bona fide Danish importers should become the consignee of all imported meat products and give guarantees against re-exportation, and firms importing other contraband goods should give similar guarantees for each cargo. The Danish government would in no way be responsible for this system of assurances, and therefore its neutrality would not be involved.

It soon appeared that Clan had been instructed merely to defend the existing policy of his government and to refuse any demand that Danish dairy products be embargoed. Clan admitted that imported tinned meat might be added to the list, but he suggested that other contraband goods suspected of having an enemy destination might better be seized by the British before they reached Denmark. At the same time he made formal protest against Article 2 of the October Order in Council, even though it was the only legal basis on which conditional contraband on a continuous voyage through Denmark to Germany could be stopped.

In the course of these conversations in London it developed that the Danish government would agree to maintain its embargoes provided the Danes could continue to export freely their own home produce and to re-export contraband to Norway and Sweden. The Danes stood out against any proposals that the government should become the consignee for certain contraband goods, that they should add to the embargo lists except for domestic reasons, or that any institution similar to the Netherlands Oversea Trust be established in Denmark.[49] Grey still was unwilling to press the Danes too far, although after the detention of the ship *Kentucky*, with another large cargo of foodstuffs, Sir Eyre Crowe urged him to declare Denmark a base of enemy supply.[50] Grey clearly feared retaliation in the form of a stoppage of Danish agricultural products to England, which could only result in benefit to the Germans. Moreover, Grey believed it was important that negotiations with one of the northern neutrals should not break down, for such a failure would certainly be reflected in the negotiations that were going on at the same time with the others. This seemed to be a particular danger since the meeting of the three Scandinavian kings at Malmö on December 18 and 19 indicated the possibility of a co-ordinated policy in the future, even though nothing very concrete had been decided by them at this time.[51] At any rate King Christian instructed Andersen to urge the importance of reaching an agreement. In the end Grey decided that a limited agreement with the Danes was preferable to none at all.

By the beginning of January the general principles of such an agreement were decided upon, and a document, dated January 9, 1915, was duly signed. In it the Danish government declared its firm intention to maintain existing embargoes and not to grant licenses to export even if supplies became abundant.[52] The prohibitions were to include not only the raw materials named but also alloys, half-finished products, and manufactured goods. Denmark was to be permitted to export her domestic meats and lard so long as the importation of these goods into Denmark did not exceed normal amounts. The British thus left open the possibility of raising the question of excessive importations that released an equivalent amount of similar domestic goods for exportation to Germany; the article foreshadowed the later application of "produits similaires" clauses and rationing. The British, however, agreed for the moment not to raise any question of importations releasing domestic products, and for this they were rewarded by the addition of lard to the Danish embargo list on January 10, 1915.[53] The Danes were left free to export contraband to neighboring neutrals if the goods were included on the latters' embargo lists.

On the other side the British made a rather general promise that ships bound for Danish ports would only be detained when they contained contraband goods not on the Danish embargo lists or when the British had conclusive evidence of the ultimate enemy destination of their cargoes. The British agreed that for the present the Allies would not apply Article 2 of the October Order in Council, and that it would give due notice if compelled to do so in the future.

With this agreement the foundations for British control of Danish trade with Germany were laid. Although the Danish government had signed an accord with the British government, which the Dutch government refused to do in any circumstances, the end result was not so comprehensive. There was no control of particular kinds of cargoes, and except for the agreement secured with Captain Cold, no system of guarantees was as yet set up. As had been foreseen in the discussions just completed in London, negotiations toward such an end were soon begun with Danish industrialists and merchants.

NEGOTIATIONS WITH SWEDEN

On the eve of the war agriculture was still the chief occupation in Sweden, and although the country was by no means self-sufficient in its food and fodder supplies it did export important amounts of butter, meat, and livestock.[54] The most important articles of export, however, were wood and wood products which in 1913 amounted to 215,400,000 kronor, with paper and paper pulp ranking second, to an amount of 142,800,000 kronor. In both instances an overwhelming part was marketed in Great Britain. From the beginning of the twentieth century the manufacture of machinery became an important industry in Sweden, and more than half of this category of exports went to the Entente states in 1913. In addition large amounts of iron and steel were made, for which Great Britain was by far the best customer, with Germany buying only about half as much. Sweden imported almost all of her coal from Britain so that in ordinary circumstances the

British could have exerted great pressure on the Swedish government by threatening to cut off this supply. The one thing that prevented such action was the necessity of keeping a continuous supply of war materials going to Russia, and during a large part of the year this was possible only by using the Swedish railways, one of which ran to Haparanda on the Russo-Swedish frontier. Any threats by Great Britain could be met by obstacles placed in the way of this transit trade. Since Sweden was never so dependent on imported food and forage as were the Netherlands and Denmark, strictly economic factors played a less important role in determining her attitude toward the belligerents during the first months of the war.

Late in July 1914 the Swedish and Norwegian governments discussed what their respective policies should be in the event of a general European war. From the beginning the Swedish government and Court were generally known to be sympathetic to the Central Powers, while the Norwegians inclined toward the Allies. The Norwegians, whose relations with the Swedes had on the whole been amicable since the separation of the two states in 1905, nonetheless feared the possibility that Sweden might intervene in the war and that a combined German-Swedish attack against Norway would result. It was with some satisfaction that Nils C. Ihlen, the Norwegian foreign minister, received the inquiry made on July 29 by the Swedish minister in Christiania, Baron Ramel, whether he would agree that during the European war Norway and Sweden should guarantee never to attack each other. Ihlen readily agreed and notes to this effect were exchanged on August 8.[55] Thus the first step in Scandinavian co-operation during the war was taken. In the meantime the Swedish government on July 31 and August 3 issued declarations of neutrality.[56] Indeed, in spite of any sympathies for Germany that might exist, it was clear that the majority of the Swedish Riksdag and press supported the almost fierce determination of Hjalmar Hammarskjöld, the prime minister, and his foreign minister, Kurt Wallenberg, to maintain Swedish neutrality unimpaired. As shall be seen repeatedly, there was no government anywhere that stood out more firmly against any invasion of its neutral rights, or with greater success—for a variety of reasons.

Like its neutral neighbors, Sweden immediately took measures to control its own economic life by issuing a moratorium on gold payments; undertaking a state-supported scheme for insurance against war risks; establishing an Industrial Commission (Industrikommission) with the task of regulating the industrial life of the country, securing raw materials, regulating credit facilities, and the like; and setting up a Food Commission charged with securing sufficient supplies for domestic needs.[57] On August 1 the first embargo list prohibiting the export of war materials, coal, mineral oils, cereals, and so forth was published.[58] Since goods declared to be in transit were not at first included within the scope of the prohibition, large amounts of cereals and other raw materials continued to go to Germany. This state of affairs accounts for the policy the British soon established: all vessels bound for Swedish ports were detained by the examining forces at Kirkwall and the

Downs, and release was granted only when the owners of the contraband goods on board gave a guarantee against their re-exportation from Sweden. In some cases the release was ordered after the Swedish minister in London informed the British government that the goods in question were on the Swedish embargo list. When no such prohibition existed, the owner's guarantee was delivered through the Swedish legation in London.[59]

By October the stocks of grain in Sweden were diminishing, and Sweden's old sources of supply in Germany and Russia were virtually closed. In order to facilitate overseas shipments that came through British examination lines, the Swedish government on October 9 modified its policy toward goods in transit. Only in instances where the final (non-Swedish) destination appeared in the ship's papers were the goods allowed to proceed. When goods were declared to be in transit on arrival, but with no evidence that their real destination had been determined before the voyage began, the embargoes were applied. A few days later, on October 12, a guarantee was given to the British that no grain exports from Sweden to any belligerent country would be permitted.[60]

Sir Esme Howard, the British minister in Stockholm, believed that a more satisfactory method of dealing with the supply of goods to Germany through Sweden should be found, for the practice of general detentions was most irritating to the Swedes. Late in October it developed in his conversations with Wallenberg that Sweden was willing to forbid the export of all raw materials not normally exported provided the Allies trusted the Swedish government to operate its own embargoes. But the good effect of this move was almost at once offset by Swedish reaction to the British declaration that the North Sea was to be considered a military area, for the Swedish government took the lead in securing a concerted Scandinavian protest based on international law. The Allied ministers in Stockholm agreed that some move to placate Swedish public opinion was now even more desirable.[61]

It was at about the same time that the Allied proposals were being made to the Dutch and Danish governments, on November 17 and 19, that heads of an agreement were presented to the Swedes. The first British proposal that the Swedes should embargo all goods on the Allied contraband lists was refused. The British also sought to prevent the re-export of goods sent to a named consignee which were later declared to be in transit. The Swedish counterproposals included recognition of freedom from interference in the importation of certain grains and raw materials, including copper and ferromanganese, and recognition of the right to export goods of Swedish origin. The Swedes demanded the right to export contraband goods to Norway and Denmark, and also the right to grant export licenses for minimum quantities of embargoed goods to other destinations.

Under these conditions the British Contraband Department believed an agreement with Sweden, which was not essential since counterpressures could always be exerted by wholesale detentions, would be useless. It was Howard who kept insisting that even though concessions granted to the

Swedes might be abused, it was politically preferable to make them, especially in view of current rumors that Sweden might intervene in the war. It was also understood that Sweden was under pressures from Germany, which threatened severe reprisals if supplies to Russia continued to be carried on Swedish railroads. In the end the Foreign Office agreed to Howard's position, even though the freedom of the Swedes to export goods to Denmark might well add to the flood of exports from that country into Germany, a trade which the Danish government at that point seemed powerless to stop.

Early in December the Swedish government added a considerable number of goods to its embargo list and defined more carefully the categories already included.[62] The total effect was to make the Swedish list very nearly approximate the Allied contraband lists, although as a matter of principle the Swedish government still refused to make them conform exactly. On December 8 an agreement was registered in a memorandum of the British and French ministers which was accepted by the Swedish foreign minister. By it the Allies agreed not to interfere with neutral ships carrying contraband to Sweden except to examine and verify the ship's papers if the goods in the cargo were on the Swedish embargo list and were addressed to a named consignee. On the other hand contraband goods not on the Swedish embargo list might be detained or actually seized if evidence of an ultimate hostile destination was at hand. The Allies were bound to respect their first undertaking only if half-finished and manufactured articles produced from imported raw materials were also embargoed. The Allies agreed not to interfere with the exportation of goods produced in Sweden. They accepted the Swedish demands in regard to exportations to Norway and Denmark and recognized the right to grant export licenses for small quantities in special instances.

In these negotiations there appears to have been no attempt on the part of the Allies to secure the establishment of a general consignee in Sweden. The Swedes succeeded rather well in making no great concessions to the Allies, but it remained to be seen whether either party to the December agreement would benefit much from it.

NEGOTIATIONS WITH NORWAY

The economic situation in Norway differed somewhat from that of her Scandinavian neighbors inasmuch as agricultural products were relatively unimportant in Norwegian export trade. By far the most important exports were timber, timber products, paper, fish, and certain ores. A large part of the Norwegian population were seafaring men, either fishermen or sailors on Norwegian boats. A great variety of fish was taken from Norwegian waters, and even though the year 1912 had been a very bad one in the herring fish-eries, fish and fish products totaling some 319,000 tons with a value of more than 100,000,000 kroner were exported.[63] A large proportion of these fish exports went to the Catholic countries of southern Europe, although Germany was an important buyer of herring. The United Kingdom bought heavily in the timber and paper markets in Norway. In the three years 1910–1912, 27.27 per cent of the entire Norwegian export trade went to the United Kingdom, while 19.80 per cent went to Germany. The proportion was re-versed, however, in Norway's imports: 30.24 per cent came from Germany and 25.34 per cent from the United Kingdom. Over half of the goods (by value) imported from England were coal, steamships, and tin plate; Germany was the chief source of imported machinery and tools, and competed sharply with English textiles. Norway was quite unable to provide her own food supply and annually imported some 500,000 tons of grain, more than one fifth of which was purchased in German markets in 1912. The bulk of the grain supply was imported from Russia and overseas countries. Thus Nor-way's economy was largely based on taking fish from the sea, selling them in other countries, and on carrying the products of other countries all over the world. Geographically Norway was in an excellent position to sell her own products to, and undertake a carrying trade with, Germany, but many of Norway's necessities of life were either controlled at the source by Great Britain or had to travel through British-controlled waters.

The problems that the outbreak of war created had not been entirely unforeseen in Norway where as early as 1905 a commission had been estab-lished to consider the safety of her food supply in time of war, with a view to stockpiling, and where in 1912 the Defense Department had undertaken similar measures in respect to coal.[64] Nonetheless, Norway was seized by a general panic in the first days of the war, although the government took swift measures to avert more serious consequences.[65] Somewhat against the advice of the managing director of the Norges Bank, the government on August 4 passed a provisional statute suspending gold payments. Export prohibitions on grain and flour, potatoes, coal, coke, and mineral oils were imposed the same day, followed shortly by the appointment of a Food Commission with powers to fix prices and control distribution. Norway was, of course, faced with the problem of covering war risks to her merchant marine, but here a policy rather different from that of Denmark and Sweden was followed. A committee set up on August 11 to consider the matter under the chairman-ship of Johan Mowinckel, shipowner and president of the Odelsting, re-ported on August 14 in favor of a system of mutual and compulsory war risk insurance for ships, without the participation of government funds. It was felt that the population and the financial resources of the state were too small in relation to the size of the merchant marine for the government to undertake financial responsibility for any insurance scheme, particularly, as Wilhelm Keilhau says, since "Norwegian shipowners were known for their inclination to charter their ships for dangerous voyages when high profits were tempting." A law establishing such mutual insurance was passed on August 21, 1914, to be executed by a War Insurance Board, five members of which were appointed by the government. On September 8 a corporation, the Norsk Varekrigsforsikring, was established to cover war risks on cargoes, with 20 per cent of the risk taken up by this company, 40 per cent by the state, and 40 per cent reinsured with other Norwegian insurance companies.

In contrast with the Swedish government, the Norwegian cabinet led by Gunnar Knudsen, with Nils C. Ihlen as the foreign minister, never took such an adamant position on the questions of international law which came into play as a result of belligerent action. It is true that Norway issued proclamations of neutrality on August 1 and 4, and that, as we have seen, it entered into a nonaggression agreement with Sweden on August 8.[66] Ihlen, who was chiefly responsible for negotiations with the belligerents, was a businessman who had no interest in pressing legal arguments, who believed that the war would be short and that Norway would get on better if he took no strong measures and followed a "policy of postponement." In the early part of the war the Norwegian cabinet met with very little trouble in the Storting, which had been called into special session on August 8. Although there was no formal Burgfrieden, the Opposition showed no inclination to embarrass the moderate liberal government. The Opposition apparently did not seek even a coalition government. Knudsen was later to suggest that one of the reasons the Conservatives were so anxious to end party strife was that they wished to slow up the reform program to which the government was pledged.[67]

During the first few months of the war the British Restriction of Enemy Supply Committee noticed no unusual increase in Norwegian importations except that large grain orders were placed in North and South America.[68] It was recognized that these were probably made necessary by the failure of the usual European sources of supply. The British nonetheless detained many ships bound for Norwegian ports, often on general suspicion. The demands to Scandinavian ministers for guarantees against re-exportation became part of the routine business of the British Foreign Office, but their regularity made the practice no less vexatious to neutral shippers and merchants. Sir Mansfeldt Findlay, the British minister to Norway, had no reason to doubt the good intentions of the Norwegian government in executing its embargoes. He stressed the seriousness of Norway's supply problem. Although some leakage of imported goods to Germany was inevitable, Findlay believed it was better to put up with it than to create ill will in Norwegian governmental and business circles.[69]

The November announcement that the North Sea would be considered a military area was received with general indignation in Norway. No other neutral was so much affected by this threat to the continuation of merchant shipping in northern Europe. Findlay had in mid-October made efforts to persuade the Norwegians to avoid the difficulties involved in carrying goods for bona fide neutral consumption by having ships call voluntarily at a British port.[70] This attempt foreshadowed British policy undertaken more generally in November, and although the Norwegian government was fore-warned that did not prevent the German minister's exploiting the situation to the full. The Norwegian government immediately sent a protest to the British government on November 5 and then joined in another protest in common with Sweden and Denmark on November 13, which was directed to France, Russia, and Germany as well.[71] This instance of Scandinavian co-operation was viewed with apprehension by Findlay who feared this united action would make future negotiations more difficult for the British. However, the feeling of extreme irritation against the British changed gradually to one of toleration when the losses from German mines were compared with the inconveniences of calling at a British port for directions for a safe course.

In the third week of November, the British presented demands to the Norwegians similar to those made to the Dutch and the other Scandinavians. The Norwegians were slow to reply and when Findlay pressed Ihlen for an answer, the latter reminded him of Grey's statement, made early in November, that the British were satisfied that Scandinavian embargoes were a sufficient guarantee against re-exportation.[72] Ihlen maintained that no further negotiations were necessary, and he made no answer at all to the general proposal that all articles on Allied contraband lists should be embargoed. The French and British ministers in a second memorandum reminded Ihlen of the discrepancies between the two lists and asked for assurances in regard to copper, aluminum, nickel, lead, iron ore, rubber, and petroleum, of which only rubber was on the Norwegian embargo list at that time.[73]

Norway was then making heavy importations of copper for electrical purposes, but at the same time was exporting native copper and cupreous pyrites, which were much in demand in Germany for the manufacture of sulfuric acid. Ihlen, however, refused to give any guarantees concerning the exportation of metals from Norwegian mines; Norway insisted it must reserve the right to sell its own products to whomever it wished. Ihlen did admit, however, that his government might forbid the exportation of imported metals if the Allies recognized Norway's right to trade freely with Denmark and Sweden as well as the right to grant exemptions from the general prohibitions. He promised to notify the Allied ministers of these exemptions in advance and suggested the possibility of adding other articles to the embargo. Although the British Contraband Department disliked to admit the right to grant licenses, it was well satisfied with the concessions that the Norwegians offered on the other points.

Thereafter the British negotiators were most concerned with the enlargement of the embargo lists, and in practice Ihlen met Allied wishes. On December 11 copper and copperplates were embargoed, on December 16 jute and scrap iron and steel, on December 24 aluminum and lead; and on January 5, 1915, nickel was added.[74] By that time the lists were so comprehensive that the Allies decided not to press their proposals on the Norwegian government any further at the moment. Instead they preferred to begin negotiations with particular trades and trading houses for guarantees and concessions. It was believed that this policy would, in general, involve the Norwegian government less and would decrease the possibility of the formation of a close union of the Scandinavian states.[75]

THE PRACTICAL ACCOMPLISHMENTS OF ALLIED NEGOTIATIONS

Because of its ability to exert pressure on neutral trade by detaining overseas supplies, the British government succeeded by the end of 1914 in enlisting the aid of the Scandinavian governments in controlling the transit of contraband goods to Germany. The concessions made by Dutch merchants and shipowners were even more comprehensive. The crucial point in the agreements or tacit understandings was the promise of these neutral governments to maintain embargoes that, in practice, were comparable to the Allied contraband lists.

Up to this point in the economic war the British were trying to do no more than stop contraband trade with Germany; there was as yet no attempt to stop all German imports and exports. The absence of sufficient information on which to take all suspected cargoes before a prize court explains why the British were satisfied with the agreements respecting neutral embargoes. Even these agreements were not uniform, nor, indeed, could they be because of the differences in the economic policies and political points of view of the neutral governments involved. However, to some degree, any agreement made by one of these governments with a belligerent was unneutral, and whether these agreements survived or were extended depended on Allied military and naval victories. Moreover, the British quite appreciated the embarrassment these agreements might cause neutral governments and therefore, by the end of 1914, had come to the conclusion that it was desirable to deal directly with neutral merchants, manufacturers, and shipowners. The results of the first negotiations with the Netherlands Oversea Trust proved the wisdom of this policy.

It was equally important to the British government, once it had made these agreements, that their operation should not become the subject of protest by the United States. From late October onward the Department of State sent almost daily inquiries concerning British intentions toward American ships and cargoes, and protested not infrequently against what were alleged to be unwarranted detentions and seizures. It is important to note, however, that although the State Department knew in advance that the British were carrying on negotiations with the border neutrals, the United States made no move to block them. Even though the State Department on

November 7 protested to Spring Rice against the detention of the *John D. Rockefeller*, the *Platuria* and the *Chr. Knudsen* pending the conclusion of agreements with Denmark guaranteeing the nonexportation of oil, no objection of any sort was made to British demands to a neutral state for such guarantees.[76] At the same time the United States government quite properly refused to take even a tacit part in the establishment of neutral importation trusts.[77]

In its desire to facilitate trade necessary to industrial production in the United States, the State Department went even a step further in tolerating the British policy of demanding guarantees of nonexportation for goods produced in the British Empire. Numerous inquiries had been made on behalf of American manufacturers of textiles, rubber, and steel as to whether exemptions from British and French embargoes could be made to permit the exportation of wool, hides, raw rubber, manganese and chrome ores, and plumbago.[78] Page reported on November 6 that such requests were entertained by the British government only when the neutral government guaranteed that neither the goods nor any articles manufactured therefrom would be exported from its territory.[79] Page took it for granted that the United States government could give no such guarantee. Various American importers had offered to give guarantees against re-exportation and as a consequence William Jennings Bryan informed Page on November 11 and 12 that "the Department [of State] will consider reasonable arrangements to secure against exportation of wool so obtained from United States to countries at war with Great Britain."[80]

Page was able to report on November 17 that Chandler Anderson, special legal adviser to the embassy, was conferring with the Foreign Office.[81] Anderson suggested that the United States government should recommend to the British the firms that desired to import particular British goods, and it should also furnish the British with information about the enforcement of guarantees given by these importers. As a result of these conversations a "working arrangement" was drawn up on December 5, 1914, which covered detentions of American ships and cargoes as well as licenses to export goods from Great Britain under guarantees against re-exportation.[82] It was proposed that the United States government should give "administrative assistance" to end certain fraudulent practices that the British government alleged had been used by American exporters—shipping contraband with false or simulated descriptions or with no description whatever. It was implied in the preceding negotiations that this assistance would include a return to the practice of publishing manifests of cargoes. This practice had been stopped by a Treasury Order of October 28, 1914, which provided that such publication could not be made until thirty days after the vessel sailed, in order to prevent improper use by agents of belligerent governments of the information thus furnished.[83] It was also proposed in the working arrangement that the United States should refrain from supporting the claims of traders concerning detentions of copper cargoes destined to the enemy.

The British suggested that addressing goods to bona fide consignees in neutral ports would greatly minimize the risk of detention, since negotiations with these neutral governments respecting embargoes were well advanced. In return for these American concessions, the British government declared itself willing to negotiate for permission to export from Great Britain and its colonies to the United States, rubber, hides, jute, plumbago, manganese, ferromanganese, chrome, tungsten ore, and other ingredients of steel. Assurances were to be given that these articles would not in any form be exported to states at war with Great Britain or to neutral European countries from which Great Britain had not received satisfactory guarantees against re-exportation.

No definite refusal or acceptance was ever given concerning this "working arrangement." On December 9 Bryan said there then appeared to be no insurmountable obstacle to such a common understanding,[84] but late in December a note on detentions was sent which seemed to indicate a refusal was intended. Spring Rice reported that there was no hope of reaching an agreement, although the State Department still continued to press for the removal of certain British export restrictions.[85] The State Department refused to promise not to press the claims of American copper interests and to the British this was a necessary part of the arrangement. Once more the policy of the State Department seemed confused; indeed Spring Rice reported to his government that the situation in the State Department was "chaotic," with a good many technical questions being delegated to a variety of persons about whose conduct the secretary of state knew nothing.[86]

Even though no formal agreement was made with the United States government, Britain nonetheless secured most of its aims. It had, of course, been part of the original scheme that agreements should be concluded with American manufacturers desiring to import British raw materials. There had been nothing in the expressed attitude of the State Department to prevent their being negotiated now. During January, February, and March 1915 such arrangements were made with the rubber manufacturers, the Textile Alliance, the United States Steel Products Company, and the Carnegie Steel Corporation.[87] In January 1915 the American copper producers agreed that they would ship copper only to named consumers in neutral countries where its exportation was prohibited, to a recognized purchaser in London, or to a bank approved by the British government. Sir Eyre Crowe was much pleased with the control this arrangement gave the British authorities, and even though there was some muttering in the United States that it might make it possible for the British to corner the copper market, it did quiet a potentially angry controversy.[88] More important was the fact that the United States did actually comply to a certain extent with the British request for co-operation. On January 5, 1915, the United States Treasury issued a notice that called attention to the importance of using complete and accurate shipping manifests in order to exclude all suspicion that American exports were being shipped with the intention of concealing the true nature and destination of the goods.[89] Another step was taken by the Treasury that in fact carried out the proposal when on February 16, 1915, the order prohibiting the publication of ship manifests until thirty days after sailing was rescinded.[90] These two administrative orders were exactly what the British government had asked the United States to do. The State Department refused to make an agreement on the subject, but the government was not averse to taking the same action without one.

The British, then, had secured the beginnings of a system of trade controls over neutral commerce in both Europe and America, without evoking more than polite notes of protest from the United States government. The latter had shown itself willing to permit its citizens to make private agreements if American trade and industries would thus be benefited. It even went further and of its own accord adopted measures that made the execution of these agreements easier. Having received this degree of toleration, the British government felt quite safe in perfecting and extending its system of coercion in Europe.

IV

The Reprisals Order in Council, March 11, 1915

THE measures of economic warfare undertaken by the Allies up to the end of 1914 were, as has been shown, based primarily upon the right to intercept contraband, although agreements made with neutral governments and neutral merchants had supplemented these controls. It was the German declaration, made on February 4, 1915, of submarine warfare in the waters around Great Britain and Ireland that led to further Allied measures against enemy trade. It was the Order in Council of March 11, 1915, that laid the legal foundation of the so-called blockade of Germany.

THE GERMAN DECLARATION OF SUBMARINE WARFARE, FEBRUARY 4, 1915

The events leading up to the German proclamation of February 4 are complicated and it will suffice here to mention some of the factors that determined the German government to take this course.[1] Until that time German submarines had undertaken no large, predetermined campaign against enemy ships but had simply given chase to ships they encountered in the Channel and Irish Sea. The first proposal for a more systematic submarine campaign against British seaborne trade in retaliation against the laying of mines by the British in the Channel was made on October 8, 1914, in a report from one Captain Bauer to Admiral von Ingenohl, commander of the High Seas Fleet.[2] Both von Ingenohl and Admiral Hugo von Pohl, chief of the naval staff, received the idea with favor.[3] It was the British Admiralty's notification that the North Sea would be considered a military area that decided von Pohl to press the matter. However, great opposition was encountered, partly from Admiral Alfred von Tirpitz who believed that the navy was then unprepared for such a campaign, but most of all from Beth-mann-Hollweg, the chancellor, who feared the political consequences of such a threat to neutral commerce.[4] Von Pohl, however, was emphatic in his belief that submarine warfare would be decisive, an opinion that was backed by the reports of certain German professors of economics as to the effect a blockade would have on English supplies.[5] The fact was that submarines had never been used on a large scale, and no one knew enough about their shortcomings to refute von Pohl. By January public opinion was thoroughly aroused over the measures taken by the British to stop German overseas commerce through contiguous neutrals.[6] It was easy to make it appear that a submarine blockade of England was Germany's sole salvation.

The new naval policy, decided upon in the critical days of February 1–4, was announced in a proclamation of February 4, 1915.[7] This document gave as its *raison d'être* the actions of the British government taken in defiance of the Declaration of London and of international law: the extension of contraband lists; the abolition, in practice, of the distinction between absolute and conditional contraband; the capture of German private property of a noncontraband nature on neutral ships; the removal of German citizens from neutral ships; the declaration of the North Sea as a military area; and the great dangers to neutral shipping in Scottish waters. The Germans also protested that neutral governments had aided in the execution of British measures by yielding to British pressure to hinder "the transit of wares for peaceful purposes to Germany," by laying export and transit embargoes. In retaliation the German government then declared all the waters around Great Britain and Ireland, including the entire English Channel, an area of war. Beginning on February 18, 1915, the German Navy would attempt to destroy every merchant vessel found in that area, and no promises about the safety of goods and crews could be given. Neutral ships were warned against entering the war zone because the British government had ordered its ships, when in danger of capture, to fly neutral flags as a *ruse de guerre*, and "the contingencies of naval warfare" made it impossible always to prevent neutral ships from becoming the victims of torpedoes. A zone free from such peril was marked off around the Norwegian and Dutch North Sea coasts.

This German announcement occasioned almost immediate protests from neutral governments.[8] The Dutch government asserted that it had protested against every measure taken by belligerents that was, in its view, opposed to international law and injured Dutch interests. It insisted that the decline in exports and transit of goods to Germany was not the result of measures taken by the Allied governments at sea, and that in any case the Dutch government had refused to give any guarantees that goods brought in from overseas would not be forwarded to Germany. Dutch embargoes had been issued solely to preserve domestic supplies. The Dutch government stated that while it had protested against the British declaration respecting the North Sea, that decree had up to that time in no way influenced Dutch shipping: Dutch ships continued to follow their regular routes and no part of the Dutch coast was blockaded.

The charge that the British had misused neutral flags was viewed very seriously by the Dutch. It was true that on February 2 the British Admiralty had issued instructions to British merchant-captains on the Dutch route that, in order to avoid being sunk, they were to hoist a neutral flag when submarines were known to be about. The Dutch as well as the United States, Italian, and Swedish governments protested to the British against this order.[9] The British contended that the use of a neutral flag by a belligerent ship to avoid capture was a recognized *ruse de guerre* which in no way increased the burden of the ordinary legal obligation of a warship to determine the nationality of the vessel and the nature of its cargo before making a capture. This duty was one which still rested on German ships.[10] The Dutch reply to this argument was typical of those given by other neutrals: the use of a state's flag without its own consent was always an abuse, and was even more grave in time of war when doubt was thus thrown on neutral ships that were flying their own flag.[11] It must be admitted that this furor died down very soon, for other marks that clearly distinguished neutral ships were soon used—e.g., floodlighting at night on large symbols painted on the sides of the ship.

The effects of the German submarine campaign were not immediately felt by neutrals, for on the day the campaign began only two German submarines were at sea. By the end of February, eight had been in action, and seven ships, all of British registry, had been sunk. In the month of March only twenty-one merchant ships, with a total of 25,000 tons, were sunk of the five thousand that entered and left English ports.[12]

ALLIED CONSULTATIONS AND THE AMERICAN PROPOSAL FOR A WORKING ARRANGEMENT

Even before the severity of the new German policy could be fully realized the Allied governments decided to take measures of reprisal. It was Admiral Moreau of the French Navy who first, in a conversation with Jean Gout, expressed the idea that the time had come to stop all of Germany's foreign commerce.[13] The proposal was forwarded to Théophile Delcassé, the French foreign minister, who was then in London, and with his approval special representatives were sent to London to confer with the Admiralty and Foreign Office. The French wished to put as few burdens on neutrals as possible and suggested that a fund be created from the sale of enemy prizes to reimburse neutral losses, and that the Allies should first attempt to make agreements with the northern neutrals to cause them to end their trade with Germany. The British refused to consider this last proposal because they did not want to make retaliation against Germany depend in any way on negotiations with neutrals. They knew such a procedure would consume valuable time and would only give a chance for concerted neutral resistance to the Allied measures. The French withdrew their proposals and by February 20 agreed to act with the British who had already, by February 9, formulated a draft of a new order in council. By February 26 the order, somewhat amended in details, was ready for publication.[14]

There seems to have been no great public demand in England that retaliatory measures should be taken against Germany. The attitude of the London *Times* and its correspondents seemed to be that the German threats were rather futile, an opinion which became more confirmed as time went on.[15] That some action was contemplated by the government was made clear to the public by Asquith in the House of Commons on February 11.[16] Lord Charles Beresford had suggested that an extension of contraband lists should be made to include all food and raw materials. Asquith expressed the hope that he could shortly announce the new measures the government intended to take. Their general nature was indicated to the House by Churchill on February 15, when he said that the immunities of neutral ships carrying goods to and from German ports must be reconsidered in view of the fact that Germany had placed itself outside all international obligations. The new declaration, he said, "will have the effect for the first time of applying the full force of naval pressure to the enemy."[17]

There are indications, however, that even after Asquith's statement, Grey might have been willing to compromise. The chief basis for such an assertion is the reception he gave to the American proposal addressed to Germany and Great Britain on February 20, 1915, that some working arrangement in regard to the use of mines, neutral flags, and submarines should be made.[18] The note proposed that submarines should not be used to attack merchant vessels except to enforce the right of search. This, obviously, would have involved a great concession on the part of Germany. On the other hand, Great Britain was asked to agree not to make foodstuffs absolute contraband and not to detain shipments of foodstuffs consigned to certain agencies in Germany that would be designated by the United States government. Such food would only be distributed to licensed retailers who would sell solely to noncombatants.

The American note was the subject of a conversation between Grey and Page on February 23. Grey was noncommittal but appeared to favor the proposal at least in principle, although he told Page that it would be necessary to submit the matter to the cabinet before an answer could be given. This was probably done on February 24, the same day that a revised draft of the retaliation order in council was approved.[19] Opinion in the cabinet was against acceptance of the working arrangement; a memorandum by Maurice P. A. Hankey, urging that no compromise be made, was circulated. By February most people in the British government had arrived at the conclusion that little was to be gained by attempts to pacify American opinion, and that the chief considerations of policy should be Britain's self-interest. On the whole the advantages in the American proposal seemed to the British to be on the German side, for by it England would save a few steamers from the—thus far—rather feeble submarine campaign, while Germany would receive unlimited food supplies for its civilian population. The British were by this time putting a certain faith in the coercive power of their economic war, and to accept the principle of the immunity from capture of the enemy's civilian food supply would nullify the effect of the contemplated retaliatory measures.

The British were relieved of any odium of refusal by the answer made on February 28 by the German government. The German government was not much attracted by the American proposals at this particular time, for, having announced its submarine campaign, it could hardly abandon it without loss of prestige, both at home and in foreign countries.[20] Moreover, it was doubted by some whether adequate neutral tonnage would be free and willing to import food from America. Germany feared that even if this compromise were accepted, England would put some new hindrances in the way of importation. The German note accepted less than the American propositions in regard to mines and submarines, and made the modification of submarine practice depend upon the abstinence of British merchantmen from flying neutral flags and arming themselves.[21] What definitely ended the possibility of the proposal being accepted was the German demand that not only should regulated food importations be permitted through neutral as well as German ports, but also that similar facilities should be given for importation for civilian use of raw materials mentioned in the Declaration of London.

The British reply was sent to the American government on March 13,[22] after the German reply had been published and after reprisals against Germany had been announced by the Allied governments. Britain's refusal to accept the proposal ended the attempt to secure a *modus vivendi* that would reconcile the illegal features of the economic campaigns of both belligerents.

THE BRITISH AND FRENCH JOINT DECLARATION AND THE REPRISALS ORDER IN COUNCIL

Identic notes to neutral governments were delivered by the British and French governments on March 1, 1915, declaring their intention to undertake new measures against enemy trade.[23] The violations of international law committed by German submarines were cited—failure to take captured ships into prize courts, failure to discriminate between neutral and enemy vessels, and failure to make provision for the safety of the crew and passengers of the vessels they sank. The whole method of submarine warfare was said to be outside the scope of any of the international instruments regulating operations against commerce in time of war. The Allied governments stated that they were therefore "driven to frame retaliatory measures in order in their turn to prevent commodities of any kind from reaching or leaving Germany." The note promised that these measures would be carried out without risk to neutral ships and to neutral or noncombatant life, and then asserted that the Allied governments "would feel free to detain and take into port ships carrying goods of presumed enemy destination, ownership or origin." Only ships or cargoes otherwise liable to condemnation would be confiscated, and ships that sailed before March 1 would not be affected.

The Allied declaration was put into effect by a British Order in Council on March 11 and by a French Decree on March 13, 1915.[24] The Order in Council merits close attention. Article 1 provided that no merchant vessel sailing from its port of departure after March 1, 1915, would be allowed to proceed to any German port, and unless it received a pass permitting it to proceed to some neutral or Allied port its cargo was to be discharged in a British port. Contraband goods would presumably be confiscated, and noncontraband articles could either be requisitioned for government use or restored to their owners on such terms as the prize court would deem just. Similarly, according to Article 2, no merchant vessel would be allowed to proceed on her voyage from a German port after March 1, and the whole cargo of any ship so proceeding could be requisitioned, detained, or sold under the direction of the prize court. No proceeds of such sales were to be paid out until the conclusion of peace unless it could be shown that the goods had become neutral property before the Order in Council was issued; in the last instance the amount realized on their sale might be released to the owners. Article 3 provided that goods of enemy destination, or goods of enemy ownership,[25] found on ships bound for non-German ports might be required to be discharged in a British or Allied port; they might be released only under the conditions set up in Article 2. The same procedure might be required of goods of enemy origin or ownership on ships sailing from non-German ports (Article 4), but nothing in the Order should prevent the release of neutral property of enemy origin to the proper British authorities. At the same time it was stated that relaxations of the provisions of the Order could be made in respect to the merchant ships of any country that declared that no commerce intended for or originating in Germany or belonging to German subjects should enjoy the protection of its flag.

Here, for the first time, the British government attempted to stop all German trade, imports and exports alike, without reference to its contraband or noncontraband character. As has been shown, the only legal means known to international law by which a belligerent could prevent all egress and ingress of ships and supplies to its enemy's ports was by declaring a blockade and enforcing it with ships stationed off those ports or closely patrolling the waters around them. While this British Order in Council had the same aim as a legal blockade, none was declared and, in fact, the British government rather studiously avoided that characterization of its new measures. The penalties for violating the Order in Council were not those which attached to running a blockade. No penalty of confiscation attached to the ship unless it carried a cargo that was one-half contraband, or unless it rendered unneutral service—i.e., the penalties were those laid down in the Declaration of London as amended by the Order in Council of October 29, 1914. The neutral goods brought in under the new Order might be condemned only if they were otherwise liable, e.g., as contraband goods.

In the absence of a declared blockade there had been no legal means by which noncontraband goods destined to German ports could be captured, and none by which all goods exported from German ports—unless they were found on enemy ships—could be captured. Certainly enemy property had not been generally liable to capture since 1856, when noncontraband enemy property on board neutral ships had been specifically exempted by the Declaration of Paris. This principle was now clearly set aside when the intention to capture all goods of enemy ownership, origin, and destination was carried out.

The March Order in Council also restated and extended the doctrine of continuous voyage so that it not only applied to contraband goods destined to a neutral port and ultimately to the enemy, but also to all goods owned by the enemy or ultimately destined to enemy territory. This extension of power gave the British a means of dealing with a larger amount of indirect trade through neutral territory, for noncontraband goods could now be stopped. Of course these goods were to be released to their neutral owners on certain conditions, but they were prevented from reaching the enemy. Although this appeared to make it unnecessary to declare goods contraband,

it was still considered better policy to do so; neutral governments would protest less over the seizure of a cargo of contraband than they would over one
seized by some such right as that set up by the Order in Council.[26]

The British and French governments made no pretense that the new
Order and Decree were in accord with the rules of international law governing blockade and contraband. They were quite frankly undertaking these
measures as a reprisal against Germany's illegal methods of submarine warfare. International law recognized the right of a belligerent in the face of a
grave and persistent violation of the rules of warfare by an enemy, to take
measures of reprisal when all legal methods of combating the violation had
failed.[27] The reprisal measures might be illegal, but they were tolerated because of the first violation by an adversary. International law recognized that
the acts of retaliation need not be of the identical character as the wrong
suffered, but they should be in just proportion to the offense and should
terminate when the first wrong ceased to exist. However, international law
did not define the extent to which a belligerent government might infringe
upon the rights of neutrals in the name of carrying out reprisals. When
Asquith read the Allied declaration in the House of Commons on March 1,
1915, he recognized the fact that neutrals would suffer inconvenience and
loss; he added a statement of some significance: ". . . under existing conditions there is no form of economic pressure to which we do not consider
ourselves entitled to resort. If, as a consequence, neutrals suffer inconvenience and loss of trade, we regret it, but we beg them to remember that this
phase of the war was not initiated by us."[28]

The British prize courts were in time called upon to decide the validity
of the March Order in Council, particularly as it affected neutral property.
The prize courts did not concern themselves very much with the compatibility of the Order and the law of nations, but in the case of the *Stigstad*
some indication of the attitude of the court was given by Sir Samuel Evans
in his decision.[29] He said,

> According to the judgement of the Privy Council in the case of the
> *Zamora*, although the recitals as to the case for reprisals are con-
> clusive, the Court is not actually bound to hold that the means of
> meeting emergencies by way of reprisals are the best or only means.
> The Privy Council further declared that no party aggrieved is pre-
> cluded from contending ". . . that these means are unlawful, as
> entailing on neutrals a degree of inconvenience unreasonable, con-
> sidering all the circumstances of the case." If I have to express my
> opinion on that, I express it without doubt, that the means adopted
> in this Order in Council did not entail upon neutrals a degree of
> inconvenience unreasonable considering all the circumstances of the
> case, and that, therefore, it cannot be said that by reason of those
> means the Order in Council is in itself unlawful.

As Jan H. W. Verzijl very pointedly remarks, the prize court passed in silence the question of the invalidity of the Order in the light of written law, formulated in the second rule of the Declaration of Paris.[30]

A further justification for the reprisal measures that were later undertaken by the British was found by Lord Sumner in the case of the *Leonora*: ". . . in estimating the burden of the retaliation, account must be taken of the gravity of the original offence which provoked it, and that it is material to consider not only the burden which the neutral is called upon to bear, but the peril from which, at the price of that burden, it may be expected that belligerent retaliation will deliver him."[31]

NEUTRALS AND THE REPRISALS ORDER IN COUNCIL

The first reaction of the United States government to the British and French declaration of March 1 was one of uncertainty as to its exact implications. On March 8, 1915, Page brought to Grey's attention the points that most troubled the State Department: the fate of detained noncontraband goods, the fate of goods of enemy origin (1) owned by a neutral or (2) owned by an enemy subject, and the fate of ships that carried goods out of Germany.[32] Page said that while his government was fully alive to the possibility that new methods of warfare, particularly the use of the submarine for both defensive and offensive purposes, might make the former means of maintaining a blockade physically impossible, it felt that there should be some limitation on the radius of activity, especially if the Allied declaration was to be regarded as constituting a blockade.

After the State Department received the text of the Order in Council, Page presented on April 2 a more detailed criticism and note of protest to Grey.[33] The United States took exception to the inclusion of neutral ports and coasts within the area of what the United States called the blockade. It regarded all acts taken beyond the ordinary right of visit and search to prevent shipment of contraband as a distinct invasion of the sovereign rights of states whose ships and commerce were interfered with. But again the note made an admission, very welcome to the British, that the United States was not oblivious to the great changes that had occurred in conditions and means of naval warfare, and that it might be ready to admit that the old form of close blockade was no longer practicable. The United States still believed that it was possible "to conform at least to the spirit and principles of the established rules of war." The minimum it would require was that free access to neutral ports should be permitted for everything except contraband in transit to the enemy, even though the blockading lines might extend across the approaches to neutral harbors. A general protest was made against the argument that the unlawful action of the German government was sufficient justification for the illegal measures undertaken by Great Britain.

At the same time, then, that the United States recognized that new conditions might make it necessary to adapt the old rules of blockade to meet new weapons, it still demanded that goods with a bona fide neutral destination should be allowed through the British cordon and that the right of American vessels carrying noncontraband to approach neutral ports must remain unrestricted. Yet the British believed that the blockade of Germany could be made effective only if noncontraband goods could be stopped in their transit through neutral territory. They realized that in the end the execution of the Order in Council would depend on neutral toleration. On the whole the United States government had been friendly in its protest,[34] and if the border neutrals agreed to accept the restrictions that the Allies wished to place on their trade, the United States would probably acquiesce.

The three Scandinavian states once more took counsel together and on March 17 they presented identic notes to the British and French governments.[35] The notes were short and the protest no more than a formal one, that was sent in order to reserve their full neutral rights under international law.

NEW ADMINISTRATIVE ORGANS IN GREAT BRITAIN AND FRANCE

The machinery already set up in England and France to administer the orders in council and decrees respecting enemy trade was soon supplemented by new committees. The British government was gradually collecting a large body of information about shipping companies, importers and exporters, and all their commercial relationships. The censorship of cable messages formed one of the most important sources of information, since the British and French governments were in a position to read all of the messages sent from overseas into Central Europe. The German transatlantic cables, which ran through the Channel, had been cut in the early days of the war.[36] All other transatlantic cables had at least one of their terminals in British or French territory and were thus subject to censorship.[37] The cables connecting England with the Scandinavian countries, through which messages would ordinarily be transmitted to Germany and the rest of Central Europe, were owned mainly by a Danish firm, the Great Northern Telegraph Company, but here again one terminal in England gave British authorities adequate opportunity for censoring messages.

All of the information from cables, together with that gleaned from intercepted letters, and confidential reports made by Allied agents, dealt with innumerable commercial transactions. Early in the spring of 1915 a special organization, the War Trade Intelligence Department, was set up in London under Hankey's direction to collate and index the information as it came in. The War Trade Intelligence Department was itself a division of the War Trade Department which had been established by Treasury order on February 17, 1915, as a result of a decision reached by the Committee of Imperial Defence in January.[38] The first duties given the War Trade Department had been to deal with requests for export and import licenses, work which the Trading with the Enemy Committee and the Licensing Committee had formerly done. Lord Emmott was director of the War Trade Department and Sir Nathaniel Highmore its secretary.

Another division of the War Trade Department, the War Trade Statistical Department, was soon created to have special charge of collecting figures on the imports and exports of the northern neutral countries. Weekly and monthly reports were issued for the use of other governmental departments on the amount and destination of all goods passing through the British lines at the Downs and in Scottish waters, as well as the number of licenses issued for British exportations.

The Contraband Committee, which was still an important part of the organization, also dealt with ships and cargoes. The information collected by the War Trade Intelligence Department on any detained cargo was forwarded to the Committee to facilitate its reaching a decision as to whether to send the cargo to the prize court, to detain it for further investigation, or to release it at once. The ownership and ultimate destination of such a cargo were always first considerations in reaching the decision, but it was also necessary to determine whether the cargo was covered by agreements with neutral shipowners or traders. If adequate guarantees against re-exportation were given, the cargo would be allowed to proceed. The number of cases processed by the Contraband Committee rose sharply in March and succeeding months, and the proportion of detentions to releases also increased. This was all part of a deliberate policy made clear in new fleet orders, approved by the cabinet on March 10, 1915, to put pressure on neutrals and discourage their trading with Britain's enemies. Generally speaking the guarantee of the Netherlands Oversea Trust was regarded as sufficient, and for political reasons connected with the Allied hope that Italy would soon throw in her lot with them, cargoes destined to Italian ports were treated with special mildness.[39]

The new Allied attempt to stop all goods of enemy origin made necessary a new committee, the Enemy Exports Committee.[40] This committee, sitting at the Foreign Office, was established in March 1915 and was composed of representatives of the Foreign Office, Admiralty, and Board of Trade. Commander Frederick Leverton Harris presided over it until June 1916. Very soon the practice of sending goods accompanied by properly attested certificates of origin was adopted by neutral tradesmen. The decisions of the Enemy Exports Committee were greatly facilitated, for it thus became easier to distinguish between goods of enemy and neutral production.

Organization for economic warfare in France still lagged behind that developed in Great Britain. In November 1914 Delcassé, who had taken due note of the establishment of the Restriction of Enemy Supply Committee in England, recommended to his government that a similar body should be set up in France in order to co-ordinate the work of the various ministries dealing with enemy trade.[41] He proposed that this committee should not only recommend measures to be taken against enemy supply but it should also purchase certain foods and raw materials in neutral markets in order to prevent their acquisition by the enemy. Representatives of the Ministries of War, Foreign Affairs, Commerce, Agriculture, Marine, Finance, and Justice met and reached agreement on a very complete project which was then submitted to the cabinet. This first plan was abandoned on the ground that it would be an infringement of parliamentary prerogative to allow a committee such an extended right to purchase goods whose utilization by France or her allies was problematic.

However, the need for some control organization to deal with contraband and to recommend changes in the contraband lists became increasingly apparent. In January 1915 upon the return of the government from Bordeaux to Paris, Delcassé again took up the question. For the time being the proposal to buy foreign goods on government account was dropped.

The new body, the Comité de Restriction des Approvisionnements et du Commerce de l'Ennemi—commonly known as Comité R., held its first meeting on March 13, 1915.[42] In the beginning it was made up of Admiral Moreau, who was the president; Gout, who was vice-president; Chaptal, director of civilian food supply in the Ministry of Commerce; Jean Branet, director-general of customs; Carrier, chef du cabinet of the Ministry of Agriculture; Controller-General Jules Boone and Lieutenant-Colonel Théry of the Ministry of War. The Ministries of Justice, Public Works, and Colonies were also represented. The powers of the Comité were fixed by Article 2 of the Decree of March 22, 1915, in these terms:

> The Comité will receive and centralize all information and documents on the foreign commerce of the enemy, importation as well as exportation; on the supplies that the enemy states try to obtain from outside; on the needs and resources of all kinds that exist in enemy states; on the products whose exportation from France, French colonies or French protectorates ought to be prohibited in order to prevent their use by the enemy countries; on the products that the various French Departments can procure outside in the interest of the national defense or to meet the necessities of war.[43]

To the Comité were soon attached experts of all kinds to study the needs of the Central Powers and of neutral states, in order to recommend what goods might be allowed to proceed to neutral destinations. Studies were made of the uses to which various raw materials might be put, the stocks available in neutral countries, and the action that France should take in regard to these materials. The reports of the Comité that are now available show quite clearly that the important decisions on the importations of the Netherlands and the Scandinavian states were left to the British government, while French action in these matters was secondary. The bulk of the French reports dealt with the policy that should be adopted toward Swiss trade, for this problem was left, by prearrangement between the Allies, primarily for French consideration. As in the instance of the British committees and departments, the work of Comité R. increased in scope as the aims of the Allied economic measures became more extended.

V

Rationing Agreements, 1915

━━━━━━━━━━━━━━━━━━━

ALTHOUGH it was the British government that had undertaken the negotiations that led to the first agreements with the northern European neutrals in 1914, the French government was kept informed of British progress and gave its approval of the principles involved. The French were anxious that the measures already adopted to prevent materials from reaching the enemy should be vigorously carried out and that some immediate steps should be taken to co-ordinate British and French efforts in the economic sphere. In January 1915 the French government proposed a meeting of technical experts to consider more effective means of dealing with imports by neutral countries. There were at least two sets of circumstances that impelled the French to this move: (1) the existing state of British trading with the enemy legislation, and (2) the abnormal export trade between Great Britain and the border neutrals.

ALLIED LEGISLATION ON TRADING WITH THE ENEMY

Hitherto nothing has been said in this study about the legislation of Great Britain and France that dealt with trading with the enemy. It will suffice here to point out the main divergences between French and British practice, which resulted in what the French came to regard as a distinct abuse.

It was a general maxim of international law, as interpreted by the Anglo-American school and by certain Continental writers, that war interrupted commerce between the citizens of states at war.[1] In the instance of Great Britain the character of municipal legislation enforcing this rule had varied more or less with the degree of peril felt and the state of public opinion. When a mercantile theory of trade was the basis for economic policy, the British government had never allowed a strict theory of law to interfere with the trade of its citizens, even though articles in that trade might be destined to the enemy. Thus during the Napoleonic Wars an easy system of licensing permitted British commerce to continue with the Continent—even with France, for it was considered all-important that money should continue to be available for the war and that English commercial supremacy should remain unchallenged.[2]

When the question of trading with the enemy was considered by a subcommittee of the Committee of Imperial Defence in 1911 and 1912, the representatives of the Board of Trade admitted the necessity of prohibiting direct trade between Great Britain and Germany, but they also believed that indirect trade between the two countries could not be effectively reduced. It was contended that nothing would be gained by prohibiting trade with German nationals residing in neutral territory who could send goods on to Germany; other neutrals would certainly enter such markets and secure the profits that British merchants might otherwise have. Although the customs authorities believed that by requiring declarations of ultimate destination for all exports, they would be able to control indirect trade with the enemy, the opinion of the Board of Trade prevailed even for some months after the outbreak of the war.[3]

The first British proclamation relating to trading with the enemy, issued on August 5, 1914, set up a purely territorial definition of enemy trade.[4] All persons within the British Empire were prohibited from supplying to or obtaining from, any person within the German Empire, any goods; or from supplying to, or obtaining from any person, any goods that were being transmitted to or from the German Empire. Thus direct trade with Germany was prohibited, and in addition trade with persons acting as intermediaries in a transmissory sale was forbidden. However, trade with branches of enemy firms established in neutral states or even in British territory was permitted, provided that it was not a transmissory sale and did not involve the head office of the firm, situated in enemy territory. There was no prohibition against trading with alien enemies resident in Great Britain who were acting as free agents.

Later proclamations and statutes made the prohibitions, especially those relating to financial transactions, more specific. The only important change in principle made during 1914 was contained in Article 6 of the proclamation of September 9: branches of enemy firms established in neutral territory in Europe were excluded from the general permission to trade with enemy firms outside Germany.[5] By September the relationship between German firms and their branches in Scandinavia, the Netherlands, and Switzerland had been found to be so close that transactions with the branches could not be distinguished from those with the main company.

The French view of what constituted trading with the enemy was much more inclusive. French law, based on Article 77 of the Penal Code of February 22, 1810, was founded on two principles: nationality and domicile.[6] Thus French citizens were prohibited from trading with citizens of enemy countries, wherever the latter might be. This article was brought to the attention of French citizens at the beginning of the war when it was published in the *Journal officiel* on August 14, 1914. Its principle was emphasized in a decree issued on September 27, 1914, that also added another provision to existing law: trade was prohibited with all persons residing in enemy territory whatever their nationality, and enemy subjects were prohibited from trading directly or through intermediaries with persons in French territory or French protectorates.[7]

It is evident that French citizens were put under much more severe restrictions than were British subjects. It was not at all strange, then, that the French government should suggest a co-ordination of Allied policy in the matter of trading with the enemy legislation. Before long, voices already heard in the country were raised in the Chamber of Deputies against maintaining such strict regulations to the detriment of the immediate interests of French trade.

This dissatisfaction was first heard in the Chamber on March 11, 1915, during debate on two bills designed to ratify the decree of September 27 and to provide penalties for its violation.[8] Although most of the speakers were very anxious that the penalties suffered by those in France who dealt with Germans and Austrians should be most severe, several doubted the wisdom of applying the same rules to French citizens who dealt with enemy-owned companies established in neutral territory. Considerable efforts had been made to stimulate the expansion of French business in markets hitherto held by German and Austrian interests. It was pointed out that the continued operation of existing legislation would only serve to paralyze the economic life of the country and make it less possible for French merchants to trade in neutral states. Particular attention was called to the English system that allowed British subjects to trade with enemy citizens resident in neutral countries. However, Gaston Thomson, minister of commerce, under-took to show that in South America, where the differences in Allied legis-lation would have the greatest effect, the situation of the two states was not the same. Many English companies had been established there for years, and nothing could be gained and much might be lost by breaking existing commercial relations with enemy houses of trade. On the other hand, French businessmen had not set up their own branches in South America and had been content to trade through German establishments. Nothing would be gained by French business if these ties with German companies were al-lowed to continue. In fact, the German firms would only be preserved in full vigor to continue their trade after the war.

Partly as a result of the representations of the French government, British trading with the enemy regulations were modified once more on June 24, 1915.[9] Now it was forbidden to trade with enemy nationals resi-dent or carrying on business in China, Siam, Persia, or Morocco, and, thus, so far as these particular countries were concerned, British legislation was brought into line with the French. The first important step was taken toward applying the nationality principle.

When debates on trading with the enemy legislation took place in the French Senate in July, amendments to the bill dealing with substantive law, which had been passed by the Chamber in March, were accepted, which allowed greater freedom in exportation trade with non-European countries.[10] Considerable satisfaction was felt with the recent changes made in the British system, but several senators urged that negotiations be continued until the two sets of legislation were identical. Upon the passage of the bill a motion was carried inviting the government to continue such negotiations with the Allied states.[11]

ALLIED EXPORTATION POLICY

The second cause of alarm to the French government and to many people in the British government was the evidence, included in British sta-tistical reports, of the great increases in the export trade of the United King-dom with the neutral states bordering on Germany.[12] It was true that the total export trade of Great Britain had been affected very adversely by the war. In 1913 exports of articles grown and manufactured in the United Kingdom had been valued at £329,938,481 but in 1914 the total had fallen to £259,091,859. The effect of the war can be seen even more clearly in a comparison of the statistics for the last quarter of these years: 1913—£84,-170,820 and 1914—£44,457,122. The same general tendency, but to a lesser degree, was evident in the movement of British re-exportations of foreign and colonial goods: in 1913 the total value was £95,959,662 and in 1914 it was £83,216,430. In the last quarter of 1913 the total value of re-exportations was £23,990,395, and in 1914 it was £16,119,848. It would appear, therefore, that only British merchants and British officials anxious to keep up British income would be disturbed by these figures. But when the details of these exportation and re-exportation statistics were examined, alarm spread, and for another reason.

British export trade in the last quarter of 1914 to the northern neutral countries was slightly above normal, except in the case of the Netherlands where the decrease was great. But British re-exportations to these states were excessively high, which goes far to account for the fact that the total decline of such re-exports from the United Kingdom to all destinations was about 30 per cent, as against a 50 per cent decline in exports of United Kingdom products. In the last quarter of 1914 British re-exportations to Sweden increased 294 per cent above the amount for the same period in 1913; those to Norway, 259 per cent; those to Denmark, 933 per cent; and those to the Netherlands, 292 per cent.

With a few exceptions it is impossible to determine from the published statistics of either Great Britain or the states of destination what quantities of particular goods were exported or re-exported from the United Kingdom to the border states each month.[13] From the British annual statistics which enumerate and classify the goods exported according to their destinations it can be seen that re-exportations of cocoa, coffee, tea, colonial grains, cotton, fats, and fertilizers to the Netherlands increased many fold in 1914.[14] The largest increases in trade to Sweden were in re-exportations of cocoa and certain oils and fats, although there was a slight decrease in re-exportations of lard and a considerable decrease in meat. Norwegian importations of colonial and foreign goods through Great Britain showed large increases in cocoa, tea, coffee, soda ash, raw cotton, corn, and bread grain. Danish importations of petroleum from Great Britain, in addition to these other articles, also increased.

In considering these statistics one must be cautious about reaching any hasty conclusion that all of these excessive amounts of goods were destined to Germany. It should be remembered that the war had disrupted many of the regular channels of trade and that reliance had to be placed on new markets. Thus grain purchases in Germany and Russia fell sharply, and soda compounds used in bleaching textiles had to be sought largely from non-German sources. Trade statistics published later by the neutral governments show that the total importations of some of these goods from all sources actually fell between 1913 and 1914, but this was something which as yet the British government did not actually know, and in many instances this was counterbalanced by a tremendous increase in these exports in 1915. In view of the fact that the British were detaining many cargoes from neutral sources that were bound for northern European destinations, and were requiring guarantees from neutral governments and consignees before release was granted, the lack of scrutiny of British exportations was, to say the least, peculiar. British exportations were not covered by the guarantees demanded for neutral cargoes, since British exporters gave only a simple declaration concerning the ultimate destination of their shipments and they asked no guarantee from the neutral consignee that the goods would be consumed in the neutral state. Nor did the British government ask for any such guarantee, even though it knew that the system of certificates of ultimate destination could not be effectively enforced.

The increasingly large exportations of coffee, tea, and cocoa to the border neutrals undoubtedly provided these comforts, if one cannot call them necessities, to the enemy by early 1915. The enterprise provided a handsome profit to British merchants and plantation owners at the expense of other producers—those in the Dutch East Indies, for instance. It had been the policy of the British Board of Trade to expand trade during the war, and therefore little could be hoped for in the way of positive restrictions on this prosperous traffic. Indeed, quite unconsciously, the departments of the British government charged with executing blockade measures aided in the realization of the Board of Trade's program, for as goods from neutral origins were detained or stopped, British trade tended to increase in proportion. The problem of restricting the supply of goods to the enemy was really much closer home than some British officials wanted to admit.[15] The French might well think that a co-ordination of policy was in order.

In France a different attitude was taken toward importations by neutral states. In the opinion of the Commission des Dérogations, which issued licenses to permit exportation of embargoed goods from France, all goods imported by a neutral state in excess of the normal amount should be considered to be destined for the enemy. On this basis the Commission examined the prewar trade statistics of the neutral states and then granted licenses for exportation from France only within the limits of these peacetime, normal figures. French exportations to the four northern European neutral states showed a considerable decrease in 1914.[16]

The first request of the French government that the two allies should meet to consider their economic policies met with discouragement from the British Board of Trade, although the civil and military authorities responsible for the measures against enemy trade approved.[17] An Anglo-French-Italian conference was held in Paris on June 3–9, 1915, at which the British Board of Trade apparently was not represented. The delegates dealt mainly with technical questions of administration and considered additions to embargo lists. However, it was the first attempt of the Western Allies to consider jointly the details of their economic policy. By this time the operation of the March Order in Council was resulting in a greater number of neutral ships detained, but little progress had been made in restricting the questionable British re-export trade.[18] The British representatives, Cecil Hurst, Admiral Sir Edmond Slade, and Longden, made no vigorous defense of their government's policies, realizing that until the Allies systematically controlled their own exports it would be difficult to defend wholesale detentions of American goods, for instance, to these same neutral markets. It was left to the French delegation to make constructive proposals for action.

The French suggested that the system of rations based on the normal importations made by neutrals in peacetime, already applied to exports from France to European neutrals, should now be extended to trade between neutrals.[19] Henri Fromageot, the legal counsel of the Ministry of Foreign Affairs, believed that the practical difficulties of applying a system of rationing in its most general form were too great, but he thought the March Order in Council could be carried out in such a way that all goods imported by neutrals in excess of their normal needs would be considered to be destined to the enemy. As Louis Guichard says, a sort of "sufficiency presumption of enemy destination" would thereby be created. At any rate, the idea was accepted for further investigation.

Once the conference was over, it remained for the British Foreign Office to convince the Board of Trade that a change in British export policy was necessary.[20] The Board gave its consent to restricting British exports to neutrals only if a system of rationing imports from neutral sources to these countries was undertaken at exactly the same time. Administrative preparations were made in July and the whole question was then submitted to another Allied conference that met in London during August. On their return to Paris, the French representatives, Moreau, Gout, and Fromageot, gave a full report to the Comité de Restriction of the problems discussed: controversies with the United States over the treatment of cotton cargoes, the negotiations with Sweden for a general agreement, the censorship of mails on neutral ships, and the treatment of ships transferred to another flag during wartime; but no great progress could as yet be reported in the matter of rationing neutrals. The Comité had already recognized one of the great difficulties involved in this operation—the fact that the neutrals bordering on Germany had either suspended the publication of their trade statistics or published them after such long delay as to make it impossible to check whether excessive importations were being made. It was believed, however, that the British cruisers on contraband control duty in the North Sea could give a sufficiently accurate estimate of the goods reaching these neutral states to make it possible for them to detain any beyond the normal amount. French cruisers would be given orders to apply the Decree of March 22, 1915, in this sense as soon as the British agreed; it was expected that at least one or two French cruisers would be attached to the British North Sea fleet to give an appearance of greater Allied solidarity.[21]

The chief difficulty foreseen by Sir Eyre Crowe in operating a rationing system was that prize courts might rule illegal those captures of goods which, if allowed to proceed, would swell the neutral's importation figures above normal. Crowe regarded it as extremely doubtful whether a prize court would uphold a presumption of enemy destination based on such statistical evidence.

An answer to the question of what the status of statistical evidence would be in a prize court was provided in September 1915 in Sir Samuel Evans' decision in the case of the Kim.[22] The Kim and several other vessels carrying large cargoes of American meat packers' products, which had been shipped in October and November 1914, for Copenhagen, had been brought in and placed in prize. Most of the bills of lading were drawn "to order," and many of the agents of the American packers in Copenhagen had formerly carried on their business in Germany and still maintained certain relations with German merchants. Moreover, large parts of the cargoes were of such a character or were packed in such a way that it was almost certain that the goods were intended to be army rations. All of these points were important factors in the court's decision that most of these cargoes were destined for consumption in Germany, and that the consignment to the consignor's agents in Copenhagen was but part of a predetermined and continuous voyage. It was only in conjunction with this evidence, gained to a great extent from intercepted mails and cables, that the court considered the statistical evidence. Since importations of meat products into Denmark were so much greater than normal, a presumption of the ultimate enemy destination of a large portion of the goods could be set up. In the judgment Sir Samuel said:

> These facts [referring to an increase in American lard exports to Scandinavian countries from 2,125,579 lbs. in August–December, 1913 to 59,694,447 lbs. during the same period in 1914] give practical certainty to the inference that an overwhelming proportion (so overwhelming as to amount to almost the whole) of the consignments of lard in the four vessels we are dealing with was intended for, or would find its way into, Germany. These, however, are general considerations, important to bear in mind in their appropriate place; but not in any sense conclusive upon the serious questions of consecutive voyages, of hostile quality, and of hostile destination, which are involved before it can be determined whether the goods seized are confiscable as prize.[23]

The British government therefore realized that if it were to set up a system of control that would hold neutral imports to a normal amount, it could not rely on an occasional favorable decision in a prize court when the particular circumstances of the case lent additional weight to statistical evidence. Instead it seemed even more important to reach agreements with neutrals who would guarantee domestic consumption of imported goods and who would also accept restrictions on the amount allowed by the Allies to reach them.

Certain administrative matters had to be arranged before these new negotiations could be begun. First it was necessary to gather detailed statistics on the importation and possible re-exportation by neutrals of all the commodities that were to be rationed. It had to be decided what units of time would be used in operating the system: whether the ration should be set for the year, the quarter, or the month. The longer period would make close supervision more difficult, whereas the smallest unit would probably not allow sufficient flexibility to meet the needs of bona fide neutral trade. It had already been shown by experience that some central organization responsible for the distribution of the rationed amounts of goods in the neutral state was needed; otherwise unscrupulous traders could buy up the whole ration, export it, and leave the native population to go without. Even if the merchants were honest, it was still desirable that there should be an equitable distribution of business among merchants of good standing. The whole system would have to be built up bit by bit, and details would have to be fitted to circumstances.

The next sections of this chapter will show how existing Allied controls were extended, and how rationing agreements were made and put into effect in the Netherlands and the Scandinavian states.

THE NETHERLANDS OVERSEA TRUST IN 1915

The development of the Netherlands Oversea Trust (N.O.T.), immediately after the conclusion of its first agreement with the British government on December 26, 1914, was mainly an internal one. Contracts were signed very quickly by importers and shipping companies. Between March and May 1915 contracts were made with certain warehouse companies in order to control speculative trading in supplies once they had been delivered by the N.O.T. The warehouse men agreed that goods put in storage by importers approved by the N.O.T. would be given up again only with the Trust's consent.[24] The control exercised by the Trust was also much increased when the original importers who brought in goods under N.O.T. consent demanded money guarantees from their customers that imported goods would remain in the Netherlands; all traders who dealt in N.O.T. goods thus had a monetary interest in carrying out the guarantees given by the N.O.T. to the British government.[25]

While the Trust was consolidating its control over imports, the British suggested on February 12, 1915, that the British authorities grant licenses to British exporters desiring to send goods to the Netherlands upon a simple declaration that the goods were not intended for the enemy and were consigned to the N.O.T., without it being necessary to secure the consent of the Trust to such consignment in advance. Surely this proposal must have originated in those circles that were anxious to further British trade in neutral markets. The N.O.T. refused to permit its name to be used as a consignee until it had been given an opportunity to investigate the intentions of the exporter and the importer. The "good faith" of the British merchant was not something upon which the N.O.T. cared to risk its reputation.

The position of the Trust was soon made more difficult by the Allied reprisal measures against Germany. The protest of the Dutch government was only a formal one, and it was evident that both government and press believed that the practical problems resulting from the Order in Council should be left to the businessmen.[26] The new burdens on Dutch trade were of a twofold nature: because of the Allied effort to prevent German exports, the proper provisioning of Dutch colonies was more difficult; and because of the effort to prevent supplies reaching Germany, all shipping bound to Dutch ports was subjected to closer surveillance. As a matter of practice, goods bound for the Netherlands which were detained in British ports under the March Order in Council were released only when they were consigned to the N.O.T.

In the expectation that the British would scrutinize outward-bound Dutch trade very carefully, the N.O.T. provided all ships sailing from Dutch ports with a declaration that the goods they carried had passed from foreign ownership into Dutch possession before March 1, 1915. On March 26 the Executive Committee of the N.O.T. proposed naming a special committee to secure and regulate the use of goods from Germany and then to license their exportation in sufficient quantities to meet the needs of the Dutch Indies. Within a few days Joost van Vollenhoven went to London to lay the proposal before the British authorities. He was able to report on April 6 that almost everything the N.O.T. wished in regard to trade with the Dutch colonies was acceptable to the British.[27]

The new regulations of Dutch trade were set forth in a letter to the N.O.T. signed by H. G. Chilton, the first secretary at the British legation; it constituted the agreement of April 11, 1915, on behalf of both the French and British governments.[28] The Committee for Dutch Oversea Interests, which was actually set up two days later as Subcommittee A of the N.O.T., and was made up of van Aalst, L. P. D. op ten Noort, and van Vollenhoven, was to supervise the trade which the British would allow the Dutch to carry on in derogation of the March Order in Council. Certificates of origin issued by Dutch customs officials and factory inspectors were to be regarded as prima facie evidence of the Dutch origin of the goods they covered, but in case of doubt the Committee would furnish complete information to the British legation. The test of what constituted an article of Dutch manufacture was set forth as follows: "Manufactures exported from Holland will not be deemed to be of German origin unless more than 25 per cent of their value consists of materials which are of German origin, or of German labour employed in their manufacture." This, indeed, was the test the British used for some time in determining the neutral or enemy character of manufactured goods that might be subject to detention or seizure under the March Order in Council. It was agreed that the British would not demand certifiates of origin for certain articles of particular interest to Dutch trade, such as bulbs, cheese, butter, condensed milk, eggs, fish, candles, and gin.

Dutch ships sailing from Dutch ports were to be permitted free passage if they called at the Downs or at a British or French port for verification of their papers, and providing that the manifests of cargo were endorsed by the Committee for Dutch Oversea Interests, which guaranteed that the cargo consisted only of "licensed" goods—i.e., goods of enemy origin that fit into one of the following categories: (1) they had been paid for by a neutral before March 1, 1915, (2) they were intended for use in Dutch colonies and had been acquired under a contract made before March 1, (3) they were covered by certificates of origin, (4) they were required for the factories or public services of the Dutch colonies and were not procurable from other sources,[29] (5) they were already licensed by the British authorities, or (6) they were necessary to the health of the inhabitants of the colonies. Presumably the sixth category was to include medical supplies. Other articles in the agreement concerned with Dutch importations provided that Dutch ships on their way to Dutch ports would not be detained if their cargoes were consigned specifically to the Committee or to the N.O.T., although certain Dutch colonial goods, such as tobacco, coffee, and cinchona, were exempted from this requirement if they were consigned to agents of the producing plantation, in Holland, where they were to be sold at auction. Mediterranean fruits were also exceptions to the consignment rule, provided that they were licensed by the British authorities and were carried by regular Dutch shipping lines.

When the official announcement of the establishment of the N.O.T. was made to the German government by W. A. F. Gevers, the Dutch minister in Berlin, on January 13, 1915, the German government was asked to declare that contraband goods exported to the Netherlands from Germany on consignment to the N.O.T. would not be stopped.[30] It was in response to a very real need of the Netherlands and Dutch Indies for certain German goods that this request was made. However, up to the time that the British Order in Council was issued in March, the German government had little interest in securing guarantees against re-exportation of German goods to its enemies. It was only when the British began to stop all goods of enemy origin, thus threatening all markets abroad for German goods, that the German government became more interested in using N.O.T. facilities to export German goods to the Dutch colonies. The N.O.T. sought unsuccessfully to secure a promise that contraband goods, of whatever origin, sent overseas to the Netherlands under N.O.T. guarantee would be unmolested by German submarines.[31] No specific agreement was made, but an increasing amount of German export commerce was carried on through the Trust; the figures rose from 146,365 tons in March 1915, to 2,500,000 tons in July, to 7,000,000 tons in September, to 10,000,000 tons in October and November.

In order to prevent unscrupulous British merchants from giving careless declarations of ultimate destination, the British government took new measures that resulted indirectly in an extension of N.O.T. control over Dutch trade. Additional British customs regulations issued on April 26 1915, required that the name and address of consignor and consignee, and the ultimate destination of each shipment in the cargo be stated on the ship' papers before clearance from a British port would be granted. In addition an act was passed on June 24 that permitted the prohibition of exportation of any article that was not consigned to persons authorized by a royal proclamation to receive such articles; violators were made subject to a fine of £500. The next day a proclamation was issued naming the N.O.T. as sole consignee for all goods exported from the United Kingdom to the Netherlands except when a British export license covering embargoed goods named another approved consignee.[32] This arrangement had been considered when van Vollenhoven visited London in May, and official confirmation of his approval was given by the Trust on June 9, 1915. To make sure that no fraudulent N.O.T. consents were foisted upon the British customs, the N.O.T. agreed on June 21 that the British government should periodically send the consents it had received to the Trust for checking.[33]

These changes in procedure were made in anticipation of a new agreement which was presented in draft form by the British government on July 9. The principles involved in the proposals were acceptable to the N.O.T. and an accord was registered in a series of notes, the first of which, dated July 19, 1915, replaced the notes of December 26, 1914, and April 11, 1915.[34] The new accord took over the main features of the April 1915 agreement, but the Committee for Oversea Interests was now responsible for licensing the exportation of goods of neutral origin that had been sent to the Netherlands for reshipment, as well as goods accompanied by certificates establishing their British, French, Russian, or Italian origin. Facilities for exporting goods of German origin to Dutch colonies under contracts made prior to March 1 were continued, rather against the judgment of the French Comité de Restriction,[35] but only on condition that the N.O.T. Committee ascertain immediately what unfulfilled contracts were still valid. The promises given in earlier agreements of uninterrupted passage of cargoes consigned to the N.O.T. were now somewhat restricted, and temporary detentions of vessels on their way to a Dutch home port were permitted until the British government could communicate with the Trust. The Trust agreed to refuse delivery when any doubt about the ultimate destination of a cargo existed; if proof were given that a contraband shipment was not really intended for Dutch consumption, the N.O.T. agreed to return the goods to Great Britain for prize court proceedings.

In a separate letter sent to the British legation by the Executive Committee of the Trust on July 20, 1915, the N.O.T. agreed "to restrict importation from all sources into Holland of any article to the amount required for home consumption as defined in that agreement (of July 19). Acceptance of consignment of goods will so far as possible be limited to that amount and where goods in excess of it have been consigned to the Trust without their consent the goods will be warehoused by the Trust and they will not be allowed into circulation until the normal level of imports has again been reached."[36] Thus the N.O.T. accepted the principle of rationing, although no attempt was then made to determine exactly what amounts were necessary for home consumption, since adequate statistical estimates were lacking.

Special arrangements were made on July 18/21, 1915, to send English and French newspapers, periodicals, and books to designated Dutch firms on direct consignment to the Trust, without first securing an N.O.T. consent for each shipment.[37] This was done to permit the usual trade to continue unencumbered. Another agreement was made on August 2/4, 1915, to hasten telegrams sent through British censorship to and from the N.O.T., provided the Trust agreed to limit messages to those on behalf of bona fide Dutch merchants for whom the Trust accepted responsibility. The Trust had not been particularly anxious to undertake this new task and it soon decided to demand a high security bond from tradesmen who used these facilities and to deliver incoming telegrams only to stockholders in the N.O.T. who in turn delivered them to the addressee with whom the shareholders had some sort of contract. Thus the shareholder became responsible for determining the good faith of the addressee. A few weeks later the N.O.T. ordered that telegrams be limited to accurate descriptions of goods and cargoes covered by one of its contracts.[38]

While the British were perfecting their controls over Dutch trade and making the intervention of the N.O.T. in foreign trade transactions a practical necessity, other arrangements were negotiated with other Allied governments. On July 14 the Russian government agreed to place exportations from Russia to the Netherlands and the Dutch colonies under the regime of the Trust on the same conditions fixed in the British and French agreements, and any new arrangements made by these states were to apply to goods exported from Russia to the Netherlands.[39] In a note of September 13, 1915, in terms almost identical with the Russian note, the Italian government adhered to the latest British agreement with the N.O.T.[40] Even though Italy had not yet declared war on Germany as it had agreed to do in its treaty with Britain, France, and Russia in April 1915, the prohibition of re-exportation of Italian goods included not only the countries with which Italy was at war but also "enemies of Allied states which had adhered to the Trust." Strangely enough some weeks passed before the French brought their agreements with the N.O.T. into harmony with the latest arrangements made by Great Britain.

The Trust now attacked the problem of discovering a practical basis for putting the principles of rationing, agreed upon in the note of July 20, into effect. Studies made by the N.O.T. of the amounts of goods needed for home consumption soon revealed the inadequacy of Dutch official statistical publications. On the other hand the Trust had not yet been able to accumulate sufficient evidence upon which it could even begin general negotiations. It was therefore found necessary to conclude several separate agreements on the rations to be allowed the Dutch. The first such accord was signed on September 1, 1915, on behalf of Dutch cotton spinners and manufacturers. It covered raw cotton, cotton linters, cotton waste, and cotton yarn.[41] The ration for the totality of these articles, except yarn, from all sources was set at 10,000 metric tons per quarter, and imports of 3,200 metric tons of cotton yarn and thread per month were permitted. These goods were to be covered by the July 19 agreement, and special regulations were laid down concerning the clearance of ships carrying the ration, and for the inspection of the importers' books. In order to replenish depleted stocks in the Netherlands, the British agreed to issue at once licenses for the exportation of 3,000 tons of raw cotton, linters, and waste beyond the agreed ration.

The condition of Dutch trade continued to be perilous. Smuggling over the frontiers persisted, supplies were hoarded to be sold later at higher prices, and in consequence goods failed to reach the consumer. Detentions of goods in British ports continued, and although the Dutch government still refused to permit its willingness to decree embargoes to be used as a quid pro quo in negotiations with the belligerents, the Trust urged the government to reconsider its position in order to smooth the way for a better understanding with the Allies.

Early in November Joost van Vollenhoven went to London to discuss the pending agreement between the Netherlands and France and to reach an agreement on rationing with the British.[42] He took with him statistics prepared by the N.O.T. on the amounts of goods needed under normal circumstances in a three-month period. The British agreed to his request for 225,000 tons of corn and rye per quarter, on the condition that rye should no longer be used as fodder, but they insisted that the proposed rations for oil cake and meal be reduced to such a degree that it seemed to the Dutch that they were virtually being encouraged to export cattle and meat to Germany.

Soon after van Vollenhoven's return an exchange of notes took place between the Trust and the British, on November 13/23, 1915, which regulated the trade in vegetable and animal oils and fats, certain grains, and petroleum.[43] The British accepted the N.O.T. statistics on normal Dutch consumption, and agreed to permit imports up to these amounts on condition that exportations of Dutch margarine to the United Kingdom did not fall below 43,750 cwt. per week. If, however, the exports of margarine exceeded that figure, the British would provide the raw materials required for the manufacture of such excess.

This was the first successful attempt to secure a substantial proportion of the products of Dutch industry for the Allies; it was the forerunner to much more ambitious purchasing agreements that the British entered into with all the northern neutrals in 1916 in order to prevent their goods from reaching Germany. The note of November 23 enumerated Dutch rations of overseas imports from all sources as follows: corn and rye, 225,000 metric tons per quarter; linseed, 50,000; oil cake and meal, 70,000; oleaginous seeds and nuts, 18,265; vegetable oils and fats, 20,500; animal fats and oils, including fish oil, 12,810; lard, 3,000; mineral lubricating oils, 5,000; refined petroleum, and oil used in stoves and lamps, 41,000; naphtha, benzine, gasoline, 12,000; gas oil and fuel oil, 20,000 in the period October 1 to December 31, 1915, 20,000 in the period January 1 to April 30, 1916, and none in the period May 1 to September 30, 1916; and raw wool, 3,000. The question of Dutch pork exports was left unregulated, although the British did consider instituting a purchasing program.

On December 6, 1915, the long-awaited agreement between the French government and the N.O.T. was concluded. It is difficult to see why it should have been so long delayed, for the Comité de Restriction seemed to be agreed as early as September 4 that the principles involved in the July agreement signed by the British were acceptable. Certainly the lack of co-ordination had caused some difficulties. One example of this was that French regulations had never gone so far as to require that goods exported from France be consigned to the N.O.T.; the Comité de Restriction had only proposed in July that a notice be sent to French chambers of commerce recommending that this procedure be followed. The French Customs had attempted to demand that all nonembargoed goods be consigned to the Trust, but this rested on no decree and it was doubtful what kind of penalties could be imposed for infringement—those for trading with the enemy, or only those for violating a customs regulation. All this was particularly embarrassing since some French merchant ships carrying goods to Dutch ports had been detained by British cruisers because their cargoes were not consigned to the Trust.[44] The new French—N.O.T. agreement followed almost exactly the British agreement of July 19, 1915, and on December 7, the N.O.T. reiterated its promise to restrict Dutch imports to the quarterly rations agreed upon with the British and French governments.[45] However, the Trust went one step beyond the obligations it had hitherto undertaken, when it agreed not to permit the exportation of goods already in the Netherlands or goods produced there that might be freed for exportation because of the importation of similar or equivalent goods from overseas on consignment to the N.O.T. If, in spite of the Trust's advice, the Dutch government issued export licenses, or if no embargoes existed to cover the goods in question, the N.O.T. would refuse to grant consents for an equivalent amount of goods. This attempt to control the exportation of "produits similaires," it will be seen, opened up a whole new field for argument.

Even after the conclusion of all these agreements, relations between the N.O.T. and the Allies at the end of 1915 were not particularly amicable. Reports of increasing exports of fodder, corn, and hides, with prices rising by leaps and bounds—as much as ten to fifty guilders per cwt. of corn in a day—made the British authorities very suspicious of the good faith of Dutch traders. On December 3 the British legation warned the Trust that unless the exportation of hides to Germany ceased, all overseas cargoes on ships bound for the Netherlands would be detained regardless of their destination or the nature of the goods.[46] In order to calm the situation the Executive Committee decided to refuse temporarily all consents for the importation of Indian and American hides, so that the British could not object to the exportation of domestic hides.

Great difficulties arose in the execution of the November rationing agreement, largely because the Dutch government insisted on buying fodder independently of the N.O.T. and without regard to the obligations the Trust had undertaken. In December the rations to the N.O.T. were detained by the British. As a result of conversations held by F. E. Posthuma, Dutch minister of agriculture, industry, and commerce, with representatives of the Trust on December 7, it was announced through the State Bureau for the Distribution of Grain and Flour that the government wished all rye and corn to be consigned to it. Thus the N.O.T. would no longer be responsible for the distribution of these grains, and a cause of contention between the Trust and the government, and between the Trust and the Allies, would presumably be removed. The British, however, regarded this arrangement as a breach of faith on the part of the Trust, for their carefully balanced plan of control over Dutch grain importations was made useless. But the British were not without a weapon: they simply detained grain cargoes consigned to the Dutch government on the ground that a misconception existed as to the true meaning of "home consumption."[47]

Nor was it only the British who were agitated about Dutch trade with Germany. The agreement between the French and the Trust was no sooner signed than the Comité de Restriction recommended, on December 11, the conclusion of a new arrangement that would ration Dutch imports of copper and other metals, as well as hides and tanning extracts. Early in January 1916 concern was expressed over excessive trade in tobacco and coffee of Dutch colonial origin.[48] In fact everything pointed toward the renewal of negotiations with the Trust at an early date, on a number of questions.

By the end of the first year of its existence the N.O.T. had expanded its operations greatly. At the beginning of 1915 total importations into the Netherlands compared with those made through the Trust stood at 40 to 1, but at the end of December 1915 the ratio was 2.6 to 1. Goods imported through the Trust in 1915 amounted to 557,000,000 guilders, invoice value.[49] A more exact picture of its activities can be gained, however, from an examination of the new departments and committees established by the N.O.T. In addition to the Committee for Dutch Oversea Interests (Subcommittee A), which dealt with marketing Dutch goods and providing certificates of origin to cover them, a Committee on Trade with Foreign Countries (Commissee voor het Handelsverkeer met het Buitenland), known as Subcommittee B was set up in April after negotiations between the Trust and Posthuma, minister of agriculture. Representatives on this committee, besides those named by the Trust, were appointed by the Ministry of Agriculture, Industry, and Commerce, by the Subcommittee on Industry, and by the Committee for Feeding Men and Beasts, both of these committees being attached to the Royal National Relief Committee.[50] The work of Subcommittee B was to gather information on importations from Germany and to regulate the whole exchange system with Germany, maintaining imports and exports at a determined level. No export licenses were to be granted by the government for any destination, nor any embargo laid, without the advice of this body.

In the course of negotiations with various trades and industries in the Netherlands, the N.O.T. established special divisions of experts to deal with problems of supply and control of the raw materials brought onto the Dutch market. Most of these committees will only be named here,[51] but attention will be given to one of them to show how the control actually worked. By the end of 1915 four committees were dealing with the tobacco trade: one set up on April 13, 1915, dealt with American tobacco imports, one to control Java tobacco was established on October 29, another on Sumatra tobacco on November 8, and the fourth, which dealt with control of non-Dutch Indies tobacco was set up on December 14. Trade in quinine was regulated by a Control Committee; a Committee on Dutch Indies Coffee was named at a meeting of Dutch merchants on October 16, 1915, and it became part of the Trust organization. The Permanent Committee of Tea Traders reached an agreement with the N.O.T. on May 14, 1915, and the Tea Warehouse-Masters of Amsterdam signed one on June 7. On December 17, 1915, the Executive Committee announced the establishment of a Tea Committee, which soon appointed inspectors to control both importers and retailers.

Probably the most important single control exercised by the N.O.T., judging from the Dutch and American interests involved as well as from Germany's need and demand, was that established over traders in fats and oils. The Dutch margarine industry had received a great impetus as a result of heavy demands from both belligerents. Most of the raw materials, which undoubtedly fell within the British definition of contraband foodstuffs and forage, came from overseas, and in order to keep British intervention and detentions at a minimum it was necessary that stocks within the country should be carefully controlled. Since there seemed to be a temporary oversupply on the Dutch market the Executive Committee on May 28, 1915, decided to refuse all consignments of fats and oils, allowing only a few exceptions for existing contracts.[52]

Immediately opposition arose from almost all manufacturers and importers. The market was anxious and prices fluctuated widely. A meeting of persons interested in oil and fat importations was held on June 2 with the Executive Committee, at which the Committee explained the situation and insisted that the Holland-Amerika Line refuse in the future, cargoes of oil and fats, to save its other cargoes from detention. The Committee believed that the Dutch market would not suffer because enormous supplies had already been sent by the American meat packers to their agents in Rotterdam. The businessmen at this meeting represented divergent interests and opinions. A few of the manufacturers were large importers on their own account and many others were dependent on Rotterdam importers. It soon appeared that one of the largest margarine manufacturers, who had a branch in England, had a special agreement with the British government that allowed him to forward vegetable oils, except from America, to the Netherlands, and in return he made large exportations of margarine to England. The little manufacturers were not interested in such a system; they wanted freedom of trade and lower prices. The supply of cottonseed oil appeared adequate, judging from the current cotton crop; the American packers were widening their sources of supply for premier jus[53] to South America. Thus if nothing interfered, the little companies stood a good chance of making handsome profits. The representatives at the meeting were unable to reach any agreement concerning regulating their own trade, however, so the Executive Committee decided that it would have to act for them.

The next day the N.O.T. named an Advisory Committee on Oils and Fats to which all requests to consign these goods to the Trust would first be submitted. New N.O.T. consents would be required for all shipments on the high seas or lying on American wharves, and on June 16 it was announced that all incoming cargoes of oils and fats would be warehoused until their buyers had been licensed by the N.O.T. This regulation hit the little manufacturers hard, for, having no storage space of their own, they were forced to buy from the large manufacturers who did. Good raw materials were scarce, because many were detained by the British, and the large manufacturers charged high prices for those they had in stock. As these supplies were used up, the N.O.T. little by little allowed small consignments of oleo oil and premier jus to be imported. In time, large and small manufacturers alike became more or less dependent on the Trust.

Difficulties with British detentions continued, for, so long as Dutch pigs, pork, and lard were being sent to Germany, the Allies were reluctant to permit overseas cargoes of fats and oils to reach the Netherlands, since these imports would only release more Dutch products for exportation. The Trust decided that the only way to make sure of a just distribution of overseas supplies was to establish a central purchasing agency which would buy and allocate supplies for the whole margarine industry. This plan was not at all to the liking of the American meat packers. Moeller, Hammond and Company's Rotterdam agent, represented the scheme as originating with van den Bergh and Jurgens, the two largest Dutch margarine manufacturers, who saw in the existing difficulties a chance to "use the power of the N.O.T. for carrying out their old favorite plan of joint buying, by which, as you will understand, they get another means to strangle the competition of the smaller churners."[54] Moeller pointed out that after the establishment of such an agency there would be only one buyer with whom the packers could deal. He had protested to the N.O.T. against this interference with freedom of trade; he had been asked by the Trust: "What are the United States doing to find a way out of the difficulty? Let your friends in America see what they can get done to do away with the continuous molestations from the part of the British Authorities." The letter continues, in somewhat curious English: "This statement shows in our opinion, the way which has to be followed and seems to indicate that even the N.O.T., although she is certainly nothing more than a better grade of English policeman on duty in our country, begins to feel sick of the far-going arrogance of the British authorities and should welcome anything which could relieve her of the pressure under which she is now, although partly through her own fault."

The small churners likewise protested against this new scheme, for they feared the power that it would put into the hands of the large manufacturers, as well as the possibility that the organization might survive after the war. This protest may explain why the officers of the Jurgens and van den Bergh companies were not made members of the purchasing committee as they, at least, had originally intended. Instead the three brokers who were already on the Advisory Committee on Oils and Fats, with four others, were named to the new Bureau for Edible Fats and Oils.[55]

Moeller's description of the operation of the Bureau was somewhat as follows: Every week all churners and importers were required to give an exact statement of the stocks of raw materials on hand, what goods were on order, and what their requirements were. When churners requested new stocks all of this information was sent to the N.O.T. Executive Committee. There it was decided what amounts could be purchased by the Bureau and how they were to be distributed among the churners, in order to prevent stock-piling. Moeller added that the statements made by the churners were carefully checked by the N.O.T. inspectors, and any frauds or misstatements were dealt with severely. The Bureau bought a particular type of goods at one certain price on any day, and then distributed the order among the packers' agents who had offered that commodity for sale. Thus it was suggested that the agents should all agree to offer goods at the same price, for any one packer who offered goods at a reduced figure would set the price for all.[56]

The regulation of copra, the dried kernel of the coconut from which coconut oil is extracted, became the province of a special Copra Bureau, established by the Trust on July 27, 1915.[57] The Bureau immediately made contracts with the shipping companies engaged in the Dutch Indies trade. After September 1 an N.O.T. shipping consent was required for every shipment of copra not sold through the Bureau. Applicants for a consent agreed to sell the copra within four weeks to a manufacturer approved by the Trust, in order to control stocks more easily.

After August 1, 1915, the Trust also required that margarine made from imported raw materials should not be exported to a belligerent country, although it was still possible to export to England margarine produced from British raw materials. This, of course, placed a premium on purchase from agents in London. In the execution of this new order the Dutch government co-operated to the extent that it required exporters of margarine to declare the source of the ingredient materials; thus the N.O.T. was able to fine churners who might try to ship goods to Germany that were imported under N.O.T. contracts. In practice similar exportations to England were permitted to proceed unmolested.[58]

Once all these measures were taken by the Trust the "soft" contracts, which provided that the article should not be exported but said nothing about derivative products, became a thing of the past so far as oils and fats were concerned. Mair, head of Swift and Company's foreign sales department, pointed out: "The soft contract has left a considerable opening for trade with Germany. For instance, butterine manufactured from imported materials, sausage casings stuffed with meat of Dutch production, compounds manufactured from imported raw materials—all could be shipped into Germany."[59]

Great difficulties for both the Dutch government and the Trust arose from the attempt to secure the required certificates of origin. Margarine was made from a great variety of oils and fats, some of them domestic and some foreign. There was nothing to prevent the exportation under license of truly Dutch margarine; the problem was to identify it. Almost all of the margarine contained some Dutch milk, but the proportion was never high enough to make that a determining factor. It was only at the end of December 1915 that the confusion abated, after the Dutch government proposed that the Trust should require manufacturers either to use foreign oils exclusively or not at all.[60]

The Trust also regulated after November 1915 the retail trade in margarine when it set up a Margarine Consumption Control Bureau which permitted sales to storekeepers on the basis of consumption needs on January 1, 1914, with increases up to 20 per cent being allowed if good cause could be shown.[61]

All this reveals the extent to which the Trust found it necessary to go in order to satisfy the British government. There is ample evidence that the Dutch traders and manufacturers, the agents of the American packers, and, it would seem, even the N.O.T. itself, were far from pleased with this interference in Dutch trade. The Dutch government was still perfectly willing that its people should do all possible trading with Germany, but neither the government nor the manufacturers really wanted to run the risk of being cut off from supplies of raw materials or excluded from the English market. They had little alternative but to comply with British "requests."[62]

NEGOTIATIONS WITH THE DANISH MERCHANT GUILD AND THE CHAMBER OF MANUFACTURERS, 1915

The first agreement negotiated in London by J. C. T. Clan on behalf of the Danish government and signed on January 12, 1915, was primarily concerned with the maintenance of Danish embargoes. It was understood that the British government would seek guarantees from Danish importers to cover certain goods, in much the same way that Dutch imports were guaranteed by the N.O.T. The Danish government had resisted any suggestion that a Trust should be set up in Denmark, but the British found that other organizations of traders and manufacturers already existed which could be made to serve the same ends.

The two organizations with which the British government made agreements were the Grosserer Societat (or Merchant Guild), and the Industriraad (or Chamber of Manufacturers). The Guild, established by a royal order on April 23, 1817, was made up of all licensed traders and importers in Copenhagen and was therefore representative of the whole mercantile community. The Raad, established in 1910, was a company in which the chief industries and industrial organizations, not individuals, were members. In 1915 some 1,800 industries either singly or through membership in pre-existing trade associations were included. Both organizations had regulations governing the business activities of their members and fines were levied for nonobservance of the rules. Since all of the important traders and manufacturers in Denmark belonged to one of these bodies, and since a system of sanctions already existed, it was fairly easy to extend their scope and make these societies organs through which belligerents might seek to control Danish trade. The Danes, like the Dutch, wanted certainty in their trade, but at the same time they sought to avoid its direct control by foreigners.

Soon after the January agreement was signed, H. P. Prior, who had been the first president of the Raad, went to London to confer with Walter Runciman and Sir Francis Hopwood about arrangements to cover exports of goods of British origin, embargoed in England, which were not on Danish embargo lists. On February 11/18 a rather limited agreement was registered in an exchange of notes, under which the Raad agreed that certain goods, such as wool, wool yarn, turpentine, tin plates, hides, graphite, steel wire, copper sulphate, cotton waste, and so forth, imported by its members under British export licenses would not be sent to Germany in any form. In case of violations the offending importer would be removed from the Raad's membership list. It was arranged at the same time that K. Mygind, who had accompanied Prior to London, would remain there to aid Danish interests in securing British export licenses.[63]

After the March Order in Council was issued, both sets of belligerents had a greater interest in regulating Danish trade. It appears that the Guild and the Raad, at the request of the Danish Ministry of Foreign Affairs, made the same basic proposal to the German and British governments. While they offered to enforce the guarantees given by their members to foreign governments, they refused to become general consignees for goods imported under those guarantees as the N.O.T. had done. Bills of lading would still name the individual Danish importer as the consignee.

It was the German government that first began negotiations, sending a delegation to Copenhagen in May with a proposal that a strict compensation system be set up, whereby German goods would be exchanged for Danish goods of equal value. The first German proposals met with considerable opposition, particularly from Max Ballin, one of the most important industrialists, who feared that Danish industry would fall too much under German control. Later new negotiations were undertaken by Alex Foss, president of the Raad, with Dr. D. Toepffer, the German commercial attaché, who acted with the full support of Count Ulrich von Brockdorff-Rantzau, the German minister to Denmark. Apparently Brockdorff-Rantzau and the German Foreign Office were not in accord with the German Ministry of War, which recommended a much stiffer trade policy toward Denmark; in general the Foreign Office opinion prevailed. An agreement was reached on August 24, 1915, between the Raad and the German government that provided that goods imported from Germany by members of the Raad should not be re-exported to Germany's enemies, nor used in manufacturing war materials intended for Germany's enemies. The individual importer was required to sign declaration forms attached to the agreement. A similar accord was signed by the Merchant Guild on September 27, and on November 9 the Austro-Hungarian government arrived at identical accords with both of the Danish associations.[64]

The execution of these agreements raised some new problems. The Germans returned to the idea of an exchange system as a basis for trade with Denmark. In practice they proved to be most reluctant to accept Danish bacon or dairy products for the grain, coal, machinery, and dyestuffs which the Danes wanted to import from them, on the assumption that these domestic products of Denmark would in any case find their way to German markets where prices were high. Instead the Germans demanded horses, rice, lard, cocoa, and imported grains. Since many of these articles were obtained by Denmark from overseas only on the sufferance of the British authorities it would be necessary to make some new arrangements with Great Britain. Probably the Germans recognized this fact, for they later took a rather lenient view concerning re-exports of Danish manufactured goods containing some German raw materials to Great Britain. It was also necessary to make arrangements with the Danish government to grant licenses to export goods on the Danish embargo lists. Thus on November 22, 1915, an accord was signed by the Danish Foreign Office on the advice of the Raad, permitting the exportation of ten thousand horses in exchange for German exports of zinc and zinc plate, potassium salt, dyes, caustic soda, medicines, tobacco, iron and steel goods, that would suffice for five or six months.[65]

In order to carry on the compensation trade with Germany, the Danes also had to secure the consent of the British to the re-exportation of at least small amounts of goods. The British Foreign Office realized that Germany might undertake reprisals against Denmark if the British government refused these concessions. Even if Germany undertook no military measures against Denmark, the Allies would be under a moral obligation to provide the Danes with the articles they usually imported from Germany. This would involve a reallocation of raw materials and tonnage at a time when the scarcity of tonnage was becoming a problem of greatest importance to the Allies. The Danes were in an excellent position to play one belligerent off against the other, a circumstance which was used to advantage both at this time and later, in 1916, when purchasing agreements were being negotiated.

Before the British took up serious negotiations with the Danish Raad and Guild in the summer of 1915 they had already secured a new agreement with Captain C. M. T. Cold of the United Steamship Company on May 20 which renewed and somewhat extended the assurances he had given in November 1914 that the goods carried on his company's vessels would not be re-exported to Germany. The company also agreed that none of its ships would carry copper, nickel, rubber, petroleum, or lubricating oil to Norway or Sweden without its first investigating the trustworthiness of the consignees. The British government reserved the right to detain cargoes on the company's ships whenever it appeared that the embargoes laid by the Scandinavian states were not being enforced. A similar agreement was reached with the East Asiatic Company and the Orient Line on December 30, 1915.[66]

In July and August 1915 Dr. Holger Federspiel, sent by the Merchant Guild, and Rudolph Schou, on behalf of Danish agricultural interests, went to London.[67] Federspiel offered a more comprehensive agreement under which the Guild would legalize all guarantees given by Danish merchants to foreign officials, and would limit Danish re-exports to Norway and Sweden to a very well-defined list of goods. The British refused to give any assurance of free importations from other neutral states to Denmark, and, indeed, pressed for a recognition of the rationing system. Consultations were held in Copenhagen between representatives of the Guild, the Raad, and the Danish Foreign Office; Foss protested particularly against the one-sidedness of the obligations whose burden fell almost entirely on the Danes, and the fact that Danish trade with her Scandinavian neighbors would be crippled. Although these wider negotiations had no immediate consequence, the Danes were willing to accept limited agreements covering only raw cotton imports. One was signed by the Industriraad on August 23, 1915, and another with the Guild on September 24, 1915. By these agreements a definite and regular supply of British cotton was secured by the Danish textile industry, in return for guarantees concerning the disposition of its manufactured products. All cotton coming in was to be consigned directly to the spinners who were members of the Raad, the request for a British export license having been accompanied by a certificate of guarantee from the Raad. A copy of the guarantee forms to be signed by the consignee was attached to the agreement; the names of violators were to be reported to the British legation in Copenhagen. The Raad also admitted that the average monthly consumption of raw cotton in Denmark did not exceed 625 metric tons, and Article 5 implied that the total importation from all sources would not exceed that amount. As an act of grace the British agreed to permit the exportation of 875 tons of raw cotton from the United Kingdom between

August 10 and 31, 1915, in order to fill depleted stocks. Arrangements cover-ing cotton waste and cotton yarn were reserved for a later accord. It is plain to see that the British had succeeded on a fundamental point: the Danes had agreed to rationing for an important item, and Britain could now hope to extend the principle.[68]

On October 24, 1915, a new Danish mission went to London, with Alex Foss and C. C. Clausen, representing the Raad and Guild, respectively. The chief British representatives who dealt with them were Sir Eyre Crowe and O. Sarjeant, while R. M. A. E. Turner, the British commercial attaché in Copenhagen, was kept in close touch. The Danes believed that the moment was favorable for reaching an agreement, since British Foreign Office influ-ence in determining blockade policy was in the ascendancy over the more purely military point of view of the Admiralty, and Britain was more apt to make it possible for neutrals to maintain their economic neutrality in order to avoid new controversies with the United States. A single accord was signed by the Raad and Guild with the British government on November 19, 1915.[69] The British government disclaimed all intention of preventing the passage to Denmark from neutral countries of goods for Danish bona fide home re-quirements, and then proceeded to define "home requirements" as includ-ing (1) goods for Danish home consumption, (2) certain goods for re-export to Norway and Denmark, (3) certain manufactured articles made of no more than 20 per cent imported materials, for export even to belligerent countries, and (4) goods required for the exchange trade with Germany. The goods that might be sent to Sweden and Norway, which were to be covered by guarantees identical to those under which they were originally imported, were limited to quarterly rations which in most instances were set at the average of Danish imports in the years 1911–1912–1913 (for such things as tea, tobacco, wines and spirits, paper, salt, soda, fine woods, grass seed, per-fumes, glass, earthenware, hardware, carpets, and draperies); some were set at a fixed figure (coffee and cocoa); others (steel and iron plates, pipes, tubes, fittings, and fruits) were to be fixed by later agreements. It was also possible to send vessels built in Denmark for Swedish or Norwegian owners, and specified amounts of leather goods made from Danish hides tanned with imported tanning materials, whereas telephone cables could be sent only to Norway. Articles made of imported noncontraband goods which could not be reduced to their original constituents and which were covered by guaran-tees that could be legally enforced in Sweden or Norway might also be ex-ported. A list of goods that might be sent to branches of Danish firms in Sweden and Norway was to be drawn up later.

More important from the point of view of British blockade policy was the recognition of the right of the Danes to send to Germany such things as akvavit, china, earthenware, toys, printing ink, coloring materials for butter and cheese, rennet, and certain machinery—dairy, agricultural, washing, ironing, cement-making, and shoemakers' machines as well as stokers, ship winches, and so on, all up to specified values per quarter, to a total of £90,000.

The goods which might be sent in the exchange trade with Germany included beer, matches, leather goods made of Danish hides but prepared with imported tanning materials, malt, coffee, chocolate of Danish manufacture, tea, fresh and dried fruits, women's and children's clothing (provided that cotton, rubber, or wool were not essential parts of them), and clocks and watches. Other articles in the agreement set up the machinery for forwarding the guarantees to the British government—through the War Trade Department in the case of goods to be exported from the United Kingdom, India, or British colonies, and through the British legation in Copenhagen for goods sent from non-British ports. The names of all those who violated their guarantees were to be sent to the British government; such people were probably added to the black lists.[70] If the British found it necessary to detain cargoes covered by Danish guarantees, they agreed "so far as is reasonably possible" to inform the Raad and Guild of the reasons. It was understood that nothing in this agreement was to affect the importation of British coal and coke; raw cotton, cotton yarn, and waste; petroleum; tin plates from the United Kingdom; motor tires and tubes; or gold, silver, and materials intended for making coins or paper money. Nor were any agreements made with Danish shipping companies to be affected. The British agreed to accept certificates of origin issued by the Raad as conclusive evidence that Danish goods did not include more than 25 per cent by value of enemy labor or materials.

Simultaneously with the negotiation of this general agreement, a supplement to the cotton agreements was arranged, something which had been foreseen in the original accords signed in August and September. Now, on November 24, Crowe and Mygind specified the amounts of cotton waste and cotton yarn which the Danes might import from all sources.[71]

Although the November agreement went into effect on December 7 with respect to imports from the United Kingdom and on December 21 with respect to all other imports, actually the British continued to detain Danish cargoes and to refuse permission for British exportations because, as shall be shown below, the British blockade policy was under severe criticism in Parliament and the press. It was apparent by February 1916 that if the Danes were to get any considerable benefits they would have to take up negotiations once more in order to meet British demands that rations be set for a large number of items. Foss again went to London, where Crowe made it clear that Britain wanted a great reduction in Danish imports, particularly of American packing-house products.[72] The estimates of normal home consumption which Foss took with him were based on statistics of purchases and sales made by the industries and retailers concerned. The British refused to accept these and insisted that the ration should be based on Danish import and export statistics for the years preceding the war, taking due account of the importance of Denmark as an entrepôt in the Scandinavian trade. The differences in the two calculations were great: the British estimated the need of animal oils and fats at 8,000 tons per year, the Raad and Guild set it at 24,000 tons; the estimates for vegetable oils and fats were 14,400 tons as against 26,000 tons; for oleaginous nuts and seeds, 40,000 tons as against 100,000; for cocoa and cocoa beans, 2,400 tons as against 14,000. The British had not properly considered the changes in dietary habits brought about by the war, for more margarine materials were necessary when forage imports, and the consequent production of animal fats, were reduced. In some instances, also, neutral industries—e.g., the Danish soap industry, had been able to expand at the expense of their German rivals and additional raw materials were therefore necessary.

Foss complained very forcefully that British export licenses were denied many times to Danish importers, often "the best and finest houses in the country," who had been guaranteed by the Raad or Guild, without the British communicating the reasons. He charged that such British action was taken "not on evidence but on suspicion." He foresaw a total undermining of all faith in these organizations, and believed that importers would in the future try to apply directly to British authorities for all licenses and permissions. He pointed out how impossible it was for the associations to achieve an equitable distribution of imported materials among Danish firms if the associations never knew which importers would be acceptable to the British authorities as consignees. He asked that a list of suspected persons be sent at once so the associations could clear up their statuses or restrict the guarantees given so that they might be reissued to other consignees. Foss also objected to an unnecessary widening of the list of rationed items, protesting that feedstuffs should not be included and that the British should not attempt to tie their granting of free passage for such goods to increased Danish exports of dairy produce and bacon to Great Britain in a kind of compensation system.[73]

Later Foss conferred with Grey, with Sir E. M. Pollock, chairman of the Contraband Committee, with Lord Emmott, director of the War Trade Department, and took part in committee meetings at the Board of Trade and at the Admiralty. Finally on February 19 Foss said quite bluntly that the Danish associations would have no further interest in such a trade agreement as the British were proposing. H. N. Andersen, who had had an important part in the conversations, used his influence to prevent a complete break in the negotiations. Just what quick concessions were made it is impossible to say, but on February 29, 1916, Crowe drew up a rationing agreement that the Danes found acceptable. No text of this note is available, but seventy-five items were included.[74] The whole position of the Guild and Raad was ultimately much improved by this agreement, especially after a Danish Trade Office was set up in London on a more permanent basis under the direction of Christian Rottbøll, with Mygind continuing in his special capacity as representative of the Raad. Other agreements that took over the provisions of this English accord were concluded with France on March 17, 1916,[75] with Italy on December 21, 1916, and with Russia on February 13/26, 1917.

It is interesting to see what reaction the signing of the November 1915 agreement with the Danes had on the British political situation, for as a result of the publication in Denmark of what purported to be a text of this accord, the whole question of British trade policies got a thorough airing in the Northcliffe press and in Parliament.[76] Several members of both Houses tried to force the government, early in December 1915, to lay before Parliament a copy of the official text; this the government flatly refused to do. The arguments, however, are instructive both as to the opinion of several politicians regarding trade with neutrals, and as to the extent to which the government was able and willing to take the public into its confidence on the existing measures of economic warfare.

It was argued in the Commons on December 9, where the opposition to the agreement was led by Sir Henry Dalziel and Sir Arthur Markham, both frequent critics of the government, that any agreement with private persons in a neutral state was undesirable. It was believed by many, and the government didn't contradict them, that neither the question of entering into such an arrangement nor the accord itself had been submitted to the cabinet. This whole argument marked another stage in the struggle, which will be noted elsewhere, between those who thought that the Foreign Office and other civil branches of the government were deliberately taking steps, against the better judgment of the Admiralty, which hampered the British fleet in its treatment of enemy trade. The feeling in this instance persisted even though the Marquess of Crewe stated specifically in the House of Lords that the Admiralty was strongly represented on the committee that considered the agreement, and that the Admiralty had approved the final text.

The chief objection to the agreement, whose details were quite accurately reported in the British press, was that it recognized the right of the Danes to export goods to Germany. This, it was alleged, was in direct contravention of the policy laid down in the March Order in Council. What these parliamentary critics forgot was that part, at least, of the goods which the British so graciously allowed the Danes to export were products of Danish industry over which the British had no direct control. Indeed, the Order in Council could be applied only when the goods were encountered on the high seas, and then only if proof of their enemy destination was at hand. It is understandable that the critics should have felt alarm over the exportation of non-Danish goods to Germany, for they had not been given the facts which had led the government to foster to a certain extent the Danish-German exchange system.

The answer on behalf of the government, given by Lord Robert Cecil in the Commons, did very little to explain away the difficulties. The substance of his speech was: "This Agreement, in common with every other step in the blockade of Germany, has been solely with a desire to make that blockade as effective as it can be made. It has been concluded, and the terms have been arranged in such a way as to produce the most effective blockade with the greatest freedom to neutral trade that can possibly be devised."[77]

Cecil's statement now appears to be true, but members of the House of Commons could not have come to this conclusion on such information as was given them.

Quite similar arguments were brought in the House of Lords against the Danish agreement by Lord Strachie, the Earl of Portsmouth, and Lord Devonport on December 16. In addition the character and nationality of merchants who were members of the Danish associations were brought into question; it was said that many of them were German.[78] Portsmouth found fault with the facilities given by the accord for re-exportations from Denmark to Norway and Sweden where, he believed, it was impossible to secure adequate guarantees against exportation to Germany. He objected that the agreement which relaxed the execution of the Order in Council gave preferential treatment to Denmark. This was undoubtedly true, but, since no legal blockade had been declared, there was no legal necessity for maintaining in all circumstances the measures undertaken in retaliation when policy dictated otherwise.

The defense of the agreement in the House of Lords was much more informative and satisfactory than that made in the Commons. The Marquess of Lansdowne stated that none of the other agreements made with neutrals had been made public and the government had no intention of setting a precedent in this case, for it would only make future negotiations more difficult.[79] To the charge that special treatment was given to Denmark, he replied that uniformity in these agreements was impossible and that the government could only try to make the blockade as effective as possible by reaching agreements most favorable in existing circumstances. He explained that the government's policy had been to reach an understanding on the amount of goods necessary for the normal and legitimate domestic consumption of the neutral states and then to secure an admission that goods imported in excess of that amount might be presumed to have an enemy destination. Proper institutions to assume responsibility for receiving and distributing neutral importations had been found or established in these states. Lansdowne then spoke of the danger of smuggling and of the charge that the fleet was being restrained from using its full force, and added:

> My Lords, your Fleet may be never so powerful but it will not be able to prevent goods passing through what I may call the back doors through which our enemies obtain most of the things they require. Unless you can obtain a working arrangement with the neutral country itself, an arrangement which that country will respect and which it will endeavour to carry out to the best of its powers, I believe you will be helpless to prevent the passage of almost unlimited quantities of supplies to your enemies. And let it be remembered that unless you set up some responsible body of this kind in the neutral country to conduct the business for you the mere fixation of a limit

representing the normal consumption of certain classes of commodities by the neutral Power will not help you in the least.[80]

Crewe continued the argument by saying that apparently the critics of the agreement had forgotten that international law placed severe limita-tions on the free exercise of British sea power:

> No noble Lord has mentioned the fact that before a cargo can be dealt with it has to be brought into a prize court and condemned. I do not know whether noble Lords suppose that the prize court is ready to condemn all cargoes or ships which it may be convenient for the Government of the country in which it sits to have con-demned. . . . It is quite true that absolute contraband, which it is most important to keep out of the enemy country, would always be condemned. But as regards conditional contraband, it is quite well known that unless an enemy destination can be proved it will be allowed to go through.[81]

The third speaker for the government, Lord Emmott, was especially competent to speak on the subject because of his experience as director of the War Trade Department. He pointed out that two things were desired: to deprive Germany of necessities for her existence and prosecution of the war, and to break down its exchange. If Germany continued to buy luxuries and nonnecessities from neutral countries it would have an adverse effect on her exchange. He asserted that in spite of easy access from Scandinavian and Dutch markets to Germany, the government had been quite successful in depriving Germany of necessities; as proof he referred to increases in prices of meat, grain, and metals in Germany. The agreement with Denmark would give the British even more control over the goods that Denmark might ex-port to Germany, and it would certainly smooth commercial relations be-tween Great Britain and Denmark.

Most of the comments on these debates in Parliament which appeared in the London *Times* during December 1915 were extremely critical of the government's policy, and especially of its failure to disclose the text of the Danish agreement.[82] A single letter written by M. L. Bramson, a Dane resi-dent in London, on behalf of the agreement appeared in the *Times* on De-cember 20.[83] He called attention to the freedom of trade in noncontraband and nonembargoed goods between Denmark and Germany that had hith-erto existed, and pointed out that contraband goods had also been sold to Swedish buyers who maintained a thriving business with Germany. The let-ter continued: "It would therefore appear to be altogether a magnificent and most powerful stroke against Germany, if, in order to cope with these diffi-culties, the British Government has been able to find an arrangement by which it obtains practically the entire control of the German Scandinavian trade, even at the expense of having to formally consent to transactions which previously took place without consent, and on a much larger scale."

Although Bramson somewhat overstated the degree of control the British secured over Scandinavia's trade with Germany, his appreciation of the situation was essentially correct. Undoubtedly the recognition of the rationing principle by the Danes was a distinct gain for Allied policy, while the Danish merchants obtained more certainty in their supply of oversea goods, and, to a limited extent, the means of continuing their trade with Germany and their Scandinavian neighbors.

ACCORDS WITH NORWEGIAN TRADERS AND MANUFACTURERS, 1915

It will be remembered that, in contrast to the situation in the other northern European neutral states, no agreement of any kind had been reached by the Allies either with the Norwegian government or with any private Norwegian associations, at the end of 1914. Despite the absence of a written agreement, the Norwegian government had complied with British requests to add to the Norwegian embargo lists until they included the most important articles on British contraband lists. [84]

In 1915 the British government undertook negotiations with the Norwegian government for a general agreement, and with associations of Norwegian traders to limit their imports and control the distribution and use of the goods concerned. Only the second group of agreements will be discussed in this chapter; the more complicated matter of the official negotiations will be reserved for Chapter VI.

The first accord concluded was one with the Norwegian Cotton Mills Association on August 31, 1915, signed by W. Langley on behalf of the British and by Ole Mörch for the Association. [85] Mörch went to London well supplied with statistics and the agreement was rather easily reached. It covered raw cotton, cotton waste, and cotton yarn, and followed exactly the same pattern as the one concluded with the Danish Raad a week earlier. The Norwegian ration of raw cotton was set at 360 metric tons per month, or not to exceed 1,440 tons in any four-month period. Cotton yarns might be imported up to 170 tons a month or 340 tons in any two-month period. The accord went into effect on September 15, 1915, but in order to fill the ordinary stocks of cotton, the British government agreed to authorize the exportation of 2,800 bales of cotton between August 24 and September 14. This cotton was to be released from the cargoes of the *Nordic* and the *Helge*, already consigned to Norwegians but which had been detained in the United Kingdom. Only 1,000 bales of this amount were to be counted against the ration fixed in the agreement. The Association was left to devise its own methods of dealing with its members except that it had to secure free access to their books. The Norwegian government took no direct part in the negotiations, but it pledged itself not to issue dispensations from its embargoes for cotton exports except for shipments to Great Britain or its allies.

During September 1915 negotiations were carried on between the British and certain margarine and glycerine companies. On September 24 one agreement was reached with the Aktieselskab Lilleborg Fabriken and the Aktieselskab Christiania Dampoliomolle, and another with O. Mustad and Son.[86] The Mustad Company owned refineries and manufacturing plants not only in Norway but in Sweden, England, Germany, and Austria-Hungary, but it insisted that each enterprise was conducted "exclusively in the country where the factory is located and each provides for the domestic market of that country with the exception of the Norwegian and Swedish factories which export only to countries not at war with Great Britain." In order to secure a British promise not to intervene "more than is necessary" in shipments of raw materials consigned from neutral countries, the company agreed not to resell any part of the raw materials, except with British consent, nor to sell any products of its Norwegian or Swedish factories except against guarantees. Each month the company was to furnish information concerning stocks on hand, sales, imports, and exports, and it also consented to the examination of its books by an accountant chosen by the British authorities. The rationing principle was recognized in this agreement, since the British were not obligated to permit the shipment of raw materials beyond those which the official Norwegian and Swedish statistics showed to be necessary for home consumption.

An accord with the Association of Norwegian Tanners and Leather Manufacturers was signed on November 12, 1915, which provided for guarantees covering both skins and tanning materials imported from any source.[87] The Association accepted a ration of 9,000 tons of tanning materials a year, and in return the British promised to facilitate transit of these goods as much as possible. The Association agreed to establish a central office to handle import problems and to permit the British legation access to its books. Moreover, it agreed to secure at least "the unofficial approval" of the Norwegian government to the whole arrangement.

The British and French governments joined on September 23, 1915, in making a common agreement with the Arendal Smelteverk which guaranteed against the exportation of metals it produced to countries at war with France and Great Britain.[88] Other rationing agreements were signed by the British with the Porgrunds Elektrometallurgiske Aktieselskab on November 29 in regard to metals; by the British and French governments with the Norsk Svovlsyrefabrik on December 14 in regard to sulfuric acid; by the British with the Automobile Club of Norway on December 17 in regard to tires and inner tubes; and by the British with the Aktieselskab Valloe Olieralfineri on December 29 respecting importations of oil and raw petroleum. In the agreement with the Automobile Club, which Sir Mansfeldt

Findlay, the British Minister, sent to Sir Edward Grey on December 19, the British agreed to grant export licenses each month for 750 tires and 400 inner tubes for automobiles, and 65 tires and 65 tubes for motorcycles, but importations from any other country were to be deducted from this amount. The Club agreed to distribute the tires only after guarantees had been given to the Norwegian minister of finance by the member of the Club receiving them. Findlay also enclosed a letter, dated November 27, 1915, from Nils C. Ihlen, the minister of foreign affairs, in which Ihlen agreed that his department would advise Norwegian merchants who wished to import tires and tubes to seek all necessary assistance from the Club. Ihlen, however, refused to give the Club access to official statistics which would enable them to check the importations made under the rationing provisions of the agreement.[89]

The British government also succeeded in 1915 in arriving at agreements with Norwegian shipowners similar to those made with certain Danish companies. Eight Norwegian lines signed agreements, each of which in general provided that the company would investigate the ultimate destination of cargoes carried by their ships, that it would refuse all cargoes of German destination or origin, and that it would warehouse all cargoes until the British government gave permission for their delivery to the consignees. The British agreed to permit free passage of these vessels to neutral destination without their first undergoing search in British ports.[90]

These agreements formed, from the British point of view, a valuable complement to the other accords and measures that constituted the blockade of Germany, and early in 1916 they sought to widen their scope.

RATIONING AGREEMENTS IN SWEDEN, 1915

The political and economic situation in Sweden in 1915 was so complicated that a discussion of it and its effect on negotiations between the Swedish and British governments will be left for Chapter VI. In spite of the difficult relations between the two governments, and in spite of the active disapproval of the Swedish government, the British were fairly successful in reaching private trading agreements.

The first of these arrangements was concluded on June 24, 1915, with the Association of Swedish Cotton Spinners (Svenska Bomullsspinnereiforeningen); Crowe signed it on behalf of the British government, and C. L. Schönmeyr and G. Boothius for the Spinners.[91] The agreement was of a provisional and temporary nature, being intended to cover the period from June 3 to July 17, 1915, or until negotiations for a definitive agreement in regard to cotton owned by the Spinners which was then detained in

British ports could be concluded. Cotton valued at some 16 million kronor was involved. The British agreed to release immediately 15,000 bales of the detained cotton, which would represent the Swedish ration for one and one-half months. The cotton was to be consigned to the Association, which would guarantee that the cotton would be used exclusively by Swedish mills whose owners in turn guaranteed that neither the raw cotton, cotton waste, nor cotton yarn would be re-exported. Details about freight charges resulting from the detention and transshipment of the cargoes were included. It was agreed that if the definitive agreement was not reached by July 17, the British would release another 10,000 bales to the Association to cover the period until August 17. Any importations of cotton from other sources were to be deducted from the amount that Great Britain promised to put at the Association's disposal.

Other arrangements were made late in 1915 concerning Swedish importations of petroleum and petroleum products. The first of these was concluded on October 22, 1915, with the Vacuum Oil Company, represented by H. E. Stoner; it was supplemented by another arrangement made on December 20, 1915.[92] The Company gave guarantees against re-exportation of its products from Sweden, and further agreed that all ships owned by it and carrying its cargoes should call at a port in the United Kingdom. Similar agreements that applied to Sweden were made with M. M. Olsen and Company on December 24, 1915, and with the Scandinavisk-Amerikansk Petroleums Aktieselskab on December 29, 1915. Some accords were made that covered the trade of the parties in all the Scandinavian countries. The three companies mentioned above entered into such arrangements, as well as the Asiatic Petroleum Company on December 23, 1915, and the Danske Petroleum Aktieselskab of Copenhagen on December 29, 1915.

The significance of these agreements will appear in better perspective when the course of negotiations with the Swedish government is presented. Each of the companies with which the British dealt was important, but in the absence of government co-operation in executing these undertakings, the effectiveness of the agreements was questionable.

VI

Negotiations with Sweden and Norway for General Agreements in 1915

IN 1915 attempts were made by the British to solve difficulties in Swedish and Norwegian trade by reaching general agreements with these two governments, in the hope that their trade could be controlled on somewhat the same basis as that of the Netherlands and Denmark. The negotiations in both instances failed, but it is none the less important to trace their course and to see what principles were involved.

SWEDEN

Relations between Great Britain and Sweden had not been materially smoothed by the conclusion of the agreement of December 8, 1914. Although the Swedish government had extended its embargo lists as it had promised to do, the British were never satisfied with their execution. The

Swedes maintained the right to grant special export licenses, and then re-fused to make any accounting to any foreign government of the amount of goods those licenses covered, or to whom or where the goods were sent. Re-ports from British consuls and commercial agents came in showing that unusual exportations of fats, meat products, lubricating oils, oil cake, and metals were being made to Germany, and, indeed, before many months passed it was realized that Swedish ports had been substituted for Copen-hagen as way stations in the German trade in American meat packers' prod-ucts. While British officials knew that the total importations of many goods into Sweden were far in excess of actual Swedish needs, it was extremely diffi-cult to find evidence that would justify seizure of any particular cargo. De-tentions of large numbers of ships bound for Sweden were ordered, particu-larly after the March Order in Council was issued, in the hope that the Swedes would be forced to undertake new negotiations.[1]

The Swedish government was not without weapons to combat these tactics. The most serious inconvenience that Sweden could threaten was a general prohibition of the transit of goods to Russia over Swedish territory. Although a temporary arrangement had been reached in October 1914, new Swedish measures soon upset the status quo. Even though the Swedish government had given assurances that goods declared in transit upon their entry into Sweden, and which were accompanied by papers to prove their immediate foreign destination, would not be stopped, a decree issued on January 9, 1915, prohibited entirely the transit of arms, ammunition, and certain goods used directly in war.[2] Transit of other supplies was still per-mitted on the old terms, but the decree was a severe blow to an icebound Russia badly in need of war materials. The Swedish government upheld its action on the ground that it was a necessary step in the maintenance of a strict neutrality. By mid-March there were suggestions that in the future the Swedish government would balance any permissions to export or to transit goods to Russia with licenses to export an equal amount of goods to Ger-many. Here was the basis for the "compensation system" that was to become the foundation for Swedish foreign trade throughout most of the war. The transit trade was even more closely controlled after May 4 when it was re-quired that a Swedish license be obtained for the re-exportation or transit of all goods that came in by sea.

It was inevitable that the detentions ordered under the March Order in Council should bring new difficulties. The first important case concerned the *Sir Ernest Cassel*, which had been captured while carrying a cargo of magnetic ore from a Swedish port to Germany. The Swedish government on April 12, 1915, sent a protest to the British government, contending that the March Order in Council was illegal, that magnetic ore had never been de-clared contraband, and that in any case Great Britain could not legally stop the exportation of domestic goods from Sweden. Sir Edward Grey's answer to the Swedish protest was made early in May.[3] In it he argued that the agree-ment made by Sir Esme Howard, the British minister, on October 4, 1914,

:o the effect that magnetic ore would not be treated as contraband, was in
no way involved since the cargo had been seized not because it was contraband but because it was destined to Germany. In order to calm the Swedes,
Grey proposed that the British government should buy at a reasonable price
all the ore which would otherwise go to Germany. Actually arrangements
for such purchases were made only in 1918 as part of the Allied-Swedish
Agreement of May 29, 1918.

To Grey's reply was attached a memorandum on the subject of the
December 1914 agreement.[4] Count A. M. H. Wrangel, the Swedish minister
in London, had been informed by the British on April 12 that this agreement
was not giving satisfaction to the two parties and that it ought to be altered
or at least completed by a new note defining contested points. Grey now
was anxious to prove that recent British action was not contrary to the December agreement, for presumably any new accord would be made on somewhat the same basis. He also asserted the right of Great Britain to apply its
reprisal measures to neutrals just as if a legal blockade had been declared,
and insisted that nothing in the agreement could be interpreted as limiting
Britain's right to establish a blockade.

At about the same time the British Foreign Office prepared a draft
memorandum which it proposed should serve as the basis for negotiations
for a new Anglo-Swedish agreement. Whether this document, or a similar
one, was ever actually sent is now unknown. However, since Paul Cambon
told his Government when he sent a copy of this draft on May 10, 1915, that
"the present project represents very exactly Foreign Office opinion in regard
to the question of Swedish commerce," it is important to discuss it in some
detail.

The memorandum set forth succinctly the dissatisfactions the British
government felt, together with suggestions for improvement. It stated that
the British had signed the December agreement because it seemed to provide a means of securing importations into Sweden of raw materials and
other articles declared contraband by the Allies or included on British and
French embargo lists. In return Sweden had given assurances that the goods
would be consumed domestically. On March 19, however, the British government had been obliged to make known that its confidence was shaken,
for British interests had not been given the security the British government
had the full right to expect. The note cited the fact that the Swedish government at the end of April had closed to the British legation and consuls, all
sources of information on Swedish imports and exports, and that the Swedish
government had not itself published any official statistics. The British government had therefore been obliged to use statistics from other sources, presumably those gathered by British searching parties in British ports and by
agents in Swedish ports. It was said that American statistics supported the
allegation that Swedish imports from the United States were excessive, and
that "they demonstrate officially the point that during the War Sweden has

become the supplier for Germany." In regard to this the memorandum continued:

> His Majesty's Government has full confidence that the Swedish Government adopts all measures necessary to carry out the accord of December 1914, but it trusts very little certain classes of Swedish traders whose anti-English sentiments are only too notorious. In general, the trader is not only interested in supplying Germany, he is desirous of doing it; the metal market in Sweden daily receives new and unknown recruits desiring to handle contraband; information comes from all parts indicating the existence in Stockholm of a vast organization for revictualling Germany; and the cases of the rerouting of Swedish ships, apparently with the complicity of Swedish consignors, are always more frequent and cause serious anxiety to His Majesty's Government.[5]

The British were pleased to note that Swedish customs officers had been given discretionary powers to prevent the export of certain alloys in ways that evaded Swedish embargoes, but, the note went on to say, this measure would have been more in order on December 10 than on April 22!

The opinion of the British government concerning the Swedish government was not altogether complimentary, since it was charged that evasions of Swedish embargoes had not only been rendered possible but had been authorized in the name of the law. At the same time that Swedish imports of certain goods had increased many fold, the Swedish government claimed that Great Britain should issue an unlimited number of British export licenses for goods on Swedish embargoes and should permit an indefinite importation from other countries.[6]

Coming down to practical problems and possible solutions, the British memorandum said that the opposition of the Swedish government to the creation of an organization similar to the Netherlands Oversea Trust was understandable, and it would not be insisted upon. The British proposed as an alternative that syndicates or associations of importers and distributors— one for each of the groups dealing in the same products, should be established and made responsible for receiving and distributing imported goods. On the other hand goods essential to all the Swedish people, such as grains and forage, or petroleum products, might be consigned to government commissions. The British also asked the Swedish government to present statistics on existing domestic needs, and then promised to do everything possible to facilitate the passage of these goods to the contemplated trusts or commissions, and to grant export licenses for goods on British embargoes so far as English and allied supplies permitted. That a rationing system was contemplated was made clear by the proposal that whenever Swedish imports in any month exceeded a twelfth part of the normal annual consumption figure less a twelfth part of the annual domestic production figure, the British could then inquire of the directors of the associations the reasons

or this increase. It was expected that the Swedish government would en-
arge its embargo lists, inflict proper penalties on violators, and define precisely the word "small" as applied to the number of licenses issued in derogation of Swedish embargoes. On the other hand, the British reserved their
 right to interfere with shipments of goods sent otherwise than through the
rusts, as well as those which were addressed to German agents.

To this draft memorandum was attached an annex dealing with the
ransit of goods to Russia. The British protested against the Swedish decree
of January and regarded it as a repudiation of assurances that Kurt Wallenberg, the foreign minister, had given in his memorandum of October 16,
1914. They requested that goods should be sent to Russia on a "through
bill of lading," as a means of reducing the possibility of fraudulent rerouting
of imported goods to Germany; up to this time the Swedish State Railways
had refused to carry goods under any such "through bill."

Before more serious discussions were undertaken, the Swedish government decided to establish a new bureau that would regulate Sweden's
foreign trade, and would, among other things, be responsible for execution
of Swedish embargoes, granting licenses and maintaining a balance between
licenses for exports to Russia and Germany. By royal decree the State Commerce Commission (Statens Handelskommission) was established on June
8, 1915, with E. B. Trolle, ex-minister of foreign affairs, and ex-minister to
Germany, as its chairman, and Karl A. Fryxell as its vice-chairman.[7] In carrying out its functions the Commission also applied another kind of compensation principle, for exports of goods from Sweden to a belligerent state were
permitted only if that state sent goods of equal amount or value to Sweden.
Thus if finished or half-finished manufactured goods were exported, the
Swedes frequently demanded raw materials in return, or if goods on the
Swedish embargo were sent, for instance to Germany, the Germans would
be required to issue licenses for exportation of goods on their embargo lists.
Still another kind of concession might be demanded by Sweden—the right
to send unhindered, certain Swedish products to the opposing belligerents.
Thus, a system was evolved by which Sweden sent horses to Germany and
the German government permitted Sweden to export pit props to the Allies.[8]
The exchange arrangement was constantly extended to an increasing number
of articles.

Almost immediately after the appointment of the Commerce Commission, Anatoli Nekludov, the Russian minister, began conversations to secure
some relaxations from the general rule that all goods in transit to Russia
must be covered by a Swedish export license. He soon reported that the
heart of the matter was that Sweden wished by this requirement to put pressure on England to secure the release of cotton, rubber, and other products
necessary to Swedish industries.[9] Wallenberg said quite frankly that as soon
as he received concessions from England, transit to Russia would again be
permitted. The question was, of course, called to the attention of the British

government, and the Russians asked their ally to keep in mind Russia's spe cial interests.[10]

During the spring of 1915 the political situation and the state of publi opinion in Sweden became increasingly disgusting to the Allied govern ments. Although there existed a strong desire among many people—the Labor party, the greatest part of the farmers, the industrial, mercantile, an financial circles—to maintain the true neutrality of Sweden, there was also a persistent agitation carried on by the friends of Germany who wanted a wa against Russia at any price. Nekludov reported that this actively pro-German party included the Swedish Court, the aristocracy, a large majority of the officers and the entire rank and file of the army, a considerable body of Lutherans, the middle bureaucracy, literary and intellectual circles who felt strongly attached to German culture, and the whole of the Conservative press.[11] British reports generally agreed with this appreciation of the situa tion, but the British government believed that although the Court party with its press could make a great clamor, its parliamentary leaders were dull and not too capable.[12] Both the British and Russians realized that even those Swedes who did not share in the veneration of the German government and culture, but who admired England, felt great distrust for the Russian gov- ernment. This feeling was largely the result of fears of the territorial ambi- tions that Russia might at any time display on the frontier of Finland or in the Aland Islands. In general, however, although the Swedish middle classes disliked Russia, they were not prepared to embark on a military venture on the side of Germany unless Russia had overwhelming victories. They clearly hoped that the war would end to the marked advantage of neither side. Hjalmar Hammarskjöld had, therefore, to pursue a policy of neutrality, while at the same time he issued occasional strong statements warning of possible Swedish intervention in order to stave off pressures from the Court party. Thus at the time of Italy's intervention in the war in May, there were fears that Sweden might enter as a counterforce on the side of the Central Powers,[13] but later in the year Russian military reverses served to strengthen the neutral position of Sweden. Throughout 1915 the Swedish Socialists continued to criticize the government's failure to regulate the economy of the country more effectively, but they were in a difficult position, for much as they wished to oppose their own army and aristocracy, they hated even more the entire Russian system. Howard was in frequent touch with Hjalmar Branting, the Social Democratic leader, who was certainly friendly to the British and was critical of the Ministry of Foreign Affairs for permitting the controversy with the Allies to go on.

Some Swedish circles professed to fear that the Allies might undertake preventive military measures against Sweden, and it was to quiet them that the British, French, and Russian ministers in Stockholm renewed their earlier guarantees of Sweden's independence and territorial integrity. The occasion for giving these assurances was offered in a speech made by Gustav V early in May in which he stressed the necessity of Swedish military prevaredness. It was Grey who took the initiative in arranging for the joint Allied declaration, made on May 12; the British were prepared to give similar assurances in Christiania and Copenhagen.[14] Wallenberg at once answered that Sweden had not and did not intend to mix in the war, and that the Allied notes of guarantee presented on August 6, 1914, were considered very valuable by the Swedish government. Wallenberg said that, therefore, he could see no necessity for the Allies to remind him of the assurances.[15]

Even before the formal presentation of the declaration, the three ministers became aware that Wallenberg had no intention of publishing it; thus its desired effect of calming the Swedish press and public opinion would be lost. Nekludov advised against the publication of the note in the press of the Allied states because Wallenberg would then become very disagreeable in later negotiations. Apparently the matter was not pressed, and there followed an increase in Swedish agitation against British detentions of Swedish shipping.[16] Sergei Sazonov, the Russian foreign minister, was very much alarmed over the situation, and he reminded Benckendorff, Russian ambassador in London, that if war should come with Sweden the burden of the struggle would fall on Russia. He therefore instructed Benckendorff to urge the British to moderate their policy toward Sweden and make substantial concessions in the matter of transit of goods and mails to Sweden. General Janushkevich, chief of staff of the Russian High Command, wrote to Sazonov on June 20 that, from a military point of view, it was desirable to attempt all possible means to prevent a clash with Sweden, and Great Britain should again be informed of the threatening danger to Russia. He believed that Russia should even agree to a reduction in transit of goods to Russia through Sweden, since that compromised Sweden in German eyes.[17]

Evidently the Swedish government was equally upset over the dangers to its neutrality policy. After long conversations between Wrangel and Sir Eyre Crowe in London, Wallenberg suggested in the middle of June that the British and Swedish governments should come to a temporary accommodation on a few urgent matters, and should at the same time open negotiations for a general agreement. Both sides were convinced that the December accord was no longer workable.[18] As a result of negotiations in Stockholm and London, the British government did release a considerable amount of rubber and cotton that had been detained in British ports. The agreement reached with the Swedish Cotton Spinners on June 24, 1915, was one part of this arrangement.[19] Great Britain stipulated that in return the Swedes must grant a limited number of licenses for exportations to Russia.

The bases of discussion that the British delegation, which was shortly to go to Stockholm, would use in its negotiations for a general agreement were decided upon by June 19, 1915.[20] They included: the removal of all obstacles to free commercial interchange between the United Kingdom and Sweden for their respective products; the removal of obstacles to the passage of letters and telegrams between Sweden and neutral countries;[21] freedom of importation into Sweden of all goods from neutral countries in the quantities necessary for home consumption; security that goods imported into Sweden on the basis of such an agreement would not be re-exported as long as their exportation was prohibited; and regulation of the transit trade across Sweden between Great Britain and Russia.

The British delegation, made up of Robert Vansittart, H. Lancelot Smith, H. M. Cleminson, and E. Hambro, arrived in Stockholm in the last days of June and began its negotiations on July 2. The Swedish government appointed Admiral Arvid Lindman, parliamentary leader of the Court party, Trolle, C. G. Westman, Axel Wahlberg, Gustav Dillner, and C. L. Schön meyr as its representatives in the negotiations.[22]

It became clear in the next few weeks that the chief British objective was to reduce Swedish imports to normal quantities. Although Vansittart still believed that the most effective method of administering any quota system would be through a central agency similar to the N.O.T., he was willing to consider as an alternative a series of consignee-distributing associations such as were proposed in the Foreign Office draft memorandum of May. This would leave essential control of Swedish trade in Swedish hands, and would assure a proper distributing system among Swedish traders.

The British delegation soon reported to Grey that it was generally met by hostility and that only Wallenberg appeared to be anxious to have the negotiations succeed.[23] The civil functionaries had done their best to prevent any contact being made between the delegates and Swedish commercial men, and warnings had even been issued through the Conservative press to merchants who might not be averse to reaching an agreement favorable to themselves. Trolle was reported to be anxious that no settlement be arrived at, for then Wallenberg would resign and in all probability he, the favorite of the pro-German group, would become foreign minister. Westman, who was regarded as a tool of Hammarskjöld, was inclined to sympathize with Trolle's point of view.

Before the British proposals were discussed at all, the Swedes presented a proposal that if Great Britain granted to Sweden goods in excess of her own needs that might be re-exported to Germany, then an equal amount of goods would be permitted to proceed in transit to Russia. The Swedes agreed that British goods might be guaranteed against re-exportation, but they expected to receive undiminished imports of overseas goods regardless of whether the consignees were suspect or not. The Swedes insisted that all delays of Swedish shipping be removed and that the alleged right to requisition detained goods be renounced by the British government. The Swedish government reserved the right to prohibit entirely transit of war materials across its territory, and finally protested against the British Order in Council of March 11, 1915, as a violation of the December agreement.

The British delegation found this memorandum quite impossible as a basis for discussion, but believed that probably the Swedes had presented it under pressure from the Germans.[24] Wallenberg, however, revealed to Howard that he expected in the course of time, after discussion, the Swedish delegation would modify its proposals; he felt no alarm that an agreement would not be reached. In any case on July 8 Nekludov reported that the Swedes had retired their inadmissable proposal on the balancing of Russian and German transit, and that the British had made their counterproposals. However, the Swedes refused to admit that any cargo could be detained under the March Order in Council unless the goods concerned had been declared contraband. They also held that the Swedish government alone was responsible for calculating the normal importation of various goods, and they refused to discuss these statistics with a foreign power. Again they insisted that Swedish embargoes must be regarded as adequate guarantees against re-exportations. The Russian government continued to urge moderation on the British, and Sazonov even instructed Benckendorff to suggest that the concessions desired by Sweden be made to run for a certain length of time as an experiment that could be cancelled if the Allied military situation improved or if the Dardanelles were opened.[25] For a time the entire breakdown of negotiations was feared.

Sometime between July 10 and 15 the British finally admitted that Swedish embargoes would be considered satisfactory guarantees, and gave up for the time being any hope of establishing import associations.[26] Attention was then concentrated on rationing and transit problems. The British proposed a licensing system that would permit British exports of hemp, jute, rubber, tanning materials, and coal to Sweden, while the Swedish government would be given the sole responsibility for the control and distribution of these goods. This was regarded by the British as quite unsatisfactory but the best they could hope to achieve. Sweden, in return, was to grant no licenses for exportations of arms, ammunition, other military equipment, metals, leather, woolen yarns, and mineral oils; importations of other contraband goods into Sweden were to be limited to normal amounts.

The attitude of Hammarskjöld seemed increasingly menacing. On July 18 he addressed a deputation of Swedish pacifists, saying among other things, "The Swedish government intends to maintain neutrality so long as is possible, but not at every price. Besides a hostile attack there exist other considerations which could force Sweden to retreat from her neutrality." Nekludov believed that this speech was directed to the English delegation as a warning and a threat.[27] In addition measures preparatory to mobilization were taken —horses, automobiles, and boats were commandeered, railway facilities were made available for the free passage of troops, certain workmen in essential industries were exempted from any mobilization, and so on.

By the first week in August, a draft was agreed upon that fell far short of British hopes. It provided that questions of transit to Russia and exportations of goods by Sweden to other destinations were to be handled by mutual exchanges, the amounts to be settled at the beginning of each month. Whether transit to Russia was to be exactly countered by Swedish exports to Germany was not really decided, although Lindman denied that this was his government's intention. The central part of the agreement was contained in Article 3 which set up a list of goods (List A) which might be imported by Sweden only in normal quantities and whose exportation was to be absolutely prohibited. Goods on List B were likewise to be imported in normal amounts, and they were all to be included in Swedish embargo lists. Presumably these goods could be exported under Swedish licenses.[28] In deference to the Swedish demand, no provision for estimating or publishing figures on normal Swedish consumption was made and the certificate of the Commerce Commission was to be sufficient evidence that the necessary quantities of imports had not been exceeded. Thus, although the principle of rationing was admitted, no statement of what constituted the normal importation of various commodities was made. The Swedish government did agree to notify the British, before a ship sailed, what goods in its cargo would be covered by a certificate of home consumption, so that if the amount became excessive the British government might remonstrate. The Swedes did not secure the position they had taken that only contraband could be detained, for they acknowledged the British right to detain cargoes whose enemy destination was proved; the British therefore did secure recognition of one of the main principles of the March Order in Council.

It would appear that this draft was not in the end acceptable to the Swedes. Nekludov continued to report that members of the Swedish delegation seemed anxious to "spring" the negotiations and thus bring about Wallenberg's resignation.[29] The Swedish demand that they be allowed to export goods of British origin to Germany as compensation for German exports to Sweden was held by Nekludov to be absurd and quite enough to disgust the English.

Even before the draft was communicated to the British Foreign Office, the course of the negotiations had not met with general approval there. The impossibility of establishing any real rationing system was regarded as the chief fault of the proposal. The British were convinced, however, of the importance of avoiding any pretext for war, and, although the mere failure of these negotiations probably would not have that effect, some sort of agreement seemed necessary. In such circumstances it was deemed desirable to restrict the scope and obligations of the agreement and to continue negotiations as long as possible before signing. As one Foreign Office memorandum stated: "If we must have an agreement intrinsically bad merely because not to have one at all would be dangerous, it will be well to restrict our engagements as much as possible to general principles, and to avoid the difficulty of making definite and excessive concessions by resorting to the adoption of formulas sufficiently vague to slur over and leave unsettled the actual points on which agreement is found impossible."[30] The British delegation was accordingly instructed to do no more than initial the draft agreement and then refer it to the government in London. If the necessity arose, the mission could eventually be withdrawn from Stockholm without giving the appearance of breaking off negotiations. Conversations continued to little purpose until August 13. On the advice of the Allied ministers in Stockholm, only two members of the British delegation were recalled, about August 23, for consultation by Grey, with the approval of Alwyn Parker, when Grey found it difficult to accept the proposed terms. The Swedish government was informed that a decision on the acceptance of the draft agreement could not be given before mid-September.[31]

At the end of August the exchange system was facilitated by a new coal agreement between the British and Swedish governments. Britain promised to supply 50,000 tons of coal every fifteen days over a two-month period, in return for free passage through Sweden of goods in transit to Russia with a value of 1,800,000 kronor. The first transit order under the agreement, Nekludov reported, had been handled on September 3. The life of the agreement was later extended to cover November and December, so that a total of 400,000 tons of coal arrived from England in the last four months of 1915.[32]

The military situation of the Allies did not improve as much as the British Foreign Office had hoped, but pressure on Russia was sufficiently removed by the end of September to permit the British to take a stronger line with the Swedes. On the advice of Sir Eyre Crowe it had been decided that the draft agreement did not offer sufficient guarantees that the obligations would be faithfully carried out by Sweden, and, therefore, Great Britain would be better off without any agreement.[33] As a last effort, however, Britain decided about October 1 to prepare a new draft containing all the principles of control that had been put into operation in the Netherlands and Denmark, and to present it to Sweden with a statement that no modifications in it would be accepted. This was done on October 10, but Wallenberg refused the proposal and indicated that he was quite willing that Anglo-Swedish commercial relations should continue as they had been under temporary compensation arrangements. Consequently, in late October, negotiations were formally declared at an end.[34]

To facilitate the execution of the compensation system the British government in November participated in the establishment of the Aktiebolag Transito, a company through which all consignments in transit to Russia would be handled. The company was directed by Axel R. Bildt, a wholesaler, who, it was reported, held 1,996 of the 2,000 shares in his name. Closely associated with him was Lars Krogius, head of the Finnish Steamship Company. There were immediate and sharp protests against the Transito voiced in the Swedish press, which charged that the company was "a state within a state" that delivered the control of Swedish trade into foreign hands, discriminated against Swedish shipping lines, and was really managed by the British and Russian legations. English and other foreign money was believed to stand behind Bildt in this enterprise.[35] It is true that the British had, in agreement with Bildt, arranged that goods destined to Russia via Sweden should be carried by certain approved Norwegian lines to Norwegian ports, thence to Sweden where they would be in the care of Transito, which would send them by rail or by ship to the Finnish frontier, consigned to Krogius in Helsingfors (Helsinki). Transito was to be paid 2 shillings 6 pence per ton on the goods bound for Russia that it handled, and 1 krona per ton for any goods that remained in Sweden. Initially the goods remaining in Sweden were regarded as of secondary importance, although Transito imports of coffee in 1917 and 1918 later became a subject of great controversy. It was commonly reported that the Swedish government had given its permission for the establishment of Transito, and it was sharply criticized for this by such papers as *Aftonbladet*, which charged that the British were now seeking by indirect means to achieve what they had failed to get by agreement in the recent negotiations with the Swedish government. *Dagens Nyheter* and *Social Demokraten*, on the other hand, tried to calm these fears by pointing out that it was only goods in transit to Russia that were involved, and that in any case the Swedish government still controlled the granting of licenses for the actual exports of these goods and still managed the Swedish railways. There is no doubt, however, that the clamor over Transito was one of the important factors in the passage of the War Trade Law of April 17, 1916.[36]

It is interesting that although negotiations for a general agreement had failed, Anglo-Swedish relations did not seem to deteriorate. Indeed through the temporary expedients noted above, the conditions of transit traffic to Russia and of certain Swedish importations actually improved. Given the severe attitude of the Swedish government toward British trade controls, little more could be hoped for.

NORWAY

At about the same time that negotiations were proceeding between the British government and the Norwegian Cotton Manufacturers Association the Norwegian government, with the support of the Norwegian Trade Association and the Federation of Manufacturing and Industry, decided to approach the British for a general arrangement on Norwegian overseas imports.[37] The Norwegians were apparently encouraged by the reports of fairly successful negotiations between the Danish associations and the British.

The concrete suggestion that the Norwegians should begin similar negotiations came first on August 6, 1915, from the State Committee on Trade Industry, and Shipping, which had been established by Royal decree in October 1914. Nils C. Ihlen, the foreign minister, was also chairman of this committee, so the functions of this body and of the Foreign Ministry were easily co-ordinated. Toward the end of August, Consul-General H. A. N. Olsen and Einar Maseng, secretary of the Committee, were sent to England to represent the Norwegian government. It was not until September 7 that the first meeting with the British authorities was arranged, partly because Maseng's earlier articles on foreign affairs, which appeared to be pro-German, did not make him particularly welcome to the British. Between September 7 and October 6 some fifteen meetings were held, and a draft agreement was reached on October 5. As the negotiations were reported to the Norwegian government there were four important points involved. First, the British insisted that the relaxations made by them in favor of importations into Norway should affect only those products that were on Norwegian embargo lists. This demand was later withdrawn. Second, the British asked that importations of all important goods should be rationed on a monthly basis; in the end, a quarterly system of rations was agreed upon. Third, all ships which would benefit from the agreement were to submit voluntarily to search in British ports. Fourth, goods were to be re-exported to Sweden only if they were on Swedish embargo lists.

Almost every article that was imported from or controlled by Great Britain was included in the scope of the project, except those goods for which arrangements had already been made with Norwegian associations and individuals: coal, coke, cotton, petroleum, mineral oil, and castor oil. The rations were based on Norwegian bona fide needs, plus goods intended for re-exportation to Great Britain, her allies, Spain, Portugal, Holland, neutral countries outside Europe, and under certain conditions to Denmark and Sweden. Guarantees for the faithful performance of the duties imposed by the agreement were to be given by the importer to the Norwegian Trade Federation and the Federation of Norwegian Manufacturing and Industry, which were to be responsible for the actual execution of the accord.

On November 12 the draft finally was considered by the Trade, Industry, and Shipping Committee. Olsen reported that he believed the proposals were as favorable as Norway could then hope to secure, and urged acceptance. He was supported by Erik Farup, who had just returned from England. Many doubts, however, were expressed by other members, among them Ihlen, and it was decided to leave the question of acceptance in abeyance until the two associations expressed their opinions.

Before any action was taken by the associations, a note was delivered by Findlay, the British minister, to the Norwegian Ministry of Foreign Affairs on December 27, stating that the British government was no longer interested in concluding a general trade agreement with the Norwegian government. The criticism of the Danish agreement in the House of Commons had evidently had its effect and had made the British government hesitant about closing another similar agreement, at least until the storm blew over.

Had the agreement been signed, it would certainly have provided a more definite basis for the continuation of Norway's overseas trade. Norwegians who have written on the subject have generally agreed in condemning Ihlen for his slowness in considering the draft, and for his failure to urge its immediate acceptance even as late as November. If ratification had taken place at that time, the agreement would undoubtedly have been censured in England along with the Danish agreement, but the British government would hardly have repudiated it on that ground alone.

The failure of these negotiations left matters as they had been: any relaxation in British policy toward Norwegian importations could be arranged only through agreements made by individuals and trade associations. Regulation could not be accomplished to the complete satisfaction of either the British or the Norwegians, for no unified basis for the control of all Norwegian trade could be agreed upon, nor could its difficulties be adequately dealt with. For the time, at least, the Norwegian government was again outside the negotiations.

VII

The State of the Blockade at the End of 1915

THE year 1915 had brought with it many changes in methods of warfare, one of the most important being the new emphasis placed upon
the use of economic weapons. While German submarine warfare threatened
neutral shipping and neutral lives, Allied measures to prevent trade with
Germany threatened the continuance of neutral trade. Undoubtedly the
greatest single development in the field of economic warfare was the beginning of rationing, at a time when the Allies had suffered setbacks in every
land campaign that was undertaken. At the end of 1915 no real *system* could
be said to exist, but the principle had been accepted by several of the neutrals, and agreements which put the idea into practice had been reached
concerning certain commodities. These agreements were each conditioned
by the special circumstances of the country concerned, so that some, like
those made with the Netherlands Oversea Trust and the Danish associations, were fairly comprehensive whereas others, like those made with the
Swedish Cotton Spinners, applied to a single article. These accords were
effective barriers to trade with Germany in some articles, but so many goods
were left outside of controls that complete stoppage was impossible. In

these negotiations the British government had to make concessions to neutral opinion and interests, and it had to be satisfied with such control as it could get, either willingly or by threatening more onerous restrictions if its requests were not accepted. We have seen that the Danish associations and the N.O.T. agreed to wide measures of control and interference, while the Swedish government refused to allow such things to happen in its country. However, controls were exercised over Swedish, and, indeed, all Scandinavian trade through agreements with shipping companies or with producers of raw materials which these neutrals wished to import.

There had been no particularly arduous bargaining in reaching rationing agreements. These were business agreements, and neutral traders preferred to attain certainty and immediate profits rather than observance of a legal right only at the price of long delay. It was recognized that, in the last analysis, the British government was the more powerful, and it was extremely doubtful whether, in practice, the right of neutrals to trade with Britain's enemies would be left unhindered.

At the same time that relations between the British and the neutrals were being clarified by these rationing agreements, there had been great progress made in perfecting the vast British organization that carried out its measures of economic warfare. With the acceptance of the rationing principle, it became more necessary than ever to collect trade statistics through censorship of mails and cables. The success of the whole rationing operation depended on the British government being able to control all traffic on the main routes leading into the North Sea. British naval supremacy there, was, as has been shown, maintained by the Tenth Cruiser Squadron at the northern entrance of the North Sea and by the fleet stationed in the Channel.[1] Actual interception of ships in the Channel was carried out by the Downs Boarding Flotilla stationed in the Dover Straits. Every neutral ship entering or leaving the North Sea was examined unless it had already been examined and cleared in a British or allied port, in which case it would have a green card or would fly "the flag of the day" from Kirkwall indicating that it had passed inspection there.

In spite of the large number of ships that called voluntarily and received clearance from a British port—the agreements made with various Scandinavian shipping companies required this—there were still many vessels for the patrols to stop and search. Official statistics showed that during 1915 the Tenth Cruiser Squadron intercepted 3,098 vessels, including both eastbound and westbound ships, of which 408 or 13.2 per cent were of British or allied registry; 817 or 26 per cent were fishing craft; 1,130 or 36.6 per cent were neutral merchantmen which were allowed to pass after being boarded or identified at sea. The remaining ships—743 or 24 per cent—were sent in to Kirkwall or Lerwick for examination, more than two a day. The traffic in the Downs was much heavier: from 80 to 120 ships passed through daily, although almost 80 per cent were British ships requiring only instructions as to a safe route, and many were neutral ships proceeding to British east coast ports. Others had already called at Falmouth and possessed a green clearance. But there still remained about twelve each day that were sent in for search by the naval examination service.

For a ship thus sent in, examination included scrutiny of her manifest, bills of lading, and other documents; from these an analysis of the cargo was made and sent by telegram to the Admiralty, Foreign Office, and Board of Customs. Information on eastbound ships was sent to the War Trade Intelligence Department, and there it was added to the other data on the cargo already received from British consuls, from intercepted cables, wireless messages, letters, and from confidential information sent in by special agents of the government. From this array a report was made quite quickly, by 3 P.M. if the customs cable was received in the morning or at once upon arrival if the ship's manifest had been forwarded in advance. The report was sent to the Contraband Committee where the fate of the cargo was decided: whether it would be released or whether the whole or part of the cargo was to be held for prize proceedings or until adequate guarantees against re-exportation to Germany were received. From the manifests of ships examined in port or boarded at sea the Statistical Department of the War Trade Department collected figures on the amounts of each kind of commodity that went to each of the northern neutrals. Reports on the proportion of the rations already imported were made to the Foreign Office and to the Contraband Committee month by month. The British legations would warn the firms or associations which had entered into agreement with the British government when their allowances were nearly filled.

An even greater proportion of westbound ships called voluntarily at British ports to present certificates of neutral origin for their cargoes—the temptation of high prices in forbidden markets was not present for traffic in this direction. The effect of the blockade in this particular trade is easier to see than in any other.[2] The risks of detention were so great and the relative profit so slight that neutral shipping companies refused to carry suspect cargoes, with the result that German export trade reached a very low point. The shipping that continued was more or less by the grace of the British government which allowed some goods to proceed to neutral countries where a special need for them was evident, or when goods ordered before March 1, 1915, had already been paid for by the neutral purchaser. There was no indication that the neutral states contiguous to Germany absorbed the surplus goods that had been exported overseas, if, indeed, there was any considerable exportable surplus in Germany during most of the war.

Neutral importations, however, were still far enough above normal to lead the British to the conclusion that a part of these goods were being re-exported to Germany. The neutrals concerned tried, of course, to impress upon the British the fact that not every increase in their imports went on to the Central Powers. It is extremely difficult, even now, to make any estimate of the effect that the Allied blockade had on German importations. Germany never published her customs statistics for the war period, and neutral statistical publications are incomplete.[3] The British were able at the time to check fairly well, through their observers in neutral commercial centers, the exportations of certain articles; but any complete view of German importations was impossible. The next best indication of the effect of the blockade can be seen in the fluctuations in prices of food and raw materials in Germany. One must be cautious of the conclusions reached from such figures, for some rise in prices can undoubtedly be attributed to general war conditions. The statistics, however, do indicate that supplies were being depleted and that people were anxious. Meat prices in Berlin in December 1915 showed an increase over those of December 1914 of 50 per cent for veal, 67 per cent for mutton, 56 per cent for pork, 100 per cent for bacon, and 76 per cent for ham, while beef prices declined 33 per cent. Rises in prices of cotton yarns and cotton waste were steady in the last half of 1915.[4]

If it is now difficult to estimate the effects of the blockade on the Central Powers, it was even more so in 1915. It is not surprising, in view of the indecisive Allied military operations in 1915, that there should have been great concern over the efforts to stop materials useful for the enemy armies from reaching Germany. During the course of the year there appeared in the British press and in parliamentary debates ample evidence that the negotiations with the neutrals were viewed with suspicion. It was the opinion of many that the honest efforts of the Navy to stop all goods which might conceivably be destined to the enemy were being unduly hampered by the Foreign Office and other civilian branches of the government.

The cause of greatest dissatisfaction was the failure of the government to stop cotton importations into Germany. It was quite well known that cotton waste when properly treated with nitroglycerine became a basic substance for a large group of explosives. The question in the mind of the government soon became not so much whether cotton imports into Germany should be stopped, but rather what methods should be used to effect this result. Not only were military and naval factors concerned but also questions of purely political policy toward neutral states. The government realized that it was on this matter that American pressure could most easily be brought to bear, and it was against such action that the government wished to protect itself.

In October 1914 the British government decided not to declare cotton contraband and Sir Cecil Spring Rice was instructed to reassure the State Department on this point.[5] American cotton exports to the border neutrals did unquestionably increase in late 1914 high above the normal figure, and early in 1915 members of the Opposition in Parliament began to register their disapproval through the questions they addressed to the government. At the same time much was said about the excessively large re-exportations of cotton from Great Britain to the northern neutral states. On February 4, 1915, Sir J. D. Rees asked whether cotton was a usual if not indispensable ingredient in many modern explosives, and, if so, why it was not included in the contraband list. Grey, in answering, admitted that it was, but he said it had not been declared contraband because the proportion of the German cotton import used in explosives was so small that the requirements could have been supplied from stocks already in Germany at the outbreak of the war.[6] Later in the month H. J. Tennant, undersecretary of state for the War Office, said that this was a temporary position and one which would have to be reviewed from time to time.[7]

If in February the government had any great fears about German cotton importations, it believed after March, with considerable justification, that the matter could be handled adequately under the March Order in Council. The British intended that cotton, as well as every other article, should be prevented so far as possible from reaching Germany. Cotton cargoes in large numbers were detained until their owners or neutral consignees gave assurances against their re-exportation. In order to mitigate the hardship on American cotton owners who would be adversely affected by this order, the British government did agree to buy at the contract price all cotton for which contracts of sale and freight engagements had been made before March 2, 1915, provided that the ships sailed not later than March 31.[8] But against a very real desire on the part of Grey to avoid friction with the United States, even to the extent of relaxing the blockade, there continued to be two forces at work: a demand of certain people in Parliament that cotton be declared contraband, and a similar demand made by the French government. The French realized quite well that the burden of maintaining the blockade must fall on the British, as well as any onus for adverse effects these measures would have on neutral interests. So far as the blockade affected the northern European neutrals, the French knew they could only be auxiliaries, but they particularly felt that the Western Allies should be jointly responsible in matters of policy that affected relations with the United States. The French believed that seizure of cotton cargoes would be easier and controversy with the United States less if cotton were declared contraband. As early as October 1914 Colonel Théry had envisaged an Allied purchasing operation in the American cotton market, and the French government apparently wholly approved the British arrangements mentioned above.[9]

It should perhaps be mentioned here that this question concerning cotton coincided in point of time with the controversy between the United States and Germany over the sinking of the *Lusitania* on May 7, 1915. If there was division within the German government as to the role that submarine warfare should play, there was also division among President Wilson's advisers as to how the danger should be met. Whereas Lansing and Colonel House were in favor of making stern demands that submarines should apply the rules of cruiser warfare, and Germany should disavow the illegal acts committed, Bryan believed that the British and German systems of economic warfare should be treated as equally objectionable and a vigorous remonstrance should be sent to London. It was also realized in London that the submarine controversy was an obstacle in the way of Wilson's plan for mediation between the belligerents, a plan in which he set great store. It is against this background that differences of opinion within the British government should be put. Apparently Grey was in a more pliable mood and was, in mid-June, quite prepared to make relaxations in the total war against enemy trade that had been declared in the March Order in Council. Crowe, on the other hand, thought that concessions made in October 1914 had failed to satisfy the American government and that since some controversy was inevitable, Great Britain should not give up anything of importance in the hope of pleasing the Americans. He believed that this controversy would not be appreciably aggravated by declaring cotton contraband.[10]

Questions about exports of cotton from Great Britain to the border neutrals continued to be raised in Parliament during June and July.[11] On June 10 evidence of some change in the point of view of the government was given in a speech by Runciman, president of the Board of Trade, in which he said it was recognized that any cotton going to Germany might be used for explosives, and "therefore it became incumbent upon us to see that amongst the articles which we prevented passing into Germany, cotton should be included." It was particularly felt that controls should be established before the new cotton crop came in. In consequence exportations of cotton and cotton yarns from the United Kingdom were prohibited and a special Cotton Licensing Committee was set up by the War Trade Department.[12] But it was also clear that the government was not yet ready to resort to declaring cotton contraband or to a general rationing of cotton imports into neutral countries. Lord Robert Cecil on June 22 gave a very cogent statement of the government's position: cotton could be stopped just as effectively, and the method of arrest would be the same, whether cotton was stopped as contraband or simply under the March Order in Council.[13] The difficulty of finding the true ultimate destination of the cotton would remain. Cecil pointed out that neutrals could and would make great difficulties if statistics of excessive neutral imports alone were used as a basis for presuming enemy destination. This then was the situation when the House adjourned on July 28.

All during July increasingly disquieting reports came from America of large cotton shipments and dissatisfaction among American meat packers, copper, cotton, and rubber men with the whole British blockade.[14] Spring Rice could at first report nothing very definite about the probable effect that a declaration of cotton as contraband would have in the United States, except that irritation in the South would be increased, and he feared this would add support to the efforts being made to secure an American embargo on all arms and munitions. Spring Rice believed, however, that the declaration could be safely issued if arrangements were made for steadying cotton prices by purchases in the American market, and that probably a purchase of 2,500,000 bales would be sufficient. By mid-July he was urging strong and immediate action of some kind to conciliate the powerful interests that considered themselves aggrieved. Walter Hines Page, in London, also gave ample warning of the dangers of the situation in America, while Spring Rice sent careful reports on the activities of Senator Hoke Smith in inflaming the controversy. Spring Rice in mid-July urged most earnestly that Grey should lay the matter before the cabinet, and although on July 15 Page believed the British government would resist the clamor to make cotton contraband, within a week a change took place.[15] There is some indication, according to A. C. Bell, that Lansing in a conversation with Spring Rice said that he believed the declaration of cotton as contraband would probably be the best way out. At least the British had the tacit approval of the American secretary of state in this step.

On July 22 Page reported that Grey had just telegraphed to Spring Rice that the declaration would be made before the new crop came to market.[16] Sir Richard Crawford, British commercial attaché in Washington, was instructed to come to some satisfactory arrangement on the cotton purchases to be made by the British government. There was some difference of opinion among British officials as to how large these purchases would have to be. Rose, the Board of Trade cotton expert, believed they would have to be larger than those contemplated by Spring Rice, while Crawford, upon whom Spring Rice was relying, thought that occasional purchases at eight cents a pound would suffice.

Final consultations were held with the French on the subject when Jean Gout came to London in mid-August, and it was agreed that raw cotton, cotton linters, cotton waste, and cotton yarns be placed on the absolute contraband list. A royal proclamation to this effect was issued on August 20, 1915.[17] The next day a Foreign Office memorandum was published which announced the government's intention to relieve as far as possible any abnormal depression on the cotton market. Up to the end of September 1915 no such depression occurred.[18]

Actually the declaration was received quite calmly, and by November the agitation among the cotton men, led by certain American senators, had died down. It undoubtedly did serve to hasten three of the northern neutrals in concluding cotton agreements with the British; the Danish Raad signing one on August 23, the Norwegian Cotton Spinners signing one on August 31, and the N.O.T. on September 1, 1915. In the House of Commons on November 2 Lord Cecil stated that, so far as could be seen, the declaration had had no effect on the amount of cotton going to Germany, for that had already been stopped by other means.[19] Moreover no difference was seen in the price of cotton on the American market.

The chief importance of the cotton situation lies not so much in the ultimate decision to make cotton contraband as in the indications the controversy gave of the critical spirit of Parliament and the press regarding the blockade. There was a general fear that the government was not doing all that it could to stop imports into Germany, either from neutral states or from the United Kingdom itself. Once the cotton issue was "settled" the parliamentary opposition moved on to a new one. Lord Charles Beresford was one of the first speakers to voice the complaint in the House of Commons, on November 2, 1915, that the Foreign Office was not doing all it should to maintain the blockade of Germany, and was, in fact, preventing the Navy from doing so.[20] The general complaint was that the fleet brought in ships that it evidently suspected of carrying goods destined to the enemy and that the Foreign Office subsequently ordered the release of a large number of them. To Beresford it seemed almost criminal that Great Britain should have control of the seas and yet "was not using it." The fact that the Foreign Office released ships was adequate proof for him that the government had no fixed policy. In order to refute this whole charge, which was vague at best—for no one specified what sinister influence it was in the government that made them want to save Germany—Lord Cecil rose to explain just what the aims of the blockade were.[21] Not only, he said, did the government desire to weaken Germany by depriving it of all war materials possible, and exerting economic pressure on it by stopping all avenues of external commerce, but Britain also had the duty of preserving friendly relations with neutral states. It was therefore necessary to have proper regard for treaties and the general provisions of international law. This the British could not do and at the same time blockade neutral ports with British ships. Yet such a blockade, which would stop all goods coming from overseas whether bound to a neutral or to an enemy, was apparently what critics of the government advocated. Instead of that method, the government had chosen another: that of stopping all German exports. This, Cecil maintained, was more important than stopping imports, for unless Germany sold, it could not buy except with shipments of gold and loans. However, Britain had also attempted to stop imports into Germany, and had not met any serious conflict with the border neutrals. The difficulties in this policy, he pointed out, lay not only with neutral commerce but with British trade as well. It was true that in attempting to stop the excessive trade of British merchants with these neutrals, British trade with a bona fide neutral destination would be injured. Cecil advocated that a rationing system should be established, operated through some central distributing and guaranteeing agency in the neutral states concerned, in order to distinguish between legitimate neutral trade and that which was destined to Britain's enemies.

The whole agitation against the government's measures of economic war seems to have been entirely misconceived in its aim. Nothing definite could be proved against anyone in the Foreign Office, and clearly no one of those complaining had any idea of the processes by which ships were brought in, searched and either freed or detained, depending upon guarantees of consumption being given in the neutral state. To these few people it was enough that any ships were ever released to make them raise a cry about England's threatened rights at sea. It would have been much more to the point for them to insist upon some real inquiry into the excessive exports and re-exports from the United Kingdom to the border neutrals.[22] Except for a few questions in the Commons, that matter was never discussed in Parliament, not even when a bill dealing with trading with the enemy was discussed on July 20, 1915.[23] The complaints made later in the year by representatives of the Board of Trade against the Danish agreement on the ground that certain goods re-exported from England might be used in the Danish exchange system with Germany, were hardly in keeping with the general Board of Trade policy to encourage British trade with these neutrals, even against the wishes of the Foreign Office.

Early in January 1916 the Foreign Office issued a White Paper entitled *Statement of the Measures Adopted to Intercept the Seaborne Commerce of Germany.*[24] In this statement were summarized the early measures taken against contraband; those taken under the March Order in Council in regard to German exports and imports; and the guarantees demanded in respect to goods bound for the border neutrals. The principle of rationing was explained, as well as the control exercised over world commerce through agreements with shipping lines and through the limitations placed on the supply of British bunker coal. In the concluding paragraphs it was candidly admitted that the facts were not available for a complete statement on the results of these policies. The paper asserted that an almost complete destruction of German export trade had been accomplished, that there was ample evidence of shortages of food and raw materials in Germany, and that both of these results had been attained "without any serious friction with any neutral government."

This *Statement* became the object of criticism and debate in the House of Commons on January 26, 1916, during the discussion of a motion, proposed by Shirley Benn, that urged the government "to enforce as effective a blockade as possible, without interfering with the normal requirements of those neutrals [bordering on enemy territory] for internal consumption."[25] This debate gave the "Blue Water School," as Leverton Harris called one group which criticized the Foreign Office's policy, another chance to air its views. It was also the occasion for others to offer constructive suggestions for new methods of approaching the problem of stopping German trade. The government, through Leverton Harris, Cecil, Sir E. M. Pollock, chairman of the Contraband Committee, and Grey, was able to expand on the information already furnished the House concerning the means so far developed and to defend them more forcefully. The whole argument served as a summary of what had been accomplished in the economic war by the end of 1915 and pointed the way to certain changes that were soon to be made.

Some believed that a regular blockade in accordance with the rules of international law should be declared, and that then the doctrine of continuous voyage should be applied.[26] There was little argument, however, that neutrals would be more complacent about such a measure than they had been toward the March Order in Council. If this advantage did not result, it is difficult to see wherein the Allies would have been better off. Grey pointed out that the only difference would lie in the penalties involved, for the government had undertaken to stop all trade with Germany and the doctrine of continuous voyage was being applied to the fullest extent.[27] The problem, which was the same whether a blockade was declared or whether the British operated under the Reprisals Order, was to distinguish between bona fide neutral trade and that consigned to neutrals but with an ultimate enemy destination. Grey pointed out that there was no difficulty about contraband, for in fact all differences between absolute and conditional contraband had been erased. No particular attempt was now made to determine whether a consignment of conditional contraband was destined to the armed forces or governmental department of the enemy: destination to hostile territory was enough to secure its condemnation.

A more feasible suggestion was made by Leslie Scott, who seconded the motion, and who will be remembered as one of the more knowing critics of the Declaration of London in 1911. He now proposed that all goods in excess of neutral requirements should be presumed to be intended for the enemy, and all such goods should be stopped by the fleet and brought in for condemnation, presumably on the ground of attempting to run the blockade.[28] There was no suggestion that this rationing should be accomplished through agreements with neutrals; it was to be a forcible process. Scott regarded this as the crux of the whole proposal.

Other objections raised against the existing system of economic warfare were the multiplicity of methods employed and the number of committees and departments executing it. Those who criticized in this vein usually ended their argument by urging the declaration of a legal blockade. The government was given an opportunity to explain the administrative machinery, to show what duties the various committees had, and to show how necessary the work of these committees was in "filtering" neutral trade and obtaining evidence that would justify bringing a particular case before the prize court. The government recognized the need for better co-ordination of the activities of governmental departments; it was Leverton Harris who suggested appointing a minister of contraband.[29]

One group, which Leverton Harris called the "Statistical School," tried to show from figures of neutral imports that the government's policy was a failure. The statistics they used had recently appeared in the press, but the government insisted they gave a very erroneous impression in many instances. Leverton Harris called attention to the fact that Russia was dependent on the Swedish transit trade for many commodities, and that Great Britain was herself a heavy importer of essential goods from border neutrals. He made no attempt to deny that a certain amount of trade was going from these neutral states into Germany, either openly when they were domestic products and no embargo existed, or by smuggling when such a prohibition had been decreed. But, he said, whatever system of warfare against enemy trade might be adopted, it would be impossible to prevent the same thing happening. Great Britain could not forbid neutrals to export their own produce to whomever they pleased, and it could not set up a police system in a neutral state to prevent smuggling. Leverton Harris did regard rationing as a legitimate means of decreasing neutral exports to Germany, and he saw great possibilities in the pressure of withholding British bunker coal from neutral ships except under certain guarantees.[30]

W. A. S. Hewins held the view that on the whole the system supported by the government was a good one that only wanted tightening up to make it more effective.[31] Many members of the House felt it unfortunate that partisan controversy had been introduced into the subject and realized that little was to be gained by censuring the government. This group seemed more inclined toward making arrangements with neutrals than toward using more forcible methods that might well fail to attain their ends.

Many similar arguments were heard in the debate initiated in the House of Lords by Lord Sydenham (formerly Sir George Sydenham Clarke) on February 22 and 23, 1916.[32] The most revealing speeches were made by Lord Emmott of the War Trade Department and by Lord Faringdon, who had just returned from a mission of investigation in Scandinavia and the Netherlands. Both men pointed out the difficulties of dealing with the domestic production of the border neutrals, but Faringdon in particular spoke as well of the restrictive measures taken in Denmark and the Netherlands by trade associations within these countries. He insisted that British policy was determined jointly by the Navy and the Foreign Office and that charges of divergence between them were unfounded. The Marquess of Crewe, lord president of the Council, came to the defense of the committees that had been working on these problems, but he admitted that no absolute system of rationing could be applied to neutrals, since no prize court could be expected to condemn a cargo simply because it exceeded the ration.

It would seem that as a result of these debates, the members of Parliament, at least, should have gained a more precise idea of the aims and measures of the economic campaign being waged by the government against enemy trade, and the government had survived the criticism of its opponents without much trouble.

VIII

Forcible Rationing, Navicerting, Black-Listing and Intercepting Neutral Mails

———

DURING the year 1916 the Allied governments, and in particular the British government, undertook certain measures that fell outside the agreements concluded with the northern European neutrals. These measures, which the Allies usually insisted were legitimate exercises of their sovereign rights, became the subject of neutral protests, but they were persisted in and became important adjuncts of the system of blockade. The policies which fell in this category included forcible rationing, navicerting, black-listing, and finally, the interception of neutral mails. Although some of these had been put into operation to a limited degree before February 1916, it was not until after the establishment of the Ministry of Blockade that they became wholly effective.

THE MINISTRY OF BLOCKADE

Partly as a result of criticism made in Parliament and by those using the services of the various government committees—that the administrative operation of the blockade was cumbersome—and partly because of the inevitable confusion growing out of the overlapping of the duties of these organs, it was felt by those working in the government that the machinery of the economic war should be perfected. It was therefore decided to create a Ministry of Blockade whose head would be a member of the cabinet and whose chief function would be to co-ordinate the activities of the existing branches of the government dealing with the blockade. On February 23, 1916, this ministry was established, and Lord Robert Cecil, who continued to be an undersecretary of state for foreign affairs, was named the minister of blockade.[1] The central executive of the new ministry remained in the Contraband Department, which by then was divided into eight sections. Sir Eyre Crowe became the undersecretary of blockade and was especially concerned with the work of the Contraband Department. He was assisted by G. S. Spicer, who had been the Foreign Office representative on the Contraband Committee, and by Alwyn Parker. Politically the minister of blockade carried the responsibility of the cabinet on matters of blockade; he represented the ministry in Parliament and made all communications to the press. The minister was given full executive power to issue regulations and to come to decisions regarding contraband and all other restrictions on enemy trade. Cecil also, as chief of the section of the Foreign Office charged with the economic war, dealt directly with neutral governments on questions affecting the blockade. He superintended the operation of agreements with neutrals and was responsible for new negotiations to extend British controls over neutral trade.

From the administrative point of view the duties of the minister of blockade were tremendous. The two principal organizations placed within the ministry were the War Trade Department and the Contraband Department. Attached to the former, it will be recalled, were the War Trade Intelligence Department and the War Trade Statistical Department. In 1916 two other committees were added to the War Trade Department: the War Trade Advisory Committee and the Rationing Committee. The War Trade Advisory Committee was composed of the heads of all the committees concerned with the restriction of enemy supply; it was presided over by Lord Crewe and was intended to advise the cabinet on matters of policy. The Rationing Committee, set up in April 1916, determined the amounts of various articles that would be authorized to go into the northern neutral countries, and was thus similar to the French Commission des Contingents, which dealt with Swiss rations.[2]

Two other important organs functioned within the Ministry of Blockade although they were independent of either of its two main divisions. One, the Foreign Trade Department, was concerned with regulations against trading with the enemy. It was this department that established the black lists and in special circumstances delivered permissions to trade in enemy goods or with enemy persons. The second was the Section on Financial Transactions, which supervised British financial operations with neutral states, controlled banking, and adopted measures to impede enemy operations being carried on through neutral banks. In time a third department was created to supervise purchases made by the British government in neutral markets with the object of obstructing enemy trade.

Altogether the Ministry of Blockade provided the unifying force among the various committees that had been set up to deal with the trade of the Central Powers, and the efficiency of the blockade in 1916 may, to a great extent, be attributed to its creation and operation. To keep pace with these changes in the British government, the French made a similar one when on March 23, 1916, Denys Cochin, the president of the Comité de Restriction des Approvisionnements et du Commerce de l'Ennemi, was raised to ministerial rank.[3] Although no immediate changes took place in the organization of the Comité de Restriction, it now had opportunity to exert more direct influence on governmental decisions.

FORCIBLE RATIONING

Even before the Ministry of Blockade was established, the British government had considered certain ideas for extending the rationing principle. Although the agreements made with neutrals had been relatively successful, it was felt that more rigorous action was necessary to cut off German importations. In Parliament late in 1915 the government had seemed quite cool toward the idea of a general rationing of neutrals without first securing agreements. In private, however, the idea was coming to seem quite acceptable to certain officials who felt that some more regular administrative process, based on statistical evidence, for stopping or releasing neutral cargoes should be evolved. This procedure was named "forcible rationing"; it consisted of detaining all goods destined to neutral states beyond the amount required by them in normal times, irrespective of whether neutral governments or trade associations had agreed to the figure set by the British.

Late in January 1916 Lord Crewe told the Foreign Office that the cabinet had made no specific objection to the system and that it might be assumed that the policy was one which the Government intended to introduce.[4] It is not certain that Grey was in favor of putting so much pressure on neutrals; his earlier speeches in Parliament showed that he had a nice regard for neutral rights of trade. Cecil Hurst urged Grey to agree on the ground that unless all shipments to neutrals in excess of normal were held up by the British, these neutrals would soon know that more than the amounts they had secured by particular accords were coming in. In such circumstances neutrals would refuse to carry out their promises and would see no reason for giving new ones. Thus the whole system of British control, which had been gained so laboriously over a period of months, would be put in danger. Grey seems to have been convinced by February 3 that the policy should be attempted, although he thought it best not to speak too openly of rationing.

Hurst then circulated a paper among all the blockade departments suggesting that the Contraband Department should notify neutrals that certain commodities were to be rationed, and that once the normal importation figure had been reached, all overseas cargoes would be ordered detained by the Contraband Committee. It was objected by some that general trade statistics would not be accepted in a prize court as proof that any particular consignments were destined to the enemy. But Hurst, supported by John Mellor, procurator-general, considered that the government could at least hold up cargoes, and the burden of proof as to the innocence of their destination would then be on the consignee. Delay and a certain amount of confusion in neutral trade would result, but the pressure thus exerted would be enough to make neutrals seek further arrangements with the Allies. Lord Cecil circulated two papers in defense of the policy of forcible rationing, which resulted in its acceptance for the rest of the year.

A confidential memorandum by Lord Cecil, dated July 8, 1916, dealing with the procedure to be followed in rationing the northern neutrals, shows how carefully the part of each of the various governmental agencies in carrying out forcible rationing had been considered.[5] The memorandum began by stating that since importations of certain articles exceeded domestic needs in these neutral countries, it was desirable that immediate and simultaneous measures should be taken by all the services engaged in administering the blockade, in order to stop further importations, whatever their source. To carry out this proposal the Rationing Committee, together with the War Trade Statistical Department, would have the responsibility of beginning the surveillance of all important articles and of recommending to the government the measures that ought to be taken. Their recommendations would at once be addressed officially to the secretary of the Rationing Committee, and by him to the secretary of state for foreign affairs; copies of the recommendation would be sent to the other ministries and departments concerned.[6] The decision to carry out the recommendation, Lord Cecil's memorandum continued, would be made by the minister of blockade, and the secretary of state for foreign affairs would set the date on which the decision would come into effect. The decision would then be announced to these same ministries and departments who would take all necessary measures in conformity with the following procedure: (1) The War Trade Department and the committees attached to it would cease to grant licenses to export to neutral states the goods concerned in the decision. They would likewise be responsible for the revision of licenses already granted. (2) The Foreign Trade Department would inform the banks immediately to cease to give credit facilities for consignments of the goods in question, whatever their source, to the mentioned states, until some date specified in the notice. (3) The Restriction of Enemy Supply Committee would inform the president of Lloyd's that insurance facilities must cease to be accorded for consignments of the goods in question. (4) The secretary of state for foreign affairs would (a) inform British representatives in the countries to which the goods were destined and give them instructions to take whatever measures they judged necessary, (b) give a note to the press—following a set formula which was annexed to the memorandum—that no more facilities would be accorded by His Majesty's Government for the importation into certain countries of stipulated goods for a designated length of time,[7] (c) take measures to inform representatives of the American press of the text of the decision, (d) inform the ambassador at Washington that no new facilities would be given until further orders, and that requests for letters of assurance[8] must be refused except in special cases, (e) inform the French government, and, if necessary, the Italian government, and invite them to take similar measures. (5) The Contraband Committee would reject all requests for letters of assurance and would put as many obstacles as possible in the way of consignments already en route. (6) The Rationing Committee would confirm to the Foreign Office that the existing importations of the state concerned were again in exact proportion to the needs of the country, or would be by a certain date.

Unfortunately, no exact evidence is available on the results of this policy of forcible rationing, and no statistical estimate can be made of the trade that was turned away from the border neutrals by this means. According to C. Ernest Fayle, the procedure was in working order by August 1, 1916,[9] and there is no doubt that these measures, judiciously applied, in common with other means of coercion, were effective in keeping from the neutrals surpluses of overseas goods that might otherwise have been shipped on to Germany.

NAVICERTING

One of the administrative processes developed by the British to make their measures of surveillance more palatable to neutral exporters, importers, and shipping companies was that of navicerting. The system was another example of the practice in which a neutral gave an engagement and received certain facilities from the British government in return. Here the American exporter submitted his case to the British authorities before shipping his goods to the Scandinavian countries, and if the government was convinced of the innocence of the cargo, a navicert—a sort of commercial passport— was granted, which insured in most cases an undisturbed passage of the goods to their destination.

An earlier example of giving notice of cargoes and their destinations is to be found in Captain Cold's first agreement with the British, concluded in November 1914, in which he engaged to keep the British commercial attaché in Copenhagen au courant with the cargoes shipped by his company. In return the British agreed not to detain his ships.[10]

The suggestion that some method should be found by which American shippers could be given an idea of the probable fate of their cargoes before the sailing date evidently originated with Robert Skinner, American consul general in London. He had been most active in pressing the claims of American citizens against the British government, rather to the latter's discomfort, and his suggestion could in no way be ascribed to any desire to aid the British in controlling trade still further. Indeed, because he was convinced that the British would never relax their blockade, it was, he believed, better to come to some arrangement which would make American trade safer. Skinner first suggested to the state department in mid-April 1915 that manifests should be cabled to London before cargoes were shipped, perhaps under some American official guarantee that the cargo conformed to the manifest; and that American exporters should then be informed whether or not the British government approved their cargoes, in the same way that British shippers were either granted licenses, refused them, or asked for further details.[11] Skinner discussed his plan with Admiral Sir Edmond Slade of the War Trade Advisory Committee on April 19, and he was favorably impressed,[12] particularly since it would give ten days or two weeks, between the sailing of the ship and its arrival in British waters, to adjust difficulties. Late in 1915 Skinner returned to Washington where he consulted with Sir Richard Crawford as well as with Frank Polk, legal counselor of the Department of State. Officially, however, the State Department was noncommittal.

The British found during February 1916 that a similar plan tried by the Norwegian-America Line was working satisfactorily; the company telegraphed certain particulars of the cargo they intended to ship and received an answer, either that the shipment might lead to difficulties or it was not likely to do so. Indeed, the War Trade Advisory Committee was convinced that Skinner's scheme might succeed, and by February 28 Crawford had begun to establish an office at the embassy in Washington to which applications might be addressed.[13]

On March 4, 1916, a circular was issued from the British consulate general in New York explaining the new arrangements.[14] Shippers who desired to use the opportunity of finding whether their shipments would be regarded as unobjectionable under British military regulations, and, therefore, would be allowed through the naval patrol, were advised to make application at the office established in the British embassy in Washington. Applications were required to relate to particular consignments, and had to be made at least two weeks before the date of shipment. The following information was asked: the name and address of the consignor; a complete description and quantity of the goods; the name and address of the consignee in Norway, Sweden, or Denmark; the name of the steamship line which was to transport the goods; the approximate date of shipping; and, when known, the name of the vessel.

The embassy was given a digest of the commercial information collected by the War Trade Department, including a list of consignees known to be unsatisfactory, and was empowered to grant letters of assurance for goods not on British embargo lists. When applications came in for letters of assurance to cover other goods, all pertinent information respecting the consignment in question was cabled, at the applicant's expense, to London. There the request was first examined by the Foreign Trade Department, where the records of previous shipments made to the consignee were examined. Next the request was examined by the Statistical Department and the Contraband Department to determine the amount of the same goods which had already been imported by the neutral country, and what agreements were in effect concerning the commodities in the shipment. Finally the Contraband Committee passed on the question and an answer in code was sent: "nolo" meant that the request was refused, "accipe" meant that it was granted, and "pendens" meant that further inquiries had to be made and no immediate answer was to be expected. One of the chief reasons for giving the "pendens" answer was that necessary guarantees against re-exportation had not yet been secured from the Scandinavian consignee; in some cases it was necessary to refer the question to the British legation in the country of destination. A navicert, once granted, was valid for two months.

It was the hope of the British government in setting up this system of navicerts that political friction with the United States would thereby be lessened. To a considerable extent this was the result, but there is ample evidence that American exporters were far from satisfied with the way in which the plan was executed.[15] As a result of the comparative certainty which a letter of assurance gave to the steamship companies—that the consignment thus covered would not be the cause of the ship's detention—most of the shipping companies in the Scandinavian trade soon refused to accept shipments unless a navicert had been obtained.[16] However, the delays that occurred between the date of application and the granting of the navicert made it difficult for the American exporters to know what orders to give manufacturers or what orders to take for shipment. Some exporters felt that the British had almost a strangle hold on their business, for if there had been no navicerting system, the risks could have been placed on the Scandinavian buyers and American trade could have gone its own way.

Charges were also made that the British embassy was in no hurry to announce its decision once it had been made, and that by this policy British
trade was fostered at American expense.[17]

The State Department declined all responsibility for the navicerting
system and pointed out that it could do nothing to force shipping companies to accept consignments not covered by navicerts.[18] The Department
did convey some of the complaints to Sir Richard Crawford, but no protest
seems to have been made against letters of assurance in general.[19]

Later in the year the British government considered an extension of the
navicerting system which would have increased its control over American
trade. The documents available on this proposal also show something of
the way in which navicerting was operating.

As will be explained in the next chapter, the British government had
laid down conditions regulating the use of articles whose source of supply
was controlled by the British. Thus it was required that exportations of
goods manufactured from raw materials of British origin should be covered
by guarantees that they were not destined to Britain's enemies. In practice
the shipment of these goods had also been made subject to the issue of a
navicert. American manufacturers had accepted this second extension of
their obligations without too much protest, for, after all, it did facilitate
the shipment and delivery of their goods. It was on July 27, 1916, that the
Admiralty, in a letter to the Foreign Office, asked whether guarantees against
exportation of their goods to the enemy should be asked of all American
exporters who applied for letters of assurance.[20] The Admiralty advised that
the request of the Dutch government for the facilitation of a consignment
of antimony, to be shipped by an American firm, should be refused by the
British government because the firm had never signed a guarantee against
the exportation of its antimony to Germany. It also became evident that
the Admiralty wanted all American exports to Scandinavia, whether fabri-
cated from British materials or not, to carry a navicert, which would be
granted only against guarantees given by the exporter. Thus, if the consignment seemed suspect, or if the quotas had already been filled, the goods
would never be put to sea. More than this, the whole system of forcible
rationing would be strengthened.

The reply of the Foreign Office stated nicely the problems involved.[21]
The British government had been able to demand guarantees from American manufacturers as a condition of their receiving raw materials from the
British Empire or facilities for the transport of their exports. But the situation also arose where an American firm had been able to supply itself with
raw materials outside the British Empire, e.g., American tanning materials
and Chinese antimony. Such firms had neither the need nor the desire to
sign an accord with the British government respecting the disposal of their
goods. The Foreign Office reminded the lords of the Admiralty that a system demanding guarantees from all American exporters might be interpreted
as an interference in perfectly legitimate commerce between neutrals.

On the recommendation of Cecil Hurst the Admiralty's proposal was
ubmitted to a special subcommittee of the War Trade Advisory Com-
nittee.[22] Its first meeting, on September 25, 1916, was presided over by Sir
3eorge Cave. Admiral Slade presented the Admiralty's point of view and
ecommended that the navicerting system should at least be extended to
:over Dutch trade. The difference of opinion between the Admiralty and
'oreign Office was well expressed in a note written by Hurst after a conver-
ation with Admiral Dudley R. S. de Chair:

> ... I was not able to convince the Admiral that it is not reasonable
> for us to use the control that we obtain through the guarantees de-
> manded from United States firms which supply themselves with raw
> materials from the British Empire to hinder the commerce of firms
> who have not given us any guarantee in exchange for what we have
> given them. . . . The only reason that would lead firms, who do not
> wish to supply themselves in the British Empire, to give us guarantees
> would be the belief that their shipments would be stopped at sea.
> Most of our formulas of guarantee use the expression "by reason of
> your (the British Consul's) consent to deliver. . . ." This formula
> is scarcely applicable to a firm which receives no raw materials from
> the British Empire and to which, in consequence, the Consul has not
> given his consent for a delivery of goods.
>
> The opinion of the Admiral, which is I suppose that of the naval
> authorities, is that we ought to draw all of the advantages possible
> from our supremacy of the seas; we ought even to go so far as to
> dictate to the houses of neutral countries, like Holland, the names of
> the firms in the United States where they can supply themselves. I
> believe that since our right of seizure of goods at sea depends on the
> extent to which we can prove clearly before the Prize Court their
> enemy destination, it is not wise to extend so far the application of
> our mastery of the seas.[23]

The report of the subcommittee was given to the War Trade Advisory
Committee on October 9, 1916.[24] For the most part the report followed
Hurst's recommendations, pointing out that the system of navicerting was
of great importance and that it was not desirable to disturb it by imposing
new conditions unless there were very good reasons for doing so. This was
particularly true since the United States government had up to then acquiesced in the practice, and it might well raise the entire question if new
and more far-reaching conditions were added. The report stated that the
Contraband Department was opposed to the Admiralty's proposition, for
it had confidence that the information then at the disposal of the Committee would allow it to decide whether or not a consignment was ultimately
destined to the enemy. The Contraband Committee believed that any such
new guarantees might have a prejudicial effect, for an exporter who had

given a guarantee would then consider himself aggrieved if a navicert were refused to him. Such a situation would only increase tension between Great Britain and neutral governments. The subcommittee therefore decided it was not desirable to use the navicert to obtain the guarantees in question.

BLACK-LISTING

In Chapter V the changes in British trading with the enemy legislation have been traced up to the point where, in June 1915, the prohibition was made to include trade with German nationals resident in China, Siam, Persia, and Morocco. Then, for the first time, British regulations approximated those applied by the French government, which, throughout the war, had based its legislation on the principle of nationality as well as domicile.

The next step in increasing the forcefulness of British legislation was taken with the passage of the Trading with the Enemy Act of December 23, 1915.[25] This act put into effect a modified form of the principle of nationality, and was in reality a further recognition of the validity of French complaints against existing British regulations. The government was now authorized to issue proclamations forbidding trade between persons domiciled in the United Kingdom and those persons or organizations of "enemy associations" who were domiciled in neutral countries. It would thus be possible to proscribe trade with German or Austrian nationals in any neutral country; but more than that, trade with any individual or company, whatever the nationality, could be forbidden if the British government suspected him or it of lending aid to the enemy. Since the British were anxious to inconvenience their own trade relations in neutral countries as little as possible, there were distinct advantages in forbidding trade only with those firms whose enemy connections were undoubted, rather than forbidding trade with all German nationals everywhere as the French did.[26] The first list of persons with whom residents of Great Britain were forbidden to trade was issued by royal proclamation on February 29, 1916.[27] Technically the list was known as a "statutory list."

Similar lists of neutral firms or individuals who were regarded as suspect had previously been compiled by the British government.[28] In the first months of the war Lieutenant Clayton Calthorp had in the course of his work in the Admiralty collected the information coming to him in an Intelligence Manual Regarding Neutral Traders. Quite independently of him an Enemy Traders List was compiled by one Major Phillips in the Censor's Department. These two lists were later merged at the suggestion of Colonel Maurice P. A. Hankey; the new list became known as Who's Who in Relation to War Trade. In it was included every firm known to be connected in any way with trade with the Central Powers, and the sources of information in each instance. Supplements were issued quarterly from information collected by the Censor's Department and the Department of Military Intelligence. The list became a guide for the Contraband Committee in reaching decisions on the disposition to be made of ships and cargoes. The use of the list in no way meant that British subjects were prevented from trading with the suspected firms if they wished.

The preparation of the black lists provided for by statute was undertaken by the Foreign Trade Department. Three types of lists were made. The first, the statutory list proper, included those firms in neutral territory whose enemy associations were undoubted. This list was published, and all persons resident in the United Kingdom were prohibited from trading with those whose names appeared on it. The penalties for violation were those laid down by the Proclamation Relating to Trading with the Enemy of September 9, 1914, or as amended by any subsequent proclamations. In addition to this list there was a second, unpublished and secret list. The firms on this "List B" were regarded as highly suspicious and, in consequence, none of their cargoes were in practice allowed through the blockade; the mere appearance of the name of the black-listed firm on a commercial document was regarded as creating a presumption of an enemy destination of the goods in question. British export licenses were never granted for goods destined to firms on List B, and British firms were "advised" not to trade with them.[29] So far as crippling enemy trade was concerned, List B played quite as important a part, and seems to have been as effective, as the statutory list. The third list—that of all enemy and neutral traders, with all pertinent information about them—was continued for the use of the Contraband Committee; it, too, was secret. A supplementary statutory list was issued on April 26, 1916, and on May 23 still another was published, which consolidated the preceding ones.

Originally the black lists were purely a British measure, but early in June the French government began to consider the advisability of issuing similar ones. The initiative was taken by the Commission des Dérogations, which raised the question with the Comité de Restriction, with the result that a special subcommittee, made up of representatives of the Ministries of War, Foreign Affairs, and Marine and the Comité, was established to make recommendations.[30] It was assumed in a note sent by Aristide Briand to Denys Cochin on June 20, 1916, that the British statutory list would form the basis for the French black lists, and the French would particularly be able to add Swiss firms with questionable connections.[31] It was believed that this co-operation with the British was necessary to remove some of the difficulties French traders were encountering. French houses had sometimes sent goods to neutral houses inscribed on the English black lists, but about which French information was not unfavorable. The warning was given, however, that the greatest care should be taken to avoid restraining French exporta tions too much, and to prevent clashes with neutrals over arrangements already concluded, for diplomatic repercussions might follow and groups friendly to the Allied cause might be alienated. There is no doubt that French action was hastened by the recommendations made at the Allied Economic Conference held in Paris, June 14–17.[32] The formal notification of the first French black list was published on August 6, 1916.[33]

It was not until July 18, 1916, that the names of American firms appeared on the British statutory list, although some had already been placed on the secret list.[34] The publication of the names of eighty-five American firms aroused much ill feeling in the United States and became the subject of protests by the State Department. Just what the British hoped to gain by this move is somewhat difficult to see, for their ends could have been attained quite as well in secret by continuing to deal with suspect American firms through List B. One explanation of the decision to add American firms, is, of course, that the British government wanted to avoid charges of discrimination brought by other neutrals. It is undoubtedly true that the uproar in the United States was quite unexpected, since other measures had been accepted without too much protest, but once having embarked upon the policy it was difficult for the British to draw back.

The protest made toward the end of July by the United States government against the black list was not based so much on the legal rights of Americans as upon "moral" grounds.[35] The impossibility of obtaining tonnage for cargoes owned by proscribed firms, and of obtaining credit from banks, made it appear that the prohibition actually applied to neutral domestic transactions as well as to those in the British Empire. The United States government regarded the measures as extremely arbitrary, and no limit was seen to the extent to which the British might ultimately go in further proscribing legitimate American trade.

Grey's reply to the American protest was delivered to Page belatedly, on October 10, 1916.[36] The British conceded nothing, and, as might have been expected, insisted that the act and proclamation were purely municipal legislation designed to prohibit persons in the United Kingdom from trading with any persons in foreign countries who were specified in the proclamation. The right of Great Britain to pass such legislation could hardly be doubted, for nothing was done directly to interfere with rights of neutral trade, nor were neutrals condemned or their property confiscated. The note asserted that the British government could not be expected to give to those active in assisting the cause of its enemies the facilities which would flow from participation in British commerce. The note was forcefully written, and was, from the legal point of view, convincing.

The British government realized, however, that from the political point of view it had made a serious blunder in publicly listing American firms. To quiet the situation Spring Rice had already been instructed to announce that Britain had no intention of interfering with neutrals trading with neutrals, or neutrals trading with Germans, and that there would be no black-listing

)f American firms because they traded with those already on the lists.[37] The 3ritish offered to reconsider specific cases. In November Page reported that)oth Grey and Cecil were prepared to carry out this latter offer; Grey had ısked that some eminent American be sent to London to confer with him n order to "whittle the list down to the smallest number of names."[38] Page uggested that Polk, counselor in the State Department, should go, and 3rey regarded him as most satisfactory. But, although Lansing was pleased vith the invitation, he found it impossible to allow Polk to leave the De->artment for so long. Page was very much disappointed in this refusal.[39] Thus stood the conversations between the British and American govern-nents on the black lists at the end of November 1916. No definite conclu-;ion had been reached.

The opinion of the War Trade Department on the efficacy of the black-ist system was stated in a memorandum issued to refute the contention that :he statutory list was not a war measure and did not contribute to shorten-ing the war.[40] The document explained that in the first months of the war when German cruisers were still at large in South American waters, the cruisers secured a large part of their supplies and information from the Ger-man trading houses established in the large ports. The British government possessed considerable evidence of the value of the services thus rendered. Because of the inactivity of German cruisers in recent months, neutrals had come to believe that these ships would not be able to attack commerce up to the end of the war. However, the British government believed that this conclusion was at least premature, for the cruise of the Moewe[41] had shown that a German corsair could reach the Atlantic and stay there long enough to do considerable damage. Should more German cruisers venture out, these German houses would once more become important as sources of supply. So long as they had money and facilities, they could accumulate reserves of coal, oil, and the like, but if they were threatened and had to fight to keep solvent, it seemed evident that they could do less to aid the cause of the Fatherland. The British had proof that the black list was a means of paralyz-ing the activity of these German firms. Thus the directors of the Deutsches Kohlen Depot, the most important of the German overseas coal companies, which had supplied the Goeben and the Breslau as well as other enemy cruisers, had written to their agent at Buenos Aires that "the efforts of fifteen years have been destroyed."[42]

It was further pointed out in this memorandum that the effects of the black list were necessarily slow in appearing, and the longer the duration of the war, the more German trade would be tied up. Effects had been seen on the general instability of German finance, and there was an increasing anxiety among German businessmen. It was believed that "the more these interests see their future compromised by the continuation of war, and [feel] the pressure that the commercial measures of the Allies exercise on their branches established in neutral countries, the more they will be desirous of shortening the war and the more will they consent to terms acceptable to the Allies."

The third sphere where the effects of black-listing were seen was in the blockade. The memorandum stated that while the black lists were not at first intended to contribute to the blockade, they had rendered it more effective in several ways. Black-listing of certain firms in America—especially in South America where sources of supply were largely in German hands— had cut the amount of foodstuffs and raw materials coming from overseas. This was true in the instance of Argentine wheat, and of rubber, coffee, and nitrates from Brazil. So long as German firms in America had been free to send their goods it was inevitable that they should try to send them to Germany, and however vigilant the British surveillance was, a considerable amount escaped, because, lacking proofs, the government could not send them to the prize court. After the establishment of the statutory lists, these shipments had nearly ceased, since few shipowners would take the risk of having their vessels inscribed on the black list of ships or risk being deprived of coal, because they had carried goods for a black-listed firm.[43]

Another contribution to the blockade resulted from the great dislike of neutrals of seeing their names "put in pillory," which distressed them even more than knowing that they had been put on a secret list. This had been shown by the protests of the Danish Guild and the Netherlands Oversea Trust when the names of some of their members figured on the published list. A number of neutral houses had spontaneously offered to give up their business with Germany and to come to an agreement with the British government. The memorandum ended by saying: "In fact, it does not seem exaggerated to say, that the Statutory list has done more than any other measure to make neutrals sensible to the effects of maritime supremacy." It was believed in the War Trade Department that any attenuation in the black-list policy would be interpreted by neutrals as a weakening of British power and of the government's resolution to continue the war with the greatest possible vigor.

BRITISH INTERCEPTION OF NEUTRAL MAILS

. In the wars of the seventeenth and eighteenth centuries, neutral mails had been regarded by England as a legitimate source of information on the plans and activities of its enemies. Official dispatches of an enemy state were regarded as contraband, and even dispatches between belligerent and neutral governments were not inviolable. It was not until the nineteenth century and the development of postal conventions which regulated the expedition of international mails, that correspondence came to have a more privileged position than any other goods in time of war. Even so, this attitude was only a tendency, and no international law that laid down the inviolability of neutral mails could be said to exist.

Formal recognition of the principle of this inviolability took place in 1907 in Articles 1 and 2 of the Eleventh Hague Convention on the Exercise of the Right of Capture in Maritime War.[44] These provisions read:

> 1. The postal correspondence of neutrals or belligerents, whatever its official or private character may be, found on the high seas on board a neutral or enemy ship, is inviolable. If the ship is detained, the correspondence is forwarded by the captor with the least possible delay.
>
> The provisions of the preceding paragraph do not apply in case of violation of blockade, to correspondence destined for or proceeding from a blockaded port.
>
> 2. The inviolability of postal correspondence does not exempt a neutral mail ship from the laws and customs of maritime war as to neutral merchant ships in general. The ship, however, may not be searched except when absolutely necessary, and then only with as much consideration and expedition as possible.

It was argued by the German delegate, Dr. Johannes Kriege, who made this proposal, that because of the importance of belligerent censorship of the telegraph, the importance of intercepting mails had greatly decreased. This assertion was unchallenged by the British military and naval delegates, and the Hague Convention was accepted by the British government. Of the states that later participated in the World War, Russia, Italy, Bulgaria, Montenegro, Serbia, and Turkey did not sign.

During the first months of the war any British censorship of mails was carried out by the War Office, with a view to gathering information of military value.[45] Provision for this kind of censorship had been made in the War Office War Book, where it was required that applications should be made to the Home Office for warrants to open mail of suspected persons. If foreign mails were involved, the Foreign Office was consulted. On August 27, 1914, the War Office requested the privilege of opening all mail passing through England from and to Holland, Denmark, and Norway. When the opinion of the Foreign Office was asked, Sir Eyre Crowe said this was really a military matter and it would be enough if the Foreign Office was notified of any extensions later considered necessary. By the end of 1914 warrants had been granted for the inspection of the mails of all neutral states in Europe. Like most of the other weapons used in the economic campaign, the censorship of mails for this purpose developed gradually. It is not known exactly when information of an economic nature came to be taken from censored letters. At any rate a Commercial Branch was established in the Censor's Office and from it information was being sent by February 1915 to the various commit tees engaged in the economic war.

The difficulties which arose from British censorship had to do with two types of mail: parcel post and letter mail. In view of the importance attached to stopping all trade with Germany after March 1, 1915, it is somewhat strange that measures were not taken immediately to inspect parcel-post packages. It was not until late in September 1915 that such censorship was authorized by the Foreign Office. The action of the French government had been much more vigorous, for very soon after the March Decree, orders were given to the naval squadrons that parcels found on steamers were to be al lowed to pass only if they were covered by certificates of origin. The French sent to the British government information that a very considerable parcel post trade had recently developed, and dispatches from Spring Rice sup ported the French assertions. The British cabinet was willing to go only part of the way that Crowe urged, but early in September 1915 the customs authorities were empowered to open parcels entering the United Kingdom. Paul Cambon objected that even then the British squadrons did not seize parcels. As a result late in September Grey sanctioned the inspection of parcel mails found on neutral steamers on the high seas, but only on condi tion that a French cruiser should be attached to the British squadron con ducting this examination service, in order to indicate the joint responsibility of the two governments.

The censorship of letter mails originating in or destined for the United Kingdom was, as has been shown, begun early in the war, as an exercise of a sovereign right. An extension of letter censorship came in April 1915 as a means of gathering commercial information that would permit a better exe cution of the March Order in Council. By a new order, mails between Euro pean countries and the United States which were sent to a United Kingdom port for transshipment were included among the mails to be censored. It was argued that these mails were forwarded between United Kingdom ports by the British Post Office, and since they were in British territory, under British jurisdiction and protection, and were enjoying facilities of the Post Office, the right of censorship in time of war was undoubted.[46]

A systematic censorship of mails on board all ships entering United Kingdom ports, or intercepted on the high seas and then brought in, was undertaken still later. That this was a right which Great Britain might exer cise in the future had been indicated by an answer that Grey made to an interpellation in the House of Commons on October 12, 1915. Joseph King, M.P. for Somerset, asked whether the Universal Postal Convention (of June 1, 1878) contained any article which had been "so misunderstood or mis represented" as to place in an unfavorable light the action of the British or allied governments in delaying postal matter passing over belligerent terri tory from one neutral to another.[47] Grey replied that in the opinion of the government a state of war suspended the application of the Convention be tween the belligerents themselves, and then he went on to say:

His Majesty's Government find it impossible so to construe the terms of the Convention as to suppose that it binds a belligerent state to allow itself to be used as the channel for communications intended to defeat its own measures of war, and in these circumstances they feel bound in certain cases to exercise their right of examination of mails in transit over British territory between two neutral countries. I would add that every care is taken to avoid undue delay or prejudice to the legitimate interests of neutral subjects.

Given this theory, it was but a step to the censorship of mails carried by neutral ships that called at a British port or entered British jurisdiction "without any form of compulsion." In this category were included vessels owned by neutral companies having agreements with the British government. One might, of course, quibble over the phrase "without any form of compulsion," when failure to call at a British port might well involve withholding of British coal or being brought in and detained on suspicion!

Even more discontent was aroused in neutral governmental and business circles by the third type of censorship, that was begun in December 1915. On December 5, 1915, the Noordam on a voyage from the Netherlands to the United States was brought in under compulsion to a British port and the mails it was carrying were removed. On December 18 the Noorderdijk, going from the United States to the Netherlands, was brought in to Ramsgate under similar circumstances. These were the first instances in which censorship was exercised over mails that were admittedly covered by the Hague Convention.[48]

As might have been expected these measures met with protests from neutral governments. The complaints of the United States dealt with both letter mails and parcel post, the first formal protest being made by Page on January 10, 1916. In the instructions which Lansing sent to Page on January 4, he cited the recent seizure of parcel mail from the Danish steamer Oscar II, en route from the United States to Norway, Sweden, and Denmark, and from the Swedish ship Stockholm on its way from Göteborg to New York.[49] Other parcels had been seized on the Danish ship United States, and on the Frederick VIII. While the State Department was willing to admit that parcel mail should enjoy, in regard to search, seizure, and condemnation, no privileged position over goods sent as express or freight, it stated that its protests against "the unlawful bringing in of the ships for search in port, the illegality of so-called blockade by Great Britain, and the improper assumption of jurisdiction of vessels and cargoes" should apply to commerce using parcel post service for the transmission of commodities.

At the same time Page was instructed to protest against the seizures of letter mails from the Nieuw Amsterdam, the Noorderdijk, the Rotterdam, and the Noordam. Lansing stated that the Department could not recognize the British right

. . . to seize neutral vessels plying directly between American and neutral European ports without touching at British ports, to bring them into port, and, while there, to remove or censor mails carried by them. Modern practice generally recognized that mails are not to be censored, confiscated or destroyed on [the] high seas, even when carried by belligerent mail ships. To attain [the] same end by bringing such mail ships within British jurisdiction for purposes of search and then subjecting them to local regulations allowing censorship of mails can not be justified on the ground of national jurisdiction.

The United States government would not even recognize the British right to censor mails on board ships that called *voluntarily* at British ports. Its argument was that: "Mails on such ships never rightfully came into the custody of the British mail service, and that service is entirely without responsibility for their transit or safety."

This statement, however, seemed to imply that the right to censor "transit mails" which were expedited by the British Post Office was recognized.

Identical notes in answer to this protest were presented to the State Department on April 3, 1916, by the British and French ambassadors.[50] Their notes cited the practice of the German and Austrian governments in not only capturing but destroying mailbags on neutral ships, as in the cases of the *Iris*, the *Haakon VII*, and the *Germania* in August 1915. Although the German government had since announced it would desist from similar action in the future, it had declared that such seizures were fully justified. The German government had also said that because the Eleventh Hague Convention had not been ratified by all the powers engaged in the war, it would not be applicable. A further justification of the Allied seizures of various parcel-post bags, which the note averred were in no way removed from liability to visit and search, was the fact that rubber and wool—both contraband—had been found in wrappers and envelopes which might have been supposed to carry nothing but correspondence. In reply to arguments based on the Hague Convention, the governments said: "The said inviolability only detracted from the public law as far as 'correspondence'—that is to say, despatches or 'missive letters'—are concerned. . . . The result is, . . . that this inviolability would be given a wider scope than it possesses if it were regarded as exempting from any supervision goods and articles shipped by mail, even though they were contraband of war."

The place given in the note to the protests against Allied treatment of letter mails was scant. The simple statement was made that "the Allied Governments will continue, for the present, to refrain on the high seas from seizing and confiscating such correspondence, letters, or dispatches, and will insure their speediest possible transmission as soon as the sincerity of their character shall have been ascertained."

The United States government presented new and identic notes of protest to the British and French ambassadors on May 24, 1916.[51] Special attention was drawn to the failure of the Allied governments to answer the protest on seizure of mails from ships brought into port under some form of duress, or from those ships that called at British ports. The inconveniences and serious economic losses caused by long detention of legal papers relating to estates, insurance claims, income tax returns, and the like were called to the attention of Great Britain and France, and it was suggested that British firms had benefited in neutral countries from the failure of American bids to arrive in time.[52] The State Department admitted that it was only the application of the rules covering search and seizure of contraband that was in question. "Genuine correspondence," the United States agreed, should not include money orders, checks, stocks, bonds, or other negotiable instruments which could be classed as merchandise, but, on the other hand, it believed that shipping documents and money-order lists, even though they related to enemy supplies and exports, should be so regarded and should be unmolested in their passage. Again the United States demanded a radical change in the practice of seizing genuine correspondence in Allied ports.

In order to satisfy American opinion, a statement was issued to the press by the British embassy in Washington on August 10, which explained the necessity for censorship and showed exactly how long mails were detained for this purpose.[53] The delay was less if the mails were removed from the ship by which they were dispatched—i.e., if they were transited through England as a matter of course—, but even when they were removed by compulsion the maximum delay was fifteen days, and the minimum in the instance of mails from the United States to the Netherlands was three days. The necessity of centralizing censorship in London was made clear: the staff which was required, even when split up, could not be accommodated in smaller port-towns; retransmission of mails could be best carried out from London where the postal facilities were most efficient; and the censorship could work more smoothly where a larger number of people could be set to work, each group on particular mails.

A formal reply to Lansing's note of May 24 was presented much later, on October 12, 1916.[54] For the first time the Allied governments made some sort of answer to the objections raised against censorship of mails brought into port under compulsion. The note asserted that the Allies "have never subjected mail to a different treatment whether it was found on a neutral vessel on the high seas or on neutral vessels compelled to proceed to an Allied port. They have always acknowledged that visits made in port after a forced change of course must in this respect be on the same footing as a visit on the high seas, and the criticism formulated by the Government of the United States does not therefore seem warranted."

Altogether, this was not a very satisfactory reply, since it in no way explained what censorship was being exercised over mails on these ships. The British and French governments then stated that ships that called voluntarily at Allied ports did so only at their owners' orders and in so calling submitted

themselves to the jurisdiction of the port and the law in force there. Refer-
ring once more to the Hague Convention, the note held that the inviolability "only refers to mails found at sea and that it is entirely foreign to postal
correspondence found on board ships in ports." It was still not clear whether
the Allied governments intended to apply this explanation to censorship of
mails on ships that came in under compulsion.

The discontent among neutrals was not confined to the United States.
From the point of view of the annoyance suffered by the British government, perhaps the controversy with Sweden came next in importance. As
has been shown, the Swedes were in an excellent position to stop the transit
of goods to Russia. When in December 1915 the British detained the
Stockholm and the *Hellig Olav*, and removed and censored their mails, the
Swedish government retaliated by detaining all goods sent by parcel post in
transit through Sweden from or to England. The British government was
notified of this decision on December 18, 1915.[55] There followed a long
correspondence on the claim of the British to the right to treat contraband
goods carried by parcel post as they would any other contraband, with the
British denying that they had been guilty of any breach of international law.
The arguments of the Swedish government were directed against all of the
Allied measures which constituted the blockade, and it insisted that it was
"not aware that before the seizure there had been any reason to suspect the
presence of merchandise constituting contraband, and having an enemy
destination, from the British point of view." The British had said that they
found rubber in parcels on the *Hellig Olav*, but the Swedes contended that
even if rubber were considered contraband—which it should not be, since it
was on the free list of the Declaration of London—no enemy destination
could be proved.[56]

In the British reply, January 31, 1916, the application of the Hague
Convention in this case was denied, for even the Swedish minister at Paris
had, as late as January 13, in a note addressed to the French government, said
that the Thirteenth Hague Convention, respecting the rights and duties of
neutral powers in naval war, could not be regarded as operative because it
had not been ratified by all the belligerent powers.[57] The British insisted
that they were in no way bound by the free list of the Declaration of London. The rubber in question, they said, had been justifiably seized on the
basis of the doctrine of continuous voyage. In answer to the Swedish contention that no suspicion existed, and that therefore the seizure of the
Hellig Olav was illegal, Grey wrote:

> In this respect it is not unnatural that His Majesty's Govern-
> ment should have had the advantage of the Swedish authorities. They
> did have information that contraband was being shipped in the
> mails by this and other neutral vessels. Events have shown how ac-
> curate was their information. But even if this practical test were not
> now at hand, it will surely not be contended that a belligerent's right

to seize contraband is in abeyance unless and until the Government of the neutral country to which the goods were ostensibly consigned declare itself satisfied that there are sufficient grounds to suspect their innocence?

The succeeding exchanges of notes and memoranda between the two governments dealt mostly with proposals, differing only in detail, that these cases on the censorship of mails should be submitted to arbitration after the war.[58] In the end it was agreed that arbitration should be resorted to in cases of parcel mails carried on Swedish vessels where the prize court had given a decision with which the Swedish government was dissatisfied, and where all legal redress had been exhausted. As a condition of this arrangement, the Swedish government agreed to release immediately British mails in transit through Sweden.

The correspondence of the Dutch government with the British and French, which began on December 18, 1915, added little of interest to the controversy over detention of mails.[59] The Dutch tried, without much success, to distinguish in their protests between the treatment of parcel post and letter mails, holding firmly to the position that the latter were covered by the Hague Convention. Having stated its position very forcibly, the Dutch government appears after mid-July 1916 not to have pressed the question further.

Thus the British in these exchanges with neutral governments held their ground and continued to censor any or all neutral mails that came into their jurisdiction, regardless of whether they were brought in under compulsion. By censoring parcel post the March Order in Council could be more vigorously enforced, and the one method of getting overseas goods directly was closed to the Germans. The censorship of letter mails was a very useful complement to the censorship of cables, and both made it possible to compile the black lists which, in their turn, gave the Allies a means of dealing more effectively with neutral firms in the service of the Central Powers. Altogether the policies discussed in this chapter aided tremendously in discriminating between bona fide neutral trade and trade ultimately destined for the enemy. Sometimes this judgment could be based on particular information concerning the traders involved, at other times it had to be based on statistical evidence of neutral importations. It was because gaps in the systems of control were inevitable, whether the controls resulted from agreements with neutrals or whether they grew out of exercises of Allied sovereign rights, that the policy of forcible rationing was so important. By a judicious use of all other means of control together with the policy of general detention, once a certain amount of goods had passed into the neutral country, the Allies were able, increasingly as the year 1916 progressed, to make their blockade measures effective.

IX

British Controls over Goods Produced
in the Empire 1915–1916

N O serious legal arguments could be raised if a belligerent stipulated
conditions on the use to which raw materials, manufactured products,
or foodstuffs, exported from its own territory, were put by those permitted to
receive them. The control exercised over goods produced in any state was an
attribute of sovereignty: the state might prohibit entirely the exportation of
any articles it chose, it could issue licenses in derogation of such embargoes,
and there was nothing to prevent a state, in the absence of an embargo, from
requiring guarantees from the buyer concerning the consumption or re-
exportation of the goods involved. The importance of this power and the
control of neutral trade which might result, would depend, of course, upon
what proportion of the world's supply of certain key articles the belligerent
possessed. Since the British Empire was wide and produced a variety of goods,
it can be seen that the control of these commodities might be used to good
purpose in, at least, preventing them from reaching the Central Powers.

More than that, this control could be used in exacting from neutrals certain facilities and concessions which otherwise would have been given most reluctantly. It was in regulating the release of bunker coal that this British system of control was most effective.

BUNKER CONTROL

Great Britain not only was an important supplier of coal to European neutral countries for industrial and domestic uses, but, at a time when oil-burning ships were few, it also had a predominating place in supplying bunker coal to fueling stations on the main trade routes. Fayle has shown that these fueling stations were either located in British or allied territory, were controlled from the United Kingdom, or were dependent on British supplies.[1] It is true that the United States had coaling stations on the North Atlantic route, as it did on the Pacific route, but outside of the territory of the United States American coal offered very little competition to the British product. One of the chief reasons for the predominance of British coal was that the calorific content of the average American coal was much lower than that of coal produced in the United Kingdom; if American coal were used, much more of it would have to be shipped, and the space available for cargoes would be correspondingly reduced.[2] Thus nearly all of the vessels plying the North Atlantic route and all of those on the South Atlantic route used British coal. Partly as a consequence of this, British companies owning lighters and tugs for use in coaling ships had become firmly established at the Canary Islands, Pernambuco, Rio, and the Plata. American competitors would have had difficulty in breaking into this trade even if their coal had been equally good.

The possibility of restricting coal exports to neutrals for domestic purposes was seen quite early by British representatives abroad.[3] The consul at Stavanger thought that Norwegian exports of canned fish and foods might be curtailed by restricting coal exports to the canning factories. Sir Mansfeldt Findlay, the British minister, at one time suggested that coal might be refused to ships that carried pyrites to Germany, but he advised that the whole matter should be carefully considered, for hasty coercion might only make the Norwegians seek German and American supplies. The British ministers in Denmark, the Netherlands, and Sweden were consulted. It was known that German coal production had fallen and that exports had been curtailed, but if British restrictions became too great, German coal could be secured to satisfy part of the neutrals' needs—at the price of further participation in the German exchange system. Sir Esme Howard, British minister at Stockholm, reminded his government that England was drawing important supplies of iron ore and pit props from Sweden, and the refusal of coal to Sweden would hamper their production and delivery. Moreover, the Board of Trade proved reluctant at first to reduce coal exports, and it agreed to do so only when labor troubles in the mines and rising prices in British markets finally made the regulation of coal exports imperative.

On May 6, 1915, British coal exportations to all destinations abroad other than ports in British possessions and protectorates and allied countries were forbidden after May 13 except under license.[4] This Order in Council provided the legal basis for further restrictions taken during the summer. Fayle gives W. E. Hargreaves of C. I. Bowring and Company, ship and insurance brokers, the credit for suggesting that bunkering firms should be persuaded to withhold bunkers at the Atlantic islands as a means of restraining neutral trade in enemy interests.[5] A Coal Exports Committee was set up in May, and in July an "informal committee" composed of representatives of the Admiralty, Foreign Office, and Board of Trade was created to assist in formulating regulations.[6] As a temporary measure, licenses were granted freely for coal exports to the Netherlands; exports to Denmark were kept to the normal figure of 3,200,000 tons per year; and exports to Norway were controlled so that stocks there could not accumulate. In the case of Sweden, restrictions were placed on coal exports, which were later applied in principle to all neutrals: licenses were granted only if the manager of the shipping company guaranteed that the ship would bring to England a return cargo of one ton of iron ore and two tons of pit props for every three tons of coal carried to Sweden. Even then licenses were granted by the British government with reluctance, because of the large exportation to Germany of articles produced in Sweden with the aid of British coal. Consignments to the Swedish State Railways and to the Swedish government were permitted to go forward more freely.[7]

The question of coal exports to the Netherlands was discussed in July 1915 when the general agreement with the Netherlands Oversea Trust was being negotiated. On August 2 an exchange of notes between the Trust and Sir Alan Johnstone provided for British coal exports on condition that (1) no coal of any kind or origin was furnished to any vessel belonging to or trading with a country at war with Great Britain, (2) no coal would be used in the production of by-products of military value which were to be furnished to Great Britain's enemies, and (3) no coal would be sold or transferred by one importer to another without express permission from the British licensing authority.[8]

Plans for the extension of control over bunker coal were largely worked out by the Trade Division of the Admiralty, with the full support of the Foreign Office. In mid-summer 1915 licenses for the exportation of coal to coaling ports were granted on condition that it should not be furnished to the enemy, to ships known to trade in enemy interests, or to ships specified by the British government as being objectionable.[9] No coal could be transferred to another importer without special permission. A black list of ships to which coal was to be refused was sent to foreign importers.

In October 1915 a new program for bunker control was proposed by the Admiralty, and shortly thereafter, a circular was issued to explain to neutral shipowners the terms on which British coal would be supplied to them.[10] Those who accepted the British conditions were placed on a white list and were then permitted to receive bunkers freely at all fueling stations in British and allied territory or in areas under Allied control. British authorities were to be kept informed of the names of all vessels owned, chartered, or controlled by the firm; no vessel was to be chartered to an enemy subject, or company, or to any person whose name was sent to the firm; the names of vessels let on time charter were to be reported to the British beforehand and particulars of existing time charters were to be given. Vessels covered by the owner's guarantee were not to trade with any port in any country at war with Great Britain, nor were they to carry cargoes proceeding from or destined to such a country. All vessels which were bound to or from northern European ports were required to call in the United Kingdom, preferably at some Channel port, where, if their intention to call had been made known, their clearance would be facilitated. Ships bound to or from the Mediterranean were required to communicate with the British authorities at Gibraltar. In addition, all goods bound from Scandinavia were to be accompanied by certificates of origin; no goods were to be carried which were consigned "to order," and no cargoes were to be loaded that were known to expose steamers to detention by the British authorities. All bills of lading for cargoes bound to neutral ports in Europe or North Africa were to include a clause enabling the shipping company to withhold delivery of the goods until a satisfactory guarantee against re-exportation was given. Ships included in the owner's guarantee were not to carry cargoes of coal, petroleum, lubricating oil, and castor oil from neutral countries unless the consignee was approved by the British minister in the country of destination. Neither could these ships carry enemy persons of military age. They were, on the other hand, to refuse to carry contraband goods destined for the United Kingdom or to an allied country only "on reasonable grounds (e.g., that [the] ship itself becomes liable to condemnation, that state insurance becomes invalid, etc.)" Firms electing to comply with all of these conditions were asked by the circular to forward to the undersecretary of state, in the Foreign Office, the lists of their vessels; time charterers for whom the owner could not give the necessary guarantees had to make separate arrangements with the British if they desired bunkering facilities.

It is true that certain Scandinavian shipowners had already signed agreements with the British, in which bunker controls had played no part at all, but now new incentives were provided to induce many more to do so. Many of these accords included promises to charter a certain proportion of the ship's carrying space to Allied interests. By the end of 1915, 70 per cent of Scandinavian shipping was bound to the British by formal agreements;

most of the rest was engaged in the coastal or Baltic trades and could, presumably, secure fuel from other sources.[11]

In order to carry out the requirement that neutral consignees of coal, petroleum, and the like be approved by the British minister, Findlay in Christiania made a list of coal dealers who sold to genuine Norwegian consumers, and he then entered into negotiations with them. Findlay urged his government to allow these Norwegian dealers to keep up their stocks on condition that they sell only to industries and firms approved by him. Thus pro-German companies would be refused British coal, and bona fide Norwegian firms would be given greater facilities. This, Findlay insisted, was necessary, for otherwise it could be argued that Sweden was benefiting, comparatively speaking, by her refusal to make arrangements with the British. Findlay had been urging this whole procedure since midsummer, but the Coal Exports Committee, so deeply concerned with keeping the English and Welsh miners at work, was not in sympathy with these restrictions. In fact British coal, in spite of Findlay's hopes, continued to be exported to Norwegian canning factories that were known to be shipipng their goods to Germany.

In 1915 British coal exports to Norway were at about the normal figure, while those to Sweden were considerably reduced, upon the advice of Montagu W. W. P. Consett, British commercial attaché at Stockholm. Consett counted on the shortage of German labor and the poor quality of German coal to prevent its replacing British coal on the Swedish market.[12] In this he was deceived, for by the end of the year there was ample evidence that 200,000 tons of German coal were being sent to Sweden every month—more than was normally sent in a year.[13]

Under these early regulations it was still possible for a ship not on the white list to secure bunker coal if it brought a cargo or promised to return with a cargo to a British or allied port. On occasion even a black-listed owner could secure coal if he time chartered his ship to some British or approved neutral firm which carried on shipping in Allied interest. As losses in ships in both the British and neutral merchant services became more numerous, the British more often demanded some service in Allied interests in return for coal, particularly since it was so difficult to replenish stocks at the overseas coaling stations.

Nor was it difficult to find useful work for neutral ships to do. Not only was there the necessity of supplying military and civilian needs in Great Britain itself, but Britain had undertaken the responsibility for supplying its allies—France, Russia, and Italy—with food, raw materials, and coal. One of the most important steps in the solution of the tonnage problem was the adoption of a centralized chartering system for all Allied services, under the management of the firm of Furness, Withy and Company of London.[14] While Danish shipping companies were very active in the trade with Portugal, France, Spain, and other Mediterranean countries, Norwegian ships were used in all kinds of tramp trade, and Norwegian colliers found steady employment in transporting coal to France. An idea of the importance of this maritime service can be gained when one considers that Norwegian tonnage represented 25 per cent of the total cleared from United Kingdom ports for France in 1915, and Scandinavian shipping together accounted for 25 per cent of clearances from British ports for all destinations, and for 13 per cent of all entrances at British ports.

The British were reluctant to put too onerous conditions on companies that were serving Allied interests so well. In December 1915 the practice of forcing white list ships to carry cargoes both ways was tried, but it was far from being general, partly because the Port and Transit Executive Committee found that undue delays would result in British ports, which were already congested, and the effect might well be to deter neutral ships from coming to British ports at all. White-listed vessels had protested that they were being discriminated against by this requirement, and cited instances where British ships made return voyages in ballast. To remove this source of complaint British owners were asked by the Board of Trade in January 28, 1916, to use every possible care to avoid returning without cargoes.[15]

Not only did the British sometimes demand that ships receiving British coal make a return voyage with a cargo to a British or allied port, but they also stipulated what the cargo should be.[16] During December 1915, when the need for pit props from southern France, Spain, and Portugal was great and tonnage was difficult to obtain for what appeared to be unpopular work, the British required that all non-white-list vessels receiving bunkers for a voyage with coal to French Bay, North Spanish, or Portuguese ports should return with cargoes of pit props from those ports. By this same method tonnage was secured for the conveyance of Spanish iron ore. At one time the shortage of iron ore in England was so acute that the possibility of bringing in the whole supply in requisitioned tonnage was considered, but no decision to do so was ever reached.

The pit-prop situation was equally bad, for Scandinavian shipowners in the coal trade found it more profitable—just as they did in normal times—to return in ballast to a British port and be ready to take more coal consignments out in a given time. By April 1916 the shortage of tonnage in the Scandinavian trade was sufficient to evoke new measures from the British side. It was decided that after April, all ships, whatever their nationality, which took coal to Norway, Sweden, Denmark, Iceland, or the Faroe Islands would be required to bring back a cargo, or a certificate approved by the Board of Trade that no return cargo was available. This proved to be a special hardship on colliers going to Denmark, for bacon and dairy products, the chief Danish exports, were not suited to such carriage. It was arranged that these ships should go in ballast from Denmark to a Swedish or Norwegian port and there obtain some bulk cargo, such as timber, ore, or wood pulp, to fulfill their obligations to Great Britain. In order to placate Danish owners, and at the same time to relieve French needs, some Danish ships were permitted to make an extra voyage carrying coal to France instead of bringing back a cargo from a Scandinavian port. Similar arrangements were made in June 1916 in order to facilitate the supply of coal to Italy.[17] Thus Dutch and Scandinavian vessels which usually went during the summer in ballast to North American ports to load grain were now required to make an intermediate voyage with coal to Italian, French Bay, or Mediterranean ports, or to the Allied fueling stations at Gibraltar or Dakar.[18] Up to April the requirement that ships should return with cargoes had been applied only in United Kingdom ports, but it was then decided that ships securing coal in any port in the British Empire or at any coaling station under British control would be required to make a voyage of a nature approved by the Allies.

The British authorities not only controlled the supply of coal, but they also on May 25, 1916, set maximum freight charges for the carriage of coal, specifically in the English-French trade. Acceptance of this price was made a condition of receiving bunker coal, and many Norwegian owners, in particular, laid up their ships rather than accept the reductions. Eventually many of the Norwegian lines time chartered their ships to the British at a rate higher than those set in May.[19] Other difficulties arose with the Dutch over the application of coal regulations, particularly in the case of ships carrying grain consigned to the Dutch government, and ships carrying Dutch East Indian products, such as coffee and tobacco, which under British agreements might be exported to the Central Powers. But the greatest outcry came when the British demanded in mid-April that 30 per cent of Dutch tonnage in overseas trade be used in British interests if Dutch ships were to secure bunker coal at all. Since the British in mid-April 1916 informed the neutrals that they would regard any coal of German origin found on the high seas as subject to capture under the March 1915 Order in Council, the Dutch were in a most difficult position. The Dutch government and the N.O.T. both protested strongly, and no actual agreement on the matter was ever signed. Apparently Dutch shipping companies were left to make their own arrangements with the British authorities.[20]

Neutrals were naturally resentful of all the restrictions placed on their ships, and some of the neutral governments attempted to control the sale and chartering of their vessels to foreigners, in the hope of assuring themselves the shipping space necessary to bring in supplies for domestic use. In Denmark an ordinance of October 6, 1915, prohibited the sale of Danish ships to foreigners except with the government's consent and then only if the proceeds were used in constructing new vessels.[21] A similar Norwegian ordinance of December 3, 1915, was put in more permanent form in a law of July 21, 1916, and prohibited such sales except with the consent of an appropriate governmental department.[22] The Swedes on March 6, 1916, and the Dutch on March 18, 1916, passed similar legislation.[23]

The United States government was, for the most part, not directly concerned in these coal and shipping controls. However, late in December 1916 Lansing asked Page to investigate the assertion that certain American shipping companies had been told they could charter other neutral ships whose owners had signed bunker agreements only if they bound not only the chartered ships but their own as well to similar conditions, even though the American ships did not use British supplies. Page's reply indicated that since a large proportion of neutral shipowners had accepted these conditions, they must find advantage in them. He said that the British had only stated to the would-be charterers the conditions upon which they might use ships already covered by agreements. Page mentioned that a considerable number of American firms had subscribed to these conditions. Since American ships were not involved, the matter was allowed to rest.[24]

In the end the European neutrals were still faced with the need for fuel for their ships; they had little choice but to comply with the conditions set by the British.

CONTROLS OVER WOOL, JUTE, TANNING MATERIALS, RUBBER, AND TIN PLATES

It was mentioned in Chapter III that as a condition of releasing embargoed goods from the British Empire, the government demanded guarantees from the buyers that the goods would not be re-exported to the Central Powers. Toward the end of 1914 and early in 1915 certain American importers of British wool, rubber, and manganese made agreements on these terms with the British government—agreements with which the State Department did not interfere.

One of the most important groups to enter into such negotiations was the Textile Alliance, a body which had been formed by various textile trade associations in March 1914 to regulate the manufacture and sale of mill supplies. However, after the outbreak of war, as the situation in the wool trade became more acute—with the increasing difficulties in securing British and Australian wools, the Alliance instructed its agent in London to try to make some arrangement with the British authorities.[25] In the first agreement between the Alliance and the Board of Trade, on February 10/15, 1915, the British government declared itself ready to grant licenses for the exportation of merino and black-face wool through the intermediary of the Textile Alliance on condition that the wool should not be resold to any dealer or person not a member of the Alliance, that neither the wool nor its products should be exported from the United States, and that the exportation of American-grown wool should be discouraged. A member of the Alliance understood that he could resell the wool only if he was so authorized by the British government, in which case the new buyer would have to make similar promises against resale and exportation. In any event, although the individual company made all of the arrangements involving the sale, insurance, and shipping of the goods, consignment was made to the Alliance, which alone could release the goods.

Difficulties were also encountered in securing jute, the raw material from which burlap is made, which was produced almost entirely in India. The military demand for sandbags, as well as its usefulness as a packing material, made jute one of the key products that Great Britain controlled. Raw jute had been put on the British embargo on October 6, 1914, jute yarn and piece goods were added on February 3, 1915, and jute bags and sacks on July 8, 1915.[26] In a letter of February 24, 1916, which was acknowledged on March 23, the Textile Alliance agreed that all jute and products of jute fiber which they imported would be used exclusively for industrial purposes in the United States, and would not be sold in the United States except under a similar guarantee.[27] Eventually the Alliance included other articles in its system of supervision, under committees on sheep- and goatskins, carpets, castor beans and castor oil, cotton (with subcommittees on cotton yarn, and Egyptian cotton), flax, jute (San Francisco and New Orleans), kapok, leather, Manila fiber, mica, palm oil, and dyes.

In the summer of 1916 Britain put pressure on the Norwegian government to secure the prohibition of the exportation from Norway of goods packed in jute sacks or other jute fabric. An agreement was reached on December 22, 1916, under which raw jute, jute products, or goods wrapped in jute could be exported from Norway only when their non-British or non-allied origin was proved.[28] Exports to Sweden, Denmark, the Netherlands, Spain, and overseas states could be made only if the exporter declared to the Norwegian customs that the exportations were not in conflict with this agreement. Future deliveries of jute in Norway were made dependent on ratification of the importer's declaration by the Norwegian minister of finance and its subsequent presentation to the British War Trade Department and the British Customs.

Dutch importations of jute were regulated by the British through negotiations with the N.O.T. in December 1916 and January 1917. On December 15, 1916, the British informed the Trust that until certain conditions upon which they had been insisting for months were met, the supply of jute to the Netherlands would be stopped except for sacks and wrappers necessary to cover goods arranged for in the recently concluded British purchasing agreement with the Landbouw Export Bureau.[29] The Dutch were irked by the British attempt to control all textile coverings, whatever their constituent materials, and by the requirement that "free" Dutch colonial goods—those not subject to N.O.T. control—must be packed in matting produced in the Dutch colonies or in coverings supplied by Germany. The Trust did its best to insist that an equivalent amount of jute should be deposited in the Netherlands before any jute packing materials were sent to Germany; it required a guarantee of 25 guilders for each bag, the guarantee to be forfeited if the bag was not returned within a certain period. In the end the N.O.T. accepted the essentials of the original British demands in respect to jute.

The Dutch had already been more than a little annoyed by a rather thinly disguised demand, in August 1916, that they should buy their wool only in the British market and then should export no manufactured goods to any destination. While this was all done in the name of saving scanty supplies on the world market, the Dutch could not help feeling that the regulations saved British woolen interests from competition.[30]

The conclusion in Washington of an agreement with the National Association of Tanners, the Central Leather Company, and the American Hide and Leather Company was announced by Spring Rice on October 25, 1915.[31] Here guarantees were given against the re-exportation of all imported hides, or their products, to any country at war with Great Britain, provision being made for informing the British government in advance of any shipments of hides or leather to any neutral destination in Europe. A committee of the Association and principal leather manufacturers was to be formed to aid the British embassy in verifying the sincerity of would-be importers, and consignments from British territory had to be made to the British consul generals at New York, Philadelphia, Boston, or San Francisco, who would hand them over to the importer after the proper guarantees were given. The Accord was formally approved by the British government on November 11, and by November 30 all supplementary arrangements were concluded.

The first agreement reached with the Association of Norwegian Tanners and Leather Manufacturers on November 12, 1915, was noted in Chapter V. Apparently a supplementary accord was concluded in July 1916, and the Norwegian government agreed to give no export licenses for hides except those of local origin that were destined for Sweden.[32]

The British also made an agreement in January 1915 with the rubber manufactures of the United States, regulating the use of raw rubber imported with the permission of the British government. It was agreed that the companies would export no raw or waste rubber except to the United Kingdom or British possessions, and that manufactured rubber goods destined to European neutral countries would be sent from stocks already accumulated in the United Kingdom or would be sent to England specifically for re-exportation. Details concerning consignments to any non-European destinations were also to be communicated to the British consul at the port of shipment. The British were soon able to secure guarantees from the neutral buyers of these rubber goods, for instance those concluded with the Royal Automobile Club of Norway on December 17, 1915, with the N.O.T. on September 10, 1915, with the Danish Committee on Rubber Control on May 2, 1916, and with the Amerikanska Gummiaktiebolag of Stockholm (Goodrich and Company) on November 9, 1916. Since rubber proved to be one of the chief items in the smuggling trade over the Dutch frontier, the British in October 1916 refused to give any more facilities for rubber exports to the Netherlands, although it eventually arranged for shipments of hospital and dental supplies by the end of the year.[33]

Exportations of tin from the British Empire to the United States were first regulated by agreements concluded on July 29, and September 28, 1915, the importer being requested to give guarantees that no tin whatever would be exported by him other than to the United Kingdom. Separate guarantee formulas were provided (1) for manufacturers who used the tin themselves, (2) for dealers who sold to manufacturers, and (3) for covering sales by importers to jobbers who handled the distribution of the tin.[34]

There can be little doubt that the success of negotiations with the Norwegian Canners Union was in large part dependent upon the fact that the chief supply of tin plate used in the containers was controlled by the British. The original agreement with the Canners Union, of January 26, 1916, was strengthened by the requirement of the Norwegian government that, after July 8, 1916, exporters of canned goods should give a declaration to the Norwegian Customs that neither the products nor their constituent parts were covered by guarantees against exportation. Moreover, even these exportations were permitted only from certain Norwegian ports.[35]

Sometime in May 1916 the N.O.T. opened negotiations with the British legation in order to secure a resumption of British exports of tin plate for Dutch use. On November 16, 1916, after long correspondence over what should be included in the term "tin plate," an agreement was reached. The importer was required to guarantee that all tin plate, terneplate or black plate he imported would be used by him, that he was not an agent of a government at war, nor in any relation to any such agent, that all the products made from the tin plate as well as the stocks then in his possession were exclusively for home consumption in the Netherlands, for re-export to the Dutch colonies for use there, for re-export to the country of origin, or to British colonies, possessions, or protectorates. The Trust agreed that re-exportation to neutral countries would be permitted only on conditions arranged with the British government; re-export to Norway and Sweden would not be permitted. Any firm that exported tin plate after November 16, 1916, in violation of the agreement would never again be permitted to receive tin plate, terneplate or black plate.[36]

Enough has been said to show that these British controls followed a kind of pattern, and rather than have supplies of these goods cut off, neutral manufacturers and merchants acceded to them without much protest.

BRITISH EXPORTATIONS TO BORDER NEUTRALS

In earlier chapters it has been shown that certain branches of the British government responsible for regulating foreign trade did not always regard the blockade policy carried out by the Foreign Office and its departments and committees as being of prime importance. To the Board of Trade it seemed at least as important to maintain the place of British goods in world markets and wherever possible to have them take the place that German goods had filled before the war. Hence it was only after considerable pressure was brought by the French that British trading with the enemy legislation was made more rigorous.

There still remained another source of annoyance to the French government—the fact that British exports and re-exports to the border neutrals remained high and in some cases were far in excess of the legitimate domestic needs of these states (Appendix B). The articles in this trade that seemed of greatest concern to the French were cocoa, coffee, and tea; and repeated efforts were made in the second half of 1915 and early in 1916 to persuade the British to establish stronger controls.

Without a doubt, cocoa and cocoa products could and did serve a very important need in a military diet that was low in meat and fats. The chief producers of raw cocoa were subjects of the British Empire and there seemed to be no very good argument for permitting their trade to proceed if there was any chance that it was ultimately destined for the Central Powers. On the other hand, coffee and tea had no great food value, but they were luxuries of an undeniably comforting sort to an army in the field as well as to civilians. It was around coffee in particular that the differences between the British and French governments centered.

In the summer of 1916 a British memorandum, written by A. R. Tendy, was sent to the French government to explain what steps had been taken to regulate coffee exports from England, and to inform it of British opinion on further regulations.[37] Here it was pointed out that the possibility of depriving the enemy of all coffee had been considered by the Restriction of Enemy Supply Committee early in the war, but on December 19, 1914, it had been decided that this would not hasten materially the end of the war. The memorandum stated that increases in coffee exports to Sweden and the Netherlands had been noticed in January 1915 and that coffee had eventually been added to the British embargo list on July 30, 1915. British coffee exports to the Netherlands then became negligible, and those to Russia, which had recently developed to large amounts, almost stopped.[38] It was then, when one might speculate that commercial interests in London began to complain, that the policy was examined again by the Restriction of Enemy Supply Committee, with the result that relaxations in the embargo were recommended. In this opinion Lord Cecil and the Cornhill Committee, a liaison organ between the government and the City, joined. But the French government had remained adamant against any relaxation and the question was therefore submitted to the British War Trade Advisory Committee in September and October 1915. Even though statistics were available in late September which showed that during the first year of the war Germany had imported 135,700 metric tons of coffee from the Netherlands alone, with a total German importation of 170,000 tons being considered normal, the committee was not moved to enforce severe restraints.[39] On October 6 the committee agreed to send the following statement to the cabinet: "The objective of the Committee is not to prevent coffee from going into Germany, but to make prices rise as high as possible. To this end a considerable relaxation ought to be made in our policy of restriction, but coffee should not be removed from the list of prohibitions and no public communication should be made on this subject." The cabinet accepted this recommendation. As Sir Francis Hopwood explained the matter some weeks later: "The policy of the Cabinet has as a result that coffee can go into Germany with 'a chain to lock on the wheel.' Actually we allow coffee to go freely to the Scandinavian countries but it must be consigned with a license and, in the case of exportation to Holland, it must be consigned to the N.O.T."

Trouble arose, however, when the N.O.T. refused to take consignments of coffee unless they came directly from the country of origin. London's position as an entrepôt was threatened and immediately the London Chamber of Commerce passed resolutions, which they sent to the War Trade Advisory Committee on November 4, 1915. The committee agreed to the proposal that coffee be removed from the list of goods that were required to be consigned to the N.O.T., but since the Trust itself objected, as well as the French government, nothing was done to change this situation. However, in general, interference with coffee exports from Allied territories and even with those carried in neutral bottoms was reduced to a minimum—it was enough that the cargoes were consigned to neutral consignees. The British realized that this new policy could not remain a secret, and Cecil pointed out in a memorandum of November 18, 1915, that this in itself would cause prices in Germany to decrease and thus the British aim of encouraging the Germans to spend more on luxuries would be only partly fulfilled. Just why Cecil had changed his opinion on this matter is not known. However, his ideas were not entirely accepted in the War Trade Advisory Committee where on December 2, 1915, Hurst remarked that to return now to a restrictive policy would be troublesome for the London coffee traders, and that efforts were being made to persuade the N.O.T. to buy a certain amount of coffee in England. He regretted that he could report no progress in these negotiations.[40] Surely the British view of the blockade—even outside the Board of Trade—was sometimes a commercial one!

Trade statistics showed that coffee exports from the United Kingdom to the Netherlands increased a little in January 1916, and a great deal in February and March.[41] However, in January the N.O.T. was persuaded to accept a new arrangement respecting coffee. The total monthly ration was reduced from 100,000 sacks (17 to a ton) to 60,000 sacks, i.e., from about 6,000 tons to 3,600 tons, and the N.O.T. also agreed to accept consignments from the United Kingdom up to 10,000 sacks a month.[42] This latter amount was later raised to 20,000 sacks.

It was about this time that two members of the French Comité de Restriction des Approvisionnements et du Commerce de l'Ennemi, Jean Branet and Brally, entered into conversations with one M. Laneuville, editor of the trade journal Le Café, published in Le Havre, who was reputed to be the foremost French expert on the state of world trade in coffee. Their report to the Comité was presented on January 22, 1916, special care being taken to consider British policy.[43] Laneuville had informed them that there was then at sea en route to the Netherlands and the Scandinavian countries more coffee than these states normally consumed in one year—more than one million sacks. The Comité believed that it was urgent that the British should hold the cargoes in port, and Paul Cambon, the French ambassador in London, was instructed to inform them of this point of view. The Comité's letter called attention to abuses of the N.O.T. system which permitted passage of "free" Dutch colonial coffee without regulation by the N.O.T.; it charged that South American coffees were sent to Curaçao and were then transshipped as being of Dutch origin. Since most of the imports of these Dutch coffees went on into Germany it was understandable that the Allies were concerned. Before long the British did seek to reduce N.O.T. imports to 32,000 sacks a month, in order to offset these abuses, and used wholesale detentions in British ports of non-Dutch coffee consigned to the Netherlands as a means of forcing the Trust to a new agreement. The French Comité also returned to the question in March and urged that the new ration for the N.O.T. be reduced from 6,000 tons of foreign coffee to 3,000 tons per month, and that imports of Dutch colonial coffee be limited to 2,000 tons.[44] The Italian government was soon urged to restrict its reexportations of coffee to Switzerland.[45]

It was of some satisfaction to the French that the British government in April 1916 also tightened the controls over coffee exportations to Norway and Sweden. In fact it was decided that no more British export licenses could be granted until further notice, and that shipments from overseas would be detained on the ground that in view of the large stocks built up in these countries, they were not necessary to satisfy their legitimate internal needs.[46] This action, as the Tendy memorandum pointed out, introduced a well-defined policy of effective rationing for neutral states with whom no agreement existed; it was one of the early examples of forcible rationing. And it soon had its results, for Tendy reported that negotiations were then—in the early summer of 1916, going on with the Norwegian Wholesale Grocers Association, which sought some relaxation of these restrictions by offering to control coffee imported under an agreement. It was not until December 5, 1916, that the British made a settlement which permitted exports of coffee to Norway only if they were consigned to the association and shipped on the Olsen and Bergen Steamship Line. In negotiations with the Dutch there were long controversies in November and December 1916 over the release of detained cargoes, whether they should be counted against the current ration or only against the preceding quarter, reserving the current ration for coffees from the new harvest. A temporary arrangement was made on February 4, 1917, in which it was agreed to release 41,000 sacks from British custody in four equal monthly amounts, not to be counted in the current ration. But all this was made of academic interest by the beginning of the unrestricted submarine campaign.[47]

The regulation of coffee exports to Denmark caused even greater difficulties. Coffee was among those articles that, according to the agreement of November 19, 1915, the Danes could re-export to Germany and to other specified destinations. The Danes were permitted to import 20,000 tons a year, exclusive of re-exportations to Norway, Sweden, and Russia. Re-exportations to Russia might be unlimited so long as the amount sent was revealed to the British government at the end of each month. Statistics collected in the War Trade Statistical Department indicated that the total Danish importations for 1916 would be 38,000 tons, of which 23,000 would be exported, leaving 15,000 tons for home consumption. The French government complained that the original ration had been set at too high a figure, and that it was a mistake to permit the Danes to use coffee in their exchange system with Germany.[48] When this practice was again permitted under the Danish rationing agreement of March 17, 1916, Alexandre Ribot, French minister of finance, was very much aroused. Paul Cambon was instructed to inquire at the Foreign Office whether it would be possible to remove coffee from that category of goods. By a letter of June 13, Cambon informed Briand that Grey believed it better to leave coffee on that list in order "not to encourage the Danes, by a new restriction on Table E of the Arrangement (containing the list of goods that might be re-exported to Germany), to increase delivery into Germany of other goods whose exchange would remain authorized, such as lard, which is much more nourishing than coffee." Grey pointed out that any change in the list would necessitate opening new negotiations. The French refused to accept this as a reason for not dealing with coffee, and insisted that a government always had the right to ask for the modification of a clause in a contract when experience showed it to be inconvenient. Colonel Eduard Théry also believed the argument that it was better to permit the exportation of coffee than to encourage exportations of lard was unfounded. He said, "We continue to think that coffee at the present time represents for Germany, and especially for the feeding of her armies in the field, a primary supply which no equivalent can replace."[49] He added that lard and bacon were already used to the limit as articles of exchange and whether or not coffee was kept on the list of goods of exchange would make no difference in the amounts of bacon, butter, fats, or meat that would go to Germany. Théry's report concluded with a forceful section on the bad effect that continued indirect coffee exports to Germany, facilitated by the Allies, would have on neutral opinion.

In November the British government estimated that importations of coffee already effected were sufficient for Danish domestic needs until the end of 1916, and it refused to let new shipments go through, thus using the same methods already in effect with regard to the other northern neutrals.[50]

This whole exchange of ideas between the two allies on the coffee trade with neutrals and the resulting changes in British policy probably made very little difference in the ability of Germany to continue the war. But this fragmentary consideration of the question shows the detail with which these matters were pondered by the French government, and the way in which the French continually urged the British to increase the effects of the blockade on every possible side. The earlier sections of this chapter showed with what energy the British used their control over certain raw materials to exert pressure on neutrals. It is interesting to note that the same energy was not displayed in regulating their own export trade until relatively late in the development of the blockade, and then only at French insistence.

X

Allied Co-operation in the Economic War: The Paris Economic Conference, June 1916 and the Abrogation of the Declaration of London

ALLIED ECONOMIC CONFERENCES

IN the development of measures of economic warfare, Great Britain had taken the lead, but the other allies each had a stake in the blockade. Sometimes France, Russia, and Italy made special agreements with neutral governments or associations; at other times they simply acceded to those concluded by Great Britain. But, although there were frequent interchanges of opinion between the British and French governments on particular policies, there was no prearranged, *systematic* co-operation between them in their relations with neutrals. In 1915 various proposals for the creation of a regular plan of Allied co-operation were made, and the first steps in carrying them out were taken with only indifferent success. It may very well be that better results were in the end obtained by allowing Great Britain, commercially the strongest of the Allies, to clear the way in negotiations with neutrals, in order to establish as much control over neutral trade as the Allies were likely to get. It is true, in any case, that by the time Allied economic co-operation was established even on paper, the aims that were being sought had, for the most part, been obtained by other means.

It appears that the earliest proposals for securing united Allied action in the economic sphere came from the Italians. Italy had entered the war against Austria-Hungary alone, on May 23, 1915, and had then taken only a small part in the economic measures engaged in by France and Great Britain. In fact the French and British governments had felt it their almost constant duty to urge the Italian government to make its regulations against trading with the enemy more rigorous and to treat more severely trade destined ostensibly for Switzerland, but really for Germany.[1] The Italians were clearly in an equivocal position for, in keeping with their policy of having a foot in both camps, they had been careful not to declare war on Germany, and, indeed, did so only on August 27, 1916, after severe diplomatic pressures from the British and French governments. However, Italy had suffered economic losses as a result of severing trade relations with Austria-Hungary, and some Italians were anxious to reap whatever benefits they could from close association with their new allies. They desired aid in securing tonnage and food supplies, as well as favorable treatment for Italian goods by the customs authorities of the Allied states. One of the earliest suggestions for the formation of an economic league appeared in an article in Nuova Antologia, June 16, 1915.[2] The author, who wrote under the pseudonym "Victor," stressed the importance of unity of Allied action in the field of finance and credit, in domestic and foreign money markets, in the movement of trade, and in communications and transport, as a means of bringing about a quick and satisfactory peace.

It was on September 14–17, 1915, that, what Friedrich Kahl has called "the first step toward mutual economic aid" was taken by a group of Italian and French intellectuals, politicians, economists, and industrialists at a conference at Cernobbio on Lake Como.[3] The meeting was called by the Italians, and although it was unofficial it met with the sympathy of both governments. The aim was to consider the possibility of a cultural and economic union, and to prepare for a joint attack against the German-Austrian economic bloc. It was at once clear that the contemplated union would extend beyond the end of the war when new regulations of tariffs, railway fares, and the like between France and Italy would be undertaken. Both Edouard Herriot, Mayor of Lyon, and Maggiorini of the Italian Chamber of Deputies, spoke in favor of an Exportation Association of the four allied states. It was recognized that British co-operation would be necessary for the success of any such scheme, and that in all likelihood England would be reluctant to join.

During the winter of 1915–1916 many people in France and England worked hard to further the idea of Allied economic co-operation. Letters were sent to newspaper editors and speeches were made in which the emphasis was increasingly placed on the necessity of continuing the combined struggle against German trade after the war; economic co-operation during the war was taken more or less for granted. The lead in the campaign seems to have been taken by the French Chamber of Commerce in London, by the Franco-Russian Chamber of Commerce in Petrograd, and by the Central Council of Italian Chambers of Commerce, all of which favored some sort of Customs Union.[4]

The idea of annihilating German and Austrian trade for years to come did not spring out of mere hatred for the enemy, but was partly a continuation of prewar anxieties made more vivid by discussions, then going on in Germany and Austria, over a proposed Central European Customs Union, in which Turkey and Bulgaria would also be included.[5] The shrewd way in which Germany bargained with neutrals over the exportation of German coal, chemical and metallurgical products, Galician oil, and so forth made the Allied states consider what their own fate might be, should German commercial expansion continue unchecked. Equally disquieting were the reports of large stocks of raw materials being accumulated by Germany in neutral countries for use after the war.[6]

At a meeting of the Franco-British Parliamentary Committee in Paris late in February 1916, questions of Allied co-operation in war finance, munitions, and colonial matters were discussed.[7] More definite encouragement of the plans for wartime economic co-operation was shown in a conference of the commanders in chief of the Allied Armies, which met on March 12, 1916, at Chantilly. The meeting was called by General Joseph J. C. Joffre, the French chief of staff, to consider military measures to be taken to counter the German offensive begun on Verdun late in February. Joffre had at an earlier conference, held also at Chantilly in December 1915, drawn attention to the "necessity of effecting a close economic blockade of the Central Powers by imposing upon neutral countries a close rationing, strictly corresponding to their needs, with every source of leakage guarded against."[8] Now, to the purely military resolutions drawn up at the March conference, was added this statement: "The Conference is of the opinion that the economic blockade of Germany should be strengthened by all means possible."

The resolution of the Chantilly Conference was presented to a meeting of Allied political and military representatives, which met in Paris on March 27 and 28, 1916, to discuss further co-operation in all aspects of the war.[9] The invitation had been issued by the French government, which was anxious that the Pact of London of September 5, 1914, that provided that no separate peace should be made by the Allied Powers, should be extended to include a pledge that no commercial treaty with Germany or Austria should be made unless an understanding had been reached among all the allies.[10] Negotiations were conducted in the greatest secrecy, but a public declaration was issued to the press at the end of the meeting.[11] In addition to reaffirming their desire to achieve unity in the military sphere, the Allied governments declared their intention of putting into practice their solidarity of views and interests in the economic domain; it was left to the Economic Conference, which was to meet in Paris very shortly, to work out practical measures toward that end. In order to co-ordinate this economic action the Conference announced its decision to create in Paris a permanent inter-Allied committee; other resolutions were passed in favor of co-operation in the equitable partition of Allied tonnage and in the search for means of reducing freight rates. Apparently public opinion in both England and Russia was too much divided on the subject of the future treatment of German trade to make any decisions possible on problems of the postwar period.

Nonetheless the Conference seemed to give the French press unbounded hope for the future military and diplomatic co-operation that would soon lead to the complete and lasting ruination of German commerce. Georges Clemenceau, however, was sceptical of the ability of the Allies to carry out this common policy, and even in Italy little enthusiasm was shown for any such postwar program. The Italians were pleased at the prospect of freight and tonnage regulation, but were very doubtful whether Italy's allies could take all of the goods Italy had formerly exported to the Central Powers.[12] Russian opinion was in favor of common military and diplomatic action, but viewed the economic plans with indifference. For one thing, Russia was not anxious merely to substitute one economic hegemony —that of the Western Powers—for another. In England opinion on postwar commercial policy was still varied, for the free trade group maintained that a commercial war against Germany after the peace would lead to great British losses in central European markets, and the United States would be the gainer. It appears, however, that the protagonists of the idea of economic union gained some ground in England. Kahl even says that the initiative passed from the French to the British, but in view of later British policy, this would seem to be doubtful or, at most, of short duration.

In the interval before the next official Allied conference, the International Parliamentary Commercial Conference convened in Paris on April 27, 1916, to consider both the prosecution of the war and the problems that would arise upon the conclusion of peace—recovery of debts, measures against dumping, and the like.[13] The question of Allied exploitation of the economic conditions that a victorious peace would make possible was considered—favorable tariff regimes, transport and communications facilitation, international patent agreements, and monetary stabilization. Here was just one more indication of the seriousness with which postwar economic problems were being considered in 1916. It is not without significance that no Russians came to the conference, for thus far Russia's co-operation with her allies was at a minimum.

Elaborate preparations were made for the Allied Economic Conference which was to meet in June in Paris. The invitation was issued by the French government, and all of the Allies and associated governments accepted, although the British were somewhat reserved. In fact they decided to participate only after long conferences were held between Walter Runciman, president of the Board of Trade, and Étienne Clémentel, French minister of commerce, on February 4 and 5, 1916, at Chat Hill, Northumberland.[14] There, it was arranged that certain subjects would not be discussed at the conference, e.g., the relations of Great Britain with its dominions and colonies, the English fiscal and customs regime—the controversies over protectionism and free trade, and the state of dependence of the United Kingdom on the United States and other countries for necessary foodstuffs and industrial raw materials.

An agenda was in the hands of each of the Allied governments some time in advance of the meeting; each was expected to form its opinion on the various questions in order to reach some common basis for future economic legislation. It was very clear, however, that this was not to be a legislative conference; its decisions would have to be ratified by each of the governments concerned. Indeed, as early as March 1916 in discussions in Parliament on the instructions to be given to the British delegates, the government was urged by both the proponents and opponents of postwar economic co-operation to be careful not to commit the Empire to any decision until Parliament and the dominions had been consulted.[15] The House of Commons once more found Sir Henry Dalziel and Sir Arthur Markham at the fore in urging drastic measures against Germany. Both of these men urged that W. M. Hughes, prime minister of Australia, who was known to be a staunch supporter of a postwar commercial war against the Central Powers, should be sent as one of the British delegation. There was ample evidence, however, that many members in both Houses distrusted the intentions of some of the Allies and believed that nothing very beneficial could come from the Conference. Lord Bryce believed that it was impossible to foretell what conditions would be at the end of the war, and that to lay down an economic policy in advance was a serious mistake.

The Allied Economic Conference convened in Paris on June 14, 1916, with Clémental as its President. Other members representing France were Gaston Doumergue, colonial minister; Marcel Sembat, minister of public works; Albert Métin, minister of social welfare; J. Thierry, undersecretary of state for war; L. Nail, undersecretary of state for marine; and Jules Cambon. From Great Britain came the Marquess of Crewe, Andrew Bonar Law, Hughes, and Sir George Foster, Canadian minister of commerce. The absence of Runciman, whose illness prevented his going to Paris, removed a certain restraining influence on those who were most enthusiastic about making far-reaching postwar plans. Russia was represented by Chancellor N. Pokrovsky and B. Prilejaiev of the Ministry of Commerce and Industry; Italy, by E. Daneo, minister of finance, and Tommaso Tittoni; and other delegates came from Portugal, Serbia, and Belgium. Most of the delegation were accompanied by technical advisers.

The deliberations of the Conference were secret, but the final resolu tions received wide publicity.[16] The first section of the resolutions dealing with the prosecution of the economic war is, of course, most important fo this study. It was agreed that the legislation of the Allied states on trading with the enemy should be put into accord so that nationals and residents o: the Allied states should be forbidden to trade with (1) residents of enemy countries, whatever their nationality, (2) enemy subjects, wherever they re sided, (3) persons, houses of commerce, and companies whose business was in whole or in part controlled by enemy subjects, or which were under the in fluence of the enemy, or which were inscribed on a special list. The Allies were also to prohibit importations of all goods of enemy origin. The second resolution dealt with the sequestration of all enemy houses of trade existing in Allied territory, while the third sought to secure a unification of Allied contraband and embargo lists. The aim of this unification was to extend existing lists issued for purely domestic reasons, and to prohibit the exporta tion of all goods that had been declared contraband except under licenses when neutral trade associations or individuals had given special guarantees that could be controlled by Allied consular agents.

There was nothing new in these proposals, for the French and British governments had long been seeking to coördinate their policies. By June 1916 the British had for the most part complied with French requests: the effect of the black lists had been to stop trading with enemy nationals in neutral states, and British export licenses were granted more sparingly. Great Britain had been more and more demanding in the guarantees re quired from neutral importers, and the French had acceded to the most im portant of the agreements that regulated these guarantees. On the other hand, it was a gain to secure the co-operation of Italy and Russia in these blockade measures, for the gaps which had been a source of worry to the French seemed about to be closed. While it was possible that this Allied declaration of solidarity might have aroused neutral fears, such was not the case. Instead neutral apprehensions centered mostly about the third part of the resolutions dealing with measures to be taken in the postwar period.

Section two of the resolutions was concerned with transitory measures for commercial, industrial, agricultural, and maritime reconstruction in the Allied countries immediately upon the conclusion of peace. Provision was made for the mutual exchange of natural resources, for the prevention of dumping of German goods on Allied markets, for the prevention of enemy nationals from working in Allied territory in certain industries or professions of importance in maintaining the national defense and economic inde pendence of the Allied states.

In the third section the general proposal for an Allied economic com bination to operate against the Central Powers after the war was accepted. The Allies intended to take, at once, all measures necessary to free themelves from any dependence on enemy countries for raw materials and manufactured goods essential to the normal development of their economic life. They contemplated establishing enterprises subsidized and directed by the state, as well as scientific research projects to develop national industries and resources. To facilitate inter-Allied exchanges of goods, direct transportation at reduced rates, as well as improved postal and telegraphic communications, were planned. Technical experts were to meet to prepare measures to unify Allied legislation on patents, trade marks, and marks of origin; special rules were to be made to govern the Allied treatment of inventions, trade marks, and literary and artistic works created in enemy countries during the war.

It is impossible to know just what differences of opinion existed among the delegates in this Conference, since the minutes have never been published. The American embassy in Paris reported that the more radical delegates, who wished to isolate Germany economically for a long period, were disappointed in the results of the Conference.[17] Hughes was named as the leader of this group. The Russian and Italian delegates acted as a restraining influence, and, indeed, it appears that the Russians made wide reservations in their acceptance even of these rather harmless resolutions.[18] However anxious Hughes may have been to kill German trade, his enthusiasms were not shared by the British government. While it "approved" the Paris resolutions,[19] the British government did so with a certain scepticism about the practical results they would have. Grey was fully in favor of all possible economic co-operation during the war, but he seriously doubted that artificial restraints could or should be placed on German commerce after the war.[20]

In spite of this attitude on the part of the British government, which was nowhere announced and could not have been known to neutrals, great consternation was shown in large sections of the American press. The Paris Conference resolutions were regarded as just one more instance of British arrogance and commercial tyranny, which, in this situation, was believed to be aimed at legitimate American trade after the war. The unrest spread to the Senate where Senator William J. Stone of Missouri led an inquiry into the plans formulated by the Conference. As a result President Wilson on July 10, 1916, laid before the Senate a copy of the Conference resolutions, transmitted by the embassy in Paris, which was then published as a Senate Document. Extracts from British parliamentary debates and from the foreign press were likewise printed.[21]

CO-OPERATION IN THE BLOCKADE: THE RESULTS OF THE JUNE ECONOMIC CONFERENCE

The Conference produced some practical and immediate effects on the conduct of the Allied governments. Early in July steps were taken by the French government to put into execution more quickly and easily the recommendations of the Comité de Restriction. Unanimous decisions of the Comité on questions placed before it by ministerial departments were to go into effect automatically if, within eight days after notification of a decision to the competent ministers, no objection had been raised. If objections were raised, the matter would be referred to the cabinet for decision. When a question of general governmental policy was concerned, the decision of the Comité continued to be treated simply as an opinion, which would be communicated to the appropriate authorities. This action on the part of the French cabinet made Allied co-operation easier insofar as it expedited French action on any particular question concerning the blockade.

It was in the field of unification of Allied contraband and embargo lists that the first concrete results of the Conference were seen. It fell to the Comité Permanent International d'Action Économique, which was created by the Conference, to draft a project for the co-ordination of embargoes; a report on the subject was sent to the Comité de Restriction on September 8, 1916.[22] The report noted that although representatives of the four European Allies, meeting in Paris in mid-May, 1915, had recommended such unification, execution of this recommendation had not yet taken place. The difficulties of communication and the number of governments to be consulted had made agreement hard to attain. It was only after an inter-Allied organization was established that any degree of success could be hoped for. Such an organization, a subcommittee of the Comité Permanent International d'Action Économique, had been set up on June 30, 1916, at the larger body's second meeting.[23] The subcommittee realized that absolute unification was impossible, and that difficulties were bound to arise from the differences in the goods each of the Allies produced, differences in their respective needs, differences in terminology used by the customs authorities, and differences in the procedures necessary to put an article on the embargo list. The subcommittee believed that the lists should be identical when the purpose was to deprive the enemy of supplies useful in its economic or military life, but that variations might still result when goods were embargoed simply to preserve the goods for Allied domestic consumption.

In its meeting of August 18, 1916, the Comité Permanent accepted a list of goods in the former category and made this recommendation:

1. The list of prohibitions annexed hereto, containing the categories of goods which it is important to prohibit for military reasons, is recommended to the attention of the Allied Governments;

2. The Allied Governments are asked to assure themselves that all the kinds included in the categories of goods on the present list are contained on their lists of export prohibitions;

3. In the contrary case, the prohibitions will be issued for the goods that the study recommended above reveals as still remaining free;

4. The prohibitions recommended carry no restriction of the right of each Government to grant licenses when it does not believe that the goods will be re-exported to enemy countries.[24]

This document is at least indicative of the way in which the Allied governments went about implementing the recommendations of the June Conference. Although it would be too much to claim this co-operation as a result of the Conference, at least by the end of 1916 the *habit* of consultation among the Allies in economic matters had become fairly well fixed. From November 1915 onward the French, British, Italian, and Russian governments had co-operated through their representatives on the Commission Internationale des Contingents in fixing Swiss rations,[25] but it was not until November 1916 that it was suggested that the British War Trade Advisory Committee should have representatives from the Allied embassies in London to work with it on making ration arrangements for the Scandinavian countries. The matter was referred to the Foreign Office, but no immediate action seems to have been taken.[26]

It should, perhaps, be noted that not every suggestion for further Allied co-operation met a sympathetic reception. On one occasion the British recommended to the French that wood should be declared contraband and the French objected that Germany could be self-sufficient in wood and that therefore nothing would be gained by this step. In the British War Trade Advisory Committee on November 16, 1916,[27] Admiral Slade showed annoyance and said he thought that French disagreement ought not to influence any British decision. On the whole, however, there were relatively few instances of such differences, which, after all, were on matters of detail rather than matters of principle.

THE ABROGATION OF THE DECLARATION OF LONDON, JULY 7, 1916

In mid-1916 the British and French governments acted jointly to clarify the legal status of the measures which constituted the blockade of Germany. The British had taken the lead in promulgating the various documents that regulated the exercise of belligerent rights over enemy trade. Without exception the French government had acquiesced in this action and had in turn issued decrees similar to the British orders in council. This was accomplished by definite prearrangement, for the first time, in their joint declaration of March 1, 1915, and in the Reprisals Order in Council and Decree of March 11 and 13. Their political responsibility was joint and neutral protests were addressed to both of them.

The Allies in 1916 were still operating the blockade under the rules of capture laid down in the Order in Council of October 29, 1914, and the Decree of November 6, 1914. In these documents they had once more stated their adherence to the rules of the Declaration of London, with certain important changes. In fact the changes made outright by the Order in Council, plus those that resulted indirectly from agreements with neutrals and from the Reprisals Order in Council, had almost nullified the Declaration of London as a statement of existing legal policy and practice. One of the chief differences between the Declaration and British practice lay in the interpretation of the doctrine of continuous voyage. The Declaration, it will be remembered, had made the doctrine applicable only to absolute contraband, but under the March Order any goods with an ultimate enemy destination, whatever their character, provenance, or first destination, were subject to detention. Although the fate of such goods in the prize court rested on judicial interpretation of the rules of international law, they were often condemned. If the policy needed a more definite statement, the British government provided it in the Order in Council of March 30, 1916.[28] In this Order the right to capture—and therefore to confiscate—conditional contraband on board vessels bound for a neutral port was clearly stated, and the burden of proof of the innocence of the destination was put on the owner. Article 19 of the Declaration of London was abrogated so that goods could then be captured for breach of blockade even when they were bound for a neutral port. The concept of continuous voyage was thus definitely applied to both categories of contraband and to blockade. In practice, this, of course, was not new, but it was hoped that this statement would remove certain legal difficulties for the British.

However, even at the time that this Order in Council was issued, the British government was not satisfied with it. Lord Cecil believed quite rightly that constant modification of the rules of maritime law created a feeling of insecurity, which made all relations with neutrals more difficult. Of the five maritime Orders in Council issued since August, 1914, four had modified the Declaration of London. So long as British sea power remained unchallenged, there seemed to be no particular advantage either to Great Britain or to neutrals in rendering lip service to this Declaration which no longer applied. Sometime late in March 1916, the Foreign Office sent to the Admiralty for criticism a draft of a new Order in Council which would abrogate the Declaration of London. At the Admiralty it underwent a careful examination.[29]

Before anything further was done, the British government was forced by the judgment handed down by Lord Parker in the appeal of the Zamora case, on April 7, to consider more minutely its entire application of maritime law.[30] Lord Parker stated very decidedly that the prize court was a court that applied international law, and it therefore could not, even in doubtful cases, take its orders from the Crown. That being so, the court was not bound by Orders in Council unless it found them to be in accord with international law, or unless they amounted to a mitigation of the Crown's rights in favor of the enemy or the neutral claimant, as the case might be. In the case before it, the court found that a certain provision of the prize court rules, in regard to the requisition of vessels or goods before a judgment on them was given in the prize court, if construed as an imperative direction to the court, was not binding.

Since it had, therefore, been decided that an order in council could not alter the law to be administered by the court, it immediately became advantageous to make it clear that the prize court was bound only by the customary rules of international law. The British government had contended all along that its measures against enemy trade were but justifiable extensions of its belligerent rights. Neutrals, however, contended that the Declaration of London constituted a valid statement of these rules, and obviously British practice was far removed from the Declaration. Since the British government had not the slightest intention of following the Declaration, Lord Cecil contended that it was better policy to get rid of all mention of it in maritime orders in council.

The Admiralty did not in principle oppose this suggestion, although from the point of view of the action of the fleet, it could see no particular resulting advantages. It was true that if the Declaration were abrogated, greater freedom would result in blockade, the treatment of contraband, search of ships, and so forth. But as a matter of fact, no blockade of Germany had ever been declared, and the measures taken in retaliation had never been seriously or effectively challenged. Contraband lists already included almost every conceivable article. The Admiralty therefore realized that the abrogation was a matter of foreign policy and something which the diplomatic branches of the government should be allowed to deal with. The only conditions which the Admiralty laid down were that the instructions to the fleet should remain unaltered and that the instructions given to the Allied fleets by their governments should all be brought into harmony before the formal repeal of the Declaration of London took place.[31]

When the French government was approached, Cecil's plan met with considerable opposition. The French believed that the Declaration of London had marked an advance in the development of international law, and that, in a way, it had been a triumph for the Continental school of interpretation as expounded at the Hague Conference in 1907 and the London Naval Conference in 1909. In any case, abrogation would lead to an outburst of neutral protests, which the French government believed distinctly undesirable. More than that, if the Declaration were nullified, France and Great Britain would each return to its traditional maritime practice, and on many points, as earlier conflicts had shown, these practices did not coincide. Perhaps another reason for the lack of French interest in the abrogation was that the French government had no such problem in dealing with its prize courts as the British did. French prize courts were unquestionably bound by written laws and decrees; they made no pretense of applying an international law independent of those decrees, for the decrees were assumed to be in accord with international law.[32]

On May 30, 1916, Cecil, Slade, and Craigie went to Paris to consult with Denys Cochin and Léon Bourgeois. There, the British succeeded in convincing the French that the differences between British and French maritime practice could be rendered negligible. It was Admiral Marie Jean Lucien Lacaze who was mainly responsible for formulating, on June 1, a set of principles that was satisfactory to both governments. The French agreed to the British proposal on condition that the abrogation was preceded by a joint declaration which would reassure neutrals that their legitimate interests would be respected.[33]

The Allied decision to abrogate the Declaration of London was announced in the House of Commons on June 28, 1916, by Lord Cecil, in answer to a question by W. A. S. Hewins on the results of Cecil's recent visit to Paris. Cecil stated that a joint declaration and an order in council withdrawing the other orders in council would soon be issued.[34]

The memorandum, the British Order in Council, and the French Decree were all issued on July 7, 1916.[35] The memorandum stated that the chief reason for the abrogation of the Declaration of London was the unsatisfactory character of the rules, which did not "provide belligerents with the most effective means of exercising their admitted rights." Moreover, new developments of naval warfare made the conditions of modern war wholly different and thus placed the rules of the Declaration under too great a strain. Since the successive modifications of the Declaration by the Allied governments had exposed the purposes of the Allies to misconstruction, it had been concluded that "they must confine themselves simply to applying the historic and admitted rules of the law of nations."

The Order in Council itself reiterated the usual presumptions of hostile destination required for the condemnation of contraband; in addition it included consignment "to or for a person who, during the present hostilities, has forwarded contraband goods to an enemy authority, or an agent of the enemy State, or to or for a person in territory belonging to or occupied by the enemy." Thus the black list policy was again made a part of the rules governing enemy trade. The doctrine of continuous voyage was made applicable to both absolute and conditional contraband, and likewise, following the principle enunciated in the Order in Council of March 30, 1916, to blockade. The liability to capture of a ship carrying contraband extended to the end of its next voyage; this provision first appeared in the Order of October 29, 1914. The principle that a vessel might be condemned when her cargo was more than half contraband was taken over from Article 40 of the Declaration of London. The validity of the March 11, 1915, Order in Council was declared to be unchanged.

In the French Decree nothing was said about black-listed firms, nor about the application of continuous voyage to blockade. However, the French recognized the liability to seizure of goods bound to a neutral port when they constituted an amount in excess of the normal imports of the country, and thus created the implication of hostile destination. In any such case, the burden of proof was put on the claimant.

In spite of the theoretical change this made in the basis of the maritime law applied by the Allies, neutral governments made very little commotion over the new Order in Council. Polite notes were sent by most of them, reserving their right to claim compensation if neutral citizens were injured by practices in conflict with the recognized rules of international law.[36]

XI

Allied Purchasing Agreements

IN 1916 the Allied governments undertook a policy that was intended not only to increase the amount of foodstuffs available to their own people, but also to prevent those same articles from reaching Germany in excess of the amounts normally exported from the border states. This new policy was carried out by a more or less systematic purchasing scheme, which was defined and registered in various agreements with neutral fishermen and producers of agricultural products.

It will be remembered that as early as November 1914 Théophile Delcassé, minister of foreign affairs, had recommended that the French government should establish a committee charged with buying, in neutral countries, foodstuffs and materials necessary to the conduct of the war which might otherwise be acquired by the enemy.[1] This proposal was rejected on the ground that purchases involving such large sums could not be carried out through the proposed committee without infringing upon parliamentary prerogative. There is no evidence now available to show that the project was urged upon the British government, although Henri Allizé, French minister at The Hague, continually proposed the Allied purchase of Dutch goods.

The Comité de Restriction in some of its earlier meetings—April 9 and 30, 1915—recommended the purchase of part of the iron pyrites produced by the Italian firm, Montecatini, and also that the Norwegian market, rather than the Spanish market, should become the source of supply of pyrites for war purposes, in order to prevent their use by the Germans in the manufacture of sulfuric acid.[2] Except for the proposals made by Allizé, the only instance during 1915 in which the purchase of foodstuffs in neutral markets was urged by the French government was that of Rumanian grain. The Comité de Restriction ordered a study made of the question, and it was reported in July that the British had accepted the proposal in principle.[3]

The circumstances that finally caused the Allied governments to decide upon a far-reaching purchasing policy appeared slowly, and it was some time before their importance was recognized. The Allies did not become aware that an ever-increasing proportion of the products of neutral agriculture and fisheries was being deflected from Allied to German markets until the trade had gathered a certain momentum. Allied efforts had been chiefly aimed at stopping overseas goods from reaching Germany, and little thought was given to controlling the exportation of native products from the border states when overseas material made up only a small part of them. Any controls over these exports would be only on nonlegal bases, and could be secured only through the good will of neutral producers or as a result of threatening unpleasant consequences for nonconsent. It was not until a truly great deflection took place from the United Kingdom markets that the British government felt it necessary to seek such controls. Indeed, for a time early in 1915, British imports of agricultural products kept up with, and in some cases exceeded, those of the previous year. But in April 1915 importations of Danish bacon and salt pork suddenly decreased, by September Danish butter had decreased also, and except for April and May 1915, Danish egg imports were much lower than usual throughout the year. Late in 1915 a similar movement was seen in importations of cheese from the Netherlands, but butter and egg imports varied from month to month.

At first it was believed that these decreases simply reflected the decline in the total agricultural production of these states. The European neutrals had been complaining constantly about the lack of forage, and it was expected that their exports of dairy products would decline. Since the border neutral governments had failed to publish their trade statistics, there was no way of knowing in many instances how much was being shipped to Germany, and it was not until reports came in from British consuls and ministers that the gravity of the situation was realized. At about the same time the matter was reviewed by the French Comité de Restriction, which recommended that a French Committee on Purchases in Foreign Markets should be established and that its work be co-ordinated with that of similar bodies set up by the other Allied states. This recommendation was not accepted by the French cabinet, which instead gave the duty of supervising purchases in neutral markets to the Comité de Restriction; since the cabinet neglected to deal with the matter of financing purchases, the French seem to have done relatively little to carry out the scheme.[4] On the other hand, in London the Restriction of Enemy Supply Department, within the Ministry of Blockade, was given the task in June 1916 of evolving a purchasing program. Leverton Harris, its head, was in close contact with the British ministers in the border states, although the Department soon appointed its own agents to supervise the actual purchasing.[5]

NEGOTIATIONS WITH DENMARK

In early 1916 when the negotiations for a rationing agreement were proceeding, the deflection of Danish produce from United Kingdom markets was sufficiently pronounced to make the British government consider taking action. Therefore, in February 1916, Sir Eyre Crowe had insisted in a letter to Alex Foss that the Danes must admit the possibility that later negotiations be undertaken to secure a certain proportion of Danish agriculture products for the British market.[6]

The Danish government had already undertaken the regulation of fodder imports and their distribution, as well as of meat and dairy products exportations.[7] An agreement had been reached on March 23, 1915, between the Danish government and pork-packing houses which gave the latter the sole right to export Danish pork and at the same time required them to supply domestic requirements at prices fixed by the Ministry of Interior. A special committee was also set up to earmark certain percentages of the slaughtered animals for Great Britain and another proportion for Germany. Thus in 1915 Great Britain received about 75 per cent of the total pork exports, but at a loss to Danish farmers of some 100,000,000 kroner. This seemed to be a good reason for British liberality in setting a fodder ration.

In October 1915 a Butter Committee was also set up when the difference between German and British prices became very great: 402.50 kroner per 100 kilos against 288.50 kroner. As a result Britain received 58 per cent of Denmark's butter exports in 1915, although the prewar proportion had been 75 per cent. Ostensibly these controls were set up to insure an adequate supply of butter on the Danish market, but according to information published in the Comité de Restriction *Bulletin* early in November, the Danish public was not at all confident that this would result. "They think," the *Bulletin* said, "that all the friends of the Ministry will act with the same license as before and that only the men of the Opposition will feel the rigors of the new legislation."[8] The French, later in November, viewed with alarm a Danish decree which permitted the exportation of up to 60 per cent of the Danish lard production. "Because of this," the article read, "it will be possible now to justify all exports of fats which are easily dignified with the name of lard."

It was not until the spring of 1916 that the differences between German and British egg prices became great, and in April, therefore, the Danish government set up an Egg Committee. In March 1916 only 14 per cent of Denmark's egg exports went to the United Kingdom, as against 80 per cent before the war, but at the end of April the amount was raised to 30 per cent, and ultimately to 50 per cent.[9]

It was clear to the Danes that a continuation of the flourishing state of their dairying industry depended upon importations of fertilizers and fodders. In a note presented by H. de Grevenkop-Castenskiold, the Danish minister in London, on February 15, 1916, the British were reminded that any further reduction in these supplies would necessitate the slaughter of animals, which would increase meat exports to Germany. In spite of this warning, and even though the United Kingdom market had recently received a larger part of Danish food exports, the British pressed for a reduction of the fodder ration. In mid-March 1916 they suspended the exportation of rice from India to Denmark until the Danes came to terms not only on the fodder and fertilizer rations but also on apportionment of Danish products.[10]

The reply of the Danes to these proposals was based on two lines of argument. One was that any scheme for guaranteeing a fixed amount to the British market would result in a financial loss to Danish farmers. The Danish government was reluctant to force this situation on their citizens. The other was that the Danes feared an invasion by Germany if they acceded to British demands; the Danish minister in Berlin, Count Carl Moltke, had warned his government that the Germans would not hesitate to occupy Jutland. Although the Germans had protested against the earlier agreements made with the British, they appeared to recognize that the Danes were powerless to resist British controls, but if the Danes agreed to curtail the exportation of their own goods, that would be another matter.

The British were in no position to protect Denmark in the event of a German invasion, so it was decided not to attempt any sudden coercion through coal control, refusal of letters of assurance, or general detention of all food and forage cargoes bound for Denmark. The British believed that something, at least, could be secured through negotiation.

The Danish government agreed to negotiate and sent delegates, including H. N. Andersen, Christian Sonne, Th. Madsen-Mygdal, Fabre and C. C. Clausen, who arrived in London in the last week of May 1916.[11] Sir Henry Rew, and Thompson of the Board of Agriculture, with E. G. Forbes Adam of the Foreign Office assisting, represented the British government. It was soon evident that the Danish delegates had been instructed to be as noncommittal as possible. They were willing to establish a Meat Committee to regulate distribution so as to insure a sufficient supply for the Danish market, and thus prevent excessive exports to Germany—in other words simply apply the principle already in operation in the case of pork, butter, and eggs. The Danes pointed out that English buyers of Danish butter had recently reduced their orders and that they had sent all that the British market was willing to absorb; this the British had to admit. The British also had statistics from their commercial attaché in Copenhagen, R. M. A. E. Turner, showing that total Danish exports in many branches of trade had fallen. In the end the Danish delegates gave general promises—not in writing—to increase Danish exports to the United Kingdom as much as possible, while Danish imports of fodder and fertilizers would be kept at their prewar averages. The Danes gave no assurances about their lard exports, which they insisted were a necessary part of the exchange system with Germany. It was understood that the Danes would be given two months in which to carry out their promises. By the end of that time the degree of German pressure on Denmark could be better estimated.

At the end of July, when this trial period was almost over, Forbes Adam wrote a memorandum for the British government in which he admitted that although the exact situation could not then be known, since the Danes had not communicated their customs statistics, the prospect was not promising.[12] British imports of Danish bacon, butter, and eggs had all been considerably lower in June 1916 than in the preceding month. On the other hand Turner's estimates indicated that exports of meat and livestock to Germany had fallen to about 3,000 head per week (600 tons) although butter and lard exports were nearly stationary. Some satisfaction was felt in the establishment of a Meat Committee about July 7, and in the requirement that after July 10 exports of cattle, sheep, and goats were permitted only under licenses and after payment of a tax of 10 øre per kilogram to subsidize those who sold meat on the domestic market. Forbes Adam believed that applying pressures on the Danes in the form of withholding supplies would not in the end increase exports to the United Kingdom, and that only a vigorous purchasing system could do so. He further advised that the Russian government be urged to enter the Danish market, rather than buying American meat, in order to keep Danish goods from the Germans. On the whole he was satisfied with the results of the measures taken by the Danes.

There is no indication that the British attempted any further negotiations, for they believed that the situation was continuing to improve. The French, on the other hand, viewed the Danes with suspicion. The Comité de Restriction *Bulletin* for January 11, 1917, gave information, emanating from the French consul at Esbjerg, that of a total of 1,200 animals brought to the market there on December 7 only 134 were bought for domestic consumption, while 1,066 were acquired by German agents.[13] In the first week of December a total of 1,766 head of cattle was exported from Jutland to Germany, an increase of more than 200 over the preceding week. In the spring of 1917 Edmond Bapst, French minister at Copenhagen, sent statistics on Danish meat exports to Germany: 1913—a total of 150,000 head; 1914—188,000; 1915—250,000; and 1916—300,000.[14]

No attempt was made until the early autumn of 1916 to reach any agreement with the Danes concerning fish. This may be explained by the fact that Danish fish exports to the United Kingdom had actually increased proportionately more than those to Germany. Danish newspapers reported that exports to Germany, which amounted to about 33,000 tons in 1913, had more than doubled in 1915 and 1916. But exports to England had increased as follows:

	kg. of eels	kg. of fish
1913:	275,000	3,650
1915:	678,000	1,762,000
1916:	1,000,000	2,628,000 [15]

When pourparlers were begun, the British first asked that an embargo be placed on fish, but that British agents should be allowed to purchase in the Danish markets.[16] This was, of course, refused, again because of fears of German reprisals. However, the Danish government, in an order issued in September 1916, permitted the exportation of fish only by authorized institutions, at fixed maximum prices. The difference between the higher prevailing market price which the exporter paid to the fishermen and the set export price was refunded to the exporter by the Danish Treasury. This represented quite as vigorous action as any undertaken by the Danes to regulate agricultural products, yet the British were dissatisfied. Against the advice of some of its experts, the British government on December 14, 1916, ordered that all exports of fishing supplies—nets, petroleum for fishing boats, and the like, from Great Britain to Denmark should cease. Arrangements were then made with Danske Petroleums Aktieselskabet to halt deliveries of all petrol and lubricants to Danish fishermen who sent their catches to Germany. It was unfortunate for the Allies that this attempt to exert pressure on the Danes failed, the reason being that the Rumanian armies had been defeated and the country overrun by the Central Powers. Rumanian oil wells were soon put back in repair by the invaders and made to serve Austrian and German interests. Although their output was below normal, the Central Powers secured enough oil by the end of 1916 to use in their exchange system with the neutrals. According to the *Berlingske Tidende* of December 15, 1916, the representatives of the German Zentraleinkaufsgesellschaft in Esbjerg immediately offered to furnish Danish fishing boats with petrol from Rumania on condition that they reserve their fish for Germany.[17] The newspaper may have been overconfident, but it did report that this oil was already en route to Denmark. At any rate it was not long before Germany did carry out this plan, and all British hope of participating in the Danish fishing catch failed.

THE PURCHASING AGREEMENT WITH ICELAND

While these inconclusive negotiations were being carried on with the Danish government, an agreement concerning exportations from Iceland was reached in London. Iceland was partially dependent on Denmark, but its government carried on its own foreign relations.

Iceland's economy was based chiefly on production of wool, stock raising, and fishing, and the export trade in these items amounted to more than 15,000,000 krónur in 1912. It was difficult to estimate either the amount or value of Icelandic exports in 1915, but it was certain that prices rose sharply between July 1915 and March 1916.[18] The war had brought almost a complete reorientation of Iceland's trade, for while before 1914 about 90 per cent of its wool and a large part of its herring catch went to America, by 1915 the Austrians and Germans all but monopolized Icelandic markets. Most of Iceland's wool and fish went to Copenhagen, Bergen, and Göteborg, and then, presumably, on to Germany. Early in 1916 the British War Office purchased wool in Iceland on behalf of Russia, and by April the Comité de Restriction *Bulletin* reported that a more general purchasing scheme was being studied.[19] A partial regulation of the fishing fleet was secured by withholding British coal from those owners who sold fish to German agents. It was realized that something more than occasional purchases was necessary, and quite soon, for the fishing season was about to begin.[20]

While the groundwork for an agreement was carefully laid by A. G. Coates, British consul at Reykjavík, actual negotiations were carried on in London between J. Fountain of the Board of Trade and Svein Björnsson, representing the Ministry of Iceland. In an exchange of notes of May 16/ June 27, 1916, the Icelandic government agreed that ships would be given clearance from Icelandic ports only when the captains gave an engagement to call at a British port en route to their destination except such ships bound for America as the British consul at Reykjavík might approve.[21] The British government renounced "all intention of interfering in the legitimate commerce of Iceland with the United States, the Allies, and neutral countries," at the same time that it stated its intention to purchase through local agents that part of Icelandic products which could not be sold elsewhere without risk of its reaching countries at war with Great Britain. The Icelandic government agreed to facilitate British purchases of all kinds of fish, fish oil, cods' roe, fish meal, mutton, wool, and hides. The prices to be paid were fixed in Annex I of the agreement, on the understanding that if the cost of coal, salt, petrol, boat motors, or labor increased or decreased in Iceland, the two governments would negotiate these prices anew. The British agreed, so long as the purchasing agreement remained in effect, to assure supplies of coal and salt from the United Kingdom, and to aid Iceland in obtaining other indispensable items elsewhere. It was assumed that Icelandic ships would transport as many of these goods as they could, but if they proved to be insufficient the British agreed to do their best to assure a sufficient tonnage at current rates. This was a concession indeed, and one which the British had given to no other neutral down to this time. A British credit of £500,000 was established in Icelandic banks to finance the purchasing scheme.

The Icelandic government published a law on June 27, 1916, which contained the regulations concerning ship clearances and exportations of goods that were foreseen in the agreement.[22] Violations by a ship's captain of his declaration as to destination made both him and the exporter of the goods involved liable to fines up to 10,000 krónur unless the captain could plead *force majeure*.

The French consul at Reykjavík informed his government that the arrangements made by Björnsson did not satisfy all of the merchants who were in the habit of receiving the enormous prices paid by the Germans.[23] The price of herring, for example, fixed by the agreement at 45 krónur seemed disadvantageous since the price at Bergen had risen to 120 kroner.

The importance of this agreement to the Allies for stopping Iceland's exports from reaching Germany can be indicated to a certain extent by a comparison of the values of imports into the United Kingdom from Iceland and Greenland in 1915 and 1916:[24]

	1915	1916
	£ Value	
Fish	288,510	848,998
Fertilizers	12	2,884
Fish oils	231	9,648
Skins and furs	0	39,375
Wool	12,901	23,608

It must be admitted, of course, that the amount of goods which might have succeeded in reaching Germany was not large. But the British and their allies were arriving at the point where they believed that every effort should be made to prevent even small amounts of goods from going to the enemy. It is interesting to note that the Icelandic accord was the only case in which a purchasing agreement resulted in 1916 in an absolute increase of imports into the United Kingdom above the 1915 figure; in all other cases the increase was only in proportion to the amount sent to Germany from the same source.

PURCHASING AGREEMENTS WITH
THE NETHERLANDS

While Allizé, the French minister at The Hague, continued on May 4, 1915, to urge that a policy of purchases in Dutch markets should be undertaken, Joseph S. Gallieni, the French minister of war, doubted whether Dutch exports of meat to Germany were sufficiently large to justify their purchase by the French government. Briand was inclined to a different opinion and took the matter up with Gallieni on June 15.[25] As a result on June 27 the Direction de l'Intendance Militaire informed the Ministry of Foreign Affairs that the Ministry of War adhered to the *principle* involved. Soon after—on July 13—Allizé reported that the Dutch minister of Agriculture had promised that the French would be given all possible facilities for the purchase of meat in Holland. The plan seemed to be well on the way when it received another setback. On August 1, 1915, Gallieni informed Briand that since an enabling bill, introduced by Henri Cosnier, had not been voted in Parliament the only purchases of foreign meat which the French government could make were those already arranged for through the Hudson Bay and Morgan Companies of Canada and the United States; the War Administration could not then undertake to use any Dutch meat.[26]

The next move was made on August 7 when Clémentel, minister of commerce, was asked whether Dutch meat could be used for the French civilian population. No answer was forthcoming, but without any such encouragement the Ministry of Foreign Affairs proposed on November 27 that the Dutch government should be asked to sell a certain amount of meat to France at the price prevailing on the Dutch market in exchange for French deliveries of oil cake to feed Dutch cattle. When Gallieni's opinion was asked, he answered, on December 10, 1915, that "it is not absolutely necessary that the Cosnier bill be voted in order to be able to proceed to purchases of meat in foreign countries if special reasons demand these purchases. . . . For the operation of importation to be carried out, it would be necessary that the Dutch meat come in at the same price current in France, or at least it should not be much different than this price."

Clémentel now approved the purchasing scheme, and Méline, minister of agriculture, and Thierry, undersecretary of state of the Commissariat, were charged with carrying out the purchases. However, on January 5, 1916, Allizé informed his government that Dutch meat prices were almost double those in France. He offered to negotiate in order to reserve for France a part of Dutch meat exportations. This was approved only with such reservations by Thierry that the French Administration continued to supply itself in America, although the Comité de Restriction again urged the Ministry of War to enter the Dutch market.[27]

However, the importance of Dutch products in provisioning the German army was recognized in at least some French military circles. General Joffre, the chief of staff, on February 22, 1916, made the question of excessive Dutch exportations of meat, fish, cheese, and butter to Germany the subject of a note to Briand.[28] He reminded Briand that the Dutch meat and fish that went into Germany in December were sufficient on the basis of the normal military ration to feed 2,567,000 men for one day, a number equal to the total German forces in the Western Front in December. He called attention to the military interest in this trade, and he urged that Allied measures be taken to restrain it. He went on to say: "The increases in importations of which diplomatic agents inform you, constitute an evident demonstration that urgent efforts are necessary in this direction if one wishes that economic pressure will some day second and facilitate the military effort."

In the meantime the Germans were buying most of the meat and dairy products available in Dutch markets; on March 11 it was reported to the Comité de Restriction that all the meat which the Dutch government would then permit to be exported had been sold to German agents while the French were making inquiries and seeking ships.[29] Again, later in the month, even after the French cabinet, following the advice of the Comité de Restriction, agreed to the purchase of 200,000 tons of Dutch potatoes to prevent German agents from acquiring them to help fill a very urgent need, Ribot, the minister of finance, refused to honor the contracts entered into by the representative of the Comité.[30] One can't escape the conclusion that the French sense of thrift had prevailed over considerations of economic warfare!

In early January 1916 the British government, through Sir Francis Oppenheimer, informed the Executive Committee of the Netherlands Oversea Trust in no uncertain terms that continued importations of fertilizers would be permitted only if the Dutch sold half of their exports of agricultural products to England.[31] Joost van Vollenhoven was quick to inform Sir Francis that this was something which should be arranged with the Dutch government. It became quite clear that the British would agree to alleviate the Dutch scarcity of grain and fertilizer only if Dutch exports of pork to Germany were regulated. It was natural that the British should be upset that great exports of cattle, meat, and butter took place "with the help of the fodder which is imported with the assistance of His Majesty's Government." But they realized among themselves that however logical it might be to permit the Dutch to import only enough forage to raise products for the domestic market, in practice Dutch trade would not adjust itself immediately to these conditions. There would be a period when even more goods would be exported to Germany. Even so, as a result of the British communications F. E. Posthuma, Dutch minister of agriculture, attempted to regulate meat exports (February 4, 1916), and the N.O.T. decided to grant no more consents for the importation of grain and fodder.

In March 1916 new negotiations were begun between the British government and the N.O.T. to set rations on a number of items, as an addition to the agreement of November 13/23, 1915. A draft agreement dated March 17, 1916, was presented by the Dutch to the British[32] but van Vollenhoven, who had gone to London to conduct these negotiations, returned with the warning that unless a satisfactory regulation of agricultural and cattle exports was made, the agreement would not be put into operation.[33] In his conversations van Vollenhoven had foreseen the establishment of an association of agricultural producers to whom stocks of maize and oil cake would be sold on condition that they offered a corresponding part of their products to a purchasing agency designated by the British or their allies. It was understood by the French that the War Trade Advisory Committee had asked the Foreign Office to negotiate for these purchases and, if the situation demanded it, to use coercion to obtain them.[34]

Van Vollenhoven returned to London once more and between March 31 and April 10, 1916, the question of Dutch exports was again thoroughly considered. It was decided that it would be better if neither of the governments acted directly in the purchases which would eventually be made. Consequently some British trade experts were sent to the Netherlands in the middle of May to arrange details of purchase and payment through the Dutch banks. Prices were one of the chief stumbling blocks. Negotiations dragged; they were complicated by the question of detentions of grain and fodder cargoes in British ports and by arrangements over the use of Dutch tonnage in Allied service. Van Vollenhoven returned from another journey to London early in May, with the purchasing agreement no nearer completion.[35]

On May 17 Allizé once more raised the question of French purchases in the Netherlands.[36] He said that on the pretense of there being an excess of cattle in the country the Dutch government had authorized the exportation of 10,500 milk cows, which would be sent to Germany and Austria-Hungary. British negotiations, he reported, appeared to be stopped, and the French commissariat showed no intention of buying in the Dutch market. The note continued: "I believe it necessary then to recur to the interest that there would be in taking away from the Austro-Germans a part of the agricultural products they procure here. The prices are excessive, but as I have indicated on various occasions, it is an operation of war more than an alimentary operation. . . .   It seems to me that the best combination would be to send to Holland a Franco-British Purchasing Commission composed of specialists from both countries."

In the first week of June English negotiations took on new life when Leverton Harris was sent to The Hague. Both he and Sir Henry Rew, who had already arrived, were acting for a semiofficial organization, the British Purchasing Agency. On behalf of the Dutch who later formed the Landbouw Export Bureau, J. T. Linthorst Homan bore the brunt of the negotiations. He was already president of the Royal Dutch Agricultural Committee, executive chairman of both the Committee for Foreign Trade and the Committee for Feeding Men and Beasts; he was, according to Dr. Charlotte A. van Manen, in possession of the full confidence of Dutch agricultural interests.[37] In these negotiations he was ably assisted by van Vollenhoven, A. G. Kröller and O. Reitsma, secretary of the Dutch Milk Producers Association. Allizé, who kept his government well informed, recommended that a French Commission be sent to collaborate with the English delegates and to direct to French markets the products which England did not absorb.[38] He reported that the British government had already established a credit of 20 million francs to cover the difference between the price of purchase in the Dutch market and the lower price of resale. The transaction was regarded by the British as an "operation of war." There is no evidence that a French representative took part in these June negotiations. At any rate the British secured the acceptance of the heads of agreement on June 10, and on June 16, 1916, the accord was signed.[39]

The agreement provided that not less than half of the total monthly Dutch exports of all pork products were to be exported to the United Kingdom, not less than one fourth of the butter, and not less than one third of the cheese. The Dutch association guaranteed that certain amounts of these goods would be made available to the British Purchasing Agency at fixed prices each week: 400 tons of bacon at 1.44 guilders per kilo; 200 tons of butter at not to exceed 2.10 guilders per kilo f.o.b.; 400 tons of cheese at 65 guilders per 50 kilos for full cream cheese, with prices of other cheeses in proportion. Any part of these quantities not taken up by the Agency were to be sold by the association on the English market through the usual trade channels. A bonus was to be paid by the British on all sales in the United Kingdom in order to offset the difference between German and English prices. It was assumed, as a basis for the agreement, that at least 2,000 tons of meat would be exported to the United Kingdom before any exportations of meat to any other country took place, and that no sheep, mutton, veal, or live calves would be exported except to the United Kingdom, or hides or skins over nine kilos except to the United Kingdom or the United States. Exact regulation of the exportation of condensed milk was reserved for settlement later, but on the understanding that three quarters of the total export should be sent to the United Kingdom and that sweetened condensed milk should be exported only to the United Kingdom so long as any Dutch manufactory was dependent on imported sugar. It was also assumed that no exportations of hay and straw or other fodder, of fertilizers, or of cream and fresh milk would take place.

Other articles in the agreement arranged that up to February 1, 1917, one half of the potatoes and one fourth of the fruits and vegetables exported to the belligerent countries should be offered to the United Kingdom at prices that were calculated at the mean between Dutch prices and the average export prices paid in countries other than the United Kingdom. No bonuses were to be paid on exports sent directly to United Kingdom markets, although exports to France and the Belgian Relief Commission were to be reckoned for purposes of the agreement as being sent to the United Kingdom. The most important concession made to the Dutch in return for these facilities given to the British Purchasing Agency was that ". . . so long as this agreement remains in force, it is assumed that the imports into Holland of feeding stuffs and fertilizers, including the raw material, will continue both from overseas and from the United Kingdom in a satisfactory manner, based on any arrangements with the British Authorities, at present in operation concerning such imports." The last article of the accord stated that it was not to be published.

After the completion of this agreement the Landbouw Export Bureau was formally established on June 29, 1916; it received its charter on August 5, 1916.[40]

It seemed clear from the accord that certain exports to France were contemplated, and almost immediately the French government took steps preparatory to making purchases. At the meeting of the Comité de Restriction on June 28 Chappuis reported that the British agreement had been made, but he believed that it alone would not sufficiently restrict the supply to the enemy and, therefore, France must enter the Dutch market. But he also reported that Ribot was still adamant: it was impossible to secure guilders for such an operation. Chappuis' solution was that the British should make the actual purchases and then should hand over to France her share of the goods; thus the problem of paying in guilders would disappear.[41] Eduard Théry was still of the opinion that the best way to end Dutch exports to Germany was to cut off supplies of fodder to the Netherlands; Allizé, who was present at this meeting, said that the Dutch foreign minister had pointed out to him that in such a case the Allies "put us under the obligation of exporting our cattle." But so far as is known the matter of French purchases rested there; again in early July Ribot insisted that it was impossible for France to think of making purchases abroad beyond what was indispensable for her needs.[42]

The British soon found that their own purchasing arrangements in the Netherlands were not working satisfactorily. The co-operation of the Dutch government was not given with much enthusiasm since it wished to remain as far as possible in the background in these commercial matters. It was found almost impossible to divert large quantities of exports from Germany without some coercion being exerted; a promise of bonuses to offset differences in prices was not enough. The deliveries of cheese to the United Kingdom in July and August far from met the amounts stipulated, and in consequence a special British commission was sent to the Netherlands on September 7, 1916.[43] Allizé reported that within twenty-four hours deliveries began, and the cheese merchants had agreed to send two hundred tons of cheese to England weekly so that the arrears would be delivered in twenty weeks. Certainly a rise in exports to the United Kingdom was noted in September, a movement which continued for the rest of the year.[44] As might have been expected, the Dutch farmers were dissatisfied with being forced to sell to the British, but they were even more irritated at having to sell on the home market at prices fixed by royal decree. Certainly the Landbouw Export Bureau was in a difficult position. While the British exerted continual pressure to secure a reduction in exports to Germany, the Bureau attempted to get from the German government some assurance that cargoes of Dutch agricultural goods to England would not be interfered with, lest Dutch exports of fodder be cut off. But the Germans insisted that Britain was already getting too much from the Netherlands and threatened to stop coal deliveries![45]

Since relations with the Dutch government were in such a bad state, and since the June purchasing agreement was not to their liking, the British sometime in October approached the Landbouw Export Bureau for a new agreement. Negotiations were carried on in London by Leverton Harris on behalf of the British and General Trading Association, the successor to the British Purchasing Agency. At one point, when the Dutch proved intractable, the British threatened an actual blockade of the Dutch coast unless their demands were met.[46] The accord, concluded on November 1, 1916, no longer specified that definite amounts of goods should be sent to the United Kingdom but only set up requirements that a certain proportion of the total Dutch exports to belligerent countries should be so exported—i.e., one half of the pork products, one fourth of the butter, one third of the cheese, one third of the milk, one fourth of the fruits and vegetables, and one half of the meat up to May 1, 1917.[47] Additional limits were put on the total amounts of meat that could be exported to all belligerent countries, while Great Britain still claimed the right to receive all Dutch exports of sheep, mutton, wool, calves, and veal. Potatoes were in this class too, until deficits under the previous agreement were satisfied. Special agreements on seeds, sugar, and sugar beets were contemplated, and until they were reached these articles were not to be exported. An absolute prohibition to export cream, live pigs, blood, straw, hay, fodder, and fertilizers was required. Further arrangements were made concerning the existing deficits, as well as others on statements of sales under the agreement, payments, and bonuses. Now instead of a maximum price, plus a bonus, being set, the British agreed to pay the price on the free market plus a bonus. This agreement was to remain in force until the end of the war, unless it was terminated by default or upon one month's notice by either of the parties.

The British purchasing policy did have good results, for in three months' time the value of Dutch agricultural exports to England rose from 16 to 36 million guilders, while that to Germany fell from 46.5 million to between 16 and 20 million. Naturally the Germans were displeased and decided to make their future arrangements each month between the Deutsche Handelsstelle im Haag and the Bureau, rather than on a more permanent basis.[48]

The negotiations undertaken by the British to acquire a certain proportion of the Dutch fishing catch were quite separate from those just discussed. In this case the excuse for attempting to secure a purchasing agreement could not be that fish usually sold in British markets had been deflected to Germany, for actually British imports of Dutch fish in 1915 were much larger than in 1913. Moreover the control of neutral fishing would be a difficult thing, both in practice and in law. The fishing seasons were irregular, fishing was done in wide areas—often where British cruisers could not establish their supremacy, the ships were small, and their lack of ships' papers made control through the exercise of recognized belligerent rights almost impossible. Neutral governments could claim with considerable justification that fishing vessels were immune from capture unless they were assisting in military operation or were running an established blockade. The British government was not in sympathy with these arguments, for fishing had become a well-organized industry whose products formed an important article of diet in the belligerent states of Central Europe.

Determined to carry out some control of the fishing industry in northern European waters, Leverton Harris early in 1916 set up an advisory committee on fish.[49] This committee and other organs of the British government considered various ways of keeping Dutch fishing vessels under surveillance. Some thought that the boats might be detained on charges of mine-laying and then be released only when their owners agreed to sell the catch in an Allied port. Cecil Hurst thought that sufficient pressure might be exercised through refusals to grant export licenses for fishing gear, cork, and salt. It was also suggested that a few fishing vessels might be brought into a prize court as a test case. Lord Robert Cecil believed that this would excite too much opposition and animosity among neutrals and would only make ultimate negotiations more difficult; he had not faith that pressure alone would secure British ends. In addition, it was extremely doubtful whether a prize court would condemn a neutral catch bound for a neutral port. To clinch the matter, in March the Admiralty advised against any such operation.

The Dutch government had already taken certain steps to control the disposition of the catch of sea fish taken by Dutch fishermen. On March 23, 1916, the minister of agriculture announced that herring exports would be permitted only under license, and money guarantees for their return to Dutch ports were required of fishing vessels before they were permitted to put to sea. In March the Owners Association of the Herring Fisheries took advantage of a visit of van Vollenhoven to London on behalf of the N.O.T. to have him propose to the British that the distribution of herring be on the basis of 20 per cent for the Netherlands, America, and Sweden, and the other 80 per cent to be divided between Germany and England at certain fixed prices that represented a 40 per cent bonus above the cost price. But apparently the British were not interested. In any case a more thoroughgoing regulation was put into effect by the Dutch government on June 26,

1916, when 25 per cent of the herring catch and 50 per cent of other fish were reserved for the home market at fixed prices.[50]

However, early in June, Sir Henry Rew and Leverton Harris carried on investigations in the Netherlands of the whole fishing situation, and they returned to the idea that as many Dutch fishing boats as could be seized in the war zone should be brought in. The British vice-consul at Ijmuiden believed that it could be proved that nearly all of the trawlers were under contract to the German Zentraleinkaufsgesellschaft. This recommendation came just when the Admiralty was anxious to reap some advantage from the battle of Jutland, and they now expressed themselves (June 7, 1916), in favor of some sudden and decided action, although they did not have the Dutch fishing fleet in mind as the object of that action. A few days later the Admiralty did propose to bring in all the Dutch vessels found in the prohibited area for detention for a week or two. After some delay the Foreign Office agreed, although the exact intention of the Admiralty was not understood. The Foreign Office knew that it could bring proof that certain Dutch companies were working for the Germans, and, had their trawlers been brought into a prize court, condemnation would probably have followed. But the Admiralty exercised no such discrimination and proceeded to bring in all trawlers, some empty, some with cargoes, without citing any reasons— whether for just being in the prohibited danger zone or for carrying cargoes with an enemy destination. This action was not without some prior warning. On March 22 Sir Alan Johnstone, the British minister, had presented a formal warning to the Dutch government that there was grave danger to the fishing fleets that operated off the east coast of England, both from mines and from military operations. Later, on June 16, the British minister informed the Dutch that his government proposed to bring in and detain for search all ships encountered in this danger zone. The Admiralty's zeal resulted in some sixty-five ships being held in British ports by July 15, a figure which Dutch reports on July 19 regarded as low; they spoke of a hundred ships under detention.[51]

Dutch reaction to this new blow took several forms. First, of course, the Dutch government on July 11 presented a formal protest which generally denied the right of a belligerent to take a ship into port for search, or, by declaring a zone on the high seas a danger area, to evade its obligation to search then and there. The Dutch reserved the right to claim indemnity for every ship that was detained in a British port solely because it was found in this zone.[52] Johnstone had already indicated on July 1 and 8 that the Dutch ships would be released as soon as fish exports to Germany ceased, but unless this took place still more ships would be seized. Other notes of protest from the Dutch government continued to arrive—one on July 26, another on August 17, asserting the immunity of fishing vessels from such interference and asking indulgence from the hardships caused the poor fishermen. The Dutch insisted that if the British really wished to prevent the fish from reaching Germany they were quite free to enter Dutch markets which were open to all![53]

By the time these notes were written the fisheries owners themselves had entered negotiations. A special meeting of the owners was held on July 13, with the result that a delegation left for England four days later with full powers to sign an agreement that would secure the release of the ships in exchange for a promise to sell a fixed proportion of the catch to England. Leverton Harris had been correct in thinking that the arrests, whatever their reasons, would bring the Dutch fishermen to terms. On the basis of their instructions the Dutch negotiators proposed that Great Britain should release all the vessels and their cargoes and that no more should be seized, that the British should pay compensation to owners of the detained vessels at the rate of £50 per day for a sailing drifter, £75 for a motor drifter or auxiliary steam drifter, and £100 for a steam drifter. Of the catch which would be landed after the signature of an agreement Great Britain would receive 50 per cent at a price of 57.70 guilders per barrel of 115 kilos, and the rest would be sold on the open market.[54]

A British counterproposal was made by Leverton Harris on July 27, in which, although the vessels were to be released, no compensation was to be paid.[55] The British also asked that the whole Dutch fleet except that part engaged in "driftnet fishing" exclusively for Dutch and other neutral consumption should be laid up until December 15, 1916, the end of the season. In return the British offered to indemnify the owners of ships which were already fitted out and at sea but which would be called in, and also those owners who had ordered their ships to be fitted out. It was expected that the crews would be paid a share of this amount, as set in agreements signed before the water bailiffs at the fishing ports. In addition the British were to pay another sum for each ship to the Standing Committee of the Netherlands Driftnet Vessels Association, which would in turn pay indemnities to the workmen and small industrialists in the trades dependent on fishing—e.g., coopers and netmakers. Another sum was to be made available to indemnify merchants, commission agents, and brokers.

In spite of the indemnities offered, the Dutch fishermen regarded the proposal as impossible, for the economic loss would still have been tremendous. The outcry from the various unions of Dutch seamen, transport, and harbor workers, and from the fishermen's wives was united; protests were made to the British legation and to Sir Edward Grey, letters were written to the press, questions were asked in the Second Chamber of the Dutch Parliament.[56] The British soon realized that they would have to be content with securing a certain proportion of the Dutch catch; the question was, what proportion? Proposals and counterproposals were made—the Dutch suggested 20 per cent for Dutch use, 40 per cent for England, 40 per cent for Germany; and the British replied 60 per cent for England, 10 per cent for the Netherlands and 30 per cent for Germany;[57] the Dutch then suggested 50 per cent should go to England, France, and America. In the meantime the

British continued to bring in more ships during the early days of August, at the very time when they were offering to charter the entire Dutch fleet. On August 15 the Dutch Chamber of Commerce in London sent an address to Grey, new meetings of the owners were held in The Hague, and, as we have seen, Loudon renewed his protests to the British minister on August 17. Long lists of detained ships began to appear; van Manen lists 126 brought in between June 25 and August 27.[58]

In the end the British signed two agreements. One with the Ijmuiden Trawler Owners, who had from the beginning been outside these earlier negotiations, was concluded about August 22, under which the Ijmuiden men agreed to sell 35 per cent of their catch of fresh fish in Great Britain, in return for which the British agreed to grant export licenses for coal and fishing gear.[59] The other agreement was signed on August 26 with the herring fisheries.[60] The Owners Association of the Herring Fisheries agreed to respect the prohibited areas established by the British, to take stock of all herring landed before August 31, and to sell for exportation (i.e., to Germany) not more than 20 per cent of the total amount of herring caught thereafter in each month. The British government reserved the right to buy up to 20 per cent, and the rest of the catch which was not necessary for Dutch consumption was to be exported to the United States or some other country approved by the British. On these exportations to approved countries the British agreed to pay a bonus of 30 shillings per barrel, as well as on all fish which remained unsold by March 1, 1917. Ports of entry for landing the herring were designated—Maassluis, Scheveningen, Vlaardingen, Schiedam, Katwijk, and Noordwijk. The names of all nonmembers were to be communicated to the British and they apparently were to be permitted none of the advantages of the agreement, which included facilities for the supply of fishing gear. The British agreed to release all the detained vessels and cargoes belonging to members of the Association, but on condition that no claims be made for detention or loss of fishing profits; claims for damages to the vessels or gear suffered during detention would be considered only if the claim were made before the vessel left the British port. The agreement was designed to last for the duration of the war, or until the British gave one month's notice of its termination. An attached schedule laid down regulations concerning warehousing, examination of records, and bank guarantees.

The ships were released by the British by September 10, and thus ended one of the more vexatious of the controversies between the Dutch and the British.[61] The Dutch were pleased that part of the fishing season still remained, but they could not easily forget the losses they had suffered. The British had reason to be fairly well contented with the results of their agreements. In the first quarter of 1917 they received 40 per cent—rather than 35 per cent—of the fresh fish caught by the Ijmuiden fleet. Exports of all kinds of fish to Germany from the Netherlands remained high in the last quarter of 1916—13,482 tons or 76 per cent of the total exports, but in the first quarter of 1917 there was a sharp decline—2,887 tons or 52 per cent of the total.[62] How much this was due to the effects of the purchasing agreements and how much to the general dislocations caused by the increased German submarine campaign it is impossible to say, but it is safe to surmise that the British paid a high price for a relatively small achievement.

THE NORWEGIAN FISH AGREEMENT

The fact that excessive exports of fish were being made from Norway to Germany seems to have come to the attention of the British somewhat earlier than those made from the Netherlands. By the end of 1915 it was realized that the Norwegian fish market was almost entirely controlled by buyers acting on behalf of the German Zentraleinkaufsgesellschaft; the Norwegians also knew that the position of their fishing industry was a precarious one. In October 1915 the Social and Industrial Department of the Norwegian government set up a committee, headed by Johann Hjort, the director of fisheries, to study the situation.[63] The committee's report indicated that, for instance, of the 240,000 tons of salt herring processed in 1915 at Haugesund, 100,000 tons were for foreign account—and 41 per cent of that amount was for Germany, while 95 per cent of the fresh fish exported went to the same destination. It was recognized that the fishing industry was dependent for 85 per cent of its supplies on the British, and that undoubtedly plans were being made by them to decrease the exports of fish to the Central Powers. Already Norwegian buyers of salt were required to sign a declaration that none of it would reach the enemy directly or indirectly. Hjort, in November 1915, sought, with the co-operation of the Trade Department, to secure an arrangement concerning the importation of British coal for the use of the fishing fleet, in return for fish shipments to the United Kingdom. In the meantime the German agents were displeased when they found prospective purchases blocked by these declarations given to the British. On the other hand, the Norwegians knew that the British could cut off supplies of gear to Norway, a step which would, it was calculated, throw a hundred thousand Norwegian fishermen out of work. Therefore, the Norwegian government considered its policies toward Britain very carefully.

There seemed to be two alternatives. Conceivably the Norwegian government might buy up the entire fish catch and then regulate its distribution between the home and foreign markets. But this would require enormous funds, and the Norwegian Treasury was already hard pressed. The second possibility was to persuade the British government to enter the Norwegian market and buy enough fish to cut down German purchases. This, Hjort believed, would result in the least interference with Norwegian interests. Hjort had some reason to hope that the British could be persuaded to make what he called "blockade purchases," for as early as November 11, he had a letter from the British director of fisheries indicating that some people in England were considering the possibility of buying Norwegian fish simply to fill British needs. Hjort was quite willing to run the risk of having Norway accused of unneutral action if she entered into a purchasing arrangement with the British; that was better than having the fishing fleet laid up.

Hjort took the matter up with Sir Mansfeldt Findlay, the British minister, and with O. Wardrop, the British consul in Bergen, and it was arranged that the British government should make available £10 million for the purchase of fish in the free market in Norway during the year 1916. On January 24, 1916, Henry J. Maurice of the British Fisheries Department, arrived in Bergen to organize the scheme. The purchases were to be arranged through private traders and it was hoped that for some time it could remain a secret that they were being made on Britain's behalf, for otherwise the prices were certain to soar. On Hjort's suggestion Albert Martens, the owner of one of the largest Norwegian fishing companies, undertook this task. Horjt had kept Nils C. Ihlen, the foreign minister, and K. Friis-Petersen, minister of commerce, informed of his conversations with Maurice and of the arrangements made, in the Norwegian national interest, with Martens, and at this point these cabinet members made no protest. On February 5, 1916, Maurice and Martens came to a formal agreement in which it was explicitly understood that the British government would give the Norwegian fishing industry every facility for the importation of coal, salt, and hemp so long as the accord remained in effect. At the same time, the declaration which the British had demanded of those importing fishing supplies—that they should never reach the Central Powers, was altered. Martens soon bought large quantities of fish; by mid-April he was buying 70—80 per cent of the output and had spent more than 160 million kroner for dried and salt fish for which, in general, the British consumer had no need and which were, therefore, stored in Norway.[64]

It was clear that the cost of this policy was great, and that the British purchases could not be kept secret for long, for although Martens was buying large amounts he was always unwilling to sell any fish to German agents. Moreover, when the catch made by Norwegians in Icelandic waters reached port, British purchases might well have to be increased. To complicate the financial side even more, the Norges Bank, apparently kept in ignorance of the true nature of the transaction, decided to raise its commission for handling British funds, sent through the C. J. Hambro and Son Bank in London, from 0.25 to 5 per cent.

In order to straighten out some of these problems Hjort went to London in early April.[65] There he conferred with E. G. Pretyman, parliamentary secretary of the Board of Trade, who believed that purchasing from a few fishermen at fixed prices, rather than making general purchases in the open market, was the only feasible means of control. Pretyman and Hjort arrived at a statement which they proposed should be issued to the Norwegian public explaining what the British purchasing policy had been and asserting that purchases could continue only if fish prices were controlled, and that importations of fishing supplies could be permitted only by those approved by the British government. The British Treasury agreed to make available up to £14 million to cover future purchases. Maurice was then designated to go to Norway to make detailed arrangements.

When Maurice arrived, Friis-Petersen refused to meet him, one indication that the Norwegian cabinet was not entirely pleased with the new scheme. Another indication was that the Norwegians soon laid a high export tax on medicinal fish oils, and thereby impeded the use of those products which the British really did need. However, it was the implied denial by the Norwegian government of permission to inform the Norwegian public of the British purchasing plan that made it virtually impossible to carry it out; the heavy fishing season was then over, and the Norwegian government thought it safe to let the matter drift. Hjort was as disillusioned as Maurice,[66] and on April 23 he offered his resignation as director of Norwegian fisheries, to take effect on July 1.

His threat was sufficient to make Friis-Petersen and Ihlen grant him, on April 29, certain minimum powers to negotiate in London with the British authorities.[67] But his second trip to London brought few results. True, the British offered to furnish supplies for shipowners wishing to go to the Icelandic fishing grounds, provided they gave an option on their catch at the maximum price of 40 kroner per 100 kilos, to buyers approved by the British. But soon new difficulties arose when the Norwegian Food Commission wanted to buy some 15,000 barrels of the herring then stored in Norway for British account, at 50 kroner per barrel; the British insisted that they had purchased these fish at an average cost of 89 kroner per barrel. Since they needed ready funds to cover later purchases they agreed to sell at 60 kroner, provided the Food Commission took a larger amount of the stored fish off their hands. It appears that the British were being asked to underwrite a supply of cheap fish for the Norwegian public! In fact, the whole situation was so unsatisfactory that Lord Robert Cecil informed Hjort on May 26 that the British government had decided to cease fish purchases in Norway. Both agreed that the summer months might be used to study the situation and come to a new arrangement to cover the autumn catch.[68] However, the British agreed to furnish, up to July 31, 1916, "reasonable supplies" to the Icelandic fishermen and to offer them 45 kroner per barrel for their catch; any Icelandic fish or oil for which the British did not exercise their option was to be sold only to approved merchants who, in turn, would sell only to Sweden, Norway, or in approved markets outside Scandinavia.[69]

The whole question was reopened when Leverton Harris and James Hope Simpson arrived in Christiania to confer with Hjort on July 19. They presented to him a provisional scheme as a basis for discussion, in which they suggested the establishment of a Norwegian Fish Merchants' Association which would be responsible for providing a sufficient supply of fish for do-

mestic consumption, and for selling all other Norwegian fish and fish prod
ucts to the British government or to someone nominated and guaranteed
by it.[70] The Norwegian government would grant export licenses only to this
Association, and it would remove all export duties on fish for the duration of
the agreement. The Association was also to become the consignee for all
fishing gear imported with British permission. Leverton Harris reminded
Hjort, when the Norwegians objected to this scheme,[71] that there were many
in England who were opposed to making further purchases in the Norwegian
open market, and that some other solution must be found. British proposals
to store the whole catch until the end of the war, or to lay up the fishing
fleet for some months until new arrangements could be made, were also rejected. Hjort became convinced that too many questions of foreign policy
were involved in selling fish *only* to Great Britain, for he doubted that the
Germans would take kindly to such a scheme. He therefore recommended
that a representative of the Ministry of Foreign Affairs be associated with
him in the future. As a result on July 21 Arne Scheel, undersecretary of state
for foreign affairs, entered the conferences.

Apparently the Ministry of Foreign Affairs decided to urge that a branch
agreement, similar to those already made by a number of Norwegian industries, be reached in order to secure the importation of coal, oil, salt, and
the like under guarantees against re-exportation to the Central Powers.
Hjort, however, believed that such an agreement would be useless unless it
was accompanied by British purchases of fish, for otherwise there would be
very little sale for the catch made with the aid of these materials. On July 24
the British negotiators quite firmly gave the Norwegians two choices:
British purchases with a strict observance of Norwegian embargoes against
export (to Germany, that is), or a branch agreement without any obligation
on the part of the British to buy in the Norwegian fish market. The British
stated that if they did purchase the entire catch they would be "as liberal as
possible" in releasing cheap fish for Norwegian use. Hjort and Ihlen conferred with a committee representing the fishing industry, among whom was
included one Assersson, a fisheries' agent in Hamburg, who emphasized a
danger Ihlen already feared—that Germany would consider any agreement
to sell all of the Norwegian catch to the British as an unneutral act and
would at least undertake a commercial war against Norway in reprisal. Since
Hjort had already been asked some rather pointed questions about these
negotiations by Paul Rehbein, a director of the Hamburg-America Line, and
Rudolf Hintze, who were representing the German Zentraleinkaufsgesellschaft in Norway, it isn't surprising that the Norwegians should have sought
some compromise.

On July 29 Scheel and Hjort proposed that an agreement on imported
raw materials be combined with a recognition by the British that a certain
percentage of the Norwegian catch be made available for export to Germany,
provided no products imported from or with the consent of Great Britain
had been used in taking or processing the fish; the remainder of the catch

vas to be purchased by the British. Scheel made a good deal of the possibility of a German invasion of Norway if exports were entirely cut off. Leverton Harris began by agreeing in principle provided 10 per cent of the catch was reserved for Norwegian consumption, 10 per cent for "other countries," and the remainder for Great Britain at fixed prices. Scheel bargained for permission to export 25 per cent to Germany; in the end 15 per cent was the figure agreed upon. Since Hjort's chief aim had been to keep the British in the market and to secure fishing gear, he could be pleased to that extent.

The text of the draft agreement was sent to Hjort by Leverton Harris on August 3, 1916,[72] with an accompanying note in which it was stated: "At the request of Mr. Scheel, I have made no mention in the accord itself of the obligation of the Norwegian Goverment to furnish statistics. It is well understood, however, that Mr. Ihlen will be so good as to address to the British Legation a letter specifying that he will furnish to His Majesty's Minister all information desired on the subject of requests for exportation licences, as well as declarations concerning them, and exportation statistics of fish, fish oil and other products proving the real destination of these exportations."

The agreement was formally accepted in an exchange of notes on August 5, 1916.[73] By Article 1 the Norwegian government agreed to forbid the exportation of all fish, fish oil, and other fish products, except canned fish that was exported in normal quantities and in conformity with the Royal Resolution of July 4, 1916. The government was to make an inventory of all stocks of these articles then existing in Norway, and in the future, exportations would be permitted only when the certificate stating the amount of fish the exporter had on hand was presented to the customs, together with the export license and a declaration that the exportation did not conflict with any accord on the use of materials employed in fishing or in the preparation of fish products. Presumably only stocks on hand were to be available for export. Under Article 4 the British government agreed to buy all fish, fish oil, and other fish products that were not necessary for Norwegian consumption, at prices to be determined in a separate agreement, these prices to remain in effect until the end of the war. However, the British reserved the right, in Article 5, to cease purchases upon giving four weeks' notice, although it affirmed its intention to continue purchases of herring up to December 31, 1916, provided they did not exceed 80 per cent of the credits set up.[74] By Article 6 the British agreed to grant licenses and facilities for the exportation of coal, oil, and fishing-boat motors, within the limits that the needs of the Allies permitted and on condition that the necessary assurances were given by the Norwegian importers.

It was Articles 12 and 13 that laid down the conditions on which Norwegian export licenses in derogation of the fish embargo might be granted. Although such exports would undoubtedly be destined for the Central Powers, no such statement was made in this agreement. Thus the amount was to be limited to 15 per cent of certain types of fish (fresh and salt herring, salted fresh fish, salted dried fish, dried fish, cod-liver oil, seal oil, roe, fish meal, and herring meal), provided the exporter could guarantee that no products imported from or under the control of Great Britain had gone into their preparation. The exporter was also required to designate the names and addresses of the fishermen from whom he bought, and to secure from them similar guarantees about the coal, oil, engines, and so forth, they had used in catching the fish. The exporter then had to deposit with the Norwegian customs for a thirty-day period from the date of application for a license, a bond equal to the value of the goods exported; if any falsity in the declarations was discovered, the security would be confiscated. The Norwegian government, on the other hand, agreed in Article 15 to maintain the embargo on fish so long as the British continued their purchases at the established prices.

In order further to control sales of fish, Norwegian fishermen who used British materials were required, under Articles 19 and 20, not to dispose of their catch on the high seas or to land fish in any non-Norwegian port, and the Norwegian government was to designate the ports from which fish exports were to be made. It was further provided that the accord might be terminated by the Norwegian government six months after its signature, to take effect three months from the date of the notice to the British legation; engagements made and rights acquired prior to the abrogation would not be affected. Annexes to the agreement set up the list of prices, and a scheme for arbitration of disputes arising out of the agreement.[75]

Unfortunately neither of the parties was satisfied with the manner in which the agreement was executed.[76] As Keilhau points out, the prices fixed by the supplementary agreement were not made subject to change in step with any future variation in the price level. More than that, it was understood that Norwegian domestic prices were to be fixed at a figure not to exceed those set for British purchases. But the cost of materials went up and there was no opportunity for raising the prices paid by the British; the dealers were, to say the least, in a bad position. The negotiators of the agreement had believed that a considerable part of the British purchases would be resold on the Norwegian market at very low prices, but the British agents failed to offer enough to meet Norwegian domestic needs, and the prices were higher than anticipated. On the other hand the British were equally upset by the apparent laxity in observance of the guarantees, although in the end they had to accept this situation. The inventories of fish stocks had been taken in considerable haste, and it soon became clear that either much of the fish then in warehouses was not counted, or new catches were being passed off as old stock and thus were being sold to Germany freely. One of the great difficulties in carrying out the agreement was that Ihlen, much against Hjort's wishes, but out of fear of German reprisals, insisted that its terms should remain secret. Hjort maintained that since so many men were involved in executing the agreement, it *could not* be kept secret; in consequence he resigned his position as director of fisheries on August 11, 1916. A few days later he had a conversation with Rehbein, the German agent, who already knew that the Norwegians had entered into an agreement with the British. Rehbein then said that it was not this itself that embittered the Germans, for they understood why it was done, but rather that it had been kept secret from them.

On a higher level the Germans did protest. Count Alfred Oberndorff, the German minister in Christiania, was told by Ihlen that existing fish stocks would not be affected and that exemptions from the embargo would be made for certain amounts of the new catch. Ihlen presented the agreement as absolutely necessary in order to obtain raw materials and fishing gear from Great Britain. The Germans were not satisfied, and there seemed little doubt that the great losses of Norwegian shipping from German submarine action were a direct result.[77] To make sure of securing all the fish permitted them under this agreement the Germans established in Norwegian ports depots of articles of German origin that were necessary to the fishing industry—thus 15 per cent of the Norwegian catch almost certainly went to Germany.[78]

More open discontent with the fish agreement showed itself in the Norwegian Storting in February 1917 during the debate on the Speech from the Throne, when Hjort was severely criticized for putting the industry so much into British hands. Tønder, member from Bergen, insisted that the maximum prices for fish set by the agreement were far too low, and that there had been gross negligence in not setting maximum prices on the fisheries supplies to be secured from Great Britain. Bratlie, leader of the Opposition, held that it would have been sufficient to sign a branch agreement with the British. On the other hand, some speakers came to Hjort's defense, maintaining that the accord was as good as could be gotten under the circumstances, that without it the fisheries would have been far worse off, and would have been completely lacking in gear, petroleum, and coal. The point was made that although Germany had offered to supply these articles, actually it could not; circulars had been sent out by a firm in Kristiansand offering German gear, but none had ever arrived. One speaker insisted that the year 1916 had been a profitable one for the fisheries, a view that is amply borne out by statistics given in Hjort's book.[79]

The agreements made by the British government in pursuance of its purchasing policy were, as has been indicated, of varying success. Some of the agreements were the means of bringing to United Kingdom markets in 1916 an amount of agricultural and fish products greater than in the previous year. If the results did not always meet the expectations of those who negotiated them, they at least secured to Great Britain a larger proportion of these neutral goods than would have come to England in the ordinary course of wartime trade. Prices in Germany continued to be sufficiently higher than those in England to draw neutral products to German markets. The expense involved for the British government in securing even these increases in British imports was great and out of all proportion to the intrinsic value of the goods received. But as the French—who were not bearing the major part of the expense, so often pointed out, it was an "operation of war" de-signed to starve out the enemy, and as such was no more costly than any of the other measures taken toward that end. Just what effect these particular agreements had on the amount of food available in enemy countries is diffi-cult to say. One can do no more than point out that while these agreements were in operation the economic war was an increasing burden on Germany, and that the purchasing agreements were one of the means of bringing about that condition.

XII

Miscellaneous Negotiations with the Northern Neutrals in 1916

DURING 1916 the Allies were concerned with extending their controls over the trade of the Netherlands and Denmark through new agreements—or reinterpretations of old ones with the Netherlands Oversea Trust and the Danish associations. At the same time they sought with some success new accords with a number of Norwegian trade associations. In dealing with Swedish trade, the British were still proceeding on the basis of the compensation arrangements, which had been made following the breakdown of negotiations in 1915, and there was always the question of whether anything could be gained by renewing these conversations. It will be the purpose of this chapter to follow the threads of all these negotiations, to see to what extent they were complementary to the special agreements already discussed, and to what extent they perfected Allied economic controls.

NEGOTIATIONS WITH SWEDEN

The general conditions in Sweden that had made a settlement with the British impossible in 1915 continued to exist during most of 1916. The Hjalmar Hammarskjöld cabinet was still supported in its attitude toward Allied economic measures by the undemocratic Court party, although there was some feeling among the Liberal and Labor opposition groups, who actually had a majority in the Lower House, that relations with Britain were purposely kept unsettled in order to foster the excuse for increasing the powers of the cabinet at the expense of the Riksdag. At any rate the debate on the budget early in the Riksdag session of 1916 was extremely revealing.[1] For the first time Nils Eden, leader of the Liberals, and Erik Palmstierna, a prominent Social Democrat, entered into a thoroughgoing criticism of the government. The first charge was that government business, and particularly foreign affairs, was conducted in too much secrecy; in addition, the Riksdag itself operated under a self-imposed censorship that prevented open discussion of many vital matters. Although at no time did either speaker name Germany as the recipient of special favors, they called for a nonpartisan policy toward both sets of belligerents. Sven Hedin and his pro-German Activists were sharply criticized, and Palmstierna charged that Admiral Arvid Lindman, one of the leaders of the Court party, went so far in his support of the Activists that even the *Nya Dagligt Allehanda* (one of the most pro-German newspapers) had reservations about his speeches. Palmstierna also pointed to the revival of a Secret Committee on Foreign Affairs, which was not subject to parliamentary control, as an example of the renaissance of "dynastism" in the conduct of foreign affairs. Eden particularly urged that, in regard to the importation of overseas goods, the government should seek a *modus vivendi*, so that while Sweden did not give up her legal principles she at least made sure that she did not find herself buried under the wreckage. Other speakers in the debate made use of information which had just appeared in Volume I of Karl Hildebrand's "Gray Book," *De svenska statsmakterna och krigstidens folkhushållning*, to criticize the government's failure to control food and freight prices. In regard to the latter, Schotte recalled that in November 1915 an agreement had been made by the government with shipowners whereby the latter would make a contribution of one krona for each registered ton of shipping on all ships over three hundred tons, the money to be used to underwrite food imports. The sum collected had amounted to 600,000 kronor, but freight prices had risen so much above prewar levels (he quoted the figure of 400 per cent in North American and 500 per cent in South American trades) as to make the contribution negligible. At the same time he cited the case of one company, Axel Brostrom and Son, of Göteborg, whose contribution had been 120,000 kronor but which had earned 60,000 kronor more than this on a single voyage! Alexander Hamilton, another member, supported the complaint against the failure to control food prices, but he thought it was the millers and other middlemen, and not the farmers, who were the real villains. Ryden of Malmö, in the same vein, criticized the organization of the Victualling Commission on the ground that it was made up primarily of "paper men and bureaucrats," and not of businessmen or representatives of consumers and workers.

In spite of all the political maneuvering, Swedish sentiment in favor of intervention on the side of Germany, never strong, was now considerably weakened. Many of the Opposition saw in the negotiations then being carried on with the British by individuals and trade associations a means of thwarting the government's plans and policies. The Speech from the Throne at the opening of the 1916 session had introduced the proposal that it be made a criminal offense for a Swedish subject to make a commercial agreement with a foreign power. Although everyone must have known that the Swedish government wished chiefly to escape the pressures exerted by the Allies on Swedish trade, it would seem that certain speakers in the Riksdag took great pleasure in pointing out the arrangements that had been made with Germany. Thus Persson of Norrköping spoke of an agreement made in the first half of July 1915 between a German consortium of banks and a newly established company, Centralbanksgruppen Emissionbolag, back of which stood the Sveriges Privata Centralbank, the Aktiebolag Göteborgs Bank, the Skandinaviska Kreditaktiebolag, and A/B Stockholms Handelsbank, on the basis of which a loan of 40 million kronor was arranged for Germany. He went on to say that although the exchange had stood at 78 kronor to 100 marks, after the loan the price rose to 80 kronor. Moreover, the Emmission A/B secured licenses to import certain German goods—3 million kilos of mineral dyes, 600,000 kilos of aniline dyes, as well as potash, coal, and coke, but before Swedish purchasers could secure these goods they had to pay 4 per cent of the invoice value to the Swedish consortium as a sort of commission fee, as well as sign guarantee forms promising home consumption and recognizing the right of the Emission A/B to name a third person to inspect the books of the importer. The final blow was that prices were quoted in marks, but were to be paid for in Swedish money at the exchange rate of 89 kronor to 100 marks. It is interesting to see that the Germans had resorted to British methods and had even developed a few refinements of their own!

The answer of the government to all these criticisms was that, in comparison with Denmark and Norway, Sweden was well off. Hammarskjöld reaffirmed the desire of the government to preserve peace, and promised to work toward that end, but he went on to say, "although we must reckon with the eventuality that this is no longer possible for Sweden in spite of all our endeavours ... [we] will, on this principle work with the Riksdag."

On the other hand, the pressure exerted by British bunker controls was being felt in Sweden, and when conversations were undertaken by Swedish firms concerning the release of cargoes held in British ports, it was found that the British demanded not only the usual guarantees against re-exportation of these goods, but also suitable bank guarantees against the re-exportation of the products made from these goods.[2]

As might have been expected, the prospect of having the Allies control trade by means of private agreements with Swedish subjects was not pleasing to Hammarskjöld, and his reply was not long in coming. It took the form of a measure, which became law on April 17, 1916, entitled: Law Governing Commerce in Wartime, commonly known as the War Trade Law.[3] The cabinet had authorized the minister of justice as early as December 11, 1915, to put experts in his department to work drafting a law that would prevent prejudicial economic agreements between private persons and foreign powers. Algot Bagge, Professor Folke P. Wetten, and Sven Brisman worked on this bill.[4] Their chief objective was to rule out those agreements that seemed dangerous to Swedish independence as a sovereign state, and at the same time to make possible government supervision of such agreements as were necessary for the economic existence of the country. Thus it was made illegal for Swedish subjects in time of war or in a period of danger of war to enter into an economic agreement with a foreign power that would limit freedom of import to or export from Sweden, or which would serve the interests of a foreign power, without first securing the approval of the Swedish government. Any agreement not so approved was declared null and void, but, on the other hand, once an accord was validated any violation of it was a criminal offense that subjected the individual or company to heavy fine or imprisonment. Penalties were also imposed on those who, by giving commercial information, served the interests of a foreign power. In a Royal Order of April 25, 1916, the State Commerce Commission (Statens Handelskommission), established on June 8, 1915, was named as the proper authority to execute the new law,[5] while on August 4, 1916, one special committee was established to deal with guarantees concerning imports, and another to deal with licensing goods in the compensation trade with Germany and Great Britain.[6]

When this War Trade Law was discussed in the Second Chamber, Palmstierna professed to see in it an attempt on the part of the government to secure powers in blanko from the Riksdag, which would have difficulty in granting them without knowing the basis on which the government would carry out its trade policy. He cited Hammarskjöld's statement that the bill was "in the state's interest," which presumably meant that the government should regulate trade with foreign powers. Many, Palmstierna said, would cling to the principle of international law that trade with the subjects of a foreign power should remain free. How clever it was of Palmstierna to cite international law in an argument over Hammarskjöld's policy! Palmstierna also questioned the advisability of declaring invalid private agreements, such as the Cotton Agreement with England, the one establishing the relations of A/B Transito with England and Russia, the agreement of the Privata Centralbanksgruppen with Germany, and those made with Swedish shipowners. What would happen, he asked, if the foreign state did not recognize such a decree of the Swedish courts? In any case, Palmstierna believed that it would be better in the future for the government to make the agreements directly rather than to have it validate private accords. Surely he must have known that this idea was contrary to everything Hammarskjöld stood for.[7]

Other measures had already been taken by the Swedish government to strengthen its hand in dealing with tonnage problems. It had been found that large numbers of ships of Swedish registry had been transferred to foreign flags, so that in 1915 some 37 steamships, 44 motor ships, and 70 sailing ships had been lost from Swedish registry, while many others had been time chartered for various periods to foreigners. To control this situation in the future a law was passed on March 6, 1916, providing that no ship of more than 20 tons could be transferred to a foreigner, and no time charter for longer than six months would be valid except with the government's consent; violation made the person liable to a fine up to 20,000 kronor or imprisonment up to one year.[8] Certain loopholes in this regulation were closed by a new law of July 8, 1916, which also made it illegal for Swedish ships over 200 tons to ply in trades between foreign ports or for Swedish ships to be placed under control of a foreigner except with the government's consent.[9]

These acts taken together certainly made it more difficult for Swedish importers and shipowners to effect the kind of accommodation that was necessary to secure goods through the Allied blockade. This was particularly true because the guarantees, drawn up by the State Commerce Commission, to be signed by Swedish importers did not contain a clause against the exportation of *products* made from imported goods.[10] Although the British government did not consider these acts directly offensive to it, nonetheless it was clear that they constituted a new weapon in negotiation if the Swedes chose to use them as such.

It was probably no accident that the middle months of 1916 saw a stiffening in British blockade measures that affected Swedish trade. For one thing, there was a sharp increase in detentions in British ports of cargoes insured by the Swedish State Insurance Commission, from a total value of 32 million kronor in mid-1916 to nearly 60 million kronor at the end of that year.[11] Even so, this figure included only a part of the Swedish cargoes that were affected, for many were not insured by the Commission, and many other cargoes had been unloaded and sold in British ports on the order of their owners rather than run further risk of natural deterioration in their quality or the risk of condemnation by a prize court. The result was that in 1916 Sweden's normal importations of food and forage were reduced by 20 per cent, meat and meat products by 77 per cent, metals and ores by 85 per cent, animal and vegetable oils by 23 per cent, and wool and woolen manufactures by 38 per cent.[12]

At the time that the Swedish War Trade Law was passed, negotiations had been in progress for some months between the Swedish Cotton Spinners Association and the British government. It was the hope of both parties that arrangements could be made for a regular importation of 10,000 bales of cotton a month on condition that the Association guarantee its consumption within Sweden and that it should be distributed by the Association to the Swedish mills and other consumers in proportion to their requirements. In other words, they took up the negotiations where they had been left in June 1915, when the provisional agreement concerning cotton cargoes detained in Great Britain had been reached. During the early months of 1916 this provisional agreement had been extended, but once the War Trade Law was passed, these negotiations were suspended until the position of Sweden became clarified. Apparently the Commerce Commission did agree to the Association's giving the guarantees demanded by the British, for on August 9, 1916, an agreement providing for monthly consignments up to 9,000 bales was signed.[13]

In the meantime other private agreements affecting Swedish trade were signed. On April 28, 1916, an accord was reached with the International Harvester Company of Chicago concerning its exportation of agricultural machinery to its Swedish branch at Norrköping.[14] International Harvester agreed not to sell its own or any similar machines, or their parts, or their products, in any way that would profit directly or indirectly the government, or any resident, of a state at war with Great Britain. The company agreed to secure from all purchasers guarantees, whose texts were appended, against re-exportation of these goods. If there was any violation of these guarantees, the company bound itself to cease other supplies to such persons until the end of the war, and even the suspicion of such violation was to be communicated to the British legation in Stockholm. Furthermore, the British were given the right to name an agent to inspect the books of the company. It is of some interest that the British provided for the exportation of agricultural machinery to Russia, the amount to be indicated by the British for each agricultural season. The facilities of the A/B Transito were to be used in sending these goods. The articles dealing with the ration of machinery to be imported for Swedish use were set for the period ending July 31, 1916; presumably supplementary arrangements would be made to cover later periods. It was agreed that if at any time the Swedish government prevented the application of any clause of the agreement, the company would at once consult with the British government. Similar agreements were signed at the same time to cover the company's trade in Norway and Denmark, with the provision that the violation of any one of these agreements would invalidate all of them.

In August a whole series of agreements was signed concerning the importation of oils and lubricants into Sweden, some of these replacing accords reached in October and December 1915. Thus one was concluded with M. M. Olsen and Company on August 4, 1916; one with the Skandinavisk-

Amerikansk Petroleum A/B on August 5; one with the Vacuum Oil Company on August 5; and finally an arrangement concerning these agreements, with the Swedish government on August 7. The total effect was to permit the importation of 165,000 barrels of oil for the year, not exceeding 42,000 in any quarter, under a guarantee of the domestic consumption of these goods and their products.[15]

Another arrangement was made on August 3, 1916, with the American Corn Products Refining Company concerning its Scandinavian trade, so that all of its shipments were to be covered by letters of assurance. However, although as a part of the agreement, detained cargoes claimed by the company were released, those consigned by it to certain Swedish firms were excepted.[16]

These agreements were admittedly of relatively minor importance so far as the general issues were concerned, and new problems continued to arise. There are indications in the papers of the French Comité de Restriction that problems had been encountered in the compensation trade. The Swedes had prohibited wood pulp exportations on January 18, 1916,[17] with the intention of using their willingness to grant licenses in derogation of the embargo as a bargaining weapon, and in retaliation the French had stopped all exports of fats and oils to Sweden. In March 1916 a similar suspension took place in French exports of copper and lead in an attempt to force Sweden to limit her imports to normal needs, but apparently this move was without success.[18]

From the Allied point of view the difficulties over consignment of goods to governmental agencies in Sweden were more serious. In August 1914 the Swedish government had set up a Royal Food Commission (Livsmedelskommission) in order to insure a proper domestic supply of certain foods, and early in 1915 this body became the consignee for cereals, fats for the manufacture of margarine, soap, petrol, and benzine.[19] Such cargoes had been examined en route by the British naval authorities and had been allowed to proceed, but in mid-May 1916 Britain made a test case when it seized the Liguria, carrying a cargo of cottonseed oil, oleaginous seeds, and lard. The cargo represented a total of 2,080 tons of fats; already in that quarter 1,100 tons had been imported by Sweden—and 1,700 tons was regarded as a normal quarterly ration.[20] The British government maintained that it had no way of knowing who the consumers of these goods would be, and it could release the cargo only when such information was forthcoming, or when the Food Commission gave suitable guarantees against the re-exportation of the goods in any form. This the Swedish government refused to do, maintaining that as an independent government it could give no such promises to another state.

In the end, after long correspondence extending from May through mid-July, the Swedish government gave sufficient information on this particular cargo to satisfy the British, and the ship was released. The British made it clear that they wanted more specific arrangements for the future, to include establishment of a ration for oilseeds, vegetable oils and fats, and mineral oils and fats; effective guarantees against exportation from Sweden of imported articles and products manufactured from them; communication to the British government of the names of the consignees of goods, with the British having the right to forbid goods reaching persons on the black list; and approval by the Swedish State Commerce Commission of a declaration covering these goods.[21]

One slight hope for a bettering of trade relations with Sweden was achieved when an agreement was reached in Petrograd on July 15, 1916, concerning transit trade to Russia. Signed by General P. H. E. Brandstrom, the Swedish minister, and Sergei Sazonov, the accord provided for the construction of certain railway bridges and stations near the Swedish-Finnish frontier at Haparanda and Lihakajoki. Negotiations had been begun in a conference at Stockholm, April 4–15, 1915, and a commission of engineers had worked on the spot and then drafted a report in Helsingfors on December 1, 1915. However, the hope was short-lived, for in November 1916 the Swedes sharpened their regulations concerning the movement of goods across the Finnish frontier; additions to the number of customs officials were constantly made in this area, in order to hinder evasions.[22]

Perhaps with the idea of convincing the Swedes that it was better to reach a general agreement than to continue their existing policy and suffer, the British government on August 18, 1916, issued a general embargo on all goods destined to Swedish ports.[23] Licenses for exportations of goods of British origin would be granted only if guarantees against the exportation of these goods and their products were attested to before the State Commerce Commission and legalized by a British consular officer in Sweden. The Swedish government had little choice but to accept these conditions, although it still refused to apply the "products clause" to goods imported from or through neutral countries. Oddly enough, it agreed to regard goods imported via Denmark as being direct British imports so far as this matter was concerned. This was probably because most of the goods in question would have been carried by Danish shipping companies that had made agreements with the British to release cargoes only to persons, approved by the British, who would give guarantees against re-exportation of the goods or their products. Many such cargoes bound for Sweden had been held in Copenhagen warehouses when these guarantees were not forthcoming. One other concession was made when Kurt Wallenberg, the Swedish foreign minister, agreed on October 9, 1916, that cereals imported in the name of the Royal Food Commission would not be re-exported.[24]

But these half measures were by no means sufficient either to satisfy the British and their allies or to facilitate enough trade to Sweden. To make the latter's position even worse the British on September 10 absolutely prohibited (without the possibility of trading under a license) the exportation to Sweden of a whole list of goods, including antimony, raw materials for margarine, coffee, tea, cocoa, dried fruit, cork, bark, leather, and so forth. None of these goods, whether of British origin or those merely transited through the United Kingdom, reached Sweden, and manufacturing was, of course, severely hampered where it was not completely stopped, as in the instance of margarine.[25]

It was this situation that compelled the Swedish government to undertake more general negotiations with Great Britain; very soon, at the request of the British, the French and Italian representatives were associated in the conversations.[26] The Swedish delegation, consisting of J. Hellner, E. Frissell, Marcus Wallenberg, and C. G. Westman, with C. L. Schönmyer as secretary, left for London on October 31. Later John Fredholm and Dr. Moritz Marcus, secretary of the Royal Food Commission, were added to the delegation.

The Swedes reluctantly accepted the principle of rationing. They knew that the British had recently tightened up on the rations of grain and fodder permitted to other neutrals, in the hope of reducing the supply of meat and dairy products going to Germany, and the Swedes expected that similar demands would be made of them. The British soon showed that they were equally interested in the establishment of a guaranteeing body, set up as a commercial corporation, so that the Swedish government would no longer be a general consignee for the many kinds of goods that were not used for official purposes. Although little is known directly about the give and take in these negotiations, there are good indications of the attitude of the Swedish press to them.

From the outset the Conservative press foretold the failure of the negotiations with England, and undertook to warn of the danger of German reprisals on Swedish trade if any arrangements were made. It continued to maintain that Sweden could, with German help, be independent of the Entente and the blockade, a conclusion that most Swedes refused to accept. In fact, the answer of the *Stockholms Tidningen* was indicative of another body of opinion:

> According to Germany's view, real neutrality consists in contributing to Germany's supplies, even though it be at the expense of what is wanted for ourselves. By not submitting willingly, we shall not only lose the exchange of goods that Germany has at her disposal, but shall expose ourselves to the same kind of reprisals that are being visited on Norway, whose real crime seems not to be the submarine regulations [issued by the Norwegian government on October 13, 1916, excluding submarines from Norwegian territorial waters], but her unwillingness to supply Germany with herring. That is why the Norwegian mercantile fleet is treated as though it belonged to an enemy Power, for the punishment of Norway, and as a warning to Sweden.[27]

Aftonbladet, which was regarded by the *Dagens Nyheter* as but an echo of the Wilhelmstrasse Press, in spite of its Liberal tradition, warned against accepting the establishment of any trust as a general consigning agent, and insisted that Sweden must demand the abolition of black lists, the right to refuse transit of war materials, and freedom to continue to export her own produce to Germany. If, this paper went on, it was a question of breaking with Germany or England, the matter would be decided by the fact that Sweden's Baltic coast was dominated strategically and economically by Germany, and by the fact that "Britannia does not rule the waves." By mid-November the London correspondent of Nya Dagligt Allehanda reported that in British governmental circles there was a genuine wish for an agreement and that it was a matter of indifference whether a trust was formed or whether imported goods were distributed by separate companies, particularly since the agreement with the Cotton Spinners was generally regarded as working well.[28] There were, on the other hand, many rumors that an important difference of opinion existed in the Swedish cabinet over these negotiations. It was reported that during a recent illness of Hammarskjöld some members of the cabinet had offered further concessions to the British minister, a rumor that was later denied officially. However, the printing of the report was doubtless aimed against Kurt Wallenberg, the foreign minister, whose brother Marcus, director of the Stockholms Enskilda Bank, was a member of the Swedish delegation then in London. The latter had already been the target of attack by the pro-German press. In early December, Aftonbladet and Nya Dagligt Allehanda, the leaders of this section of the press, carried the news that the owners of Norwegian pyrites mines had formed a trust, and had agreed to sell part of their surplus to Sweden at a price six times the prewar level, and the rest to England, presumably at a lower price. These papers went on to say that "certain Swedish financiers" were interested in the Norwegian trust and that the contracts provided that part of the by-products from the pyrites was to be returned to copper works in Norway owned by a company in which Marcus Wallenberg and one Nachmanson, whose brother was also a director of the Enskilda Bank, were directors. The implication was that Marcus Wallenberg was too much involved in commercial transactions in which the British had some controls to be a fit representative of Swedish interests.[29]

Certainly the Swedish public could not have looked to the future with much confidence when the pro-German Stockholms Dagblad reported on December 21 and 22 that Germany intended to raise the price of coal on January 1 by amounts varying from 8.50 kronor to 16.50 kronor per ton. The figures for coal imports for the first ten months of 1916 showed that Sweden had secured 4,069,291 tons from Germany and 1,369,871 tons from England. Even Stockholms Dagblad asserted that Germany was taking advantage of the fact that it was known that England could not supply the deficiencies if German exports were to cease, and had by the price increase sought to equalize the recent fall in the exchange rate for marks.[30]

When the Riksdag opened its new session for 1917 the debate on the budget, begun on January 22, was singularly unrevealing so far as negotiations with England were concerned, for the matter was referred to only obliquely.[31] Most of the debate was given over to the old criticisms of the Hammarskjöld government: (1) its failure to deal with price controls, and speculators and middlemen who made large profits, (2) the size of the expenditures of special commissions, (3) its failure to limit the Activists, and (4) above all its continued secrecy in dealing with foreign affairs. Although a Secret Committee of Riksdag members had been established to consult with the cabinet on foreign policy, it was so restricted in its freedom that Eden, one of its members, complained that not much about its work could be revealed to the Riksdag, and, in any case, that it had no real influence on the formulation of policy.[32] Ryden, a Social Democrat, complained that too many documents on military affairs were marked "confidential" and that the Riksdag did not have sufficient information to exercise its constitutional authority over the budget. In contrast with the position of the Danish and Norwegian parliamentary bodies, and even in contrast with the Russian Duma, he said, "the Swedish Riksdag finds itself in the role of unimportant marionettes." The only matter related to the blockade was the revelation by Palmstierna that the Swedish agricultural consul in London had informed him that the British had tried to make a bargain providing for the exportation of 500 tons of fodder per month in return for Swedish exports to England of all food that Sweden did not need for itself, or at least a proportionate share of this surplus. Palmstierna charged that the Swedish government hadn't troubled to accept this arrangement because the German Zentraleinkaufsgesellschaft had established an office in Sweden and offered greater profits to Swedish exporters. He asserted that it was not until December 1916 that the Swedish Ministry of Agriculture had seen the error of its policy.

For all that, there was not such an acrimonious tone in these criticisms as in those of the preceding year, and certainly there was no indication that the days of the Hammarskjöld government were numbered. On the other hand, if the Socialists in the Riksdag remained fairly circumspect, the Socialist press now campaigned more openly for Hammarskjöld's resignation, arguing that he did not understand the role of a constitutional minister and that he played with the Riksdag as the Russian government played with the Duma.[33] The chief difficulty was that the Socialists did not have a majority in the Riksdag, and—even worse—the Young Socialists were threatening to secede from the party. On the whole it was believed that this breach would be healed because the majority socialists did control the trade unions. Nor were Socialist-Liberal relations any better. *Dagens Nyheter*, therefore, seemed to waver between advocating a Liberal-Socialist cabinet on party lines and a coalition government, without Hammarskjöld, that would include some of the Conservatives.

It is against this domestic situation that the Anglo-Swedish negotiations must be viewed. When an agreement was drafted on February 2, 1917, the rationing system and all it implied were admitted; the "products clause" applied to all goods, whatever their origin, but the supervision of imported goods was to be in the hands of several trade associations; governmental departments could continue to act as consignees. So far as goods in transit to Russia were concerned, the Swedes agreed that not less than 3,000 tons a week should be carried by the Swedish railways to Haparanda, winter and summer, and an equal amount should be carried on other lines so long as the ports in the Gulf of Bothnia were open to navigation.[34] Sweden also agreed to supply Great Britain with certain amounts of iron, steel, ball-bearings (which were essential to the Allied war effort), pit props, and perchlorate of ammonia, and the British admitted that Sweden must be able to export small amounts of tin, nickel, aluminum, and rubber to Germany in exchange for manufactured goods containing equal amounts of these raw materials. The negotiations over the exact rations, which were the chief concern of Marcus Wallenberg and Kurt Harwood, were long and involved, but in the end a comprehensive list was established. Two items were left for future negotiations: coal, and cereals, which the British hoped to tie to arrangements for purchasing Swedish dairy products. As a matter of fact these omissions were so serious, in view of Sweden's urgent need for grain, that the Swedish government felt in no immediate hurry to sign the agreement.

While the draft agreement was under consideration new problems arose and partial solutions for some old ones were found.[35] Thus there was trouble over the detention of cargoes of nitrates which were released only in mid-March. Negotiations with Russia over the compensation trade led to an agreement on February 14, 1917, in which the rationing principle was applied. However, events outside these negotiations moved more quickly: the German declaration of unrestricted submarine warfare and the fall of the Russian monarchy upset the calculations of everyone. Sweden itself passed through a crisis when Hammarskjöld's cabinet resigned on an army budget issue on March 4, 1917.[36]

There was no denying that the refusal of the government to institute the drastic controls that the Allies desired had contributed to the depletion of goods in the Swedish market, and that many of Sweden's own products had been attracted by the higher prices paid in Germany. Swedish prices had risen and the British became even more suspicious of permitting importations of foodstuffs from overseas. Thus, as Kurt Bergendal points out in his study of Swedish economy, regular Swedish business suffered and wartime profiteers went on profiteering.[37]

Once the United States entered the war neither the Swedes nor the British wanted to complete an agreement which had been drafted under quite different circumstances, and indeed it seems simply to have been dropped by tacit consent. So again, although Swedish imports were regulated by forcible means—and promised to be more so in the future, there was no general agreement covering Sweden's overseas trade, a condition which the new Swedish government soon tried to remedy.

NEGOTIATIONS WITH NORWEGIAN
TRADE ASSOCIATIONS

The failure to reach a general agreement with the Norwegian government in 1915 had led the British, as we have seen, to undertake negotiations with many Norwegian trade associations. British blockade policy therefore had as one of its chief aims in 1916 the extension of these so-called branch agreements already reached and the conclusion of new ones with other groups. The major negotiations were with a variety of manufacturers associations, in which the Norwegian government played only an incidental role, except in the case of the regulation of the Norwegian copper trade.

One of the most important series of negotiations undertaken early in 1916 dealt with the importation of fats. The British had regarded their agreement with O. Mustad and Son, the largest Norwegian margarine manufacturer, reached on September 24, 1915,[38] as only a beginning. The British Board of Trade had recently made an analysis of Norwegian imports of edible oils and fats and of the number and capacity of margarine factories in Norway. It discovered that on the basis of production in 1911–1913 from certain amounts of imported raw materials, the Norwegians had imported enough in 1914 to produce 27,000 tons of margarine, whereas only 24,800 tons actually had been manufactured, and in 1915 the discrepancy was even greater: 47,500 tons estimated as against some 30,000 to 37,000 tons. The British therefore concluded that raw materials equivalent to some 10,000 tons of margarine had been re-exported from Norway.[39] This knowledge added new impetus to the negotiations and a whole series of accords was signed, one on March 11 with the margarine manufacturers of Stavanger, Kristiansand, and Haugesund; another with those of Trondheim, Melbo, and Tromso; with those of Bergen, Kristiansund, and Ålesund; and on March 28 with those of Christiania, Drammen, Tönsberg and Fredrikshald (Halden).[40] They all followed the same pattern including promises against re-exportation of raw materials or their products, acceptance of rationing, and so forth. Early in November 1916, simultaneously with the opening of negotiations with other wholesale food associations, the British drew up a new agreement with the margarine manufacturers that would revise the rations set for four associations. Strangely enough the rations were to be increased by 2,805 tons, but the associations were to give greater co-operation in withholding stocks in Norway from any manufacturers to whom the British refused deliveries.[41]

Controls over lubricating oils were established in an agreement reached by Sir Eyre Crowe with representatives of the Oil Branch of the Union of Machinery Wholesalers (Oliegruppen av Maskingrosisternes Forening) on

March 18, 1916.[42] One provision of some interest, since the British soon sought to include it in agreements with other Norwegians, was that in which admission to membership in the association was to be denied to any person, firm, or company operated or owned by any person who was or had been a subject of a country at war with Great Britain or its allies; old members who fell into that category were to be denied the right to import goods. No lubricating oils of British origin were to be provided for ships that carried goods to Germany, or to any factory that sold goods to Germany; current contracts with any such firm or person whose name was sent to the Association by the British were to be cancelled. Within a short time the Norwegian government indicated that this agreement was too far-reaching, and a note registering certain "observations" was sent by Ihlen to the British legation on April 13. This led to discussions in Christiania on May 16 between Scheel and Einar Maseng for the Norwegian government and Clive Cuthbertson and Paus for the British. These came to naught, but eventually the British did retract their demand for the breaking of current contracts, and Norwegian firms owned by German subjects were not forbidden to buy imported oils. Even so the Norwegian Foreign Ministry refused to sanction the agreement, although it permitted imports to take place under its terms while the negotiations continued.

As Keilhau points out, it was these negotiations that showed the dangers of permitting private individuals or trade associations to come to arrangements with foreign governments. Thus the Foreign Ministry sent a warning to the food associations on May 12, 1916, that any agreements then being negotiated must be settled in co-operation with the government. The letter called attention to the Swedish War Trade Law and said that a similar one might be passed in Norway; in the meantime the government trusted to the loyalty of the associations not to evade the proposed statutory provisions.[43] On May 23 a circular was sent from the Finance Department to the customs authorities calling attention to the fact that action in the matter of the re-exportation of goods must follow closely the text of the consignment documents unless permission for a change was given by the competent department; agreements made by the importers or the steamship company with foreign authorities which laid down a different procedure, such as returning the goods to a country through which they had passed on their way to Norway, were not to be accepted in lieu of such authorization.[44] When representatives of the Foreign Ministry were in London in June 1916 the opportunity was taken to explain fully the Norwegian attitude on these branch agreements to their own legation. The government felt that it would not be enough for the British simply to advise the association in question that a particular firm could not trade under the agreement, but they must provide specific reasons. Moreover, no new conditions were to be introduced regulating trade with Sweden and Denmark; there must be no retroactive provisions concerning goods imported before the agreement went into operation; there must be no demand that ships carrying imports should call at a British port for search; both parties were to be on an equal footing in their ability to suspend the accord; and so on.[45]

On the other hand the Norwegian government did indirectly comply with British wishes when it introduced a bill in the Storting to extend the law of June 11, 1915, concerning the violation of guarantees given to cover imports and exports. Originally the law was intended to secure the execution of Norwegian embargoes, but for some time the British had asked that duplicate copies of the guarantees given by importers to their associations should be sent to the Norwegian Finance Department so that legally a violation of the branch agreements must be construed to constitute a violation of the Norwegian law. When the new bill was passed on June 23, 1916, its penalties applied to violations of declarations given to any private institution or association which was authorized by the Department to receive such declarations.[46]

Once this matter was cleared up, the British were more anxious than ever to complete agreements with a number of other trade associations. With the full knowledge of the Norwegian legation in London, negotiations were carried on with the paper manufacturers, the oil and paint merchants, and the soap manufacturers. The Norwegian government on July 8 asked the British to bear in mind that the accords would be judged in relation to the defense of Norway's rights, and certainly the drafts which the Norwegians took home were in many respects more pleasing to them than the agreement on lubricating oil had been.[47] Two conditions were still not acceptable to the Norwegian government: that Norway should grant no licenses in derogation of its own embargoes on goods covered by the agreements, and that ships carrying these goods should call at a British port. Some compromises were made and the first of this new series of agreements was signed in Christiania on September 18, 1916, with the Association of Norwegian Paper Manufacturers and the Association of Norwegian Pulp Manufacturers.[48] Although the agreement specifically covered all importations of materials used in paper manufacturing, it really controlled the disposition of all paper products manufactured by the Associations even though most of the raw materials were of domestic origin. It provided that goods consigned from overseas or from Great Britain should be carried only on lines that had a regular service between the country of origin and Norway; presumably the British could expect to secure their guarantees concerning call at a British port directly from these shipowners. The usual promises about re-exportation were given, it being stipulated that exports to Sweden could be made only when the receiver gave a guarantee that was legal in Sweden, while those to Denmark were to be consigned to the Danish Merchant Guild. Any importations from the Netherlands were to be handled through the N.O.T. It is interesting to note that in spite of Norwegian governmental protests the accord was to apply to all stocks on hand, and also all imports in the future were to be limited to the average annual imports made by each member in 1911, 1912, and 1913. British interference with Norwegian trade was made more certain when the agreement reserved to the British the right to report to the appropriate association at any time the names of persons or companies to whom the Association ought not to permit the advantages of the agreement, and to whom no member could sell paper or pulp. The British did agree to notify the Association in strict confidence the reasons for such action unless the person or firm in question was already on the British black list. If, on the other hand, the association had any suspicion that one of its members was violating the guarantees, it was to inform the British government immediately, begin an investigation, and, in the meantime, hold under its control all consignments to that member. If the suspicion was proved, no further facilities were to be given by the Association and its other members were to be informed that they must have no dealings with the backsliding member. At all times the British had the right to have an appropriate person of Norwegian nationality examine the books of the Association, and, on demand, the Association would undertake a similar check of the books of its members, the accountant in either case to be agreed upon by the British legation and the Association.

On September 25, 1916, a very similar agreement was concluded by the Norwegian Association of Oil and Paint Merchants concerning importations of paraffin wax, terebenthine, varnish, linseed oil, resin, animal and vegetable fats and oils, borax, soda compounds, and so forth.[49] Just as in the accord with the lubricating oil dealers, it was agreed that the Association would accept as new members any person or company established in Norway and engaged in the paint trade, but no facilities would be given to any person or firm controlled by anyone who was a subject of a state at war with Great Britain or her allies. In addition it was specifically provided that the Association could demand as a surety a deposit equal to the total value of any consignment, calculated on the highest price in any European market, before delivering the consignment. The appended guarantee form to be signed by members of the Association provided, in case of its violation, for a fine of double the value of the goods involved. In fixing the rations for quarterly periods, it was agreed to assume that no exportations of these materials, whether of Norwegian origin or not, would be permitted, and if such exportations did take place the ration would be correspondingly reduced.

To increase the effectiveness of this agreement the most important match manufacturers in Norway (the Nitedals Match Company of Christiania, Bryn and Halden of Christiania, Mauritzens Sons of Stavanger, and the Helios Manufacturing Company of Skien) all acceded to this agreement just four days later, and indeed became members of the Paint Merchants Association.[50]

Still another agreement growing out of these negotiations was signed on October 5, 1916, with the Norwegian Association of Soap Manufacturers,[51] and on the same day a supplement to the one made with the Lilleborg Company and the Christiania Steam-Oil Mill Company on September 24, 1915, was also concluded.[52] As in the other agreements, detailed information was to be given to the British government concerning the stocks of oils, resin, and the like on hand, and the amounts under contract for importation in the year 1916, with the understanding that these both should be deducted from the rations set in an annex to the main accord. To both of these agreements was appended a letter from Ihlen to Findlay (undated in the Vincennes file) acknowledging receipt of the agreement and registering the approval of the Norwegian government, with the further statement that violations of the engagements given to the Association or its members would be punishable under the law of June 23, 1916.

However, if the Norwegian government was willing to accept these agreements, it was not so accommodating in the matter of accords that covered grain, flour, meat, and so on that were arranged by the British with the wholesale provision merchants, the wholesale grocers, the importers of grain and flour, and the importers of forage.[53] These agreements, all drafted on November 7 and 8, as well as an agreement with the Importers of Cycle Tires, drafted on December 16, 1916, and one drafted in January 1917 (undated at Vincennes) with the Chocolate Manufacturers, were all under discussion when difficulties arose between Norway and Britain over the execution of the fish and copper agreements. The result was that these new accords were never signed, although the restrictions included in them were apparently applied anyway, the British using the restrictions as a means of pressure in the other negotiations.[54]

At the same time that the British negotiated with these associations, they also undertook new conversations with the Norwegian government concerning foodstuffs consigned to the State Food Commission. On November 7 an exchange of notes took place between Sir Eyre Crowe and Harald Pedersen, director of the Food Commission, in which the British permitted such consignments, charging them against the rations agreed upon in the accords with the various food associations.[55] It was left to the Norwegian government to make its own arrangements with the associations on the division of the ration.[56] The Commission agreed that none of the articles it imported would be exported from Norway in any form whatever, and that it would demand a similar guarantee from any retail merchant to whom it distributed these goods. Just as in the case of the food associations, the Commission was obligated to furnish information to the British every three months on the stocks it held. The agreement also bound the Commission to instruct its shippers in the United States to apply for letters of assurance, thereby enabling the British to facilitate regular importations by the Commission.

On December 22, 1916, the Norwegian government also agreed to publish an ordinance prohibiting the use of jute or cotton in packing goods that were to be exported to countries at war with Great Britain, and permitting their use in packing goods destined to Sweden, Denmark, the Netherlands,

Spain, and overseas countries only if the exporter gave a declaration to the Norwegian Customs that the shipment had been approved by a British consular agent in Norway and that no jute produced in the British Empire would be used for the profit of an enemy country.[57] This made it possible for the British to control many Norwegian exports where other agreements did not necessarily apply.

The last series of branch agreements concluded early in 1917 by the British were with various canners associations—those of Kopervik-Haugesund, Stavanger, Bergen, and the North of Norway on January 16; those of Christiania on January 17; and of Trondheim on January 18.[58] With the exception of the Stavanger group,[59] these associations were set up particularly to undertake these controls. Under the accords, which were chiefly supplemental to the Fish Agreement (since fish was the chief article preserved in Norwegian canneries) the use of tin, vegetable oils, and tomato pulp was regulated for the industry as a whole; the unions agreed to admit other canneries that applied for membership provided they were not owned by enemy subjects. Milk canners were also, as a practical matter, required to seek such membership if they were to receive a supply of tin, although an extra ration was to be arranged for them. Canned milk thus processed was to be used only for Norwegian consumption or for export to Great Britain or her allies. The general provisions of the agreements followed the pattern of earlier branch agreements.

So far as is known from available sources these agreements worked without too many difficulties prior to the intervention of the United States in the war. From the Allied point of view it was a source of satisfaction that in January and February 1917 the French government, on the recommendation of the Comité de Restriction adhered to almost all of the British-Norwegian agreements.[60] It is true that temporarily some trouble was encountered by the Wholesale Provision Merchants in importing meat from the United States because the Food Commission had already contracted for sufficient quantities from British-owned packing houses in the Argentine to fill the Norwegian ration for the next six months, but in April 1917 the British did permit the Association to make some contracts with the Chicago packers.[61] It was inevitable that all of those merchants and importers who lived near Christiania should be in a better position to deal with British agents and that those farther away should suffer inconveniences. It was therefore soon clear that central offices for most of these associations were being established in the capital, and thus the organization of the entire commercial and industrial life of the country went in the direction of cartelization.[62] This whole development, of course, could not be kept secret, and, indeed, Ihlen gave considerable information about the trade controls exercised under these agreements in the Storting debate on the Speech from the Throne on February 21, 1917. In his remarks he indicated that the Finance Department had some right to check the guarantees given to the British.[63]

THE NORWEGIAN COPPER AGREEMENT

It has been pointed out in Chapter XI that the attempts of the Norwegian government to deal directly with the British in settling problems connected with the fishing industry had not been entirely happy. The negotiations concerning Norwegian copper were no better.

Since the late spring of 1915 both the British and French governments had been concerned with the continuation of the supply of Norwegian copper pyrites to Germany. The British had already secured wide controls over American copper exports to northern Europe, and since the Norwegians imported considerable amounts of certain types of copper, chiefly for electrical uses, at least a beginning had been made in preventing the exportation of manufactured copper goods from Norway.[64] But the disposition of copper produced in Norwegian mines was another matter.

So far as available documents show, it was the French Comité de Restriction that first began to study the possibility of the purchase of Norwegian pyrites, its interest arising not only from the copper involved but also because of their sulfur content, which could be used in the manufacture of sulfuric acid, a component of munitions. On April 30, 1915, the Comité recommended to the Ministry of War that its contractors should seek supplies of pyrites in the Norwegian market, as well as in Spain, while at the same time a similar recommendation was made concerning Sicilian sulfur.[65] It was reported at a meeting of May 21 that pourparlers with the Norwegian producers had already begun and that the British had been put au courant of the negotiations.[66] However, little progress was made until late in the year when an Anglo-French agreement was reached with the Norwegian Sulfuric Acid Company (December 14, 1915), in which the company agreed not to sell any of its products nor any raw materials employed in their manufacture to any country at war with England and France, or to Sweden, Denmark, or the Netherlands, unless, in the last instance, they were consigned to the N.O.T. Similar guarantees were to be secured from all the customers of the company, with the added assurance that a security double the value of the sale should be posted, and, in event of violation of the guarantee, forfeited. A similar agreement was signed with the Haaøen Fabriker in early January 1916.[67]

British negotiations with the Norwegian importers of copper began in March 1916 when representatives went to England in hope of securing a branch agreement. Before these conversations progressed very far the British tried to secure from the Norwegian government the imposition of an embargo on copper exports. The first definite proposal from the British, on April 7, was that an exchange agreement be reached which would balance exports of Norwegian copper, under license, against the imports of refined copper that Norway wished to make.[68] Moreover, it was suggested that when Norwegian exports were made to Germany they, too, were to be balanced by the return of manufactured goods with a comparable copper content. The exchange with Great Britain was to be arranged in a separate agreement with the Metal Consumers Union, on the understanding that the British would agree to purchase a minimum of 10,000 tons of copper annually from Norway. The Norwegians, as neutrals, were not pleased with the tone of Findlay's memorandum that charged them with responsibility for the "death and disablement" of British and allied soldiers because Norwegian copper was used in the manufacture of German shells. Ihlen's reply of April 13, 1916, maintained that there was no obligation upon a neutral state to forbid its citizens to trade with belligerents, and he went on to point out that, were such a rule applied, the exportation of many articles important for the British war effort would have to be stopped!

The negotiations continued through exchanges of notes. In May the Comité de Restriction heard a résumé of the situation by Denys Cochin in which he stated that the Norwegian government had asked for time to make arrangements with Germany, and that at most it had proposed to send but one third of its copper and pyrites exports to Britain.[69] Cochin believed that the Norwegians were trying to arouse American opinion against the British demands concerning copper, and therefore the Comité agreed to instruct the French representatives in Washington and Christiania to give all their support to the British position. Again the question of the purchase of Norwegian pyrites was raised. The fear was expressed that whatever amount the Allies might purchase, the Norwegians would simply increase their production in proportion, and thus the aim of preventing the supplying of Germany would not be attained.

Certainly the information that the French Comité collected indicated the grave importance of Norwegian pyrites in the production of German munitions. The total needs of the Germans and Austro-Hungarians were calculated at about two million tons of sulfuric acid a year, of which less than one quarter was produced at home. Since the Allies had very nearly cornered the pyrites market in Spain and Portugal, only Norway and Turkey were left as sources of supply to the Central Powers. The result was that Norway had increased her exports to Germany from 6,000 tons a month at the beginning of the war to some 22,000 tons a month by mid-1916. It was further calculated that in order really to deprive Germany of her Norwegian supplies, the British and French would have to be prepared to purchase some 450,000 tons a year.[70]

By June 21, 1916, Paul Cambon was able to report from London that the British had decided to concentrate on securing a Norwegian export prohibition on copper, copper ore, and pyrites containing copper, excepting exports to the other Scandinavian states up to a total of 8,000 tons a year and then only on condition that Norway receive back an equivalent amount of manufactured copper goods. Likewise the British would permit the importation of 8,000 tons of copper by Norway, with Britain having the right to buy a similar amount of Norwegian copper in the form of copper, copper ore, and pyrites containing copper.[71]

The lines of the agreement were well set by early August, and it only remained for the British to make purchasing arrangements with a specially formed Association for the Export of Norwegian Copper, which included all companies owning mines that produced pyrites containing more than 1 per cent of copper.[72] The British made arrangements for the immediate purchase of 200,000 tons of pyrites, and the French Munitions Service agreed to take one quarter of that amount. In the meantime producers of pyrites containing less than 1 per cent of copper were led to understand that they would remain outside the Association and outside the restrictions placed on Norway's exports of copper.

The final drafting of the agreement was of some importance. The original draft was drawn up by the Norwegian Foreign Office and sent in Norwegian to the British legation, where a translation was made into English. The final draft was sent by the Norwegians on August 28, and Findlay wrote a letter of acceptance on August 30, 1916.[73] On September 1 the Norwegian government issued an export prohibition in order to implement the agreement.[74] The Norwegian texts of both the agreement and the proclamation included the phrase "kobber, kobbermalm, kobberholdig svovlkis, kobberholdig kisavbrand," which the British translated as "copper, copper ore, pyrites containing copper, purple ore containing copper." The Norwegian interpretation usually given to "kobberholdig svovlkis" was that this meant cupreous pyrites or those containing more than 1 per cent of copper, while the British took it to mean pyrites containing any copper at all. And herein was to lie the difficulty. The chief provisions of the agreement have already been indicated above, but some details may well be mentioned. In the exchange trade between Britain and Norway 5 per cent was to be allowed for waste in the refining or manufacturing process, and, in view of the cessation of imports from America for the past several months as well as recent strikes in the Norwegian mines, an immediate release of 3,000 tons of copper to Norway was to be permitted. It was agreed that the price for British imports of Norwegian copper was to be arrived at by the Norwegian exporters and the British government. Moreover, and this later caused some trouble, until the exchange for this amount was completed, Britain was to have first call on all Norwegian pyrites. One other concession was made by the British: electrolytic copper up to 20 tons monthly might be exported to Sweden on an exchange basis, although, in general, exports to the Netherlands, Denmark, and Sweden were not to exceed the amount that had been imported by these countries in recent years for their domestic use, and in no case were they to exceed 10,000 tons of cupreous pyrites per year to Sweden, or 20,000 tons to Denmark. Trade with the Netherlands was to be on a slightly different basis, for in exchange for every ton of Norwegian pyrites consigned to the N.O.T. the British would allow free passage from Rotterdam to Norway of one ton of iron or steel for ship construction whenever these materials could not be obtained from Great Britain.

It was not long before there was sharp disagreement over the interpretation of this accord.[75] On September 8 a circular sent to the Norwegian customs authorities announced that pyrites containing less than 0.5 per cent of copper were freed from the embargo. The British government at once responded with a sharp note on September 21, to the effect that this represented "a breach not only of the letter but of the spirit of the agreement." The Norwegian government's reply maintained that the copper content of the noncupreous pyrites would be so small as to be of no importance as compensation. What the Norwegians seem never to have recognized was the fact that the Allies were almost as anxious to stop the supply of sulfur as that of copper to Germany. The British doubtless believed, on the other hand, that they had neatly achieved both of these aims in this one agreement. This part of the difficulty was settled when, on the basis of an agreement reached on October 11, the Norwegian government on October 30 extended its embargo to all pyrites.

A new phase of the disagreement arose almost at once over the methods used by the British in purchasing pyrites in the Norwegian market.[76] Here the British used as their agents the Rio Tinto Company, which was the chief competitor of the Norwegian companies, and whose largest holdings were in Spain. It was only after pressure from Ihlen that the Norwegian companies accepted, late in October, a contract at very low prices which they regarded as most unfair, for when the domestic price stood at 1.50 kroner per unit the Rio Tinto Company paid only 30 øre. Again, the Rio Tinto Company had originally agreed not to sell pyrites to Sweden so long as the Anglo-Norwegian agreement remained in effect, but this did not prevent their selling Norwegian pyrites on the Danish market at a much higher price than they had paid for them. Even Ihlen was disgusted with this turn of affairs, for all of his concessions to the British had apparently gone for nothing. The British soon raised new complaints that their "first call" on the Norwegian market had not been fulfilled when the Norwegian government permitted the Stordø mines, which produced pyrites containing much less than 0.5 per cent of copper, to renew their exports to Germany when the Germans were willing to ship back in exchange the comparably small amounts of copper involved. When these exports continued, the British, from December onward, after the formation of the Lloyd George cabinet, considered new means of pressure. One method, as we have already seen, was to withhold their signature from some of the branch agreements; another was to step up protests against what they regarded as the nonexecution of the Fish Agreement. As a result of the protest of Lord Cecil to Benjamin Vogt, the Norwegian minister in London, on December 18, 1916, a new inventory of fish stocks was ordered by the Norwegian food minister on December 22, and it was announced that export licenses would be granted to Norwegian fish exporters only when their requests were accompanied by the new inventory records. The Norwegians offered to send representatives to London to discuss the problem, but the British insisted that what they wanted was not a new agreement but the execution of the old one. Perhaps the most important pressure used by the British, however, was their decision, reached on December 23, to stop all coal exports to Norway beginning December 31. In the exchanges that resulted, it became clear that the British really were seeking still another end: a greater use of Norwegian tonnage in Allied interests.

If the British were thus stepping up their controls over Norwegian trade and were taking countermeasures to offset the gains made by Germany, Germany was undertaking retaliation for the concessions made to the Allies. As a result of the news that Norway had closed the agreements on fish and copper, there was a noticeable increase in German submarine activity directly off Norway's coast in September and October with the result that a number of ships and many Norwegian lives were lost.[77] There was a great public outcry in Norway, and the government on October 13 issued a proclamation forbidding submarines to cruise or linger in Norwegian territorial waters, excepting those craft that "because of bad weather or disability" sought "Norwegian territorial waters in order to save life."[78] Such ships were to stay above the surface, fly their national flag, and leave the territory as soon as the reasons for their presence were removed. As might have been expected, the German government protested against this decree and demanded its withdrawal. The Norwegian government showed no signs of giving in, and Norwegian ship losses continued to rise from thirteen in August 1916 to forty-eight in October, twenty-eight in November, thirty-five in December, and forty-four in January 1917. Simultaneously Germany protested against the fish agreement and by November 10 there were signs that Germany might be contemplating a declaration of war on Norway.

This was not to be the last time that a threat of German invasion hung over the head of a neutral state that had been, from the German point of view, too compliant with Allied demands. The British were now, as both they and the United States were later, put in the position of having to weigh the real extent of the danger of such a German invasion and their own ability to aid Norway, against the advantages to be secured from a continuation of their own economic policies toward Norway.[79]

There was no doubt that Norway wished to maintain her neutrality, and equally that the British had no real desire to see Norway as a cobelligerent. So far as evidence is available it appears that the reports of the British military and naval staffs were based on the fundamental belief that it would not be to Germany's own advantage to declare war, but that, conversely, Britain and her allies were not really equipped to give any considerable aid in either troops or equipment to Norway. Sir Eyre Crowe, viewing the situation from the point of view of economic warfare, saw the German move as a threat to the whole British blockade. He felt that if the Norwegians gave way on any of the matters complained of, the Germans would at once present new and more embracing demands which, if complied with, would make all of the British trading agreements with Norway inoperable. Not only that, but this would be the signal for every other neutral that had economic agreements with Britain to make the same calculation: whether it was better to continue in the British system or to break away from it. Therefore, Crowe believed that Norway must be encouraged to resist German demands even if it provoked war. It was Crowe's opinion that prevailed, and Norway was advised in late October not to give way and was promised the full support of the Allies if she should be invaded by Germany. The Norwegians told the British that one of the chief reasons they were reluctant to go to war was their inability to defend certain industrial sections of their country against aerial bombardment. This was regarded as a broad hint to the French in particular that their supplies of nitrate of ammonia from this region might be endangered, and that it would therefore be better to accept with good grace whatever concessions Norway might have to make to Germany.

In any case some general concessions that had little to do with the submarine issue were made by the Norwegians. An agreement was drafted and eventually signed on January 23, 1917, to the effect that Norway and Germany should exchange commodities to the best of their abilities, Germany giving licenses for the exportation of machines, dyes, and medicines, while Norway should not up to March 1, 1917, embargo exports of nickel, molybdenum, carbide of calcium, ferrosilicon, saltpeter, or tinned fish.[80] It is true that on December 2, 1916, the instructions to the Norwegian Navy concerning the treatment of submarines were slightly altered, and the Germans accepted this as sufficient.[81] However, "to grease the wheels" a bit, Norwegian bankers agreed to float a 7,500,000 kroner loan for Germany.

This was the situation in Norway's relations with both sets of belligerents when the declaration of unrestricted submarine warfare was issued by Germany.

DENMARK IN 1916

Once the exchanges of correspondence that were intended to put into effect the Agreement of November 1915 had taken place in the early months of 1916, British negotiations with Denmark were of minor importance so far as the blockade as a whole was concerned. This does not mean that the British were completely satisfied with their controls of Danish trade, for a number of minor questions were still being discussed with the Danish associations. For example, the British were anxious to prevent so far as possible the exportation from neutral states of goods containing materials of enemy origin, and therefore they sought to restrict the conditions under which certificates of neutral origin might be issued by British consular authorities. It had been admitted by the British that manufactured goods might have up to 25 per cent of their component materials secured from enemy sources and still be considered "neutral." But the question was whether the 25 per cent rule should be applied to the invoice value of the finished product or to the value of the original raw materials, exclusive of labor and other manufacturing costs. The second alternative was recommended by the British War Trade Advisory Committee on July 6, 1916,[82] but it was not until September 25 that the British legation in Copenhagen informed the Industriraadet of its new decision.[83] It was then announced that Article 167 of the November 1915 Agreement should be modified so that if an article having an invoice value of 100 kroner contained raw materials of 40 kroner value, only 10 kroner worth of those materials might be of enemy origin. Hitherto it had been possible for such goods to contain 25 kroner worth of enemy materials and still pass as goods of neutral character. The Raad entered vigorous protests, particularly since the new rule interfered with the exportation of Copenhagen porcelain. No satisfaction was received, and indeed even a more stringent rule was to be applied by the British in March 1917.

Another question on which the British sought greater satisfaction was that of regulating re-exportations from Denmark to Norway and Sweden. It will be remembered that the November 1915 Agreement had provided for the free re-exportation to these destinations of a list of goods, both to Swedish and Norwegian buyers and to branches of Danish firms in Norway and Sweden, provided the consignees in turn gave suitable guarantees. There are some indications that a vigorous campaign was waged in both the Swedish and Norwegian press against importers in these countries being bound by any agreement made by the Danes with the British. It was reported that the Norwegians would respect the guarantees they gave, but this was just one more of the factors that led to the passage of the Swedish War Trade Law in June 1916.[84] In July 1916 the British informed Christian Rottbøll, the head of the Danish Trade Office in London, that they wanted a new definition of these parts of the agreement.[85] It was evident that since the British had increased, or expected to increase, their direct controls over Norwegian and Swedish trade, they now wanted to bring their agreements with the Danes into line. It was proposed that cocoa should be removed from the list of goods that might be re-exported from Denmark—this in keeping with Allied attempts to control neutral trade with Germany in this article, but a number of other items were to be added to the list, such as agricultural and leather-working machines, certain iron articles, certain textiles, and so forth, but all within figures calculated on the basis of normal Danish exportations in 1911, 1912, and 1913. It was specified now, too, that in the case of re-exportations to Sweden the goods must be covered by guarantees sanctioned by the Swedish State Commerce Commission and those to Norway by guarantees approved by the Norwegian Ministry of Finance, and that all goods thus re-exported should not be capable of manufacture or further change in form, presumably to make control over their consumption easier. The French government took up a study of its exports to Denmark with a view to determining which of them might safely be permitted to enter this re-export trade to the other Scandinavian states, in order to bring French practice into line with that of the British government.[86] It was not, however, until November 2, 1916, that the Danish associations formally agreed to the changes the British had proposed, and they indicated at the same time that they, too, wished to raise come questions concerning the interpretation of the 1915 Agreement.[87]

At no time did any serious difficulties arise over consignment of goods to the Danish government, because the Danish associations apparently agreed that any such goods would be considered as part of the rations accorded to them by their agreements. Actually the government's consignments seem to have been limited to a very few articles—copper, antimony, nickel, all materials necessary to the manufacture of munitions, as well as oil and cotton waste. There was never any reason to suspect that the informal guarantees given by the representatives of the Danish government against the re-exportation of these goods were ever violated.[88]

At the end of 1916 it was to be expected that the rations for the year 1917 would be discussed.[89] Although the British refused to increase the amounts of resin, cocoa, copper, cork, graphite, leather, tin, antimony, paraffin, and turpentine that might be imported, they were willing to continue the rations already in operation. The question that interested the British most was the limitation of the imports of margarine materials, since it was closely associated with Danish exports of lard and live cattle to Germany. The Danes, however, stood firm on their existing rights under the 1915 Agreement, although they were in the process of making some concessions when the German declaration of submarine warfare changed the situation materially.

There is no evidence that the negotiations with the British had such deep repercussions on Danish politics as was true in Sweden and Norway. It was true that not all parties were satisfied that Denmark's best interests were being served by permitting the British to interfere so much with the country's economic life, and these people urged closer co-operation with Germany. In contrast with their Swedish confrères, the Danish Social Democrats were pro-German, perhaps partly because the Danish government of the day was more pro-Entente and an anti-British policy was, therefore, forced on the Opposition for tactical reasons. Although there is little evidence that the Danish government was really more open in its diplomacy, the Danish Rigsdag debates contain none of the thoroughgoing denunciations of the secrecy of its policy that were then current in the other Scandinavian Parliaments and press against their governments. Carl T. Zahle, the prime minister, in a speech before the Lower House on March 3, 1916, took it for granted that all members of the body knew that the Industriraadet and the Merchant Guild had concluded agreements with "foreign countries," and that goods passing into their control would be covered by guarantees concerning their use.[90] Zahle pointed out that violations of these promises made the member liable to a fine imposed by the associations, but not to any criminal action. This situation, he said, "everyone would recognize as not desirable," and he promised that a bill would be introduced to remedy it. When the bill was introduced in early April, Zahle pointed out that it was to the honor of Danish importers that the Raad had not collected any great amount of money in fines, and that it would only be "outsiders" who would be touched by the new legislation.[91] In any case the bill became law on April 5, 1916, so the authority of the government was added to that of the associations in supporting the guarantees given to the Allies against re-exportation of imported goods.[92]

One great problem which Denmark faced was that of securing shipping to transport the goods coming from overseas that were necessary to her economic life, and this in spite of the size of the Danish merchant fleet (nearly one million tons), which was largely engaged in the more profitable extra-European trades. Since in normal times much of Denmark's own trade was carried by German and Austrian ships, it was not unexpected that the extreme need of the Central Powers had brought about the withdrawal of these vessels from Danish service. In early 1916 the government raised the question of regulating freights that might be charged by Danish ships with the aim of keeping food prices on the Danish market within reason. In the end, after consultation with shipowners, it was decided that rather than set up a complicated system of freight rates it would be better to lay a special tax on shipping company profits, the proceeds to be used for subsidies to food producers, in order to assure an adequate supply being brought to the domestic market. It was calculated that the bill which became law on May 12, 1916, would bring in 11,040,000 kroner in the year 1916.[93] In addition, the shipping companies were required to provide vessels to carry coal at reduced rates. This law also set up a Shipping Committee (Fragtnaevn) of eight members, to be named by the minister of interior after consultation with the Danish Steamshipowners Union, which was to recommend the best and cheapest means for securing tonnage.[94] By June 13 the Committee was at work and soon had some twenty-five people on its staff helping to make arrangements for chartering vessels. It was able, for instance, to secure carriage for 50,000 tons of bread grains in September 1916 and 110,000 tons of corn in November. Since the powers of the Committee were not sufficient to compel obedience to its recommendations, a Royal Order was issued on January 6, 1917, which prohibited the time chartering of Danish vessels except with the consent of the Ministry of Commerce.[95] The law of May 12 was extended by a similar one on December 22, 1916, by which time such opposition as there had been to the tax, as being discriminatory against one industry alone, was modified, so that the major complaint was about the use to which the money was being put—to the subsidies being paid on fish, for instance.[96] It is interesting to note that the profits of Danish shipowners had exceeded expectations, so that the tax actually brought in some 16 million kroner in 1916, about 4.5 million kroner more than was predicted when the law was passed.

Clearly the Danes were not suffering too much from the effects of the blockade, for even one of the Social Democrats, L. Rasmussen, declared in the Folketing's budget debate, on October 19, 1916, that Danish agriculture was enjoying a great increase in its income, trade had flowered, and manufacturing and industry were in a luxuriant state, that, in short, things were better than in peacetime. His only complaint was that the profits were not being passed on to the workers.[97]

THE NETHERLANDS AND THE BLOCKADE IN 1916

In previous chapters it has been shown how much the Dutch became involved in Allied attempts to prevent or hamper the supply of goods to the enemy during 1916 through their regulations of goods produced in the British Empire, through mail censorship, through shipping controls, and through purchasing Dutch fish and agricultural products. Over every one of these matters there had been long, and sometimes rather acrimonious exchanges between the British, the Dutch government, the N.O.T., and other trade organizations. There still remain for discussion a few problems that did not fall specifically within any of these subjects.

It had been considered a victory by the British to have secured so far-reaching a rationing agreement as was signed with the Netherlands Oversea Trust on November 13/23, 1915. But, in the British view, it was necessary to watch the execution of that agreement very carefully and to consider what other articles were being imported beyond the needs of Dutch consumption so that rations might be set for them. This attempt on the part of the British to tie in permissions to import even the amount of grain and fodder agreed upon in November with a regulation of Dutch exports of cattle, meat, and dairy products has already been discussed in Chapter V. So far as the N.O.T. was concerned the question was complicated by the fact that some grain shipments were consigned directly to the Dutch government, which, of course, felt itself in no way bound to confine its imports within the limits set by the rationing agreement, and had, indeed, purchased more grain than was permitted for the quarter. In order to secure a partial solution of the problem, the N.O.T. decided on February 4, 1916, to issue no more import consents for grain until certain government cargoes actually arrived.[98]

In mid-February the British insisted that the scope of the rationing agreement must, in any case, be extended, a demand which they said had been foreseen in the November letters. They also raised with the Trust the question of returning for action in British prize courts goods that had already arrived in the Netherlands from overseas. The Trust had very little choice, if it wanted to secure other goods from overseas, but to take up negotiations on these points. Therefore the N.O.T. sent a memorandum to the British on March 17, in which it proposed that permission be given to import, per quarter, 5,000 tons of cocoa beans, 325,000 tons of rice, 525 tons of crude tin, 150,000 hides and skins, 125 tons of leather, 2,775 tons of tanning materials, 500 tons of asbestos, and 11,000 tons of paraffin wax.[99] No cocoa powder or cocoa butter would be imported and the Trust would take over all "free stocks" of these articles already in the Netherlands, allowing no exports to the Scandinavian countries. Likewise, no rice was to be exported except to the Commission for the Relief of Belgium, and 80 per cent of that imported was to be secured from British India. The N.O.T. offered to refrain from granting further consents for the importations of a number of articles (such as raw rubber, kapok, pepper, cork, flax, hemp, and so forth) until they were needed for Dutch home consumption, and then only within stated amounts; the Trust was to present statistics on normal Dutch home consumption of pyrites, rosin, gums, and fresh and dried fruits, with a view to setting rations for them, too. The Dutch proposed to postpone consideration of coffee imports.

Apparently, the British were not satisfied with the state of the trade in rice and coffee and therefore when they eventually made counterproposals on June 28, 1916, these subjects were again postponed.[100] The British for the most part accepted the March proposals, while adding considerably to the list of goods for which the Trust was to issue no more consents until further notice—anchovies, sardines, cinnamon, cassia, mace, dried fruits, gums, eggs, and so on. On June 30 the Trust accepted this note, which thus constituted an addition to the November 1915 rationing agreement.[101] A similar exchange of notes took place between the French government and the Trust on July 20/21, 1916.[102]

But although this one aspect of Dutch foreign trade was bettered, difficulties arose in another direction. Partly to forestall undue British pressures on the N.O.T. and on Dutch agricultural interests who were then negotiating with the British, the Dutch government issued a decree on May 10 taking under its control all imports of fodder including corn, barley, oats, and oil cake, thereby taking from the Trust any jurisdiction over these articles.[103] The Allies were displeased, for they had no great faith in the efficacy of the Dutch government's controls and much preferred to deal with the N.O.T. However, the British did press the Dutch government for guarantees similar to those given by the Trust, and asked that they be extended to wheat and wheat flour consigned to the government,[104] and that notoriously suspect houses which had been put on the British black list be excluded from receiving these articles.

In the meantime the British used their usual means of pressure: detentions of ships and of cargoes, consigned in some cases to the government and in others to the N.O.T. It was difficult for either of them to get much satisfaction, for these negotiations were at a time when some people in England were questioning the good faith of Sir Francis Oppenheimer (his name alone seemed to make him suspect!), who had been responsible for most of the agreements made with the Trust, which thus shared in all these suspicions.[105] The N.O.T., in turn, felt aggrieved since it was seldom informed when cargoes consigned to it were detained, or of the reasons for the detentions, as it had a right to expect under its agreement. It recognized that the British wanted to put pressures at every possible point of Dutch economic life in order to secure a general regulation of trade with the enemy, and that until the Dutch government's controls over grain and fodder were perfected, both the Trust's and the government's consignments would be withheld. The N.O.T., therefore, tried to secure a promise from the government that it would not deliver goods to anyone to whom the Trust refused facilities.

But while the Trust might refuse to deal with those on the British black list, it was difficult for a neutral government to do so without compromising its position. Exchanges of letters between Oppenheimer, the Trust, and the Dutch government in July and August finally brought about a settlement whereby 50 per cent of all feedstuffs imported would be consigned to the N.O.T., the rest to the government, and the Trust would control all sales of these goods in the Netherlands—the government first reporting to the N.O.T. any sales of its imports.[106] Wheat was still to be consigned to the government, but it had to inform the Trust of the amounts necessary for home consumption, since the N.O.T. was still to make all rationing arrangements with the British. The Dutch government was to submit to the Trust, and it in turn to the British, a list of all the houses from which it intended to buy these supplies. It was suggested that the British would provide a list of British firms that would, of course, be regarded as suitable.

It was a time of great tension, and at one point Sir Alan Johnstone threatened the Dutch with a British invasion if they refused to accept British demands. Although there were later disagreements as to exactly what the ration should be,[107] the British compelled the Dutch government to retreat from the position it took up in May, although it neither made promises directly to the British nor specifically accepted rationing. Perhaps the legal position of the neutral states was protected by this evasiveness, but the practical effect was compliance with the British system. On the other hand the Dutch secured the release of thirty-eight grain ships from British ports on August 27, but, since a large part of the Dutch fishing fleet was still held, this passed almost unnoticed. There was no doubt that the Dutch grain supply situation remained a serious one; on August 19 a much more stringent distribution law was passed,[108] and on December 27 a system of bread rationing was begun.[109]

The most complete information now available about the actual working of the rationing system comes from Dutch sources. Late in 1916 in order to keep interferences with Dutch trade at a minimum, the N.O.T. asked the British, when the quarterly ration had been filled, to permit up to

50 per cent of the amount for the succeeding quarter to go forward in advance. The British would, at most, agree to 25 per cent proceeding on this basis, and countered with a demand that the Trust should cease to grant consents in such cases until British permission to resume was given. Even so, other problems arose over storage charges for goods held in United Kingdom ports which had arrived after the ration and the overdraft were filled. The British insisted that the N.O.T. must bear the expense; in the end the Dutch paid.[110]

It was inevitable that the Dutch should regard many British trade regulations as quite unreasonable and unnecessary. For instance considerable resentment was felt that, at a time when the British demanded that certificates of origin issued by the British consuls at Amsterdam and Rotterdam must cover Dutch exports to overseas destinations, these same officials were permitting exports of German dyes, porcelain, and gelatine to go through to America. The Dutch did not understand that the British might hope to calm relations with the United States government by making these rather minor concessions in their blockade policy. No such reasons, however, could have justified the continued supply of German beer bottles to the United Kingdom, when the greatest difficulties were put in the way of the export of Dutch gin.[111]

The Dutch did, however, have to face the fact that there was a lively smuggling trade still going on with Germany directed from the German consulate in Rotterdam.[112] The enormous prices paid in Germany were adequate reason for these transactions, particularly when, as in the case of rubber and margarine, small amounts could readily be concealed under other guises. In fact in 1916 there was practically no legitimate trade in rubber, and in early October the British, hoping to control the situation, decided to stop all Dutch imports of rubber, exceptions eventually being made for certain hospital and dental supplies. Smugglers' hangouts on the beaches flourished; at Nijmegen a cafe whose garden was half in the Netherlands and half in Germany did a large business until Dutchmen were forbidden access to the German section. As might be expected the Allied governments had evidence of this situation and on several occasions urged the N.O.T. and the Dutch government to tighten their regulations. The question had been considered at various times in the Dutch Staten-Generaal in late 1915, and although an occasional member insisted that in most instances the smuggler was merely a man carrying a little food or kerosene over the frontier to help out relatives or friends, most members regarded the question seriously, as one affecting public morality.[113] As a result on December 31, 1915, a much more stringent law was passed, which increased the penalties, permitted the expulsion of convicted smugglers from frontier districts, permitted the complete prohibition of trade in certain goods in these areas, and increased the district under state of siege. But it was apparent by the summer of 1916 that the regulations were applied with great moderation, and therefore in July a representative of the French legation undertook a tour of the frontier, as a result of which he concluded that only an increase in the number of customs officials and in their zeal could help.[114] Reports to the Trust and the Dutch government resulted in new measures, among them a supplementary credit granted by the Staten-Generaal in order to increase the salaries of frontier officials. At the same time the number of judges hearing cases in these districts was increased in order to clear court dockets more quickly. The practice of selling at auction in the frontier areas, goods seized by the officials was now stopped, and sales were moved to places in the interior where only reputable merchants who were willing to give guarantees concerning the use of the goods were permitted to bid. In several places special associations of merchants committed to the purpose of combatting smuggling were formed in 1916, in the interests of maintaining the good name of Dutch tradesmen.[115] The Trust, of course, had a black list of its own of all N.O.T. contract violators, which acted as a "preventive," since no one on that list ever again secured N.O.T. goods. But still the temptations of high profits were great and N.O.T. fines were not always a sufficient deterrent.

On the whole the criticism of the government's policy in the Staten-Generaal remained quite moderate in tone. Much of it centered around the failure of the government to take adequate measures to control exports, to secure imports, and to regulate prices. The government's answer that conditions in the Netherlands were much better than in any other European neutral country was regarded as quite inadequate by the Socialists who were most active in pressing the issue.[116]

XIII

Accomplishments and Effects of the
Blockade at the End of 1916

$$\diamond$$

B Y the close of 1916 the Allied blockade of Germany was, with few
exceptions, as effective as it could be made without the intervention
of the United States in the war, with its consequent direct co-operation to
prevent the exportation of American goods to the enemy. This long-distance
blockade was made effective by measures that fell into four categories—
those based on belligerent maritime right, those undertaken as reprisals
against the illegal action of German submarines, those that constituted an
exercise of sovereign rights, and lastly those of pure policy. It may be well to
recapitulate some of the essential features of these measures before proceeding to a consideration of their effects and the hopes and plans of the
Allied governments for the future.

Some of the measures that were said to be but justifiable extensions of
recognized belligerent rights were taken almost immediately upon the outbreak of war, and most of them, in some form or other, had been used by the
British before the end of 1914. The first contraband lists issued on August 4,
1914, had made but few changes in those included in the Declaration of

London, but the lists issued on September 21 and October 29 made severe inroads into the "free list" of articles which had been set outside the contraband categories by the Declaration. More than that, the doctrine of continuous voyage had been extended by the Order in Council of August 20, 1914, to apply to conditional as well as absolute contraband, and although the subsequent Order in Council of October 29 purported to rescind that interpretation, it still remained possible to attain the same end if a declaration was made by the British government that a neutral port or state had been assimilated to enemy territory so far as the treatment of contraband goods bound to it was concerned. In the course of 1915 the difference between absolute and conditional contraband ceased to exist in practice, and the doctrine of continuous voyage was applied to all goods bound ultimately for the enemy. It was a great innovation when, in the case of the *Kim*, Sir Samuel Evans accepted statistics of neutral imports in excess of normal as evidence that particular goods, consigned to a neutral port, would probably ultimately reach the enemy. It will be remembered that the court had not considered statistical evidence as absolute proof of such destination, but it had considered it a strong presumption. This decision did much to strengthen the British government in its determination to secure a further regulation of neutral importations through agreements with neutral governments and merchants. On the procedural side an equally great innovation was made when the burden of proof of the innocence of a cargo was placed upon the claimant.

From the point of view of its far-reaching effect and the number of subsidiary measures which it evoked, the Order in Council of March 11, 1915, was undoubtedly the most important development in Allied economic warfare made at any time during the war. This Order was undertaken as a reprisal measure and under it the British claimed the principal rights and privileges that would have resulted from a declaration of a legal blockade of all German ports. But the Order meant more than that, for in addition to preventing trade through German ports without the onerous responsibility of putting such a blockade in force, it provided the means of stopping indirect trade to and from Germany through adjacent neutral territory. By a judicious application of the doctrine of continuous voyage, the British were successful in stopping the greater part of Germany's overseas trade. The real burden of the operation undoubtedly fell upon the border neutral states and their citizens. It was in order to make this burden less severe and to increase the effectiveness of the blockade that the British government sought agreements with these neutrals.

The new measures undertaken by the British government in 1915 and 1916 were either based on an exercise of the sovereign rights of a state or were achieved on the sufferance of neutrals. It has been demonstrated that the British government regarded its censorship of cables and of mails found on ships entering British ports as justifiable on the ground that these communications were within British territorial jurisdiction. Whatever the reason for a ship's presence in a British port, once it came there its mails were liable to search. In the absence of treaty obligations, which the British government denied existed in the case of neutral nonofficial mails, there was nothing to prevent Britain from using any information gained from intercepted mails and cable messages. Indeed it was the minute knowledge of the activities of neutral firms secured from these two sources which made it possible for the Allies to make some distinction between bona fide neutral trade and that with a hostile destination. It was, likewise, this information, and that reported by Allied representatives abroad, which made possible the compilation of black lists. Here again when neutral governments protested they were met with a simple statement that the black lists were merely an extension of British trading with the enemy legislation; no one could presume to deny Britain's sovereign right to prohibit her citizens from trading with whomsoever the government might indicate. The British government insisted that any prejudice to neutral trade resulting from the black lists was wholly incidental to the main purpose, and for such prejudicial effects the government denied all responsibility.

In this same class of measures, which were considered as an exercise of sovereign right, might be placed the prohibitions of exports laid by the British government, and the consequent agreements made by neutrals in order to secure derogations of these embargoes. Neutral importers who received goods produced within the British Empire were required to give adequate guarantees concerning their use and the consumption of their manufactured products. This control in the case of British bunker coal was of prime importance in regulating neutral imports, neutral manufacturing and industry, and in securing the use of neutral tonnage on Allied behalf. Certain neutral industries, notably the rubber and wool industries in the United States, were to a large extent dependent on British sources of supply for their raw materials, so that the British government was able to exercise minute control over these American companies and the disposal of their goods. After the entrance of the United States into the war this type of control, effected through a general embargo, was even more important in bringing the neutral states of Europe more completely within the Allies' system.

Other developments were made in the realm of pure policy without there being any attempt by the British government to justify the measures on legal grounds. Whatever could not be accomplished by direct action based on belligerent or sovereign rights seems to have been secured through negotiations with neutral governments or their citizens. Late in 1914 the British concluded their first agreements with the Netherlands Oversea Trust, with the Swedish government, and early in 1915 with the Danish government. These early agreements were limited in their scope and dealt mainly with the embargoes to be laid by the neutral governments. In the latter part of 1915 by this same means the British government secured neutral recognition of its decision to permit only enough goods for bona fide neutral needs to proceed through the British naval cordon. These rationing agreements provided a means of preventing overseas goods from reaching Germany, but always at the expense of an expanding neutral trade. The year 1916 saw the conclusion of many more agreements on these same lines which tightened the control over Dutch trade and created a similar control over Norwegian importations. The British have subsequently been pleased to point to the ease with which these rationing agreements were made as an indication that the northern European neutrals were co-operating in these controls and hence could not really have been suffering very badly from them. The explanation of the willingness of the neutrals—and, in particular, neutral merchants—to begin negotiations was never as simple as that.

The real object of the neutrals was not to join in the Allied system of economic control but rather to escape the consequences of noncompliance with British demands. The neutrals realized that any other policy was unlikely to succeed. Given the geographical position of the Allies and their supremacy on the seas, which together made it possible to withhold overseas goods from the border neutrals whenever occasion demanded, the neutrals had no choice but to comply. And the consequences of resistance to Allied requests were usually made quite plain: wholesale detentions of cargoes, costly prize court proceedings, and, perhaps, finally, confiscation of goods essential to neutral needs. The neutrals were seeking, and to a considerable extent secured, a regularity and certainty in their business enterprises. Even the N.O.T., which was everywhere regarded as most pro-Ally, found itself forced either to accept British interference in every part of Dutch economic life or to become responsible for a total stoppage of Dutch imports. On the other hand, the Swedish government never made a far-reaching agreement with the British, although negotiations for one seemed to be well advanced at the end of 1916. The Swedish government had rather effectively prevented its citizens from making agreements similar to those concluded by the N.O.T. and the Danish associations, by requiring all contracts made by Swedish subjects with foreign powers to be approved by the State Commerce Commission. The British, however, were forced to admit to themselves that the Swedes fared much better at Allied hands than did many of the other neutrals who accepted British terms. The Swedes, having in their control of transit trade to Russia a means of pressure which other neutrals lacked, were able to exert a counterpressure on the British. Even at the time, neutrals realized that the value of reaching agreements with the British was questionable, for during 1916 detentions continued to be ordered on the same pretexts as before the accords were signed and sometimes in greater numbers. The British answer to complaints always was that it was doubtful whether the guarantees given for a particular cargo could or would be effective.

The element of coercion, even where agreements existed, was still strong throughout the system. By 1916 the British were perfectly well able to resort to forcible rationing whenever agreements were unsatisfactory or where neutrals were so "unreasonable" as to refuse to make an accord. The British could, of course, point out that neutrals might have been treated more severely and that where neutrals fulfilled their obligations under the agreements they received a regular supply of goods. It seems, however, that the British were everywhere dominated by a keen consideration of their own interests, and only when it appeared likely that some positive injury would result to British or allied trade, or that one of the neutral states—such as Sweden—might align itself with the Central Powers, was coercion relaxed.

A second measure in the realm of pure policy to which the British resorted was navicerting. In justice to the British system of economic warfare it should be pointed out that navicerting did lend a valuable aid to the transportation of neutral cargoes at a time when tonnage was becoming more and more difficult to obtain. The British quite readily gave a commercial passport for cargoes which were covered by adequate guarantees. Shipping companies were virtually assured of the nondetention of these cargoes and therefore accepted them for shipment in preference to other goods. It was only by these means that American industries were able to send, and the Scandinavian states to receive, the cereals, textiles, and important raw materials on which they had negotiated. Had it not been for the navicert the whole negotiations might have been without practical result or alleviation of the precarious situation of the border neutrals.

The third type of operations motivated by reasons of policy were the purchasing agreements concluded in 1916 which assured the British that a certain proportion of the agricultural and fish products exported from the border neutral states would be sent to the United Kingdom. The effect of these agreements was twofold: necessary supplies were secured for British civilian use, and at the same time excessive exportations of neutral products were diverted from German markets.

By the end of 1916 all of the measures and policies which together constituted the blockade of Germany were in full working order. It was inevitable that a certain proportion of the products of neutral agriculture and industry should continue to go to Germany, for higher prices and habits of trade continued to prevail over British attempts to subsidize exportations of these goods to the United Kingdom. In some instances these exportations to Germany were part of an exchange system which the Allies were unable to alter. It remained true, also, that some goods imported with the assistance and permission of British authorities found their way over neutral frontiers. The British naturally protested against the violations of guarantees given by the importers. However, for the most part the guarantees were faithfully carried out so far as the importers and subsequent owners of the goods were able. Montagu W. W. P. Consett in *The Triumph of Unarmed Forces* has gone to much trouble to point out the leakages that occurred, but their existence by no means made the system of Allied control as ineffective as he implies.

All this being true, it is necessary to consider whether the Allied governments were entirely satisfied with the blockade. Some indications can be gained from debates in the British Parliament. It will be remembered that at the end of 1915 and early in 1916 both Houses heard some warm discussions of the government's policy in regard to Danish trade. Although later in 1916 questions were put at various times that indicated dissatisfaction with matters of detail, there were few instances of general condemnation of the line of policy. Even so, it is interesting to see which parts of the economic campaign were discussed and how far the government was willing to go in revealing information.

Some of the government's critics who persisted in believing that the Foreign Office was acting contrary to the recommendations of the Navy, asked what they thought were pointed questions about the membership of the Contraband Committee, the suggestion being that the Admiralty was not properly represented by officers who had had experience at sea.[1] At one time Sir Frederick Banbury asked whether Admiral Jellicoe, commander in chief of the Naval Forces, had protested that the Contraband Committee had released ships which the Navy had captured, but the government refused to answer on the ground that such correspondence was confidential.[2] Along the same line, Lord Leith asked in the House of Lords on May 31 whether the Contraband Committee was appointed with the full concurrence of the Departments represented. The Marquess of Crewe replied with some asperity:

> There ought to be no colour for the statement that the Board of Admiralty takes any exception to its representation either on the Contraband Committee, or on the War Trade Advisory Committee, or on any other body in which it is interested. My noble friend started again what was rather a familiar hare—namely, that of the supposed chagrin of certain officers in the Navy at finding that ships which had been brought into British ports, sometimes with great difficulty and at considerable risk to themselves and their crews, had afterwards been released. . . .

He went on to state that naval officers had been informed of the necessity for the release of certain ships.[3]

When Major R. Hunt on July 5 asked in the Commons whether the recent policy of tightening the blockade meant that all ships arrested by the Navy on suspicion of carrying goods to the enemy were to be adjudicated by a British prize court without interference by the Foreign Office or any other authority, or whether such interference was in some or many cases still practiced, a more explicit answer was given by Lord Cecil. He explained that under conditions of modern war it was necessary to send almost all ships bound to neutral countries adjacent to Germany, which did not call voluntarily, into a British port for search. It would only be after such search that any judgment could be formed as to the probable ultimate destination, based on the nature of the cargo, character of consignors and consignees, the amount of similar articles recently imported into the neutral country, and perhaps other information of a secret character. It would be determined in London, where all of this information was collected, whether there were grounds for putting into prize court the ship, the cargo, or any part of it. "To put into Prize Court all vessels and their cargoes which are sent into port as explained above, as apparently my hon. Friend suggests, would be neither just nor wise."[4]

Another subject on which several questions were asked was that of shipping controls. It was, of course, realized that shipping space was at a great premium, and the government was urged by indirection rather than by specific criticism to deal more sternly with the problem. Thus, in February one speaker urged the establishment of some centralized controlling body that could fix freight rates,[5] and in March and April others asked whether neutral governments had considered requisitioning German merchant ships lying in their ports in order to relieve the shortage, and, if not, suggested that the British government should urge them to do so.[6] Cecil's reply was that the government knew of no such suggested measures and that it was a question for neutral governments to decide for themselves, although the British government would be willing to consider any proposal that ships so requisitioned be made immune from capture. Later in the year other members asked for statistics on the number and tonnage of British ships that had been sold to neutrals since the outbreak of war, as well as the number being built for neutral account.[7]

It has been noted in Chapter X in connection with the Paris Economic Conference that while Parliament generally agreed that it was well to secure identical Allied black lists, embargoes, and contraband lists for the war period, plans to continue controls over enemy trade in the postwar period were regarded with extreme suspicion, especially by those Liberals who were still Free Traders at heart.[8] Although the government set up a committee under the chairmanship of Arthur James Balfour to consider the feasibility of postwar economic measures, no report was issued by it down to the end of 1916, and Parliament's interest in the matter temporarily waned. Much more time was expended on the alleged failure of the government to wind up enemy businesses in the United Kingdom, to intern all enemy aliens, and to prevent Germans from changing their names to good British ones. Government spokesmen—who were called on in all these matters on an average of once a week!—explained carefully that there was no legislation that prohibited naturalized British subjects to change their names, and even though such changes might seem to give them commercial advantages, no steps could be taken against them unless they were proved guilty of actually trading with the enemy. It is perhaps understandable that Sir Arthur Markham should have been upset when one of these aliens took *his* name, but one can only get amusement from the concern felt because one Herr Buchner, who proved to be a naturalized subject and a resident of twenty-one years standing, was still bandmaster to the viceroy of India![9]

Slightly more instructive were the replies to questions about the trade of the northern neutrals, for here the government showed to what limited distance it was willing to go in revealing details of its economic policy. On July 13 Lord Cecil denied that the British government was subsidizing Dutch butter producers but stated that arrangements had been made with them whereby additional supplies would be furnished to England through regular trade channels. Cecil's denial was not altogether correct since the British had agreed to pay a bonus on these supplies.[10] Equally meager information was given on July 31 concerning the Dutch Fish Agreement, although Cecil offered to provide further details to members who asked him privately on this or on questions concerned with American trade.[11]

Minor tempests still raged around the Danish agreement, about which more was known by the public and which therefore served as a convenient object of attack. In the House of Lords on March 15 the Earl of Portsmouth asserted that this agreement had brought new antagonisms with Sweden and Norway, because of controls exercised over their trade with Danish firms, but Lansdowne firmly denied the allegation. He also said that the government would not be led into making disclosures of information which they wished to withhold, and ended with a statement that this agitation "seems to be inspired by sentiments which are neither wise nor patriotic."[12] Sir Henry Dalziel on August 23 questioned the efficacy of the agreements with both the Danish associations and the N.O.T., citing one instance where a Dutch trader who paid a £25,000 fine was reputed to have said that he did not mind since he made £75,000 on the transaction.[13] Cecil admitted that it was not easy to produce proof concerning the trade of neutral states, and he was conscious "even in what I am now saying, . . . it might be better not to say anything." Although Cecil admitted that there were leakages, he stated very forcefully that the British government had every reason to be satisfied with the working of the agreements with the Danes and the N.O.T. Within the past few weeks the situation with regard to the exportation of Dutch agricultural products to Germany had much improved. Members of Parliament were, on the other hand, not unmindful of the importance of keeping America's good will, and Dalziel, who was usually convinced that the government was acting with insufficient energy, questioned the wisdom of including so many American names on a public black list. Cecil replied that if you made it a criminal offense to trade with anyone of enemy nationality or association, you must give public notice of it—you could not wait until you summoned a person to a police court to inform him that he had transgressed the law. It is obvious, however, that this was not a complete answer since the British still used an unpublished black list without any apparent qualms.

What was American reaction to the blockade during 1916? At various times the State Department had made protests against mail censorship, black-listing, use of certificates of interest, and the like, and, although the British realized that the success of their economic warfare depended on the tacit consent of the United States, there was not much inclination to modify the essentials of their policy unless some specific retaliatory actions were taken. Generally, the British believed that they could count on the friendship of Wilson and the State Department, who would take countermeasures only if driven to them by pressures from Congress or interested business groups. For a time this event seemed about to be realized when on September 5, 1916, amendments to a revenue bill were introduced in the Senate that would give the president power (1) to prohibit the importation of foreign products from countries that had prohibited the importation of American products, (2) to withhold clearances of belligerent vessels of any state that had subjected American ships to any undue prejudice, disadvantage, or discrimination in their ability to carry freight or passengers, and (3) to refuse use of the United States mails, and facilities of express, telegraph, cable, or wireless companies in similar circumstances. The third proposal fell by the wayside but the other two were passed by both houses of Congress on September 8, with very little debate.[14]

Joseph M. Byrns, representative from Tennessee, said that the first of these measures had been prepared in response to the specific request of a conference of tobacco growers from Tennessee, Kentucky, Virginia, and Maryland held in Washington; he said that the State Department had given its approval. The British had recently reimposed more severe restrictions on tobacco imports to the Netherlands and Denmark, after they had given assurances, in November 1915, of the free passage of such cargoes. Byrns argued that the Imperial Tobacco Company, a British concern, would profit from its ability to buy American tobacco at low prices and hold it in American warehouses until the end of the war or until prices advanced. Alben W. Barkley, then a member of the House, went on to say that some people charged that these regulations were taken in collusion with the governments of Italy, France, and possibly Spain, all of which had a government monopoly, in order to reduce the price which those countries would have to pay for the American product. He went on: "If this be the intention of Great Britain and her Allies, then it is not only a breach of good faith but it is so unjustifiable as to call for the strongest protest and most radical action possible on the part of our own Government to protect our people from this injustice."

Here is a good example of the rather vague accusations made by American businessmen that their British competitors were somehow benefiting at American expense from British belligerent trade controls, a charge that is now very difficult either to prove or disprove.

It was one thing for Congress to pass this legislation and another for the executive branch of the government to enforce it. It seems most unlikely, in spite of Byrns's statement, that either the State Department or the Department of Commerce had been consulted before its passage, for certainly they showed no enthusiasm in proceeding to its execution. The secretary of commerce, William C. Redfield, submitted a long report to the State Department on October 23, 1916, in which he stated the belief that "a prohibition of imports by the United States as a retaliatory measure is likely to react more to the disadvantage of consumers, importers, and the trade generally in this country than to the detriment of exporters in the United Kingdom."[15] He feared that such action might lead to retaliation in the form of additional British embargoes. He showed to what extent the British controlled the sources of supply of cotton, thread, yarn and cloth, wool, woolen goods, and liquors, and he discounted any long-run gain being made by encouraging American manufacturers to produce goods which had hitherto been imported and for which the United States had no natural economic advantage. Redfield also pointed out the difficulties of trying to enforce an embargo against British goods which arrived from a neutral port, for then it would become necessary to require proof of origin for all goods. The United States might thereby have become involved in a minor way in the same kind of discriminations against which it had been protesting! Any application of the shipping provisions, Redfield believed, would only tie up a large amount of tonnage which American commerce needed badly, British seizures of other ships would probably increase, and in the end American goods would reach their overseas destination only if convoyed by an American naval vessel, with an imminent danger of armed conflict resulting. It was doubted whether even a general refusal to clear vessels carrying war materials would be as effective as it might have been a year earlier, for by 1916 more factories in the United Kingdom had been converted into munitions plants, and hence British needs were not so pressing. Since the British had given large contracts to American firms, any American embargo might prove more injurious to American manufacturers than to the countries at war. Redfield went on: "We have suffered the effect of embargoes and orders in council for a long period, under protest but without retaliation. The restrictions are no more hurtful now than a year and a half ago. . . . Before any action is taken, however, one other point must be carefully weighed. For success in commerce after the war we need the friendship of the belligerents if it can be obtained and held without undue sacrifice. Is not their good will then likely to be worth more to us than the present temporary restrictions have cost us?"

One concrete proposal was made: that a conference of neutral nations be held in order to counter the Allied Economic Conference that had met in June. This Conference of Neutral Governments would discuss means to insure the "open-door" policy in Europe and consider the general question of international tariff relations after the war.

There was nothing new, of course, about a conference of neutrals, for the Swedish government had been urging some such plan since January 1916. But the United States government had not previously shown any interest. Toward the end of December A. G. Schmedeman, the American minister in Norway, reported that the Swiss and Dutch governments had accepted an invitation of the Scandinavian governments to hold a preliminary meeting to call a general conference of neutral powers, but whether such a meeting was held would depend on Spain's answer. He said it was expected that Spain, under Allied pressure, would refuse to attend.[16]

Whether or not the British ought to have taken more seriously this American threat of retaliation is still a question. It has been suggested that Wilson really initiated the whole action, in the hope of having some weapon in reserve if the Allies proved recalcitrant when he launched his long-intended move to mediate between the belligerents. But the British also recognized the powerful means of pressure they could use against American trade, and decided to run the risk of American displeasure.

Did the Allies at the end of 1916 seriously contemplate any large extensions of their economic campaign? The answer must be yes—and no. Certainly there were no active negotiations in progress then, except those with the Swedes. Had these been completed, the British would have had agreements covering the trade of all four of the northern neutrals, and they would then have aimed only at tightening these controls. However, they recognized that any further decrease in the goods allowed to reach Denmark would result in a decline of Danish exports to the United Kingdom, and these goods could only be secured from other sources by a greater use of an already depleted tonnage. Further coercion of Norway was likewise impolitic, because of the restrictions that Norway might put on the supply of munitions to France. The possible application of greater pressure on Dutch trade was more carefully considered, but the position of the Board of Trade was that Great Britain would lose more in the ability to market British goods than it would gain in depriving the Netherlands and perhaps Germany of these same goods. Again the Board was thinking of the need for income from foreign trade if the expenses of the war were to be met, as well as the need for Dutch produce to supply the British consumer.

There is no evidence that the advent of the Lloyd George War Cabinet in December 1916 brought any change in blockade policy. Lord Cecil continued at his post as minister of blockade, and his staff went on with their tasks as usual. It was the German decision to begin unrestricted submarine warfare that in time altered some of the bases of Allied economic warfare.

In 1916 the position of France in regard to the blockade remained almost unchanged. Generally speaking, the French were inclined toward a more severe regulation of neutral imports and toward exerting every effort to keep neutral domestic products from reaching Germany. In this matter the financial and military branches of the French government did not always agree with the Comité de Restriction on the necessity of spending treasury funds to purchase these goods. The entire French government, however, was united in urging its British ally to strengthen controls exercised over British exports to border neutrals! Certainly this was a serious gap in the blockade, and one which the French and neutral governments alike might well resent. Although the British had made important concessions in some matters, the French were never quite satisfied with the British "commercial" view of the blockade, and they had high hopes for the future application of the resolutions of the Paris Economic Conference.

THE EFFECTS OF THE BLOCKADE ON THE
CENTRAL POWERS

It has not been the purpose of this study to consider in any detail the effects of the Allied economic operations on Germany. Some general indication might well be given, however, of the extent to which the Allied hope of starving the German people and disabling their industries and whole economic life had materialized by the end of 1916.[17] Just what effect the blockade had on the German army is difficult to say, but, so far as the Allied military leaders were aware at the end of 1916, German soldiers were well equipped. Ammunition and guns continued to be supplied in spite of severe shortages of manganese. In the process of steel making, substitutes for this steel-hardening material had been found, and the same was true in many other industries. By the end of 1916 leather and wool for shoes and clothing were scarce, and prices were high, but again substitutes were used. It is very certain, however, that the brunt of the burden occasioned by the Allied blockade was borne by the civilian population, who were expected to sacrifice everything for the military needs of the state. It is from the point of view of the well-being of the German civilian population that the effects of the blockade must be measured.

As might have been expected the degree of suffering varied among different classes. Upper-middle-class families continued for some time in 1916 to fare better than those of the lower classes; they usually had some cheap meat once a day, and milk in small quantities was still available for children and invalids, although bread was of a very inferior quality. Prices, however, continued to rise and progressively the middle classes came to suffer. By the end of 1916 communal kitchens, run by municipalities, had been established, and the poorer classes were able to get fairly decent food at cheaper prices than they could prepare it for themselves. Moreover, in spite of the minute regulations laid down for marketing agricultural produce and for requisitioning it if necessary, farmers were frequently able to keep back enough to live more comfortably than people in the towns. During 1916 shortages of milk and meat became more and more acute as forage supplies dwindled and almost disappeared; time after time the rations allowed the people were reduced. And even then there was not enough food available to give everyone the amount indicated on the meat, bread, and milk cards. Discontent with the Zentraleinkaufsgesellschaft, because of conditions over which it really had little control, became more general. It was inevitable that disorders should result. Indeed the shortages were so great that neither the rationing system, nor the harvests, which each year of the war were a greater disappointment, nor the supplies received from the border neutrals seemed to have any appreciable effect on the deficiency. There was not much hope of improvement while the war lasted; labor, horses, agricultural implements, and wagons were all lacking, and under such conditions crops could neither be raised nor harvested.

Although the other states allied with Germany have not hitherto entered into our consideration, it should be indicated that they were no better off than Germany. In Austria-Hungary, Bulgaria, and Turkey, food supplies were subjected to a rationing system, and such severe restrictions were placed on the exportation of goods that there was little chance that one of the Central Powers could buy in the markets of the other states of the alliance. Any advantages which might have resulted from a free exchange of goods between these states were made impossible. Each government looked to its own particular interests and usually refused to aid its allies in securing food and raw materials. The union of the Central Powers in military operations was not extended to the economic sphere, and it was in this second phase of warfare that disintegration was first seen. Thus, although economic pressure is of necessity rather slow in showing definite results, it was here that the Central Powers first revealed signs of collapse. However, it is impossible to measure the exact effect of the various measures taken by the Allies against German trade or to know to what extent the internal conditions in Germany resulted from the Allied economic operations.

The close of 1916 had seen the end of any real hope for a negotiated peace; the time was propitious for those Germans who believed that only an all-out submarine campaign against the British could bring the war to a close. The development of this new phase of submarine warfare and of Allied and neutral reactions to it will be the subject of a later study.

Appendixes

APPENDIX A

DISTRIBUTION OF THE WORLD'S SHIPPING IN 1914*

	Thousand Tons Net Steam Tonnage	Percentage
United Kingdom	11,538.0	44.4
Dominions and Colonies	901.8	3.5
Total British	12,439.8	47.9
France	1,098.0	4.2
Russia	498.5	1.9
Belgium	218.8	.8
Japan	1,048.0	4.0
Total Allied	15,303.1	58.8
Germany	3,096.0	11.9
Austria-Hungary	563.4	2.5
Turkey	67.8	.3
Total Enemy	3,817.2	14.7
United States	1,195.0	4.6
Norway	1,153.4	4.4
Sweden	578.5	2.3
Denmark	453.0	1.7
Holland	909.6	3.5
Italy	871.4	3.4
Greece	515.1	2.0
Other Countries	1,193.6	4.6
Total neutral	6,869.6	26.5
World total	25,989.9	100.0

* Table taken from C. Ernest Fayle, *Seaborne Trade, History of the Great War Based on Official Documents*, by direction of the Historical Section of the Committee of Imperial Defence (New York: Longman, Green and Co., Inc., 1920–1924), I, 18–19, note 2, based on Lloyd's *Register*.

ENTRANCES AND CLEARANCES IN GERMAN PORTS
(NOT INCLUDING COASTAL TRAFFIC)*

	Ships Entering		Ships Clearing	
Year	No. of German Ships	Tonnage	No. of German Ships	Tonnage
1910	86,810	17,766,193	87,387	17,967,454
1911	86,850	18,654,655	87,421	18,689,580
1912	87,943	19,429,056	87,046	19,284,699
	No. of Foreign Ships		No. of Foreign Ships	
1910	24,987	12,164,360	25,184	12,236,302
1911	25,841	12,882,133	26,158	12,956,115
1912	26,464	13,112,402	26,885	13,321,954

* Based on tables in *Statistisches Jahrbuch für das deutsche Reich*, herausgegeben vom Kaiserlichen Statistischen Amte (Berlin: Puttkammer and Muhlbrecht), 1913, p. 163, and 1914, p. 173.

FOREIGN SHIPS, ACCORDING TO FLAG, ENTERING AND CLEARING
GERMAN PORTS IN 1912

	Ships Entering		Ships Clearing	
	No. of Ships	Tonnage	No. of Ships	Tonnage
Russian	436	167,325	444	168,099
Finnish	508	193,390	505	195,267
Swedish	5,999	2,042,100	6,058	2,071,783
Norwegian	2,199	1,404,269	2,208	1,417,430
Danish	8,042	1,812,402	8,105	1,826,486
British	5,151	5,957,123	5,220	6,061,278
Dutch	3,596	752,210	3,780	774,082
Belgian	66	63,138	80	67,474
French	179	174,219	181	179,246
Spanish	88	136,289	85	132,452
Italian	24	39,054	33	50,658
Austrian	85	198,677	89	205,348
Greek	77	141,044	75	142,106
Other Foreign	14	25,162	22	30,245

APPENDIX B

BRITISH EXPORTATIONS AND RE-EXPORTATIONS TO THE NORTHERN
EUROPEAN NEUTRALS IN 1913–MID–1916, BY QUARTERS*
(Values in Pounds Sterling Throughout)

Exports, Third Quarter, ending September 30

Destination	1913	1914	1915
Sweden	2,221,446	1,780,899	1,275,515
Norway	1,496,436	1,418,556	1,753,287
Denmark	1,479,930	1,193,772	2,260,090
Netherlands	3,401,745	2,398,251	4,019,545
Total British Exports to Foreign Countries	84,174,091	52,958,593	58,896,347

Re-exports, Third Quarter, ending September 30

Destination	1913	1914	1915
Sweden	191,644	178,894	980,441
Norway	92,350	136,347	348,704
Denmark	178,950	178,284	927,886
Netherlands	1,169,646	1,171,707	2,268,787
Total British Re-exports to Foreign Countries	20,067,534	14,526,906	20,984,160

Exports, Fourth Quarter, ending December 31

Destination	1913	1914	1915
Sweden	2,110,097	2,185,231	1,139,725
Norway	1,383,690	1,531,140	1,756,723
Denmark	1,484,440	1,644,816	1,849,194
Netherlands	4,083,750	2,840,079	5,040,093
Total British Exports to Foreign Countries	84,170,820	44,450,122	64,543,937

* Compiled from Great Britain, *Parliamentary Papers, Accounts relating to Trade and Navigation for Each Month during the Year 1915*, printed by Order of the House of Commons (London: H.M. Stationery Office, 1915); and *ibid., 1916*.

Re-Exports, Fourth Quarter, ending December 31

Destination	1913	1914	1915
Sweden	215,415	631,394	628,183
Norway	132,928	345,314	406,008
Denmark	94,520	882,402	964,285
Netherlands	1,205,217	3,521,820	2,186,665
Total British Re-exports to Foreign Countries	23,990,395	16,119,848	19,853,670

Exports, First Quarter, ending March 31

Destination	1914	1915	1916
Sweden	1,804,162	1,846,389	1,491,287
Norway	1,717,556	1,812,370	2,211,715
Denmark	1,518,310	1,782,618	2,302,318
Netherlands	4,219,713	4,465,822	5,521,480
Total British Exports to Foreign Countries	83,298,731	50,678,393	69,251,933

Re-Exports, First Quarter, ending March 31

Destination	1914	1915	1916
Sweden	194,720	1,224,917	1,018,974
Norway	149,606	688,027	434,602
Denmark	118,743	1,156,795	829,136
Netherlands	1,314,319	3,529,449	2,093,873
Total British Re-exports to Foreign Countries	26,102,441	19,091,255	22,579,775

Exports, Second Quarter, ending June 30

Destination	1914	1915	1916
Sweden	1,952,527	2,028,471	1,715,817
Norway	1,825,952	1,991,070	2,922,542
Denmark	1,476,833	1,913,399	2,756,502
Netherlands	3,907,033	4,558,234	6,513,838
Total British Exports to Foreign Countries	77,918,515,	62,166,732	83,718,444

Re-Exports, Second Quarter, ending June 30

Destination	1914	1915	1916
Sweden	257,220	1,046,389	822,929
Norway	122,152	615,058	462,395
Denmark	141,859	1,067,856	870,701
Netherlands	1,300,834	4,440,030	2,699,888
Total British Re-exports to Foreign Countries	26,466,737	26,735,552	24,221,776

APPENDIX C

MONTHLY RE-EXPORTATIONS OF RAW COTTON AND COFFEE FROM THE UNITED KINGDOM TO THE NETHERLANDS AND SWEDEN, 1913, 1914, 1915*

Raw Cotton Re-Exports to the Netherlands

	Weight in cwts.		Value in pounds sterling	
	1913	1914	1913	1914
October	2,664	14,946	7,193	37,925
November	4,351	10,606	11,246	21,101
December	3,693	28,775	9,400	63,226
	1914	1915	1914	1915
January	559	36,612	1,698	77,925
February	5,334	27,990	13,932	63,938
March	1,038	45,939	3,270	99,365
April	4,204	108,009	12,894	250,077
May	3,056	25,437	8,655	46,066
June	3,594	15,641	10,893	32,843

Raw Cotton Re-Exports to Sweden

	1913	1914	1913	1914
October	1,372	7,529	4,248	18,076
November	1,231	4,663	3,081	11,957
December	2,163	20,083	6,389	41,068
	1914	1915	1914	1915
January	5,868	32,517	16,360	60,577
February	5,017	35,462	15,667	73,606
March	959	15,407	3,590	31,255
April	2,411	30,239	6,872	64,236
May	1,492	18,651	4,216	40,873
June	2,895	10,267	9,085	21,200

* Compiled from Great Britain, *Parliamentary Papers, Accounts relating to Trade and Navigation for Each Month during the Year 1914*, and *ibid.*, 1915. Raw cotton and coffee were the only two articles for which statistics on monthly exportation to any of the border neutral states were given.

Coffee Re-Exports
to the Netherlands

	1913	1914	1913	1914
October	10,283	18,149	35,631	50,692
November	10,683	64,938	37,614	186,750
December	6,886	89,883	24,651	267,917
	1914	1915	1914	1915
January	6,942	32,824	23,909	102,071
February	11,790	29,246	18,732	62,070
March	11,665	44,087	39,388	135,875
April	14,550	80,103	49,939	247,543
May	23,409	32,313	83,283	95,045
June	18,803	70,606	62,243	205,901

Coffee Re-Exports
to Sweden

	1913	1914	1913	1914
October	3,385	2,965	12,610	9,707
November	2,033	1,952	7,820	6,801
December	476	2,754	1,783	9,789
	1914	1915	1914	1915
January	680	3,962	2,561	14,634
February	988	7,113	3,574	22,951
March	1,227	5,027	4,478	17,324
April	1,700	3,424	6,179	12,448
May	3,062	2,898	10,063	11,604
June	3,538	2,290	11,742	9,239

British Re-Exportations to the Border Neutrals
The year 1914 compared with the year 1913*
(Pound Sterling Values in Parentheses)

To the Netherlands

	1913	1914
Tea, lbs.	3,810,730	19,739,388
	(£ 151,452)	(£ 811,551)
Cocoa, raw, lbs.	2,205,282	12,203,463
	(£ 62,720)	(£ 325,900)
Coffee, raw, cwts.	105,866	282,369
	(£ 368,657)	(£ 876,267)
Grains, cwts.	28,414	757,396
	(£ 16,473)	(£ 308,749)
Fats and oils, and oil-bearing seeds, cwts.	192,083	375,898
	(£ 344,059)	(£ 723,389)
Soda compounds, cwts.	121,288	310,023
	(£ 27,445)	(£ 64,516)
Fertilizers, tons	4,669	11,247
	(£ 50,053)	(£ 109,266)
Cotton, raw, cwts.	46,334	97,285
	(£ 132,200)	(£ 243,750)

To Sweden

	1913	1914
Tea, lbs.	245,660	377,533
	(£ 12,691)	(£ 18,718)
Cocoa, raw, lbs.	149,737	2,403,733
	(£ 4,692)	(£ 67,368)
Jute, tons	988	2,350
	(£ 28,053)	(£ 78,496)
Oleomargarine and oils, cwts.	3,085	9,794
	(£ 7,715)	(£ 23,483)
Coconut oil, cwts.	2,746	21,647
	(£ 6,009)	(£ 53,717)
Tallow, cwts.	9,346	16,715
	(£ 16,345)	(£ 26,928)
Soda ash, cwts.	42,120	72,865
	(£ 7,313)	(£ 12,725)

* Compiled from Great Britain, Parliamentary Papers, Annual Statement of the Trade of the United Kingdom with Foreign Countries and British Possessions, 1914, Compared with the Four Preceding Years, Vol. I, Cd. 7968, Vol. II, Cd. 8069 (London: H.M. Stationery Office, 1915).

To Norway

	1913	1914
Cocoa, raw, lbs.	193,836	676,171
	(£ 5,636)	(£ 18,934)
Tea, lbs.	164,364	277,039
	(£ 9,188)	(£ 14,218)
Coffee, lbs.	6,758	16,941
	(£ 22,261)	(£ 54,138)
Nuts and kernels for expressing oil, tons	284	2,592
	(£ 8,413)	(£ 62,942)
Tallow, cwts.	980	1,815
	(£ 1,636)	(£ 3,511)
Soda ash, cwts.	33,677	100,822
	(£ 5,760)	(£ 17,000)
Corn and grain, cwts.	48,306	213,844
	(£ 22,054)	(£ 87,318)
Cotton, raw, cwts.	6,045	33,496
	(£ 18,326)	(£ 96,157)

To Denmark

	1913	1914
Cocoa, raw, lbs.	50,782	1,853,948
	(£ 1,386)	(£ 51,134)
Coffee, raw, cwts.	4,699	18,511
	(£ 16,384)	(£ 54,034)
Tea, lbs.	830,014	4,422,298
	(£ 37,161)	(£ 186,395)
Corn and grain, cwts.	39,232	933,186
	(£ 20,970)	(£ 330,415)
Nuts and kernels, tons	542	3,372
	(£ 14,930)	(£ 76,244)
Petroleum, gals.	43,348	86,170
	(£ 974)	(£ 2,373)
Oilseed cake, tons	3	2,002
	(£ 20)	(£ 12,465)

APPENDIX E

French Exportations and Re-Exportations to the Border Neutrals in 1913, 1914, and 1915*

Exportations in 1913
French Exportations in Thousand Francs

	Foodstuffs	Industrial Raw Materials	Manufactured Goods	Total
Sweden	7,477	13,286	4,573	25,336
Norway	2,344	2,834	5,462	10,640
Denmark	10,463	17,299	13,474	41,236
The Netherlands ..	18,426	27,951	36,303	82,680
Totals to Foreign Countries	673,882	1,753,234	3,477,143	5,904,259

Temporary Admissions
Goods Re-Exported after Manufacturing

	Foodstuffs	Industrial Raw Materials	Manufactured Goods	Total
Sweden	591	6	423	1,020
Norway	1,189	13	58	1,260
Denmark	334	3	264	601
The Netherlands ..	1,201	176	1,845	3,222
Totals to Foreign Countries	107,133	40,780	109,212	257,125

Exportations in 1914
French Exportations in Thousand Francs

	Foodstuffs	Industrial Raw Materials	Manufactured Goods	Total
Sweden	4,659	10,566	2,375	17,600
Norway	1,787	2,614	3,740	8,141
Denmark	5,921	23,862	8,279	38,062
The Netherlands ..	9,657	18,352	12,632	40,641
Totals to Foreign Countries	486,383	1,212,176	2,361,443	4,060,002

Temporary Admissions
Goods Re-Exported after Manufacturing

	Foodstuffs	Industrial Raw Materials	Manufactured Goods	Total
Sweden	244	—	201	445
Norway	1,460	1	44	1,505
Denmark	199	—	90	289
The Netherlands ..	619	56	570	1,245
Totals to Foreign Countries	81,027	11,623	44,004	136,654

* Compiled from France, Bureau de la Statistique Générale, Annuaire statistique, 1914 and 1915 (Paris: Imprimerie Nationale, 1917); and ibid., 1916 (Paris: Imprimerie Nationale, 1921).

Exportations in 1915
French Exportations in Thousand Francs

Sweden	7,843	11,286	5,593	24,722
Norway	2,918	9,435	9,978	22,232
Denmark	8,797	5,966	7,843	22,606
The Netherlands ..	8,530	9,161	26,023	43,714
Totals to Foreign Countries	482,824	698,856	2,060,125	3,241,805

Temporary Admissions
Goods Re-Exported after Manufacturing

Sweden	332	—	74	406
Norway	1,000	14	28	1,042
Denmark	187	—	69	256
The Netherlands ..	90	—	371	461
Totals to Foreign Countries	15,237	19,701	44,589	79,527

APPENDIX F

GERMAN EXPORTATIONS, 1913–1914–1915*

Destination	1913	1914	1915
United States ...... (dollars)	188,963,071	189,919,136	91,372,710
Spain .... (pesetas)	185,370,000	108,124,000	20,995,000
Argentina	597,358 (tons)	322,530,000 (dollars)	305,488,000 (dollars)
Brazil .... (pounds)	11,737,000	5,719,000	458,000
Chile .... (pesos)	81,035,995	70,930,879	9,818,052
Paraguay .... (pesos)	2,243,924	1,398,002	166,669
Uruguay .... (pesos)	7,811,135	3,175,809	749,375
Japan .... (yen)	68,394,798	44,922,005	5,919,464
China .... (tael)	28,302,403	16,696,945	160,458

* Information supplied to me by A. C. Bell.

APPENDIX G

SELECTED STATISTICS ON DUTCH EXPORTATIONS TO GERMANY
1914, 1915, 1916*

(All data are for January to November in each year and are expressed in
metric tons.)

	1914	1915	1916
Butter	17,598	33,527	30,319
Cocoa	21,564	17,094	3,302
Copra	54,287	106,613	—
Eggs	12,091	24,635	29,877
Cheese	19,108	56,526	75,984
Coffee	69,986	123,490	58,209
Margarine	18,008	24,151	2,772
Tea	12,865	5,742	2,063
Fish	81,560	148,861	145,872
Meat	14,061	66,986	47,008

* Compiled from statistics published in the Comité de Restriction des Approvisionnements et du Commerce de l'Ennemi, *Bulletin*, no. 91, January 25, 1917, pp. 15–16. The
commodities listed above were selected because they were either of Dutch production, or
had been the subject of special concern to the Allied governments.

APPENDIX H

BRITISH COFFEE RE-EXPORTATIONS TO RUSSIA AND THE
NETHERLANDS IN 1913, 1914, 1915.*

(Pounds Sterling Values in Parentheses)

To Russia (in Cwts.)

		1913		1914		1915
July		1,749		3,200		1,652
	(£	7,042)	(£	12,295)	(£	7,219)
August		930		190		2,626
	(£	3,752)	(£	685)	(£	10,945)
September		1,084		173		2,532
	(£	4,132)	(£	735)	(£	8,585)
October		2,682		127		3,243
	(£	10,993)	(£	729)	(£	13,318)
November		1,313		2,744		2,518
	(£	5,255)	(£	10,164)	(£	10,059)
December		541		5,081		3,192
	(£	2,528)	(£	19,383)	(£	10,799)
Total for the year		15,676		21,228		51,259
	(£	64,164)	(£	81,441)	(£	191,780)

To the Netherlands (in Cwts.)

		1913		1914		1915
July		7,480		15,339		52,155
	(£	25,425)	(£	52,278)	(£	154,460)
August		8,674		4,062		200
	(£	29,220)	(£	12,653)	(£	650)
September		13,788		2,840		102
	(£	46,973)	(£	8,044)	(£	310)
October		10,283		18,149		7,778
	(£	35,631)	(£	50,692)	(£	24,115)
November		10,683		64,938		5,136
	(£	37,614)	(£	186,750)	(£	14,422)
December		6,886		89,883		424
	(£	24,651)	(£	267,917)	(£	1,100)
Total for the year		105,871		282,370		354,924
	(£	368,706)	(£	876,272)	(£	1,073,952)

* Great Britain, Parliamentary Papers, Accounts relating to the Trade and Navigation for Each Month during the Year 1915, and ibid., 1916.

British Coffee Re-Exportations to the Netherlands in 1916

	Cwts.	£ Value
January	1,069	2,734
February	15,276	51,854
March	24,689	75,980
April	7,757	24,206
May	20,404	61,512
June	27,744	80,951
Total for first six months of 1916 ..	96,939	297,237
[Compare to total for first six months of 1914]	87,159	297,938

APPENDIX I

IMPORTATIONS OF AGRICULTURAL AND FISH PRODUCTS BY THE UNITED
KINGDOM FROM THE NETHERLANDS, DENMARK, AND NORWAY
1914–1915–1916*

From the Netherlands
Pork (in Cwts.)

	1914	1915	1916
January	95,711	73,891	591
February	88,276	41,669	137
March	105,020	21,084	31
April	61,117	56	—
May	40,167	542	—
June	25,515	10	—
July	22,683	—	—
August	23,090	—	—
September	81,066	—	—
October	95,978	—	—
November	92,560	24	—
December	86,553	416	—
Total for the year	817,736	137,692	759

Butter (in Cwts.)

	1914	1915	1916
January	5,241	4,578	130
February	5,120	4,298	70
March	6,087	7,009	84
April	8,904	8,340	193
May	16,871	3,516	1,507
June	27,159	6,678	612
July	19,619	4,625	1,461
August	37,779	3,091	5,472
September	34,895	1,880	7,338
October	11,871	523	5,599
November	6,354	29	7,376
December	4,099	55	6,360
Total for the year	183,999	45,544	36,202

* Compiled from Great Britain, *Parliamentary Papers, Accounts relating to the Trade
and Navigation for Each month during the Year 1916.*

Cheese (in Cwts.)

	1914	1915	1916
January	24,752	20,935	1,011
February	19,606	22,139	1,282
March	22,426	17,549	1,379
April	23,598	10,070	612
May	23,014	7,398	617
June	24,452	19,427	915
July	25,855	13,196	3,312
August	36,429	5,202	11,516
September	48,216	4,858	13,128
October	59,578	2,915	18,123
November	9,791	4,918	23,206
December	21,407	498	37,486
Total for the year	349,124	129,105	112,587

Eggs (in great hundreds)

	1914	1915	1916
January	64,719	67,233	13,409
February	106,908	135,742	23,553
March	197,600	160,837	18,422
April	131,577	76,049	3,591
May	149,873	66,145	3,534
June	131,982	29,351	2,860
July	91,148	103,594	1,193
August	66,513	62,459	1,885
September	117,610	103,651	11,374
October	74,130	34,014	460
November	37,585	30,431	340
December	22,641	4,507	4,116
Total for the year	1,192,286	874,013	84,737

From Denmark
Bacon (in Cwts.)

	1914	1915	1916
January	217,605	216,144	121,548
February	214,880	248,515	128,877
March	237,435	224,464	171,291
April	216,563	164,623	136,906
May	239,050	180,055	171,233
June	229,474	191,243	109,611
July	265,686	182,624	145,061
August	180,144	144,509	135,881
September	195,510	116,778	148,644
October	226,923	114,087	137,192
November	246,170	140,672	116,697
December	245,367	139,507	118,672
Total for the year	2,714,807	2,063,221	1,641,613

Butter (in Cwts.)

	1914	1915	1916
January	139,603	128,101	104,381
February	132,943	146,008	89,620
March	170,554	150,784	101,986
April	143,776	120,602	82,003
May	149,526	129,179	110,381
June	182,539	140,364	92,801
July	151,105	111,573	98,505
August	132,516	101,343	101,064
September	157,962	86,057	94,881
October	141,055	56,855	84,652
November	121,716	67,898	91,296
December	125,777	88,336	83,231
Total for the year	1,749,072	1,327,100	1,134,801

Eggs (in great hundreds)

	1914	1915	1916
January	238,542	165,098	81,088
February	180,220	112,420	94,648
March	341,988	265,389	46,091
April	199,696	206,432	37,808
May	271,605	276,810	148,510
June	423,558	244,690	140,170
July	442,368	246,598	164,723
August	410,492	297,976	235,079
September	438,750	354,062	182,162
October	614,676	216,093	152,995
November	435,868	179,028	102,340
December	318,137	176,329	70,566
Total for the year	4,315,900	2,657,835	1,392,061

From Norway†
Fish (in Cwts.)

	1914	1915	1916
January	87,215	110,372	4,311
February	103,869	164,899	9,078
March	307,349	262,083	98,584
April	244,479	142,549	36,960
May	93,940	42,710	2,962
June	17,554	11,019	4,368
July	9,391	11,096	1,846
August	653	3,536	200
September	442	981	605
October	893	873	50
November	1,951	1,854	27
December	52,138	21,110	10
Total for the year	920,344	773,082	159,001

† Fish importations from the Netherlands and Denmark are not specified in the British statistics.

Bibliography

MANUSCRIPTS AND PAPERS FOR
PRIVATE CIRCULATION

FRANCE

Comité de Restriction des Approvisionnements et du Commerce de l'Ennemi, *Bulletin*, nos. 1–195, April 1915—January 1919 [1915, 2 vols.; 1916, 3 vols.; 1917, 3 vols.; 1917 (October)–1919 (January), 1 vol.]. A bulletin published weekly for the use of French departments and committees concerned with the economic war. The *Bulletin*, based on reports of French diplomatic and consular agents as well as on the foreign press, noted conditions in enemy, neutral, and allied states. Apparently it was intended for wider circulation than the other papers of the Comité.

Comité de Restriction des Approvisionnements et du Commerce de l'Ennemi. A collection of papers in the Bibliothèque et Musée de la Guerre de Vincennes, Paris, includes files of the following materials:

> *Comptes-rendus*, March 13, 1915—December 6, 1916. Minutes of the meetings of the Comité. There are some gaps.
>
> *Documents divers, non-numérotés*. A short series of unnumbered documents and reports prepared for circulation among the members of the Comité de Restriction.
>
> *Documents numérotés, publiés par le Secretariat* [from March 22, 1916, to January 14, 1919]. These documents, concerned mainly with negotiations with neutrals, regulation of Allied exports, and conditions resulting in Germany and Austria, give a basis for estimating French policy in the economic war. The series also includes some British documents which had been transmitted to the French government.

277

Étude sur l'effet des mesures restrictives prises par les Alliés sur les approvisionnement et le commerce de l'ennemi du 1ère octobre 1915 au 31 décembre 1916.

Procès-verbaux, April 6, 1915—December 6, 1916. Formal resolutions passed by the Comité, presumably to be sent to higher French and allied authorities.

SWEDEN

Sveriges Riksarkivet. Statens Handelskommission Papers. Very few of the papers of this commission were open for inspection when the present study was done.

Textile Alliance. A file of documents in the Hoover Library, Stanford University, California, presented by this association of American textile manufacturers and concerned with their agreements with the Allies.

Veeder Papers. Correspondence in the possession of Albert H. and Henry Veeder, of Chicago, legal counsel for Swift and Company. The materials examined deal chiefly with negotiations between the most important American meat packers and the British government in 1915 and 1916, the manner in which the agreements worked, the packers' relations with the Netherlands Oversea Trust (N.O.T.), and protests against British action directed by the packers to the United States Department of State. Files cited in this study are "N.O.T." and "Shipments under Agreement."

GOVERNMENT PUBLICATIONS

DENMARK

Danmarks Skibsliste, 1916. Copenhagen: Kongelige Søkort-Arkiv. List of ships under Danish registry.

Lovtidende for Kongeriget Danmark for Aaret 1916. Copenhagen: J. H. Schultz, 1917. Law Journal of the Kingdom of Denmark.

Rigsdagstidende, Forhandlinger paa Folketinget, 1914–1917. Copenhagen: J. H. Schultz, 1914–1917. Debates of the lower house of the Danish Parliament.

Rigsdagstidende, Forhandlinger paa Landstinget, 1915–1917. Copenhagen: J. H. Schultz, 1915–1916. Debates of the upper house of the Danish Parliament.

Samling af Love, Anordningen, offentlige Kundgørelser, ministerielle Cirkulaerer og Skrivelser, 1914–1917. Copenhagen: J. H. Schultz, 1914–1917. Collection of laws, ordinances, public proclamations, ministerial circulars and communications.

FRANCE

Bureau de la Statistique Générale de la France, Annuaire statistique, 1914, 1915, 1916. Paris: Imprimerie Nationale, 1917–1921.

Code d'instruction criminelle et code pénal, ed. A. Carpentier. Paris: Sirey, 1927.

Débats parlementaires, 11e Législature, Session Ordinaire de 1915. Paris: Imprimerie Nationale.

Journal officiel, 1914–1916. Paris: Imprimerie Nationale.

Ministère des Affaires Étrangères, Commission de Publication des Documents Rélatifs aux Origines de la Guerre de 1914, *Documents diplomatiques français (1871–1914)*, 3e Série. Paris: Imprimerie Nationale, 1929–1936. 11 vols.

Ministères de la Guerre et des Affaires Étrangères, *Bulletin périodique de la presse hollandaise*. Paris: Imprimerie Nationale, 1916.

GERMANY

The Prize Code of the German Empire, as in Force July 1, 1915, tr. and ed. Charles Henry Huberich and Richard King. New York: Baker, Voorhis and Co., 1915.

Reichs-Gesetzblatt, 1914. Berlin: Reichsamte des Innern.

Spindler, Arno, *Der Handelskrieg mit U-Booten. Der Krieg zur See, 1914–1918*, ed. the German Marine-Archiv. Berlin: Mittler, 1932–1934. 3 vols.

Statistisches Jahrbuch für das deutsche Reich, herausgegeben vom Kaiserlichen Statistischen Amte. Berlin: Puttkammer and Muhlbrecht, 1913, 1914.

Das Werk des Untersuchungsausschusses der Verfassunggegebenden Deutschen Nationalversammlung und des Deutschen Reichstages, 1919–1928, Völkerrecht im Weltkrieg, Vol. IV, ed. Dr. Johannes Bell, in collaboration with Dr. Eugen Fischer and Dr. Berthold Widmann. Berlin: Deutsche Verlagsgesellschaft für Politik und Geschichte, 1927.

GREAT BRITAIN

Board of Trade Journal, August 1914—December 1916. Chiefly useful to this study for the notices of British, allied, and neutral embargoes, and all other regulations concerning trade.

British and Foreign State Papers, Vols. XLVI (1855–1856), LX (1869–1870), C (1906–1907), CVIII (1914, Part II), and CXI (1917–1918). London: H.M. Stationery Office.

General Staff, War Office, *Daily Review of the Foreign Press, Neutral Press Supplement*, 1916–1917.

Gooch, George P., and Temperley, Harold, eds., *British Documents on the Origins of the War, 1898–1914*. London: H.M. Stationery Office, 1926–1938. 11 vols.

Manual of Emergency Legislation, Comprising All the Acts of Parliament, Proclamations, Orders, etc. Passed and Made in Consequence of the War, to September 30th, 1914, ed. Alexander Pulling. London: H.M. Stationery Office, 1914. *Supplement No. 2 to December 5, 1914, Incorporating and Superseding Supplement No. 1*. London: H.M. Stationery Office, 1914. *Supplement No. 3 to April 30th, 1915, in Continuation of Supplement No. 2*. London: H.M. Stationery Office, 1915. *Supplement No. 4 to August 31st, 1915, in Continuation of Supplement No. 3*. London: H.M. Stationery Office, 1915.

Parliamentary Debates, 3rd Series, 1856 and 1862, and 5th Series, 1911 and 1914–1916. London: H.M. Stationery Office.

Parliamentary Papers,
Accounts Relating to Trade and Navigation for Each Month during the

Year 1915, printed by order of the House of Commons. London: H.M. Stationery Office, 1915.

Accounts Relating to Trade and Navigation for Each Month during the Year 1916, printed by order of the House of Commons. London: H.M. Stationery Office, 1916.

Annual Statement of the Trade of the United Kingdom with Foreign Countries and British Possessions, 1914, Compared with the Four Preceding Years, Vol. I, Cd. 7968, Vol. II, Cd. 8069. London: H.M. Stationery Office, 1915.

Annual Statement of the Trade of the United Kingdom with Foreign Countries and British Possessions, 1916, Compared with the Four Preceding Years, Vol. II, Cd. 8714. London: H.M. Stationery Office, 1917.

Diplomatic and Consular Reports, Netherlands, Report for the Year 1913, Trade, Shipping and Agriculture of Rotterdam and the Consular Posts in the Netherlands, Cd. 7048–132. London: H.M. Stationery Office, 1914.

Diplomatic and Consular Reports, Norway, Report for the Year 1912 on the Trade and Commerce of Norway (Supplementary), Cd. 7048–67. London: H.M. Stationery Office, 1914.

Fisheries in the Great War, Being the Report on Sea Fisheries for the Years 1915, 1916, 1917, and 1918, of the Board of Agriculture and Fisheries, Parts I and II, Cmd. 585. London: H.M. Stationery Office, 1920.

Miscellaneous No. 2 (1916), Statement of the Measures Adopted to Intercept the Seaborne Commerce of Germany, Cd. 8143. London: H.M. Stationery Office, 1916.

Miscellaneous No. 2 (1917), Memorandum Addressed by the French and British Governments to the United States Government Regarding the Examination of Parcels and Letter Mails, Cd. 8438. London: H.M. Stationery Office, 1917.

Miscellaneous No. 4 (1909), Correspondence and Documents Respecting the International Naval Conference Held in London, December 1908–February 1909, Cd. 4554. London: H.M. Stationery Office, 1909.

Miscellaneous No. 5 (1916), Correspondence with the United States Ambassador Respecting the Treatment of Mails on Neutral Vessels, Cd. 8173. London: H.M. Stationery Office, 1916.

Miscellaneous No. 6 (1915), Correspondence between His Majesty's Government and the United States Government Respecting the Rights of Belligerents, Cd. 7816. London: H.M. Stationery Office, 1915.

Miscellaneous No. 6 (1917), Report Drawn Up by the Committee on the Administration of the Order in Council of March 1915 (1916), Cd. 8469. London: H.M. Stationery Office, 1917.

Miscellaneous No. 9 (1916), Memorandum Presented by His Majesty's Government and the French Government to Neutral Governments Regarding the Examination of Parcels and Letter Mails, Cd. 8223. London: H.M. Stationery Office, 1916.

Miscellaneous No. 14 (1916), Further Correspondence between His Majesty's Government and the United States Respecting the Rights of Belligerents, Cd. 8233. London: H.M. Stationery Office, 1916.

Miscellaneous No. 22 (1916), Note Addressed by His Majesty's Government to Neutral Representatives in London Respecting the Withdrawal of the Declaration of London Orders in Council, Cd. 8293. London: H.M. Stationery Office, 1916.

Miscellaneous No. 23 (1916), Note Addressed to the United States Ambassador Regarding the Examination of Parcels and Letter Mails, Cd. 8294. London: H.M. Stationery Office, 1916.

Miscellaneous No. 28 (1916), Correspondence with the Swedish Minister on the Subject of the Detention by the Swedish Government of the British Transit Mail to Russia as a Reprisal for the Search of Parcels Mail by His Majesty's Government, Cd. 8322. London: H.M. Stationery Office, 1916.

Recommendations of the Economic Conference of the Allies, Held at Paris on June 14, 15, 16, and 17, 1916, Cd. 8271. London: H.M. Stationery Office, 1916.

Report of a Select Committee on the Operation of Burdens and Restrictions Especially Affecting Merchant Shipping, with Proceedings, Evidence, Appendix, and Index. London: H.M. Stationery Office, 1860.

Public General Statutes, 5 and 6 George V, 1914–1916. London: Eyre and Spottiswoode, 1916.

Statutory Rules and Orders, 1916. London: H.M. Stationery Office, 1917.

THE NETHERLANDS

Diplomatieke Bescheiden betreffende de Inbeslagneming door de Britsche Autoriteiten van over zee vervoerde Brievenpost. The Hague: Algemeene Landsdrukkerij, 1916. Diplomatic documents concerning the detention of overseas letter mails by the British authorities.

Mededeelingen van den Minister van buitenlandsche Zaken aan de Staten-Generaal, Juli–December 1916. n.p., n.d. Communications of the minister of foreign affairs to the States-General.

Mededeelingen van den Minister van buitenlandsche Zaken aan de Staten-Generaal, Juni 1919–April 1920. n.p., n.d.

Nederlandsche Staatscourant, 1914–1915. The Hague: Algemeene Landsdrukkerij, 1914–1915.

Overzicht van eenige in het Tijdvak October 1915 tot Juli 1916 door het Ministerie van buitenlandsche Zaken behandelde Aangelegenheden. n.p., n.d. Survey of some of the affairs handled by the Ministry of Foreign Affairs in the period October 1915 to July 1916.

Staatsblad van het Koninkrijk der Nederlanden, 1914. The Hague: Algemeene Landsdrukkerij, 1915.

Staten-Generaal, Handelingen, 1914–1916. The Hague: Algemeene Landsdrukkerij, 1914–1916. Debates of the Dutch Parliament.

NORWAY

Lover, resolutioner og skrivelser, foranlediget ved krigsforholdene, 1 august 1914–31 december 1916. Christiania: Grøndahl and Sons, 1917. Laws, resolutions, and communications occasioned by the war situation.

Norges officiella statistik, Norges handel, 1913–1916. Christiania: Grøndahl and Sons.

Norske lovtidende, Samling av love, resolutioner og skrivelser, 1917. Christiania: Grøndahl and Sons, 1917.

Oversigt over de vigtigste av utenriksdepartmentet under Krigen indtil mai 1916, Behandlede saker som egner sig for offentliggjørelse. Christiania: Grøndahl and Sons, 1916. A survey of the chief work of the Department of Foreign Affairs during the war, to May 1916.

Storting, Forhandlinger, 1914–1917. Christiania: Centraltrykkeriet, 1915–1917. Debates of the Norwegian Parliament.

RUSSIA

Die internationalen Beziehungen im Zeitalter des Imperialismus, Dokumente aus den Archiven der zarischen und der provisorischen Regierung, ed. Central Executive Committee of the Soviet government, M. N. Pokrowsky, chairman; German ed. by Otto Hoetzsch. Berlin: Reimar Hobbing, 1931–1936, 8 vols. in 11. This collection contains the only published documents on the Anglo-Swedish negotiations for a general agreement in the summer of 1915.

SWEDEN

Hildebrand, Karl, *De svenska statsmakterna och krigstidens folkhushållning.* Stockholm: P. A. Norstedt, 1916–1920. 5 vols. These volumes on the Swedish state and its wartime economy, published under governmental auspices, are sometimes spoken of as "the Gray Books."

Riksdagens protokoll, 1914–1916. Stockholm: P. A. Norstedt, 1914–1916. Debates of the Swedish Parliament.

Statens Industrikommission, *Statsmakterna och den svenska industrien under krigstiden.* Stockholm: P. A. Norstedt, 1920. An official history of the State Industrial Commission during the war.

Svensk författningssamling. Stockholm: P. A. Norstedt, 1914–1916. A collection of Swedish laws and ordinances.

Sveriges officiella statistik, Handel berättelse, 1913–1916. Stockholm: P. A. Norstedt, 1914–1918. Statistical report on trade.

UNITED STATES

Congress, *Congressional Record,* 64th Congress, 1st Session, Vol. LIII, Part XIII. Washington, D.C.: Government Printing Office, 1916.

Congress, 64th Congress, 1st Session, Senate, "Trade Agreements Abroad. Articles relating to the Resolution (S. 220) 'Requesting the President to ascertain certain information relating to a recent commercial conference held in Paris, France by certain European Nations' together with the remarks of Senator William J. Stone and Senator Henry Cabot Lodge delivered in the United States Senate thereon and the message of the President in response thereto," *Senate Documents,* Vol. XLIII, Document No. 491. Washington, D.C.: Government Printing Office, 1916.

Congress, 64th Congress, 1st Session, Senate, "Trade Agreements Abroad. Message from the President of the United States, Transmitting in response to a Senate Resolution of June 29, 1916, a communication from the Secretary of State submitting a report as to the character, form, and purpose of the Agreement concluded by the Allied Nations at Paris regarding their future joint and several industrial and commercial interests," *Senate Documents*, Vol. XLIII, Document No. 490. Washington, D.C.: Government Printing Office, 1916.

Department of Commerce, *Foreign Commerce and Navigation of the United States for the Year Ending June 30, 1915*. Washington, D.C.: Government Printing Office, 1916.

Department of State, *Papers Relating to the Foreign Relations of the United States, 1914, 1915, 1916, and 1917 Supplements*. Washington, D.C.: Government Printing Office, 1928–1932. 6 vols.

Department of War, General Staff, War College Division, "Strategic Map of Central Europe Showing the International Frontiers." Washington, D.C.

Savage, Carlton, ed., *Policy of the United States toward Maritime Commerce in War*. Washington, D.C.: Government Printing Office, 1936. 2 vols.

UNOFFICIAL DOCUMENTARY COLLECTIONS

Fauchille, Paul, ed., *La Guerre de 1914, Recueil de documents intéressant le droit international*. Paris: Pedone, 1916–1920. 3 vols.

Lloyd's *Reports of Prize Cases, Heard before and Decided by the Right Honourable Sir Samuel Evans, et al., during the European War Which Began in August, 1914*. London: Lloyd's, 1915–1924. 10 vols.

Martens, Georg Friedrich de, *Nouveau Recueil général de traités et autres actes relatifs aux rapports de droit international*, Continuation du Grand Recueil de G. Fr. de Martens par Heinrich Triepel, 3e Série, tome X. Leipzig: Theodor Weicher, 1921.

Scott, James Brown, ed., *The Declaration of London, February 26, 1909: A Collection of Official Papers and Documents Relating to the International Naval Conference Held in London, December, 1908–February, 1909*. New York: Oxford University Press, 1919.

——— *The Hague Conventions and Declarations of 1899 and 1907*. New York: Oxford University Press, 1915.

——— *The Proceedings of the Hague Peace Conferences, Translations of the Official Texts: The Conference of 1907*. New York: Oxford University Press, 1920–1921. 3 vols.

MEMOIRS AND BIOGRAPHIES

Baker, Ray Stannard, *Woodrow Wilson, Life and Letters*. Garden City, N.Y.: Doubleday Doran and Co., Inc., 1927–1939. 8 vols.

Bradford, Admiral Sir Edward E., *Life of Admiral of the Fleet Sir Arthur Knyvet Wilson*. New York: E. P. Dutton and Co., 1923.

Churchill, Winston S., *The World Crisis, 1911–1915.* New York: Charles Scribner's Sons, 1923.

Grey, Viscount, *Twenty-five Years.* New York: Frederick A. Stokes, 1925. 2 vols.

Haldane, Richard Burdon, *An Autobiography.* New York: Doubleday, Doran and Co., Inc., 1929.

Howard, Esme, *Theater of Life, Life Seen from the Stalls.* Boston: Little, Brown and Co., 1936.

Joffre, Joseph J. C., *The Personal Memoirs of Joffre,* tr. Col. T. Bentley Mott. New York and London: Harper and Brothers, 1932. 2 vols.

Morris, Ira, *From an American Legation.* New York: Alfred A. Knopf, Inc., 1923.

Seymour, Charles, ed., *The Intimate Papers of Colonel House.* Boston and New York: Houghton Mifflin Co., 1926–1928. 4 vols.

Tirpitz, Alfred von, *Politische Dokumente, Deutsche Ohnmachtspolitik im Weltkrieg.* Hamburg and Berlin: Hanseatische Verlagsanstalt, 1926.

MONOGRAPHS AND ARTICLES

Assmann, Kurt, "Die englische Mobilmachung 1914," *Berliner Monatshefte,* XIV (September 1936), 677–713.

Bach, August, "Englands Entschluss zum Krieg," *Berliner Monatshefte,* X (April 1932), 309–330.

Bailey, Thomas A., "The United States and the Blacklist during the Great War," *Journal of Modern History,* VI (March 1934), 14–35.

Bell, Archibald C., *Die englische Hungerblockade im Weltkrieg, 1914–1915,* nach dem amtlichen englischen Darstellung der Hungerblockade von A. C. Bell, bearbeitet und eingeleitet durch Dr. Viktor Böhmert. Bd. XIV, Veroffentlichungen des Deutschen Instituts für Aussenpolitische Forschung. Essen: Essener Verlagsanstalt, 1943. A pirated edition of part of a history of the blockade prepared in the British Committee of Imperial Defence for official use.

Bowles, Thomas Gibson, *The Declaration of Paris of 1856: Being an Account of the Maritime Rights of Great Britain; a Consideration of Their Importance; a History of Their Surrender by the Signatories of the Declaration of Paris; and an Argument for Their Resumption by the Denunciation and Repudiation of That Declaration.* London: Sampson Low, Marston and Co., 1900.

Clémentel, Étienne, *La France et la politique économique interalliée.* Economic and Social History of the World War, French Series. Paris: Dotation Carnegie, 1931.

Cochin, Denys, ed., *Les Organisations de blocus en France pendant la Guerre, 1914–1918.* Paris: Plon, 1926. A collaborative work on the economic war in France by men associated with Cochin in the Comité de Restriction and in other government departments concerned with the blockade.

Cohn, Einar, *Danmark under den store Krig, en økonomisk oversigt.* Economic and Social History of the World War, Scandinavian Series. Copenhagen: G. E. C. Gad, 1928. [*Denmark during the Great War, An Economic Survey*.]

"Le Comité interparlementaire franco-britannique," *Nouvelles de France*, IV (February 24, 1916), 144–146, and IV (March 2, 1916), 167–168.

"La Conférence internationale du commerce," *Nouvelles de France*, IV (April 27, 1916), 337–338, and IV (May 4, 1916), 356–358.

Consett, Montagu W. W. P., *The Triumph of Unarmed Forces (1914–1918), An Account of the Transactions by which Germany during the Great War was Able to Obtain Supplies Prior to Her Collapse under the Pressure of Economic Forces.* London: Williams and Norgate, 1923. Consett, who was British commercial attaché in Stockholm, 1912–1919, treats particularly the trade between the northern European neutrals and the Central Powers in violation of, or at least contrary to, the intention of agreements made by the British with the neutrals.

Corbett, Sir Julian S., and Newbolt, Henry, *Naval Operations, History of the Great War Based on Official Documents*, by direction of the Historical Section of the Committee of Imperial Defence. New York: Longmans, Green and Co., Inc., 1920–1931. 5 vols.

Dearle, Norman B., *Dictionary of Official War-Time Organizations*. Economic and Social History of the World War, British Series. London: Humphrey Milford, 1928.

Dubern, E. B., "Les Projets d'union économique entre les Alliés dans l'hiver 1915–1916," *Revue des sciences politiques*, XXXV (June 15, 1916), 363–376.

Ehrmann, Howard M., "The Pact of London, September 5, 1914," *Berliner Monatshefte*, XIII (March 1935), 231–241.

Fayle, C. Ernest, *Seaborne Trade, History of the Great War Based on Official Documents*, by direction of the Historical Section of the Committee of Imperial Defence. New York: Longmans, Green and Co., Inc., 1920–1924.

Gatzke, Hans W., *Germany's Drive to the West (Drang nach Westen), A Study of Germany's Western War Aims during the First World War.* Baltimore: Johns Hopkins University Press, 1950.

Greiner, Herbert, "Die französische Mobilmachung 1914," *Berliner Monatshefte*, XIV (July 1936), 515–546.

Guichard, Louis, *The Naval Blockade, 1914–1918*, tr. and ed. Christopher R. Turner. London: Philip Allan and Co., 1930. A study of the blockade from the economic point of view. Guichard was attached to the Historical Section of the French Ministry of Marine. This is probably the best of the general books on this phase of the war.

———— "La Victoire par étouffement," *La Correspondant*, CCCXIII (October 10 and 25, 1928), 47–68, and 254–284.

Hansen, Johannes, *Hovedtraek af Industriraadets Historie.* Copenhagen: Nielsen and Lydiche, 1935. [*Main Features of the History of the Danish Chamber of Manufacturers*.] Much of this anniversary volume deals with the war period.

Haslam, Robert T. and Russel, Robert P., *Fuels and Their Combustion.* New York and London: McGraw-Hill Book Co., 1926.

THE ALLIED BLOCKADE OF GERMANY

Heckscher, Eli F., *Bidrag till Sveriges ekonomiska och sociala historia under och efter Världskriget*. Economic and Social History of the World War, Scandinavian Series. Stockholm: P. A. Norstedt, 1926. [A Contribution to Sweden's Economic and Social History during and after the World War.]

—— *The Continental System, An Economic Interpretation*. Oxford: Clarendon Press, 1922.

Hjort, Johan, *Utenrikspolitiske oplevelser under Verdenskrigen*. Oslo: Gyldendal Norsk Forlag, 1927. [Adventures in Foreign Policy during the World War.] An account of Anglo-Norwegian fish negotiations written by the director of Fisheries.

Higgins, A. Pearce, "Retaliation in Naval Warfare," *British Year Book of International Law*, 1927, pp. 128–146.

Kahl, Friedrich, *Die Pariser Wirtschaftskonferenz vom 14, bis 17. Juni 1916, und die ihr voraufgegangenen Beratungen der Ententestaaten über den Wirtschaftskrieg gegen die Mittelmächte*. Kriegswirtschaftliche Untersuchungen aus dem Institut für Seeverkehr und Weltwirtschaft an den Universität Kiel. Jena: Gustav Fischer, 1917. A study of the Allied Economic Conference, based on press reports of the conference, and of Allied public and parliamentary opinion. This work places particular emphasis on the plans made for the postwar economic coöperation of the Allies.

Keilhau, Wilhelm, *Norge og Verdenskrigen*. Economic and Social History of the World War, Scandinavian Series. Oslo: H. Aschehoug and Co., 1927. [Norway and the World War.]

Knudsen, Olaf, *Dansk Industriberetning 1915–1918*. Copenhagen: Nielsen and Lydiche, 1921. 2 vols. [A Report on Danish Industry.] A publication sponsored by the Industrial Union of Copenhagen.

Laurens, Adolphe, *Le Blocus et la guerre sous-marine, 1914–1918*. Paris: Armand Colin, 1924.

—— *Histoire de la guerre sous-marine allemande, 1914–1918*. Paris: Société d'Éditions Géographiques, Maritimes et Coloniales, 1930.

La Brière, Le R. P. de, "Evolution de la doctrine et la pratique en matière de rétorsion et de représailles," in A. F. Frangulis, ed., *Dictionnaire diplomatique*. Paris: Académie Diplomatique Internationale, 1933. 2 vols.

Macqueen, John Fraser, *Chief Points in the Laws of War and Neutrality, Search, and Blockade; with the Changes of 1856, and Those Now Proposed*. London and Edinburgh: Wm. and Robert Chambers, 1862.

Maegaard, Eilert, and Vestberg, Jens, *Dansk Dampskibsrederiforening, 1884—17. Januar 1934*. Copenhagen: Fr. G. Knuedtzon, 1934. The major part of this history of the Danish Steamship Owners Union deals with the war.

Malkin, Herbert W., "The Inner History of the Declaration of Paris," *British Year Book of International Law*, 1927, pp. 1–44.

Manen, Charlotte A. van, *De Nederlandsche Overzee Trustmaatschappij, Middelpunt van het Verkeer van onzijdig Nederland met het Buitenland tydens den Wereldoorlog, 1914–1918*. The Hague: Martinus Nijhoff, 1935. 8 vols. [The Netherlands Oversea Trust, the Pivot of Relations of the Neutral Netherlands with Foreign States during the World War.] The official history of the Netherlands Oversea Trust written from the records of the company. A comprehensive treatment of the course of all Dutch trade and commercial negotiations during the war. The last two volumes contain a collection of 696 *bijlagen* (documents), reproducing correspondence of the N.O.T. with the Dutch and foreign governments, the texts of Dutch and foreign laws respecting trade, maritime warfare, and the defense of the state, as well as other documents and statistical charts that explain the work and the development of the N.O.T.

Morissey, Alice M., *The American Defense of Neutral Rights, 1914–1917.* Cambridge, Mass.: Harvard University Press, 1939.

Nolde, Boris E., *Russia in the Economic War.* Economic and Social History of the World War, Russian Series. New Haven: Yale University Press, 1928.

Oppenheim, Lassa F. L., *International Law, a Treatise,* ed. Hersh Lauterpacht. 5th ed. London: Longmans, Green and Co., Inc., 1935–1937. 2 vols.

Parmelee, Maurice, *Blockade and Sea Power. The Blockade, 1914–1919, and Its Significance for a World State.* New York: Thomas Y. Crowell Co., 1924. The blockade in the years 1917–1918 is emphasized, and especially the development of Allied organizations.

Pekelharing, G. G., "De Gemeente (in het bijzonder de Gemeente Utrecht) en de Distributie van Goederen in de Jaren 1914–1920," *Economisch-historisch Jaarboek, 1920,* pp. *1–133* [*The Municipality (Especially the Municipality of Utrecht) and the Distribution of Goods in the Years 1914–1920.*]

Phillips, Ethel C., "American Participation in Belligerent Commercial Controls, 1914–1917," *American Journal of International Law,* XXVII (October 1933), 674–693. Chiefly concerned with the agreements made between the British government and the American Textile Alliance, based on documents of the Alliance.

Piggott, Sir Francis. *The Declaration of Paris, 1856,* Law of the Sea Series, Vol. IV. London: University of London Press, 1919.

Proceedings of the Third International Conference on Bituminous Coal, November 16–21, 1931. Pittsburgh: Carnegie Institute of Technology, 1932.

Ritchie, H., *The "Navicert" System during the World War.* Washington, D.C.: Carnegie Endowment for International Peace, 1938.

Siney, Marion C., "British Negotiations with American Meat Packers, 1915–1917: A Study of Belligerent Trade Controls," *Journal of Modern History,* XXIII (December 1951), 343–353.

Stockton, Charles W., "The Declaration of Paris," *American Journal of International Law,* XIV (July 1920), 356–368.

Sweden, Norway, Denmark and Iceland in the World War. Economic and Social History of the World War, James T. Shotwell, ed. New Haven: Yale University Press, 1930. Contains Eli F. Heckscher and Kurt Bergendal, "Sweden in the World War"; Wilhelm Keilhau, "Norway and the World War"; Einar Cohn, "Denmark in the Great War"; Thorstein Thorsteinsson, "Iceland and the War." This work is an abridged English translation and adaptation of four volumes that appeared in the Scandinavian Series of the economic and social history of the war undertaken by the Division of Economics and History of the Carnegie Endowment for International Peace.

Tansill, Charles C., *America Goes to War.* Boston: Little, Brown and Co., 1938.

Thomazi, Auguste, *La Marine française dans la Grande Guerre (1914–1918)*. Paris: Payot, 1926–1929. 4 vols. Vol. I: *La Guerre navale dans la zone des Armées du nord;* Vol. IV: *Mediterranée.*

Toscano, Mario, "La Svezia e l'intervento in guerra dell' Italia," *Rassegna storica del risorgimento,* XXIII (September 1936), 1181–1195. Based on Russian documents in *Die internationalen Beziehungen im Zeitalter des Imperialismus.*

Twiss, Sir Travers, *Belligerent Rights on the High Seas since the Declaration of Paris.* London: Butterworths, 1884.

Van Alstyne, Richard W., "The Policy of the United States Regarding the Declaration of London at the Outbreak of the Great War," *Journal of Modern History,* VII (December 1935), 434–447.

Verzijl, Jan H. W., *Le Droit des prises de la Grande Guerre, Jurisprudence de 1914 et des années suivantes en matières de prises maritimes.* Leyden: A. W. Sijthoff, 1924.

Victor, "L'Inghilterra nel conflitto europeo. Di una lega economica degli stati alleati per la guerra vittoriosa e breve," *Nuova antologia,* 5th Series CLXXVII (June 16, 1915), 513–532.

Vigness, Paul G., *The Neutrality of Norway in the World War.* Stanford, California: Stanford University Press, 1932.

"Union douanière contre les Allemands," *Nouvelles de France,* IV (March 2, 1916), 177–178. Reproduction of a bulletin published by the Franco-Russian chamber of commerce in Petrograd.

Wyatt, Harold F., "England's Threatened Rights at Sea," in *The Declaration of London: National Starvation in War and the Paralysis of Britain's Power at Sea.* London: Imperial Maritime League, 1911.

Notes

CHAPTER I

1 For the history of negotiations regarding neutral rights during the Crimean War and regarding the Declaration of Paris, see Sir Francis Piggott, *The Declaration of Paris, 1856,* Law of the Sea Series, Vol. IV (London: University of London Press, 1919); Herbert W. Malkin, "The Inner History of the Declaration of Paris," *British Year Book of International Law,* 1927, pp. 1–44; and Charles W. Stockton, "The Declaration of Paris," *American Journal of International Law,* XIV (July 1920), 356–368.

2 Texts of the letter, the draft resolution, and minutes of the cabinet are printed in Malkin, pp. 26–29; and in George P. Gooch and Harold Temperley, eds., *British Documents on the Origins of the War, 1898–1914* (London: H.M. Stationery Office, 1926–1938), VIII, 204–206, editorial note.

3 "Declaration Respecting Maritime Law ...," April 16, 1856, in Great Britain, *British and Foreign State Papers,* (London: H.M. Stationery Office) XLVI (1855–1856), 26–27.

4 In a debate in the House of Lords in 1856 Lord Derby and other members of the Opposition viewed the Declaration as an abandonment of British naval supremacy. See Great Britain, *Parliamentary Debates,* 3rd Series, (London: H.M. Stationery Office), CXLII, 481–547. A Select Committee on Merchant

Shipping was appointed in the House of Commons, under the chairmanship of Thomas B. Horsfall, member from Liverpool, in January 1860. In its report the committee proposed two alternatives for adoption by the government: that immunity from capture be secured for all merchant ships and their cargoes, or that Britain revert to the ancient right to capture enemy goods on neutral ships. The committee itself inclined toward the first proposal, an idea that was later upheld by John Bright when the matter was debated in Parliament in March 1862. See *Parliamentary Debates,* 3rd Series, CLVI, 331–378, and CLXV, 1359–1392, 1599–1706. See also, Piggott, pp. 161–169, 408–410, and John Fraser Macqueen, *Chief Points in the Laws of War and Neutrality, Search, and Blockade; with the Changes of 1856, and Those Now Proposed* (London and Edinburgh: Wm. and Robert Chambers, 1862), pp. 64–88.

5 Granville to Lord Augustus Loftus, August 3, 1870, in Great Britain, *British and Foreign State Papers,* LX (1869–1870), 973–975. See Sir Travers Twiss, *Belligerent Rights on the High Seas since the Declaration of Paris* (London: Butterworths, 1884), pp. 15–16.

6 Thomas Gibson Bowles, *The Declaration of Paris of 1856: Being an Account of the*

Maritime Rights of Great Britain; a Consideration of Their Importance; a History of Their Surrender by the Signatories of the Declaration of Paris; and an Argument for Their Resumption by the Denunciation and Repudiation of That Declaration (London: Sampson Low, Marston and Co., 1900).

7 Archibald C. Bell, Die englische Hungerblockade im Weltkrieg, 1914–1915, nach dem amtlichen englischen Darstellung der Hungerblockade von A. C. Bell, bearbeitet und eingeleitet durch Dr. Viktor Böhmert (Essen: Essener Verlagsanstalt, 1943), pp. 80–81.

8 The report of the committee was transmitted to Sir Edward Grey by John L. Walton, attorney-general and chairman of the committee, on February 12, 1907. See Gooch and Temperley, eds., British Documents on the Origins of the War, VIII, no. 176.

9 Instructions to British plenipotentiaries, Grey to Sir Edward Fry, June 12, 1907, in Gooch and Temperley, eds., British Documents on the Origins of the War, VIII, no. 206.

10 James Brown Scott, ed., The Proceedings of the Hague Peace Conferences, Translations of the Official Texts: The Conference of 1907 (New York: Oxford University Press, 1920–1921), III, 844–849. Hereafter cited as Proceedings.

11 James Brown Scott, ed., The Declaration of London, February 26, 1909: A Collection of Official Papers and Documents Relating to the International Naval Conference Held in London, December, 1908—February, 1909 (New York: Oxford University Press, 1919), p. 24.

12 Proceedings, III, 777–778, 821–823.

13 Proceedings, III, 866–867.

14 Proceedings, III, 752, 779, 872.

15 Proceedings, III, 856–858. The French and British delegations carried on separate negotiations for a contraband agreement, on which a report was made by Cecil Hurst. See Gooch and Temperley, eds., British Documents on the Origins of the War, VIII, enclosure 1, in no. 245.

16 Proceedings, III, 878–880, 910, 953–954, 1149. The Continental states were united in their insistence on a blockade being actively maintained by a naval force in the whole zone, on each ship being individually notified of the blockade as it approached the lines, and on seizure being permitted only at the time the vessel attempted to break the blockade lines.

17 Proceedings, II, Annexes 88 and 89, pp. 1051–1056.

18 Great Britain, British and Foreign State Papers, C (1906–1907), 435–447.

19 Great Britain, Parliamentary Papers, Miscellaneous No. 4 (1909), Correspondence and Documents Respecting the International Naval Conference Held in London, December 1908—February 1909, Cd. 4554 (London: H.M. Stationery Office, 1909), no. 1; also printed in Gooch and Temperley, eds., British Documents on the Origins of the War, VIII, no. 263.

20 The agenda drawn up by the British included contraband, blockade, the doctrine of continuous voyage, the destruction of neutral prizes, unneutral service, conversion of merchant ships on the high seas, transfer of flag, and the enemy character of private property. The British memorandum on these subjects was prepared by Lord Desart's committee, a group that became the British delegation at the London Conference. See Crowe to Satow, December 19, 1908, in Gooch and Temperley, eds., British Documents on the Origins of the War, VIII, no. 297. The text of the memorandum is printed in Great Britain, Parliamentary Papers, Miscellaneous No. 4 (1909), enclosure in no. 2.

21 Text of the Declaration of London is printed in Great Britain, Parliamentary Papers, Miscellaneous No. 4 (1909), no. 20, and in Scott, ed., The Declaration of London, pp. 112–129. A "General Report," drafted by Louis Renault, accompanied and explained the Declaration, and in the opinion of many it was of equal weight with the Declaration itself. See Great Britain, Parliamentary Papers, Miscellaneous No. 4 (1909), no. 18; and Scott, ed., The Declaration of London, pp. 130–186.

22 Gooch and Temperley, eds., British Documents on the Origins of the War, VIII, no. 307.

23 Great Britain, Parliamentary Debates, Commons, 5th Series, XXVII, 434–548, 574–696, 814–934, and XXXII, 1597–1719.

24 Bell, pp. 89–91.

25 An example of this kind of opposition is found in the following extract from Harold F. Wyatt, "England's Threatened Rights at Sea," in The Declaration of London: National Starvation in War and the Paralysis of Britain's Power at Sea (London: Imperial Maritime League,

1911), pp. 16–17: "That freedom [of right of capture] having been abandoned at the earlier date [1856], the next step in fettering the exercise of our naval power was taken in 1907. The formation was then proposed of an International Prize Court, by which the legality of all captures by belligerents of enemy ships might be decided on appeal. By this measure the last shadow of freedom was removed from the British Navy. Formerly it could pursue the goods of an enemy under any flag which flew on the waters of the world. Then its pursuit was restricted to the goods when carried under the enemy's own flag. Now the exercise even of that last right is made subject to the consent of a board, composed mainly of foreign jurists, at The Hague. Conceive, if you can, what would have been the contempt of British Ministers a hundred years ago, if such a proposal as this had been put before them. But they were men."

26 A consideration of naval plans for economic warfare is contained in Bell, pp. 92–97.

27 Sir Edward E. Bradford, *Life of Admiral of the Fleet Sir Arthur Knyvet Wilson* (New York: E. P. Dutton and Co., 1923), pp. 239–242; Winston S. Churchill, *The World Crisis, 1911–1915* (New York: Charles Scribner's Sons, 1923), pp. 151–152.

28 Churchill, who represented the Home Office at this meeting, has written an account of it in *World Crisis*, pp. 53–64; another is that of the secretary for war, Richard Haldane, *An Autobiography* (New York: Doubleday, Doran and Co., Inc., 1929), pp. 240–245.

29 Churchill, *World Crisis*, pp. 56, 90–92.

30 Gooch and Temperley, eds., *British Documents on the Origins of the War,* VIII, no. 320.

31 Gooch and Temperley, eds., *British Documents on the Origins of the War,* VIII, no. 321.

CHAPTER II

1 Sir Julian S. Corbett and Henry Newbolt, *Naval Operations, History of the Great War Based on Official Documents,* by direction of the Historical Section of the Committee of Imperial Defence (New York: Longmans, Green and Co., Inc., 1920–1931), I, 19–23. The subcommittee was composed of high officials in the Admiralty, War Office, Foreign Office, Home Office, Colonial Office, India Office, Board of Trade, Board of Customs and Excise, and the Post Office.

2 Le Gouz de Saint-Seine to Vice-Admiral Marie Jacques Charles Aubert, February 14, 1913, in France, Ministère des Affaires Étrangères, Commission de Publication des Documents Relatifs aux Origines de la Guerre de 1914, *Documents diplomatiques français (1871–1914),* 3e Série (Paris: Imprimerie Nationale, 1929–1936), V, no. 397, and annexes I, II, and III.

3 Corbett and Newbolt, *Naval Operations,* I, 9–10.

4 On the mobilization of the British fleet, see Corbett and Newbolt, *Naval Operations,* I, 23–38; Winston S. Churchill, *The World Crisis, 1911–1915* (New York: Charles Scribner's Sons, 1923), pp. 203–246; Kurt Assmann, "Die englische Mobilmachung 1914," *Berliner Monatshefte,* XIV (September 1936), 677–713; and August Bach, "Englands Entschluss zum Kriege," *Berliner Monatshefte,* X (April 1932), 309–330.

5 On the mobilization of the French fleet in the Channel, see Auguste Thomazi, *La Marine française dans la Grande Guerre (1914–1918),* Vol. I: *La Guerre navale dans la zone des armées du nord* (Paris: Payot, 1928), pp. 32–39; Herbert Greiner, "Die französische Mobilmachung 1914," *Berliner Monatshefte,* XIV (July 1936), 515–546.

6 The disposition of British naval forces is dealt with in C. Ernest Fayle, *Seaborne Trade, History of the Great War Based on Official Documents,* by direction of the Historical Section of the Committee

of Imperial Defence (New York: Longmans, Green and Co., Inc., 1920–1924), I, 8–10, 51–52; Corbett and Newbolt, *Naval Operations*, I, 10–18.

7 In a memorandum written by Churchill on August 23, 1913, and revised in April 1914 the following statement in regard to trade-route protection occurs: "4. It is no use distributing isolated cruisers about the vast ocean spaces. To produce any results from such a method would require hundreds of cruisers. The ocean is itself the best protection. We must recognize that we cannot specifically protect trade routes; we can only protect confluences. . . ." Churchill, *World Crisis*, Appendix C, p. 563.

8 Fifty-six German vessels with a tonnage of 81,000 were seized in ports of the United Kingdom when the German government failed to take action on the British offer to allow "days of grace" to merchant ships in port at the outbreak of war. Seventy-six British ships with a tonnage of 170,000 were detained in German ports. See Fayle, *Seaborne Trade*, I, 54–58; Churchill, *World Crisis*, p. 326.

9 See Appendix A for the distribution of the merchant tonnage of the world and for German shipping statistics.

10 Great Britain, *British and Foreign State Papers*, (London: H.M. Stationery Office), CVIII (1914, Part II), 72–73.

11 William Jennings Bryan to Walter Hines Page (and the ambassadors to Russia, France, Germany, and Austria-Hungary, and the minister to Belgium), August 6, 1914, in United States, Department of State, *Papers Relating to the Foreign Relations of the United States, 1914 Supplement* (Washington, D.C.: Government Printing Office, 1928), pp. 215–216. Hereafter cited as *Foreign Relations*.

12 James W. Gerard to Bryan, August 10, 1914, in *Foreign Relations, 1914 Suppl.*, p. 216. The text of the German Prize Code is in the German government publication, *Reichs-Gesetzblatt*, August 3, 1914, no. 50, pp. 275–300; and in English translation (with amendments) in *The Prize Code of the German Empire, as in Force July 1, 1915*, tr. and ed. Charles Henry Huberich and Richard King (New York: Baker, Voorhis and Co., 1915), pp. 1–74.

13 Archibald C. Bell, *Die englische Hungerblockade im Weltkrieg, 1914–1915*, nach dem amtlichen englischen Darstell-

ung der Hungerblockade von A. C. Bell, bearbeitet und eingeleitet durch Dr. Viktor Böhmert (Essen: Essener Verlagsanstalt, 1943), pp. 100–101.

14 Great Britain, *British and Foreign State Papers*, CVIII (1914, Part II), 100–102; *Foreign Relations, 1914 Suppl.*, pp. 218–220.

15 France, *Journal officiel* (Paris: Imprimerie Nationale), August 26, 1914, p. 7674.

16 Lansing's memorandum of a conversation with Spring Rice, September 29, 1914, in *Foreign Relations, 1914 Suppl.*, p. 234. Even before the Order in Council was issued, the State Department had information that the British Admiralty had ordered the diversion and detention of vessels carrying grain and other foodstuffs from the United States to continental ports. See *ibid.*, pp. 304 ff.

17 Fayle, *Seaborne Trade*, I, 74.

18 Bell, p. 103.

19 Great Britain, *Manual of Emergency Legislation, Comprising All the Acts of Parliament, Proclamations, Orders, etc. Passed and Made in Consequence of the War, to September 30th, 1914*, ed. Alexander Pulling (London: H.M. Stationery Office, 1914), pp. 111–112.

20 Lansing to Page, September 26, 1914, in *Foreign Relations, 1914 Suppl.*, pp. 225–232.

21 Bell, pp. 105–106. The committee reported that not the Netherlands but Scandinavia, and especially Sweden, was the center of indirect trade in foodstuffs.

22 In Alice M. Morrissey, *The American Defense of Neutral Rights, 1914–1917* (Cambridge, Mass.: Harvard University Press, 1939) one finds a consideration of these and later controversies which estimates the worth and consequences of the policy pursued by the United States. Its conclusions are far from favorable to Lansing.

23 Memorandum by Lansing, September 29, 1914, in *Foreign Relations, 1914 Suppl.*, pp. 233–235.

24 Page to Bryan, September 30, 1914, in *Foreign Relations, 1914 Suppl.*, p. 235; Grey to Spring Rice, September 30, 1914, *ibid.*, pp. 237–238.

25 Page to Bryan, October 9, 1914, in *Foreign Relations, 1914 Suppl.*, pp. 244–246.

26 Lansing to Page, October 16, 1914, 1 P.M., in *Foreign Relations, 1914 Suppl.*, pp. 249–250; Lansing to Page, October 16, 1914, 3 P.M. *ibid.*, pp. 250–252.

27 Richard W. Van Alstyne in his article, "The Policy of the United States Regarding the Declaration of London at the Outbreak of the Great War," *Journal of Modern History*, VII (December 1935), 434–447, concludes that Lansing's scheme had some distinct advantages over the British draft order. It is true, as Van Alstyne says, that Lansing expected that acceptance of the Declaration would at least provide certainty as to the law and would put some check upon belligerent extensions of their rights at sea. But then he goes on with this: "His [Lansing's] proposal that Great Britain apply the law of contraband to any neutral country which allowed its territory to become a way-station in the transit of supplies to Germany was a solution of the difficulties which had been presented to him as barring the way to the acceptance of the declaration . . . . The objective was the same as that sought by the British draft order in council. But whereas the British policy meant the subjection of neutral trade to constant interference and loss, Lansing's plan would avoid these inevitable sources of irritation to innocent commerce. . . . It fixed responsibility, and would accordingly avoid dangerous controversies with this country."
28 Page to Bryan, October 19, 1914, in *Foreign Relations, 1914 Suppl.*, pp. 253–254; Lansing to Page, October 22, 1914, ibid., pp. 257–258.
29 Great Britain, *British and Foreign State Papers*, CVIII (1914, Part II), 156–158; *Foreign Relations, 1914 Suppl.*, pp. 260–263. The French decree, November 6, 1914, was published in *Journal officiel*, November 7, 1914, p. 8582.
30 Bell, pp. 110, 142.
31 Text of the Admiralty announcement appears in *Foreign Relations, 1914 Suppl.*, p. 464; documents on mines and maritime danger zones are also printed there, pp. 453–474.
32 Bell, pp. 144–145.
33 Santos A. Dominici to Bryan, December 14, 1914, in *Foreign Relations, 1914 Suppl.*, pp. 447–450; Bryan to Dominici, January 13, 1915, ibid., pp. 452–453; A. G. Schmedeman to Bryan, November 6, 1914, ibid., p. 465; Bryan to Schmedeman, November 10, 1914, ibid., p. 466; Charles Seymour, ed., *The Intimate Papers of Colonel House* (Boston and New York: Houghton Mifflin Co., 1926–1928), I, 310–311.
34 Churchill, *World Crisis*, Appendix E, p. 573.
35 Bell, pp. 99, 111–112.
36 Denys Cochin, ed., *Les Organisations de blocus en France pendant la Guerre, 1914–1918* (Paris: Plon, 1926), pp. 1–2, 14–15.

CHAPTER III

1 Charlotte A. van Manen, *De Nederlandsche Overzee Trustmaatschappij, Middelpunt van het Verkeer van onzijdig Nederland met het Buitenland tydens den Wereldoorlog, 1914–1918* (The Hague: Martinus Nijhoff, 1935), I, 26. Hereafter cited as van Manen, *N.O.T.*
2 Of the ships entering Rotterdam in the year 1913, 15.3 per cent were owned by Dutch lines, 34.4 per cent by British, 23.9 per cent by German, 7.3 per cent by Norwegian, 6.5 per cent by Swedish, and the rest by Danish, Austrian, and Russian companies. Data compiled from tables in Great Britain, *Parliamentary Papers, Diplomatic and Consular Reports, Netherlands, Report for the Year 1913, Trade, Shipping and Agriculture of Rotterdam and the Consular Posts in the Netherlands*, Cd. 7048–132 (London: H.M. Stationery Office, 1914), p. 43.
3 British-owned vessels accounted for 27.2 per cent of the number entering Amsterdam in 1913; 10.2 per cent were German and 50.8 per cent were Dutch. Great Britain, *Parliamentary Papers . . . Netherlands . . .* , p. 61.
4 Declaration of Neutrality, August 5, 1914, in *Nederlandsche Staatscourant*, August 5, 1914; printed also in Paul Fauchille, ed., *La Guerre de 1914, Re-*

cueil de documents intéressant le droit international (Paris: Pedone, 1916–1920), I, no. 285.

5 Notice respecting transit up the Rhine, August 21, 1914, in van Manen, N.O.T., VIII,bijlage no. 618.

6 A British embargo on certain warlike stores, provisions, and victuals was made on August 3, 1914. See Great Britain, Manual of Emergency Legislation, Comprising All the Acts of Parliament, Proclamations, Orders, etc. Passed and Made in Consequence of the War, to September 30th, 1914, ed. Alexander Pulling (London: H.M. Stationery Office, 1914), pp. 160–161. More detailed prohibition lists were issued by the British on August 5, 10, and 20, ibid., pp. 162–170.

7 Great Britain, Board of Trade Journal, December 31, 1914, pp. 903–904.

8 Van Manen, N.O.T., I, 40.

9 Declarations of a state of siege in respect to certain Dutch frontier districts were made on August 5, 10, and 29, September 8 and 25, and November 10 and 21, 1914. See Netherlands, Staatsblad van het Koninkrijk der Nederlanden, 1914 (The Hague: Algemeene Landsdrukkerij, 1915), nos. 375, 406, 435, 448, 463, 527, and 542. The same documents are reproduced in van Manen, N.O.T., VII, bijlagen nos. 7, 8a, 8b, 9a, 9b, 10a, and 10b.

10 Van Manen, N.O.T., I, 42. On the distribution of goods in Utrecht, see G. G. Pekelharing, "De Gemeente (in het bijzonder de Gemeente Utrecht) en de Distributie van Goederen in de Jaren 1914–1920," Economisch-historisch Jaarboek, 1920, pp. 1–133.

11 Van Manen, N.O.T., I, 43.

12 Announcement of the Commission's establishment appeared in the Dutch Press on September 17. See van Manen, N.O.T., I, 45–46.

13 Van Manen, N.O.T., I, 50, 57. See also Chapter V.

14 Van Manen, N.O.T., I, 66–67.

15 Van Manen, N.O.T., I, 68. Sir Francis Oppenheimer, British commercial at-taché, had heard of the proposed shipper's contract between the Holland-Amerika Line and consignors, and therefore Sir Alan Johnstone, the British minister in The Hague, discussed the matter with Loudon, the foreign minister, on the assumption that the plan was intended to serve as the basis for an agreement between the British and Dutch governments. Loudon soon set Johnstone right on this: it was an independent and private scheme and could not be the subject of an Anglo-Dutch agreement. In a memorandum of October 15, Sir Francis recognized this fact.

16 Van Manen, N.O.T., I, 70.

17 Johnstone to Loudon, November 2, 1914, in van Manen, N.O.T., VII, bijlage no. 45.

18 Loudon to Johnstone, November 13, 1914, in van Manen, N.O.T., VII, bijlage no. 46.

19 Circular of the Ministry of Finance respecting transit up the Rhine, October 31, 1914, in van Manen. N.O.T., VIII, bijlage no. 619.

20 The text of the memorandum is not available, but see van Manen, N.O.T., I, 72, and Archibald C. Bell, Die englische Hungerblockade im Weltkrieg, 1914–1915, nach dem amtlichen englischen Darstellung der Hunger-blockade von A. C. Bell, bearbeitet und eingeleitet durch Dr. Viktor Böhmert (Essen: Essener Verlagsanstalt, 1943), p. 115. The goods that the note suggested ought to be consigned to the government or to approved firms were: vegetable oils and their products, copper, rubber, hides and leather, and certain imported food-stuffs—lard, grains, meal, meat, preserved fish, and forage.

21 Van Manen, N.O.T., I, 71–77, covers the negotiations leading to the foundation of the Trust.

22 Text of the charter is given in van Manen, N.O.T., VII, bijlage no. 53. The charter was published in the Neder-landsche Staatscourant on November 27, 1914. The members named in the charter were: C. J. K. van Aalst, president of the Nederlandsche Handelsmaatschappij, and representing the Nederlandsche-Indische Handelsbank and the Amsterdamsche Bank; Adam Roelvink, representing De Twentsche Bankvereeniging B. W. Blijdenstein en Co.; William Westerman, president of the Rotterdamsche Bankvereeniging; G. H. Hintzen of the firm of R. Mees en Zoonen, Cornelis A. den Tex, director of the Stoomvaart Maatschappij Nederland; B. E. Ruys and H. L. Bekker of the firm of Willam Ruys en Zoonen, and directors of the Stoomvaart Maatschappij Rotterdamsche Lloyd; P. C. Adrian, director of the Nederlandsche Stoomvaart Maatschappij Ocean; L. P. D. op ten

Noort, chairman of the board of the Koninklijke Paketvaart Maatschappij and representing Boudewijn Nierstrasz, director of the Hollandsch Stoomboot Maatschappij; J. R. Wierdsma, director of the Nederlandsch-Amerikaansche Stoomvaart Maatschappij; Ernest Heldring, director of the Koninklijke Nederlandsche Stoomboot Maatschappij; C. M. van Rijn, director of the Koninklijke West-Indische Maildienst; Jan Wilmink, director of the Koninklijke Hollandsche Lloyd; A. G. Kröller, president of the firm of Wm. H. Müller en Co., and director of Wm. H. Müller en Co's. Allgemeene Scheepvaart Maatschappij.

23 Van Manen, N.O.T., VII, bijlagen nos. 59 and 60.

24 Bell, p. 116.

25 Loudon to the Dutch ministers abroad, January 5, 1915, in van Manen, N.O.T., VII, bijlage no. 50.

26 Van Manen, N.O.T., VII, bijlagen nos. 54, 55, 56a, 56b and I, 78–81.

27 Johnstone to Loudon, November 29, 1914, in van Manen, N.O.T., VII, bijlage no. 47.

28 Loudon to Johnstone, December 4, 1914, in van Manen, N.O.T., VII, bijlage no. 48.

29 Oppenheimer to Executive Committee, December 26, 1914, in van Manen, N.O.T., I, 81–83; Executive Committee to Oppenheimer, December 29, 1914, ibid., I, 83. See also Bell, pp. 116–117.

30 H. G. Chilton to Loudon, December 26, 1914, in van Manen, N.O.T., VII, bijlage no. 49; Bell, p. 117.

31 Olaf Knudsen, Dansk Industriberetning 1915–1918 (Copenhagen: Nielsen and Lydiche, 1921), I, 6.

32 Denmark, Samling af Love, Anordningen, offentlige Kundgørelser, ministerielle Cirkulaerer og Skrivelser, 1914 (Copenhagen: J. H. Schultz, 1914), p. 544; others were published on August 4, 6, and 7, ibid., pp. 552, 553, 576. Hereafter cited as Denmark, Love.

33 Law Forbidding Use of Danish Territory by Belligerent Powers, August 2, 1914, in Denmark, Love, 1914, pp. 544–545.

34 Johannes Hansen, Hovedtraek af Industriraadets Historie (Copenhagen: Neilsen and Lydiche, 1935), p. 80; Einar Cohn, "Denmark in the Great War," in Sweden, Norway, Denmark and Iceland in the World War. Economic and Social History of the World War, James T. Shotwell, ed. (New Haven: Yale Uni-

versity Press, 1930) p. 421. The more detailed Scandinavian editions in this series will be cited only when they contain materials not included in the English translation.

35 Bell, pp. 118–119.

36 Law Forbidding the Exportation of Certain Goods, August 6, 1914, in Denmark, Love, 1914, pp. 553–554; Notification of Exports Prohibited, August 6, 1914, ibid., pp. 554–555; Temporary Law on Price Regulations for Food and Goods, August 7, 1914, ibid., pp. 575–576; Temporary Law on Insurance of Danish Ships against War Risks, September 10, 1914, ibid., pp. 599–603; Temporary Law Insuring Goods against War Risks at Sea, September 24, 1914, ibid., pp. 628–630. Most of the details of the insurance scheme were arranged in consultation with the Danish Steamship Owners Union. See Eilert Maegaard and Jens Vestberg, Dansk Dampskibsrederiforening, 1884—17. Januar 1934 (Copenhagen: Fr. G. Knuedtzon, 1934), pp. 71–73. On the arrangements made with respect to foreign obligations, bank credits, and so on, see Cohn, in Sweden, Norway, Denmark, pp. 431–438; Knudsen, pp. 3–4; and Hansen, pp. 80–81, 84.

37 Grey to Howard, October 14, 1914, in United States, Department of State, Papers Relating to the Foreign Relations of the United States, 1914 Supplement (Washington, D. C.: Government Printing Office, 1928) p. 323. Hereafter cited as Foreign Relations.

38 Bell, p. 119.

39 For correspondence between the United States and Great Britain on the cases of the John D. Rockefeller, Platuria, and Chr. Knudsen see Foreign Relations, 1914 Suppl. pp. 324–326, 328–329, 335, 339–340.

40 The government's intention of introducing the bill was made known in a statement made by Carl T. Zahle, the prime minister, on October 27, when he explained the difficulties the government had in dealing with the import question. The bill was passed almost without debate. See Denmark, Rigsdagstidende, Forhandlinger paa Folketinget, 1914–1915. (Copenhagen: J. H. Schultz, 1915), pp. 866, 891, 893–894. Text of the law appears in Denmark, Love, 1914, p. 701.

41 Great Britain, Board of Trade Journal, November 12, 1914, pp. 443–445.

42 Grey to the British ministers at Chris-

tiania, Stockholm, and Copenhagen, November 8, 1914, transmitted by Spring Rice to Lansing, November 9, 1914, in *Foreign Relations, 1914 Suppl.,* p. 341.

[43] Bell, p. 119.

[44] Hansen, p. 87.

[45] Bell, pp. 120–121. Importations of meat products, in pounds, from the United States into Denmark during the period August to December 1914, compared with the same period in 1913, were as follows:

	1914	1913
beef	348,564	126,139
lard	15,455,839	3,022,957
oleo	2,135,225	1,396,732
guts and plucks	1,204,104	425,138

Bell, p. 265. Regarding the practices of the American packers in Denmark in the autumn of 1914, see Spring Rice's memorandum of October 12, 1915, in *Foreign Relations, 1915 Suppl.,* pp. 566–569.

[46] Hansen, p. 93.

[47] Letter of A. C. Bell to me, February 11, 1937. In 1916 Cold's company owned 131 steamships with a total tonnage of 175,424. See Denmark, *Danmarks Skibsliste,* 1916. (Copenhagen: Kongelige Søkort-Arkiv, 1916).

[48] The material on these negotiations is taken from Bell, pp. 118–127; Hansen, pp. 93–94; Knudsen, I, 8–9; and Cohn, in *Sweden, Norway, Denmark,* pp. 419–420.

[49] That the Danes had considered the possibility of establishing a Danish trust was shown by an inquiry made by Clan and reported by Page on December 21, 1914. Clan wanted to know whether American meat packers, copper merchants, and the like would agree to refrain from exporting to neutral European countries goods in excess of the amounts sent in normal times and whether the United States would object if other neutral countries each appointed a trustee to which all imports for home consumption would be consigned. See *Foreign Relations, 1914 Suppl.,* p. 404.

[50] The Danes at least knew of the possibility that this might happen, for Constantin Brun, the Danish minister in Washington, presented a memorandum to Bryan which gave this as a reason for asking American exporters to limit their shipments to Denmark to normal quantities. See *Foreign Relations, 1914 Suppl.,* pp. 296–297.

[51] Hansen, p. 90; Cohn, in *Sweden, Norway, Denmark,* p. 419.

[52] The embargo lists had been extended twice in December to include hematite iron ore, ferrochrome, ferrosilicon, barbed wire, sulfuric acid, motor tires, nickel ore, chrome ore, vegetable stearine, raw materials for making gunpowder and explosives, and all manufactured fertilizers and their raw materials. See Denmark, *Love,* 1914, pp. 734, 772.

[53] Denmark, *Love,* 1915, p. 7. On March 9, live hogs were embargoed, and on March 25 a list of slaughterhouses licensed to export pork, pork waste, and so forth and a statement of the conditions upon which this exportation might be made were included in a proclamation. See *ibid.,* 1915, pp. 62, 75–79.

[54] Information on Sweden's agricultural and industrial position is included in Eli F. Heckscher, *Bidrag till Sveriges ekonomiska och sociala Historia under och efter Världskriget, Economic and Social History of the World War,* Scandinavian Series (Stockholm: P. A. Norstedt, 1926), Part I, pp. 44–47, 147–153. (Hereafter cited as *Bidrag.*) These sections are not included in the English edition.

[55] Wilhelm Keilhau, "Norway and the World War," in *Sweden, Norway, Denmark,* pp. 289–290. The agreement was announced to the Swedish Riksdag by Kurt Wallenberg, the foreign minister, on August 8. See Sweden, *Riksdagens protokoll,* First Chamber, 1914 (Stockholm: P. A. Norstedt, 1914), no. 50, pp. 14–15, and Second Chamber, no. 57, p. 11.

[56] Heckscher, *Bidrag,* Part II, p. 192. Text of the royal proclamation of neutrality in the Austro-Serbian war, July 31, 1914, in Sweden, *Svensk författningssamling,* 1914, no. 107.

[57] On these various measures that were chiefly of internal concern to Sweden, see Heckscher, *Bidrag,* passim; Karl Hildebrand, *De svenska statsmakterna och krigstidens folkhushållning.* (Stockholm: P. A. Norstedt, 1916–1920), I, 7–24, 61–69, 69–75, 86–92; Sweden, Statens Industrikommission, *Statsmakterna och den svenska industrien under krigstiden* (Stockholm: P. A. Norstedt, 1920), pp. 14–16.

[58] Sweden, *Svensk författningssamling,* 1914, no. 100.

[59] Eli F. Heckscher and Kurt Bergendal,

"Sweden in the World War," in *Sweden, Norway, Denmark*, pp. 59–60.

[60] Heckscher and Bergendal, in *Sweden, Norway, Denmark*, p. 59.

[61] The chief source for materials on these negotiations is Bell, pp. 127–129, and Heckscher and Bergendal in *Sweden, Norway, Denmark*, pp. 57–61. It is interesting that no mention is made of these negotiations in Hildebrand's book, published in 1916. The text of the identical Scandinavian notes of protest, dated November 12, 1914, is printed in Hildebrand, I, 57–59.

[62] Swedish decrees of December 5 and 8, 1914, in *Svensk författningssamling*, 1914, nos. 386 and 390.

[63] The statistics in this section are taken from tables in Great Britain, *Parliamentary Papers, Diplomatic and Consular Reports, Norway, Report for the Year 1912 on the Trade and Commerce of Norway (Supplementary)*, Cd. 7048–67 (London: H.M. Stationery Office, 1914).

[64] Wilhelm Keilhau, *Norge og Verdenskrigen*, Economic and Social History of the World War, Scandinavian Series (Oslo: Aschehoug and Co., 1927), pp. 4–7.

[65] See Keilhau, *Norge og Verdenskrigen*, pp. 10–16, 21–35. An abridged translation of this material is to be found in *Sweden, Norway, Denmark*, pp. 285–286, 290–294. Texts of the governmental decrees are to be found in *Norway, Lover, resolutioner og skrivelser, foranlediget ved krigsforholdene, 1 august 1914—31 december 1916.* (Christiania: Grøndahl and Sons, 1917), pp. 6–7, 21–24, 30. Hereafter cited as *Norway, Lover.*

[66] The neutrality proclamations are in *Norway, Lover*, pp. 5–6. Notification of the joint policy with Sweden was given by Knudsen in the Storting on August 8. See *Norway, Storting, Forhandlinger* (Christiania: Centraltrykkeriet, 1914), p. 2889.

[67] *Norway, Storting Forhandlinger*, 1914, pp. 2887, 2889–2892; *ibid.*, 1915, pp. 155–156, 163–165. See also Keilhau, in *Sweden, Norway, Denmark*, pp. 296–298, for an analysis of Ihlen's policy.

[68] Exports of grain from the United States to Norway in the period June 30, 1913, to June 30, 1914, compared with those in the same period during 1914–1915 showed the following increases: wheat, from 71,895 bu. to 2,504,051 bu.; wheat

flour, from 301,397 bbls. to 967,888 bbls.; oats, from 5,920 bu. to 706,425 bu.; oatmeal, from 445,237 lbs. to 5,576,215 lbs. See United States, Department of Commerce, *Foreign Commerce and Navigation of the United States for the Year Ending June 30, 1915* (Washington, D.C.: Government Printing Office, 1916), pp. 372–379.

[69] Bell, p. 130.

[70] Keilhau, *Norge og Verdenskrigen*, p. 57.

[71] A summary of the first note and the text of the second is given in *Norway, Oversigt over de vigtigste av utenriksdepartmentet under Krigen indtil mai 1916, Behandlede saker som egner sig for offentliggjørelse* (Christiania: Grøndahl and Sons, 1916), pp. 14–17, 45.

[72] *Foreign Relations, 1914 Suppl.*, p. 341 (see note 42 above).

[73] Bell, 130–131. Rubber had been embargoed on October 20. See *Norway, Lover*, p. 40.

[74] *Norway, Lover*, pp. 46–49, 51, 228.

[75] Bell, pp. 131–132.

[76] Lansing to Spring Rice, November 7, 1914, in *Foreign Relations, 1914 Suppl.*, pp. 339–340.

[77] See Bryan's answer to Page's inquiry of December 21 in Bryan to Page, December 24, 1914, in *Foreign Relations, 1914 Suppl.*, p. 405.

[78] *Foreign Relations, 1914 Suppl.*, pp. 418–431.

[79] Page to Bryan, November 6, 1914, in *Foreign Relations, 1914 Suppl.*, p. 423.

[80] Bryan to Page, November 11, 1914, in *Foreign Relations, 1914 Suppl.*, p. 424; Bryan to Page, November 12, 1914, *ibid.*, p. 425.

[81] Page to Bryan, November 17, 1914, in *Foreign Relations, 1914 Suppl.*, pp. 425–426.

[82] Page to Bryan, December 6, 1914, in *Foreign Relations, 1914 Suppl.*, pp. 356–358.

[83] *Foreign Relations, 1914 Suppl.*, pp. 331–333.

[84] Bryan to Page, December 9, 1914, in *Foreign Relations, 1914 Suppl.*, p. 361.

[85] Bryan to Page, December 26, 1914, in *Foreign Relations, 1914 Suppl.*, pp. 372–375; Bell, p. 147.

[86] Spring Rice realized that the government had severe critics in Congress to deal with and tended to excuse the State Department's conduct, whereas Crowe was indignant over the new American protests. See Bell, pp. 148–154.

87 These agreements will be discussed in greater detail in Chapter IX.

88 Bell, 166–167. The agreement is dated January 2/28, 1915, in France, Comité de Restriction des Approvisionnements et du Commerce de l'Ennemi, "Liste des accords conclus par les gouvernements alliés avec des gouvernements ou des organisations neutres au sujet de la restriction des approvisionnement et du commerce de l'ennemi," *Documents numérotés*, no. 861. The text of the agreement is printed in van Manen, *N.O.T.*, VII, bijlage no. 117, where it is noted that it was received at the Foreign Office on February 1, 1915.

89 *Foreign Relations, 1915 Suppl.*, p. 297. It is with this document in mind, apparently, that Carlton Savage, in United States, *Policy of the United States toward Maritime Commerce in War* (Washington, D.C.: Government Printing Office, 1936), II, 14, says, "The working arrangement went into effect early in 1915." I have no document to show that this was the result of any specific agreement with the British.

90 *Foreign Relations, 1915 Suppl.*, p. 334.

<hr>

CHAPTER IV

1 The most important literature on the German submarine campaign includes the two government publications: Arno Spindler, *Der Handelskrieg mit U-Booten. Der Krieg zur See, 1914–1918*, ed. the German Marine-Archiv (Berlin: Mittler, 1932–1934) and *Das Werk des Untersuchungsausschusses der Verfassunggebenden Deutschen Nationalversammlung und des Deutschen Reichstages, 1919–1928, Völkerrecht im Weltkrieg*, Vol. IV, ed. Dr. Johannes Bell (Berlin: Deutsche Verlagsgesellschaft für Politik und Geschichte, 1927), pp. 115–360; and Alfred von Tirpitz, *Politische Dokumente, Deutsche Ohnmachtspolitik im Weltkriege* (Hamburg and Berlin: Hanseatische Verlagsanstalt, 1926); Adolphe Laurens, *Le Blocus et la guerre sous-marine, 1914–1918* (Paris: Armand Colin, 1924); and his *Histoire de la guerre sous-marine allemande, 1914–1918* (Paris: Société d'Éditions Géographiques, Maritimes et Coloniales, 1930).

2 Spindler, I, Anlage no. 1.

3 Spindler, I, Anlage nos. 2, 5, and 11, and pp. 67–69.

4 Spindler, I, pp. 37–38, 52–60, and Anlage no. 12.

5 Spindler, I, Anlage nos. 19, 20, 21, and 24.

6 For German press opinion, see Spindler, I, pp. 70–71, and Anlage no. 25.

7 United States, Department of State, *Papers Relating to the Foreign Relations of the United States, 1915 Supplement* (Washington, D.C.: Government Printing Office, 1928), pp. 96–97. Hereafter cited as *Foreign Relations*.

8 Bryan to Gerard, February 10, 1915, in *Foreign Relations, 1915 Suppl.*, pp. 98–100; the Netherlands Ministry of Foreign Affairs to the German legation, February 12, 1915, *ibid.*, pp. 135–136, and Spindler, I, Anlage no. 31; the Swedish Ministry of Foreign Affairs to the German legation, February 15, 1915, in *Foreign Relations, 1915 Suppl.*, p. 139; the Danish Ministry of Foreign Affairs to the German legation, February 16, 1915, in Spindler, I, Anlage no. 32; the Italian Ministry of Foreign Affairs to the German embassy, February 17, 1915, in *Foreign Relations, 1915 Suppl.*, pp. 123–124, and Spindler, I, Anlage no. 33; the Spanish Ministry of Foreign Affairs to the German embassy, *ibid.*, I, Anlage no. 34. On the Dutch protest see also the London *Times*, February 19, 1915, p. 10.

9 Bryan to Page, February 10, 1915, in *Foreign Relations, 1915 Suppl.*, pp. 100–101; the Italian Ministry of Foreign Affairs to the British embassy, *ibid.*, pp. 124–125; the Swedish Ministry of Foreign Affairs to the British legation, February 15, 1915, *ibid.*, p. 139. Concerning German press comments on the British misuse of neutral flags, see the

London *Times*, February 8, 1915, pp. 6, 10, and *ibid.*, February 10, 1915, p. 6.

10 This statement was presented by Johnstone to Loudon on February 7. See Spindler, I, Anlage no. 26. The substance of this note appeared in the British press on February 8 as an announcement from the Foreign Office. See *Foreign Relations, 1915 Suppl.*, pp. 97–98, and the London *Times*, February 8, 1915, p. 9.

11 Loudon to Johnstone, February 15, 1915 in Spindler, I, Anlage no. 29. For comment by the Dutch press see the London *Times*, February 24, 1915, p. 6. The Dutch government later ordered that foreign ships known to have flown the Dutch flag were to be prevented from departing from Dutch ports and from passing through Dutch territorial waters. See the London *Times*, March 13, 1915, p. 7.

12 Spindler I, p. 130, and II, pp. 14, 68, and maps 1 and 2. British Admiralty figures on departures and arrivals in ports of the United Kingdom during the first week of the submarine blockade were printed in the London *Times*, February 26, 1915, p. 9.

13 Denys Cochin, ed., *Les Organisations de blocus en France pendant la Guerre, 1914–1918* (Paris: Plon, 1926), p. 8. The initiative of the French in instituting reprisal measures is also mentioned in France, Comité de Restriction des Approvisionnements et du Commerce de l'Ennemi, *Étude sur l'effet des mesures restrictives prises par les Alliés*, p. XVI. Hereafter this committee will be cited as France, Comité de Restriction.

14 Archibald C. Bell, *Die englische Hungerblockade im Weltkrieg, 1914–1915*, nach dem amtlichen englischen Darstellung der Hungerblockade von A. C. Bell, bearbeitet und eingeleitet durch Dr. Viktor Böhmert (Essen: Essener Verlagsanstalt, 1943), pp. 220–223.

15 The London *Times*, February 8, 1915, p. 9; February 9, p. 6; February 11, p. 12; February 15, p. 10; February 19, p. 10; April 19, p. 15; April 20, p. 7.

16 Great Britain, *Parliamentary Debates, Commons* 5th Series (London: H.M. Stationery Office), LIX, 714.

17 Great Britain, *Parliamentary Debates, Commons* 5th Series, LIX 937–938. An editorial in the London *Times*, February 18, 1915, p. 11, set forth the probability that retaliatory measures would be put in force. Similar information was given

to the French press on February 20, when Jean Victor Augagneur, minister of marine, said that the Allies had resolved to tighten the network of surveillance that obstructed German attempts to obtain supplies.

18 Bryan to Page, February 20, 1915, in *Foreign Relations, 1915 Suppl.*, pp. 119–120.

19 Bell, pp. 226–227.

20 The report of a conference on February 28, 1915, at which Bethmann-Hollweg, Tirpitz, Gottlieb von Jagow, and Bachmann discussed the American proposal is printed in Tirpitz, *Politische Dokumente*, II, 322–326. The London *Times*, February 23, 1915, p. 6, reported Count Ernst Reventlow as having said that it was necessary for Germany to carry on the trade war or be exposed to ridicule and contempt.

21 Gerard to Bryan, March 1, 1915, enclosing translation of German reply of February 28, 1915, in *Foreign Relations, 1915 Suppl.*, pp. 129–130.

22 Page to Bryan, March 15, 1915, in *Foreign Relations, 1915 Suppl.*, pp. 140–143.

23 Spring Rice to Bryan, March 1, 1915, in *Foreign Relations, 1915 Suppl.*, pp. 127–128.

24 Order in Council, March 11, 1915, in Great Britain, *British and Foreign State Papers* (London: H.M. Stationery Office), CIX (1915), 217–219. French decree, March 13, 1915, in France, *Journal officiel* (Paris: Imprimerie Nationale), March 16, 1915, p. 1388.

25 In the *Progresso* Sir Samuel Evans based his judgment on the belief that there was no intention to release goods of enemy ownership to their owners, and that the apparent inclusion of such property in Article 3 was a mistake. *Lloyd's Reports of Prize Cases, Heard before and Decided by the Right Honourable Sir Samuel Evans, et al., during the European War Which Began in August, 1914* (London: Lloyd's, 1915–1924) V, 424–432. Hereafter cited as *Lloyd's Reports of Prize Cases*.

26 This point was brought out by the Washington correspondent for the London *Times*, April 8, 1915, p. 7.

27 On the subject of retaliation and reprisals see Le R. P. de La Brière, "Évolution de la doctrine et de la pratique en matière de rétorsion et de représailles," in A. F. Frangulis, ed., *Dictionnaire diplomatique* (Paris: Académie

Diplomatique Internationale, 1933), II, 556–557; A. Pearce Higgins, "Retaliation in Naval Warfare," *British Year Book of International Law*, 1927, pp. 128–146.

[28] Great Britain, *Parliamentary Debates, Commons*, 5th Series, LXX, 598–601.

[29] *Lloyd's Reports of Prize Cases*, V, 383–384.

[30] Jan H. W. Verzijl, *Le Droit des prises de la Grande Guerre, Jurisprudence de 1914 et des années suivantes en matières de prises maritimes* (Leyden: A. W. Sijthoff, 1924), p. 596.

[31] *Lloyd's Reports of Prize Cases*, VII, 363. The judgment continues: "It may be— let us pray that it may be so—that an Order of this severity may never be needed and therefore may never be justtified again, for the right of retaliation is one to be sparingly exercised and to be strictly reviewed." To this Verzijl, p. 605, says: "In short, the principles formulated in the decision cited above on the subject of the 'Reprisals Orders' of 1915 and 1917, will never be recognized by neutral Great Britain."

[32] Instructions to make this communication were sent to Page on March 5, 1915. See *Foreign Relations, 1915 Suppl.*, pp.132–133, and Page to Grey, March 8, 1915, in Great Britain, *Parliamentary Papers, Miscellaneous No. 6 (1915), Correspondence between His Majesty's Government and the United States Government respecting the Rights of Belligerents*, Cd. 7816 (London: H.M. Stationery Office, 1915), no. 11.

[33] Bryan to Page, March 30, 1915, in *Foreign Relations, 1915 Suppl.*, pp. 152–156; Page to Grey, April 2, 1915, in Great Britain, *Parliamentary Papers, Miscellaneous No. 14 (1916), Further Correspondence between His Majesty's Government and the United States Respecting the Rights of Belligerents*, Cd. 8233 (London: H.M. Stationery Office, 1916), no. 1.

[34] On the American protest, see the editorial comment of the London *Times*, April 6, 1915, p. 7.

[35] Schmedeman to Bryan, March 23, 1915, in *Foreign Relations, 1915 Suppl.*, p.158.

[36] Sir Julian S. Corbett and Henry Newbolt, *Naval Operations, History of the Great War Based on Official Documents*, by direction of the Historical Section of the Committee of Imperial Defence (New York: Longmans, Green and Co., Inc., 1920–1931), I, 45.

[37] The following transatlantic cables existed at the outbreak of the war: The German Atlantic Telegraph Co., three lines from Emden through the Channel and then one of these to Vigo, Spain, and two to New York via the Azores; the German South American Telegraph Co., one line from Emden through the Channel to Pernambuco via the Canary Islands; Western Union Telegraph Co. (American), four lines from Valencia to Holyrood, two from Penzance to Cape Canso, and one from Penzance to Holyrood; Commercial Cable Co. (American), two lines from Waterville to St. Johns, two from Waterville to Cano, one from Waterville to Cano via the Azores, three from Waterville to Minehead, and one from Waterville to Le Havre; Eastern Telegraph Co. (British), five lines from Penzance, one of which ran to Vigo, two to Lisbon, one to Gibraltar, and one to the Azores; Western Telegraph Co. (British), two lines from Lisbon to Pernambuco; Direct Spanish Telegraph Co. (British), one from Cape Lizard to Blencia; French Government Cable, one line from Brest to Cape Verde; Compagnie Française des Cables Télégraphiques, two lines from Brest, of which one ran to Cape Cod, and one to Sidney via St. Pierre. Information taken from United States War Department, General Staff, War College Division, "Strategic Map of Central Europe Showing the International Frontiers" (Washington, D. C., 1917).

[38] Great Britain, *Board of Trade Journal*, February 25, 1915, p. 527; *ibid.*, August 29, 1918, p. 279; the London *Times*, February 20, 1915, p. 12; Bell, p. 189.

[39] Bell, p. 249. The statistical table on detentions before and after the March Order in Council (Bell, p. 239) gives the following record:

A, Cases processed by the Committee; B, Number of detentions; C, Percentage of B. to A.

1915	A.	B.	C.
Jan.	198	54	27
Feb.	210	46	22
March	314	97	31
April	351	157	45
May	493	205	41
June	451	207	45
July	517	218	42

[40] Great Britain, *Parliamentary Papers, Miscellaneous No. 6 (1917), Report Drawn Up by the Committee on the Adminis-*

tration of the Order in Council of March 1915 (1916), Cd. 8469 (London: H.M. Stationery Office, 1917), p. 4.
[41] Cochin, Organisations de blocus, pp. 9–11; Louis Guichard, The Naval Blockade, 1914–1918, tr. and ed. Christopher

R. Turner (London: Philip Allan and Co., 1930), pp. 39, 64–65.
[42] France, Comité de Restriction, Comptes-rendus, 1st meeting, March 13, 1915.
[43] Cochin, Organisations de blocus, pp. 47–48.

CHAPTER V

[1] See Lassa F. L. Oppenheim, International Law, a Treatise, ed. Hersh Lauterpacht, 5th ed. (London: Longmans, Green and Co., Inc., 1935–1937), II, 262–266.

[2] On British commercial policy during the Napoleonic War see Eli F. Heckscher, The Continental System, An Economic Interpretation (Oxford: Clarendon Press, 1922).

[3] Archibald C. Bell, Die englische Hungerblockade im Weltkrieg, 1914–1915, nach dem amtlichen englischen Darstellung der Hungerblockade von A. C. Bell, bearbeitet und eingeleitet durch Dr. Viktor Böhmert (Essen: Essener Verlagsanstalt, 1943), p. 173. Consideration was given also to the question of the effect that drastic trading with the enemy legislation would have on British insurance firms and bankers. It was known that a large part of the German merchant fleet was insured by Lloyd's and that when the question of validity of such policies in wartime had been raised in the German press in 1905, Lloyd's had said that they would pay up claims in war as in peace and that there was nothing in British law to prevent them. See ibid., pp. 175–176.

[4] Great Britain, Manual of Emergency Legislation, Comprising All the Acts of Parliament, Proclamations, Orders, etc. Passed and Made in Consequence of the War, to September 30th, 1914, ed. Alexander Pulling (London: H.M. Stationery Office, 1914), pp. 375–377.

[5] Great Britain, Manual of Emergency Legislation, p. 380. A proclamation of January 7, 1915, extended the application of the principle of nationality to enemy banking firms. See ibid., Supplement No. 3, pp. 545–546.

[6] Law of February 22, 1810, Book III, Title I, Chapter I, Article 77, in Code d'instruction criminelle et code pénal, A. Carpentier, ed. (Paris: Sirey, 1927), p. 312.

[7] France, Journal officiel (Paris: Imprimerie Nationale), September 28, 1914, pp. 8068–8069.

[8] France, Débats parlementaires, Chambre des deputés, 11e Législature, Session Ordinaire de 1915 (Paris, Imprimerie Nationale), pp. 334–349.

[9] Great Britain, Manual of Emergency Legislation, Supplement No. 4, pp. 401–402.

[10] The bill laying down the penalties for violation of the decrees was declared urgent by the government, and was discussed in the Senate on April 1 and 2, 1915, and adopted on the second. See France, Débats parlementaires, Sénat, 1915, pp. 167–172, 177–186. The bill dealing with the substantive law was discussed on July 22, 23, and 29. See ibid., 1915, pp. 361–366, 372–389, 392–399.

[11] France, Débats parlementaires, Sénat, 1915, p. 400.

[12] The statistics in this section are taken from tables printed in Great Britain, Parliamentary Papers, Annual Statement of the Trade of the United Kingdom with Foreign Countries and British Possessions, 1914, Compared with the Four Preceding Years, Vol. I, Cd. 7968, and Vol. II, Cd. 8069 (London: H.M. Stationery Office, 1915); and in Great Britain, Parliamentary Papers, Accounts Relating to Trade and Navigation for Each Month during the Year 1915, printed by order of the House of Commons (London: H.M. Stationery Office,

1915). For summary tables see Appendix B.

13 These exceptions are British re-exports of raw cotton and coffee to Sweden and the Netherlands; in every instance the proportional increase became higher each month. See Appendix C.

14 See Appendix D.

15 On February 3, 1915, Sir J. D. Rees raised in the House of Commons the question of the large exportations of tea and cocoa, particularly inquiring of the Board of Trade why cocoa had not been embargoed. The reply of J. M. Robertson, the parliamentary secretary to the Board of Trade, indicated that cocoa powder was still on the embargo list and that the export of cocoa beans had been permitted because the Dutch had embargoed them and "it was considered that there was no great risk of the bean reaching Germany." The case against the Board of Trade was put more strongly by Sir Henry Dalziel when he pointed out that during the last session the president of the Board of Trade had explained the lack of an embargo on tea by saying that none was going to the enemy. But this, Dalziel said, had been disproved and the Board of Trade had altered its policy. When the trade returns up to December 31 had appeared the same proof was given in regard to cocoa, and only then had it been embargoed—after Germany had got in millions of pounds. Sir Henry said Rees was right in asking why the embargo had not been laid at once. See Great Britain, *Parliamentary Debates, Commons*, 5th Series (London: H.M. Stationery Office), LXIX. 97–98, 103–104, 106.

16 See Appendix E.

17 Bell, pp. 248–253; Louis Guichard, "La Victoire par étouffement," *Le Correspondant*, CCCXIII (October 10 and 25, 1928), 47–68, 254–284, at 54–55. In the third meeting of the Comité de Restriction on April 9, 1915, several members spoke of the necessity of coördinating British and French practice. Gout said that from December on, the French had been urging a conference, and that they had "found then a very strong resistance," but they were then anticipating a meeting soon. France, Comité de Restriction des Approvisionnements et du Commerce de l'Ennemi, *Comptesrendus*, 3rd meeting, April 9, 1915. (Hereafter this committee will be cited as France, Comité de Restriction.) In

early May the Comité requested the minister of foreign affairs to urge that a date be fixed for the conference; Paul Cambon, the French ambassador in London, replied that the preparatory work begun by the British on April 7 was not yet finished. *Ibid.*, 9th meeting, May 21, 1915.

18 See Appendix B. Some measures were taken to control tea and cocoa exportations after the formation of the War Trade Department. Cocoa powder was embargoed and licenses were granted sparingly. See Great Britain, *Parliamentary Debates, Commons*, 5th Series, LXXIII, 8–9. But raw cocoa continued to go forward in large amounts.

19 The idea that neutrals should be rationed was not exclusively French. As early as August 31, 1914, Charles Bathurst asked in the House of Commons whether it was possible under existing international law to prevent the importation of foodstuffs on neutral ships into neutral countries far in excess of the normal requirements of their own population with the object of their ultimate transferal to the territory of a belligerent power. He asked whether the government had in view the possibility of taking measures to check such abnormal importations of supplies. Herbert Asquith replied that such questions were receiving careful consideration. See Great Britain, *Parliamentary Debates, Commons*, 5th Series, LXVI, 386.

20 Bell, p. 253.

21 France, Comité de Restriction, *Comtesrendus*, 21st meeting, August 21, 1915. The cotton question will be discussed in Chapter VII, and the Swedish negotiations in Chapter VI. Unfortunately the minutes of two important meetings in which rationing was dealt with, on July 10 and August 28, are missing from the Vincennes collection. Certain of the ideas expressed can be learned from the accompanying *Procès-verbaux*, nos. 18 and 23.

22 *Lloyd's Reports of Prize Cases, Heard before and Decided by the Right Honourable Sir Samuel Evans, et al., during the European War Which Began in August, 1914* (London: Lloyd's, 1915–1924) III, 167–380, especially 172, 249, 274–275, 295, 307–315, 319, 322–324. Hereafter cited as *Lloyd's Reports of Prize Cases*.

23 *Lloyd's Reports of Prize Cases*, III, 295.

24 Charlotte A. van Manen, *De Nederland-*

sche Overzee Trustmaatschappij, Middel-punt van het Verkeer van onzijdig Nederland met het Buitenland tydens den Wereldoorlog, 1914–1918 (The Hague: Martinus Nijhoff, 1935), II, 18. Hereafter cited as van Manen, *N.O.T.*

25 Van Manen, *N.O.T.*, II, 20. The declaration form used by Swift and Co., Rotterdam, in March 1915 ran as follows: "The undersigned __1__ herewith declares to be acquainted with the obligations which the firm __2__ has entered into with the Netherlands Oversea Trust Company, and on his part agrees to enter into the same obligations against the firm mentioned, concerning __3__ which he has received from them and he binds himself to protect the firm mentioned from the consequences which might arise from any action in contradiction with the obligations. Further he takes for his account the Commission of ⅛% on the value of his invoice, which the N.O.T. has charged the firm mentioned, besides the ¼% commission which the sellers have had to pay for the Bank Guarantee. For certainty he binds himself to give a bank guarantee to an amount of __4__ before taking delivery of the goods, with __5__ ." (1. Name of buyer, 2. Name of seller, 3. Description of goods, 4. Amount of invoice, 5. Bank Guarantees). Swift and Co., Rotterdam, to Swift and Co., Chicago, March 10, 1915, from unpublished correspondence in the papers of the late Henry Veeder of Chicago, counsel for Swift and Co., file marked "N.O.T." This correspondence will be cited hereafter as Veeder Papers, with the addition of the file reference.

26 Bell, pp. 260–261, citing the *Nieuwe Rotterdamsche Courant.*

27 Van Manen, *N.O.T.*, II, 55.

28 Chilton to van Aalst, April 11, 1915, in van Manen, *N.O.T.*, VII, bijlage no. 65. The list of agreements given in France, Comité de Restriction, "Liste des accords conclus par les gouvernements alliés avec des gouvernements ou des organisations neutres au sujet de la restriction des approvisionnement et du commerce de l'ennemi," *Documents numérotés*, no. 861, indicates that this was an Anglo-French agreement.

29 These goods included cement, road machinery, and materials for harbor improvements, all supplied from the Rhineland. See Bell, pp. 259–260.

30 Gevers to Loudon, January 13, 1915, in van Manen, *N.O.T.*, VII, bijlage no. 52.

31 Van Manen, *N.O.T.*, II, 64–65, quoting a note from V. Hartogensis to van Vollenhoven, April 19, 1915, and one from Gevers to Loudon, May 21, 1915.

32 Order made by the commissioners of customs and excise, April 26, 1915, in van Manen, *N.O.T.*, VII, bijlage no. 132; Act to Amend the Law Relating to the Exportation of Articles during the Present War, June 24, 1915, *ibid.*, VII, bijlage no. 135; Proclamation Relating to the Exportation of All Articles to the Netherlands during the Present War, June 25, 1915, *ibid.*, VII, bijlage no. 136.

33 Bell, 263–264; Johnstone to van Manen, June 5, 1915, in van Manen *N.O.T.*, VII, bijlage no. 67A; van Vollenhoven to Johnstone, June 9, 1915, *ibid.*, bijlage no. 67B; Johnstone to van Vollenhoven, June 16, 1915, *ibid.*, bijlage no. 67C; van Vollenhoven to Johnstone, June 21, 1915, *ibid.*, bijlage no. 68.

34 Chilton to the Executive Committee, July 19, 1915, in van Manen, *N.O.T.*, VII, bijlage no. 70.

35 The Comité had objected even to extending these facilities until May 31, and French cruisers had been instructed to put an end to the immunity from capture on that date. France, Comité de Restriction, *Comptes-rendus*, 9th meeting, May 21, 1915. However, the British indicated they intended to move the final date for embarkation of such goods to June 15, and again the Comité protested. See its *Procès-verbaux*, May 28, 1915, no. 13.

36 Executive Committee to Chilton, July 20, 1915, in van Manen *N.O.T.*, VII, bijlage no. 72.

37 N.O.T. to Chilton, July 21, 1915, in van Manen *N.O.T.*, VII, bijlage no. 74.

38 Johnstone to Pont, August 2, 1915, in van Manen, *N.O.T.*, VII bijlage no. 77; N.O.T. to Johnstone, August 4, 1915, *ibid.*, VII, bijlage no. 78; and *ibid.*, II, 139–140. Moeller, the sales agent in Rotterdam for the G. H. Hammond Co., of Chicago, reported in November 1915 that the N.O.T. had been badly disappointed in the execution of this agreement by the British government, "and all representatives from the part of the N.O.T. for a better service have only resulted in nice promises, but have not been able to touch the British Censor in his far going mood of independence." Moeller had no complaint about the

Trust's handling of telegrams. Moeller to Hammond and Co., November 25, 1915. Veeder Papers, file "Shipments under Agreement."

39 A. N. Swetchine to N.O.T., July 14, 1915, in van Manen, N.O.T., VII, bijlage no. 69. Conversations leading to this agreement were held in Paris at the Quai d'Orsay in the presence of Jean Gout. France, Comité de Restriction, Comtes-rendus, 20th meeting, August 7, 1915.

40 Sallier de la Tour Calvello to the Executive Committee, September 13, 1915, in van Manen, N.O.T., VII, bijlage no. 81.

41 "Cotton Agreement, September 1, 1915," in van Manen, N.O.T., VII, bijlage no. 79; the text is also in France, Comité de Restriction, "Accords relatifs au coton conclus par le gouvernement britannique avec des gouvernements et des associations des pays neutres," Documents numérotés, no. 388.

42 Van Manen, N.O.T., II, 181–184.

43 Johnstone to van Vollenhoven, November 13, 1915, in van Manen, N.O.T., VII, bijlage no. 85A; Executive Committee to Johnstone, November 23, 1915, ibid., bijlage no. 85B.

44 France, Comité de Restriction, Comptes-rendus, 23rd meeting, September 4, 1915. Additional information in Comptes-rendus, 17th meeting, July 17, 1915, and 37th meeting, December 11, 1915.

45 Henri Allizé to van Aalst, December 6, 1915, in van Manen, N.O.T., VII, bijlage no. 86; Executive Committee to Allizé, December 7, 1915, ibid., bijlage no. 88. Separate notes were exchanged with regard to tropical fruits. See ibid., bijlagen nos. 87 and 89.

46 Van Manen, N.O.T., II, 193–194.

47 Van Manen, N.O.T., II, 197.

48 France, Comité de Restriction, Comptes-rendus, 37th meeting, December 11, 1915; ibid., 41st meeting, January 8, 1916; Procès-verbaux, nos. 49 and 52.

49 Van Manen, N.O.T., II, 249–250.

50 Documents on the establishment of Subcommittee B are included in van Manen, N.O.T., VII, bijlage no. 104 l, and note. The Trust named as its members Kröller, Heldring, J. van Vollenhoven, Nierstrasz, and Westerman, with Lindhorst Homan serving as executive director. See appendix F on the organization of the N.O.T. at the end of 1915.

51 Materials on the committees may be found in van Manen, N.O.T., II, 89–102.

52 Much of the information regarding controls on oil and fats is based on van Manen, N.O.T., II, 104–116. On May 28, 1915, Moeller sent his company a copy of the following circular which he had received from the N.O.T.: "We have been informed that large stocks of Oils and Fats have been accumulated in our country and that these articles are still regularly imported, although there are sufficient stocks of them here, all of which may finally lead to great difficulties. Making use of the terms specified in Art. I sub C of our contract with you, No. 55 and 55 A, dated March 4, 1915, we therefore inform you herewith, that we cannot accept further consignments of the articles named and we therefore request you to stop further shipments until further notice." Veeder Papers, file "N.O.T."

53 Premier jus is "the first running of fat obtained by heating the fatty tissues of the caul and the kidneys of cattle at a temperature not exceeding 100 degrees —120 degrees Fahrenheit." Encyclopedia Britannica, 14th ed., on "Margarine."

54 Moeller to Hammond and Co., July 23, 1915, in Veeder Papers, file "N.O.T."

55 Van Manen, N.O.T., II, 112; R. Mair to Swift and Co., August 17, 1915, in Veeder Papers, file "N.O.T."

56 Moeller to Hammond and Co., August 21, 1915, in Veeder Papers, file "N.O.T."; Moeller to Hammond and Co., August 27, 1915, ibid. In another letter of August 21 Moeller refers to the Bureau as a "penny-in-the-slot machine," saying that "The seller throws his penny in the slot (wires his firm's offer of the day to the Buying Committee in The Hague) and waits until the chocolate (an order) comes out. He has no influence on the size nor on the good quality of the order. . . . Personal influence on the buyers and a certain authority towards them, which no good salesman can do without, are of no value under the new arrangement, and the agent can neither be praised for a good order, nor blamed for a poor one."

57 Van Manen, N.O.T., II, 110–111.

58 Moeller to Hammond and Co., August 4, 1915, in Veeder Papers file "N.O.T."; Moeller to Hammond and Co., August 13, 1915, ibid.; Swift and Co., Rotterdam, to Swift and Co., Chicago, September 7, 1915, ibid.

59 Mair to G. F. Swift, Jr., August 17,

1915, in Veeder Papers, file "N.O.T."
60 Van Manen, N.O.T., II, 115.
61 Van Manen, N.O.T., II, 116.
62 Mair to G. F. Swift, Jr., August 17, 1915, in Veeder Papers, file "N.O.T."
63 Johannes Hansen, Hovedtraek af Industriraadets Historie (Copenhagen: Nielsen and Lydiche, 1935) pp. 97–99; Olaf Knudsen, Dansk Industriberetning 1915–1918 (Copenhagen: Nielsen and Lydiche, 1921), I, 16–19.
64 The text of the German agreement is in Knudsen, bilag no. I, pp. 159–166. On the negotiations with the Central Powers see ibid., pp. 21–24; and Einar Cohn, "Denmark in the Great War," in Sweden, Norway, Denmark and Iceland in the World War. Economic and Social History of the World War, James T. Shotwell, ed. (New Haven: Yale University Press, 1930), pp. 441–442.
65 Hansen, pp. 104–105; Cohn, p. 449.
66 Bell, pp. 241–246. These agreements are listed in France, Comité de Restriction, Documents numérotés, no. 861.
67 Knudsen, I, 24–26; Hansen, 106–107; Bell, pp. 269–270.
68 The text of the accord with the Raad signed by Mygind is included in France, Comité de Restriction, "Accords relatifs au coton conclus par le gouvernement britannique avec des gouvernements et des associations des pays neutres," Documents numérotés, no. 388. In a conversation with L. Brahe Christensen, director of the Textilfabrikantforeningen, in May 1939, I was told that the Textile Union actually took over the distribution among its one-hundred-odd members of the textile materials imported under this and subsequent agreements.
69 These negotiations are considered in Knudsen, I, 26–33; Hansen, 107–112; Bell, 270–271. The text of the agreement is in Knudsen, bilag no. 2, pp. 167–181. Such information about the agreement as was disclosed soon after it came into effect was sent to Lansing by E. D. Winslow, American consul general in Copenhagen on December 17, 1915. See United States, Department of State, Papers Relating to the Foreign Relations of the United States, 1915 Supplement (Washington, D. C.: Government Printing Office, 1928), pp. 289–290. Hereafter cited as Foreign Relations.
70 See Chapter VIII.
71 France, Comité de Restriction, Documents numérotés, no. 388.

72 Knudsen, I, 33–39, 48–49; Hansen, pp. 114–121. The text of an undated memorandum which Foss presented to Grey sometime before February 15 is printed in Knudsen, bilag no. 3, pp. 182–186.
73 British purchasing agreements with Denmark will be discussed in Chapter XI.
74 Among the rationed goods were animal and vegetable oils and fats, oleaginous seeds, cocoa, coffee, corkwood, graphite, hemp, jute, nitrate of soda, rubber, hides, leather, tanning materials, tin, nickel, copper, antimony, ferroalloys, malt, fish, dried fruits, rice, and so forth. Hansen, pp. 120–121.
75 The Comité de Restriction recommended that France make such an agreement on December 24, 1915, after it received a text of the English accord. See France, Comité de Restriction, Procès-verbaux, no. 51 bis.
76 Great Britain, Parliamentary Debates, Commons, 5th Series (London: H.M. Stationery Office), LXXVI, 1723–1739; ibid., Lords, 5th Series, XX, 670–693, 695–744. One of the leading Copenhagen newspapers, the Berlingske Tidende, on November 25, 1915, carried an article that explained some of the arrangements made by Foss and Clausen in regard to imports and telegrams, but it was not until the issue of December 14 that a summary was published in this paper, which explained the facilities given to trade with Sweden and Norway. The paper was strangely silent regarding those given to trade with Germany. It was stated that would-be importers whose goods did not fall within the competence of the Raad and who were not members of the Copenhagen Guild might secure permissions from the Guild if their trustworthiness was attested to by some provincial organization of merchants.
77 Great Britain, Parliamentary Debates, Commons, 5th Series, LXXVI, 1736.
78 The source of this charge may well have been in a letter, by someone who signed himself Hjalmar Olsen of Hellerup, Copenhagen, which appeared in the London Evening Standard on December 8, 1915, in which the good faith of both the Danish associations was called into serious question. He charged "they are not really bodies of great standing or representative of the business element here. There are many German-Danish members in them, ... Anybody here

can become members of these societies by a small payment, and there are as many black sheep as good members." He added that Foss and Clausen "do not carry any weight over here." The agreement, he said, would "help matters more than ever for Germany to be fed, the war prolonged, and your blockade a joke." The reaction in Denmark was immediate, especially when the Copenhagen police asserted that no person with the name of Hjalmar Olsen existed. Both of the associations issued very formal denials of the charge, with the full lists of their boards of directors appended, which appeared in *Berlingske Tidende*, December 13, 1915, and in the London *Evening Standard* of the same day. The *Standard* added the comment that "a little letter from Copenhagen seems to have created a very great stir among the interested manufacturers."

79 Page had reported that the agreement was kept secret at the request of the Danish importers, who feared German reprisals if the terms should become known. Page to Lansing, December 7, 1915. See *Foreign Relations, 1915 Suppl.*, pp. 288–289.

80 Great Britain, *Parliamentary Debates, Lords*, 5th Series, XX, 690–692.

81 Great Britain, *Parliamentary Debates, Lords*, 5th Series XX, 737.

82 The London *Times*, December 13, 1915, p. 9; December 14, 1915, p. 9; December 16, 1915, p. 11; December 17, 1915, p. 10; December 18, 1915, p. 9; December 20, 1915, pp. 8, 9; December 21, 1915, pp. 11, 12. For other press comment see the London *Morning Post*, November 29, 1915, p. 8; December 9, 1915, p. 6; December 11, 1915, pp. 6, 7; December 13, 1915, p. 8; and December 15, 1915, p. 6; the *Manchester Guardian*, December 14, 1915, p. 8; and December 17, 1915, p. 6.

83 The London *Times*, December 20, 1915, p. 9.

84 Other additions to the Norwegian embargo lists were made in the first half of 1915 as follows: various vegetable oils, March 26, 1915; glycerine, March 31, 1915; copper sulfate, April 20, 1915; antimony, graphite, molybdenum, and wolfram, April 27, 1915; raw cotton, May 20, 1915; cotton waste, yarn, and cotton goods, July 15, 1915. Norway, *Lover, resolutioner og skrivelser, foranlediget ved krigsforholdene, 1 august 1914–31 december 1916*. (Christiania:

Grøndahl and Sons, 1917), pp. 62, 64, 67, 79.

85 The text is included in France, Comité de Restriction, *Documents numérotés*, no. 388. On the negotiations see Wilhelm Keilhau, *Norge og Verdenskrigen*, Economic and Social History of the World War, Scandinavian Series (Oslo: Aschehoug and Co., 1927), pp. 97–99.

86 Both agreements are listed in France, Comité de Restriction, *Documents numérotés*, no. 861, and the text of the Mustad agreement is in "Accords anglo-norvégiens," *ibid.*, no. 880, I.

87 The text is in France, Comité de Restriction, "Accords sur le cuir et les matières tannantes conclus entre le gouvernement britannique et les associations privées neutres," *Documents numérotés*, no. 707. See Keilhau, *Norge og Verdenskrigen*, p. 103.

88 The text, signed by Findlay, the British minister, and by Abel Chévalley, the French minister in Christiania, is found in France, Comité de Restriction, "Minerais et metaux, accords conclus entre le gouvernement britannique et des gouvernements étrangers ou les associations étrangères," *Documents numérotés*, no. 448.

89 The texts of the agreement and of Ihlen's letter are contained in France, Comité de Restriction, "Accords sur le caoutchouc conclus entre le gouvernement britannique et des associations privées neutres," *Documents numérotés* no. 709.

90 The following accords, listed in France, Comité de Restriction, *Documents numérotés*, no. 861, were made with: the Norwegian-American Line, May 14, 1915, and a supplementary accord on November 20, 1915; Garonne Steamship Line, July 1, 1915; Norway-Mexico-Gulf Line, July 1, 1915; Norwegian-Africa and Australia Line, July 1, 1915; Bergenske Steamship Line, July 7, 1915; Thor Thoresen Line, October 21, 1915; Nordenfeldske Dampskibsselskab of Trondhjem, October 23, 1915; and the Otto Thoresen Line of Christiania, November 15, 1915. The guarantee form used by the Thoresen Line was printed in the Comité de Restriction, *Bulletin*, no. 23, October 2, 1915. See, Bell, pp. 245–246.

91 The text is in France, Comité de Restriction, *Documents numérotés*, no. 388. The negotiations are briefly dis-

cussed in Karl Hildebrand, *De svenska statsmakterna och krigstidens folkhushållning* (Stockholm: P. A. Norstedt, 1916–1920), I, 150.

[92] The texts of these agreements were included in France, Comité de Restriction, *Documents numérotés*, no. 678, but that document is lacking in the collection at the Bibliotheque de la Guerre de Vincennes. The nature of the accords can be deduced from the text of a supplementary agreement signed by the Vacuum Oil Co., August 5, 1916, which is included in "Accords anglo-suédois," *ibid.*, no. 860. For the other agreements mentioned in this section see *ibid.*, no. 861.

CHAPTER VI

[1] Archibald C. Bell, *Die englische Hungerblockade im Weltkrieg, 1914–1915*, nach dem amtlichen englischen Darstellung der Hungerblockade von A. C. Bell, bearbeitet und eingeleitet durch Dr. Viktor Böhmert (Essen: Essener Verlagsanstalt, 1943), pp. 296–301. Swedish statistics in most instances support the charges brought by the British. To take but one example, in 1913 Sweden imported 1,627,963 kilos of premier jus, of which 294,775 kilos came from the United States, but in 1915 it imported a total of 2,670,784 kilos, with 839,681 of them coming from the United States. Swedish exports to Germany also rose sharply, e.g., fresh pork from 672,948 kilos in 1913 to 7,807,123 kilos in 1915, and salt pork from 30,854 kilos to 6,846,-820 kilos. See Sweden, *Sveriges officiella statistik, Handel berättelse för ar 1913* (Stockholm: P. A. Norstedt, 1915); *ibid., Handel . . . 1915*, (Stockholm: P. A. Norstedt, 1917), *passim*. On the vexations suffered by Swedish shipping and their effect on Swedish public opinion, see the report of Nekludov, Russian minister in Stockholm, to Sazonov, Russian foreign minister, January 9, 1915/ December 27, 1914, in Russia, *Die internationalen Beziehungen im Zeitalter des Imperialismus, Dokumente aus den Archiven der zarischen und der provisorischen Regierung*, ed. Central Executive Committee of the Soviet government, M. N. Pokrowsky, chairman; German ed. by Otto Hoetzsch (Berlin: Reimar Hobbing, 1931–1936), 2nd Series, Vol. VI, Part II, no. 740. Hereafter cited as Russia, *Die internationalen Beziehungen*.

[2] Eli F. Heckscher and Kurt Bergendal, "Sweden in the World War," in *Sweden, Norway, Denmark and Iceland in the World War, Economic and Social History of the World War*, James T. Shotwell, ed. (New Haven: Yale University Press, 1930), pp. 70–71; Karl Hildebrand, *De svenska statsmakterna och krigstidens folkhushållning* (Stockholm: P. A. Norstedt, 1916–1920), I, 103. Notice of the prohibition appeared in Great Britain's *Board of Trade Journal*, January 28, 1915, pp. 265–266.

[3] The draft of the note from Grey to Wrangel is dated May 5, 1915, in the text included in France, Comité de Restriction des Approvisionnements et du Commerce de l'Ennemi, *Documents non-numérotés* [XXIII]; it was sent as an enclosure in a letter from Cambon to Aristide Briand, May 10, 1915, *ibid.*, [XXII]. (Hereafter this committee will be cited as France, Comité de Restriction.)

[4] The text is included in France, Comité de Restriction, *Documents non-numérotés*, [XXIII].

[5] In the margin of the document at the Bibliothèque de la Guerre de Vincennes, opposite the statement about the organized revictualing of Germany, is written, "Télégramme de M. Howard, no. 202 du 28 avril 1915." It should be said in defense of the Swedish government that it had made some attempt, in a royal proclamation of February 15, to regulate shipments of embargoed goods in the coastal trade. See Sweden, *Svensk författningssamling*, 1915 (Stockholm: P. A. Norstedt, 1915), no. 19, pp. 29–31. However, later in the year the French secured information that goods were sometimes sent from one Swedish port to another but that by prearrangement the ships would be captured just at the limit

of Swedish territorial waters by German warships. When this came to the attention of the Swedish government, it insisted that all traffic between Swedish cities must be by rail. France, Comité de Restriction, *Bulletin*, no. 38, January 22, 1916.

6 The memorandum particularly mentioned maize, for which the annual statistics show an increased total importation from 55,750,553 kilos in 1914 to 210,619,250 kilos in 1915. See Sweden, *Sveriges officiel statistik, Handel . . . 1914,* and *Handel . . . 1915, passim.*

7 Hildebrand, I, 118, 167–169; Heckscher and Bergendal, in *Sweden, Norway, Denmark,* pp. 71–72. The longhand original of the decree, signed by Gustav V is in the Swedish Riksarkivet, Statens Handelskommission. Kommissionens Ledamöter, 1915–1919, Vol. C 26.

8 For material on the exportation of horses, see A. Nekludov to A. Neratov, April 13/March 31, 1915, (two letters of the same date), in Russia, *Die internationalen Beziehungen,* 2nd Series, Vol. VII, Part II, nos. 523 and 524.

9 Nekludov to Neratov, June 12/May 30, 1915, in Russia, *Die internationalen Beziehungen,* 2nd Series, Vol. VIII, Part I, no. 103.

10 Sazonov to Benckendorff, Russian ambassador in London, June 16/3, 1915, in Russia, *Die internationalen Beziehungen,* 2nd Series, Vol. VIII, Part I, no. 122; Sazonov to Nekludov, June 20/7, 1915, *ibid.,* no. 143.

11 Nekludov to Sazonov, June 2/May 20, 1915, in Russia, *Die internationalen Beziehungen,* 2nd Series, Vol. VIII, Part I, no. 52.

12 Bell, p. 296. When the French Comité de Restriction had considered the British draft memorandum sent to it in May, it had approved the principles involved, but Gout had urged that Sweden be handled with mildness in order to prevent its taking part in the war against Russia. France, Comité de Restriction, *Comptes-rendus,* 9th meeting, May 21, 1915.

13 Mario Toscano, "La Svezia e l'intervento in guerre dell'Italia," *Rassegna storica del risorgimento,* XXIII (September 1936), pp. 1181–1195.

14 Sir George Buchanan, British ambassador in St. Petersburg, to Sazonov, May 6/April 23, 1915, in Russia, *Die internationalen Beziehungen,* 2nd Series, Vol. VII, Part II, no. 687; Sazonov to Buchanan and Maurice Paleologue, French ambassador in St. Petersburg, May 7/April 24, 1915, *ibid.,* no. 693.

15 Nekludov to Sazonov, May 14/1, 1915, in Russia, *Die internationalen Beziehungen,* 2nd Series, Vol. VII, Part II, no. 762.

16 Nekludov to Sazonov, May 11/April 28, 1915, in Russia, *Die internationalen Beziehungen,* 2nd Series, Vol. VII, Part II, no. 732; Nekludov to Sazonov, June 18/5, 1915, *ibid.,* 2nd Series, Vol. VIII, Part I, no. 130.

17 Sazonov to Benckendorff, June 19/6, 1915, in Russia, *Die internationalen Beziehungen,* 2nd Series, Vol. VIII, Part I, no. 137; Janushkevich to Sazonov, June 20/7, 1915, *ibid.,* no. 147.

18 Bell, pp. 301–302.

19 See Chapter V above. Also see Russia, *Die internationalen Beziehungen,* 2nd Series, Vol. VIII, Part I, no. 166, note 1, quoting from a telegram from Nekludov, June 25/12, 1915.

20 Bell, p. 302; Aide-memoire of Buchannan, June 22/9, 1915, in Russia, *Die internationalen Beziehungen,* 2nd Series, Vol. VIII, Part I, no. 166, n. 2. The Foreign Office letter of instructions is dated June 26, 1915, by Howard in his memoirs. See Esme Howard, *Theatre of Life, Life Seen from the Stalls* (Boston: Little, Brown and Co., 1936), pp. 243–244. The form of the letter differed somewhat from the summary given above, but the sense is the same.

21 Benckendorff reported on June 23 that postal questions would be handled separately. See Benckendorff to Sazonov, June 23/10, 1915, in Russia, *Die internationalen Beziehungen,* 2nd Series, Vol. VIII, Part I, no. 166.

22 Hildebrand, I, 149–150. A notice concerning the opening of the negotiations appeared in the London *Times,* July 2, 1915, p. 7.

23 Aide-memoire of Buchanan to Sazonov, July 7/June 24, 1915, in Russia, *Die internationalen Beziehungen,* 2nd Series, Vol. VIII, Part I, no. 253.

24 Hammarskjöld had made a short secret visit to Berlin about which speculation was current. See Russia, *Die internationalen Beziehungen,* 2nd Series, Vol. VIII, Part I, no. 147, note 1, and no. 253, note 3.

25 Bell, pp. 303–304; Sazonov to Benckendorff, July 16/3, 1915, in Russia, *Die internationalen Beziehungen,* 2nd Series, Vol. VIII, Part I, no. 324. In early July

the Russians were being driven from Kurland, suffered reverses in Galicia, and were in desperate need of supplies.

26 Bell, 305–306. The Conservative press, including *Stockholms Dagblad, Svenska Dagbladet,* and the *Nya Dagligt Allehanda,* had been particularly violent in their denunciation of any import trusts.

27 Nekludov to Sazonov, July 18/5, 1915, in Russia, *Die internationalen Beziehungen,* 2nd Series, Vol. VIII, Part I, no. 343, note 2.

28 Bell, pp. 307–308, discusses this draft agreement. List A included antimony, aluminum and its alloys, chrome and its alloys, copper, hides and leather, molybdenum, nickel, rubber, tanning materials, tin, tungsten, vanadium, and wool. List B included asbestos, bran, cereals, copper alloys, including brass and bronze, cotton and cotton waste, explosives, flax, glycerine, graphite, glutenous foods, hemp, jute and jute goods, lard, lead, lubricating oils, meats in all forms, maize, manganese ores and alloys, mercury, mineral oils, nitrates, nitric acid, oils and fats, oil cake, olein, paraffin wax, phosphates, resin, oilseeds and nuts, sulfur, sulfuric acid, and wire.

29 Nekludov to Sazonov, August 2/July 20, 1915, no. 1, in Russia, *Die internationalen Beziehungen,* 2nd Series, Vol. VIII, Part II, no. 443, note 1.

30 Bell, pp. 309–310.

31 Nekludov to Sazonov, August 21/8, 1915, in Russia, *Die internationalen Beziehungen,* 2nd Series, Vol. VIII, Part II, no. 549; Benckendorff to Sazonov, August 23/10, 1915, *ibid.,* no. 549, note 2. Jean Gout, who had been on a mission to London, reported to the Comité de Restriction on August 21 on the state of negotiations with the Swedes. He said that Paul Cambon had rather wryly remarked that "the Swedes have found in London the best of all advocates: the Russian ambassador." France, Comité de Restriction, *Comptes-rendus,* 21st meeting, August 21, 1915.

32 Hildebrand, I, p. 150; Nekludov to Neratov, September 3/August 21, 1915, in Russia, *Die internationalen Beziehungen,* 2nd Series, Vol. VIII, Part II, no. 631.

33 Bell, pp. 310–311.

34 Ira Morris, American minister to Sweden, reported the end of the negotiations on October 30. See United States, Department of State, *Papers Relating to the Foreign Relations of the United States, 1915 Supplement* (Washington, D.C.: Government Printing Office, 1928), pp. 284–285. Hereafter cited as *Foreign Relations.*

35 Howard say in his memoirs: "I found a pro-English Swedish gentleman of good family, Herr Axel de Bildt, who was willing to undertake the formation of this company. . . ." He goes on to explain that Bildt was socially ostracized, received threats and had pressure put on him from high quarters to drop the whole plan. On the other hand, Howard reported with some amusement that the Crown Princess of Sweden, a daughter of the Duke of Connaught, and even Gustav V were happy to use Transito facilities for securing tires for their motor cars, such facilities being granted, even in those cases, only when the Swedish government permitted an equal number to go to Russia. Howard, *Theater of Life,* pp. 249–252.

36 Some of the most important press articles in this controversy appeared in *Nya Dagligt Allehanda,* November 22 and 25, 1915; *Stockholms Dagblad,* November 23, which printed a letter from Bildt denying many of the charges; *Aftonbladet,* November 22, and *Svenska Dagbladet,* November 23, 24, and December 5, 1915. The United States government received word of the establishment of the Transito in a communication of Morris to Lansing, November 24, 1915 (see *Foreign Relations, 1915 Suppl.,* pp. 286–287) and through a communication of the British legation concerning Aktiebolaget Transito, which was enclosed in Morris to Lansing, December 1, 1915 (*ibid.,* pp. 287–288). See also Boris E. Nolde, *Russia in the Economic War,* Economic and Social History of the World War, Russian Series (New Haven: Yale University Press, 1928), p. 36.

37 This section is based primarily on Wilhelm Keilhau, *Norge og Verdenskrigen,* Economic and Social History of the World War, Scandinavian Series (Oslo: Aschehoug and Co., 1927), pp. 99–103; Norway, *Oversigt over de vigtigste av utenriksdepartmentet under Krigen indtil mai 1916, Behandlede saker som egner sig for offentliggjørelse* (Christiania: Grøndahl and Sons, 1916), pp. 39–40; and Paul G. Vigness, *The Neutrality of Norway in the World War* (Stanford, California: Stanford University Press, 1932), pp. 49–52.

CHAPTER VII

[1] C. Ernest Fayle, *Seaborne Trade, History of the Great War Based on Official Documents*, by direction of the Historical Section of the Committee of Imperial Defence (New York: Longman's Green and Co., Inc., 1920–1924), II, 148–151.

[2] For British statistics on decreases in German exports see Appendix F.

[3] Dutch official statistics published in 1915 were used to advantage by Allied negotiators. Extracts from these statistics were published in various numbers of France, Comité de Restriction des Approvisionnements et du Commerce de l'Ennemi, *Bulletin.* See Appendix G. (Hereafter this committee will be cited as France, Comité de Restriction.)

[4] In July 1915 cotton yarn cost 159–171 pfennigs per English pound; in December, 238–257 pfennigs. Cotton waste in September 1914 cost 35–180 pfennigs per 100 kilos; in September 1915 it was 100–315 pfennigs; and in November 1915, 156–370 pfennigs.

[5] Archibald C. Bell, *Die englische Hungerblockade im Weltkrieg, 1914–1915,* nach dem amtlichen englischen Darstellung der Hungerblockade von A. C. Bell, bearbeitet und eingeleitet durch Dr. Viktor Böhmert (Essen: Essener Verlagsanstalt, 1943), p. 280.

[6] Great Britain, *Parliamentary Debates, Commons,* 5th Series, (London: H.M. Stationery Office), LXIX, 167–168. A similar question was asked on February 8, 1915, by Joseph King but no further answer was given. See *ibid.*, 267.

[7] Great Britain, *Parliamentary Debates, Commons,* 5th Series, LXX, 23. Another question was asked on February 25 to determine what amounts of cotton Germany would need for the manufacture of explosives, with a view to finding out how long her stocks would last and how long Great Britain would continue to treat cotton as noncontraband. See *ibid.*, 391, and LXXI, 5.

[8] Public announcement by the British embassy, Washington, March 8, 1915, in United States, Department of State, *Papers Relating to the Foreign Relations of the United States, 1915 Supplement* (Washington, D.C.: Government Printing Office, 1928), p. 189. (Hereafter cited as *Foreign Relations.*) On July 19, 1915, Lord Robert Cecil stated in the Commons that since March 11, forty-nine vessels with cotton cargoes had been diverted to United Kingdom ports, and eleven to other British ports. Payments amounting to £700,000 had been made for twenty-five shipments purchased under the arrangement made with American cotton shippers. See Great Britain, *Parliamentary Debates, Commons,* 5th Series, LXXIII, 1145–1146. According to Bell, p. 281, £2,000,000 was spent on this project.

[9] Bell, p. 283. The background of France's position on the matter of cotton was given in a meeting of the Comité de Restriction by Gout on August 21, 1915. France, Comité de Restriction, *Comptes-rendus,* 21st meeting.

[10] On the submarine controversy see Charles Seymour, ed., *The Intimate Papers of Colonel House* (Boston and New York: Houghton Mifflin Co., 1926–1928), II, 1–48; Ray Stannard Baker, *Woodrow Wilson, Life and Letters* (Garden City, N. Y.: Doubleday, Doran and Co., 1927–1939) V, Chapters V, VII, and VIII; Charles C. Tansill, *America Goes to War* (Boston: Little, Brown and Co., 1938), Chapters XI, XII, and XIII. For the discussions in the German government see Germany, Arno Spindler, *Der Handelskrieg mit U-Booten, Der Krieg zur See, 1914–1918,* ed. the German Marine-Archiv (Berlin: Mittler, 1932–1934), II. On the differences of opinion within the British Government, see Bell, pp. 281–282; Viscount Grey, *Twenty-five Years* (New York: Frederick A. Stokes, 1925) II, 115–117.

[11] Great Britain, *Parliamentary Debates, Commons,* 5th Series, LXXII, 63–64, 240–241, 260, 274–276, 395–396

668–669; LXXIII, 543, 636, 978, 1145–1146, 2256, 2273.

12 Great Britain, *Parliamentary Debates, Commons,* 5th Series, LXXII, 423–426.

13 Great Britain, *Parliamentary Debates, Commons,* 5th Series, LXXII, 1115–1118.

14 On the British controversy with the American meat packers growing out of the *Kim* cases see my article, "British Negotiations with American Meat Packers, 1915–1917: A Study of Belligerent Trade Controls," *Journal of Modern History,* XXIII (December 1951), 343–353. Pertinent articles on American relations appeared in the London *Times,* July 17, 1915, p. 6; July 21, pp. 5, 7; July 23, p. 7, and July 24, p. 5.

15 Bell, pp. 283–285. Page to Lansing, July 15, 1915, in *Foreign Relations, 1915 Suppl.,* pp. 192–193.

16 Page to Lansing, July 22, 1915, in *Foreign Relations, 1915 Suppl.,* p. 193.

17 France, Comité de Restriction, *Comptes-rendus,* 21st meeting, August 21, 1915; Great Britain, *Board of Trade Journal,* August 26, 1915, p. 592; *Foreign Relations, 1915 Suppl.,* p. 174.

18 See the answers given by Asquith and Cecil to questions on government cotton purchases, in Great Britain, *Parliamentary Debates, Commons,* 5th Series, LXXIV, 563, 983.

19 Great Britain, *Parliamentary Debates, Commons,* 5th Series, LXXIV, 618.

20 Great Britain, *Parliamentary Debates, Commons,* 5th Series, LXXV, 579–581. Beresford spoke in the same sense on November 23, *ibid.,* LXXVI, 268–269. See also the speeches of Sir A. Markham on December 9, *ibid.,* LXXVI, 1730–1731, of Sir R. Cooper on December 23, *ibid.,* LXXVII, 726–727, and of Major Hunt on January 20, 1916, *ibid.,* LXXVIII, 582–583. Thomas Gibson Bowles wrote a letter on the subject to the London *Times,* November 22, 1915, p. 9.

21 Great Britain, *Parliamentary Debates, Commons,* 5th Series, LXXV, 606–619.

22 For the statistics of British exports and re-exports in the last half of 1915, see Appendix B.

23 On March 11, 1915, Basil E. Peto called attention to the increased exports of cotton yarns to Denmark. See Great Britain, *Parliamentary Debates, Commons,* 5th Series, LXX, 1547. On May 4 Sir John Lonsdale asked a question concerning the continued exports of cotton on British ships, *ibid.,* LXXI, 979. For the debate on July 20, see *ibid.,* LXXIII, 1454–1458.

24 Great Britain, *Parliamentary Papers, Miscellaneous No. 2 (1916), Statement of the Measures Adopted to Intercept the Seaborne Commerce of Germany,* Cd. 8145 (London: H.M. Stationery Office, 1916).

25 Great Britain, *Parliamentary Debates, Commons,* 5th Series, LXXVIII, 1279–1388.

26 See the speeches of Benn, in Great Britain, *Parliamentary Debates, Commons,* 5th Series, LXXVIII, 1281–1285; of J. G. Butcher, *ibid.,* 1352–1355; and of Sir Robert Finlay, *ibid.,* 1370–1372.

27 Great Britain, *Parliamentary Debates, Commons,* 5th Series, LXXVIII, 1320–1323.

28 Great Britain, *Parliamentary Debates, Commons,* 5th Series, LXXVIII, 1293. For a discussion by Lord Cecil of the administrative difficulties of such a system, where no neutral consignee association participated, see *ibid.,* 1381–1383.

29 Great Britain, *Parliamentary Debates, Commons,* 5th Series, LXXVIII, 1307–1309, 1311 (Leverton Harris), 1319 (Grey), 1335–1337 (Pollock), and 1380–1382 (Cecil).

30 Great Britain, *Parliamentary Debates, Commons,* 5th Series, LXXVIII, 1302, 1305, 1312–1314, and 1334.

31 Great Britain, *Parliamentary Debates, Commons,* 5th Series, LXXVIII, 1323–1324.

32 Great Britain, *Parliamentary Debates, Lords,* 5th Series, XXI, 72–184.

CHAPTER VIII

1 France, Comité de Restriction des Approvisionnements et du Commerce de l'Ennemi, "Sommaire sur l'organisation du ministère du blocus en Angleterre, par de Lasteyrie, chef de cabinet de Denys Cochin, 5 août 1916," *Documents numérotés* no. 283. (Hereafter this committee will be cited as France, Comité de Restriction.)

2 C. Ernest Fayle, *Seaborne Trade, History of the Great War Based on Official Documents,* by direction of the Historical Section of the Committee of Imperial Defence (New York: Longmans, Green and Co., Inc., 1920–1924), III, 36.

3 France, Comité de Restriction, *Comptes-rendus,* 52nd meeting, March 24, 1916.

4 Information supplied to me by A. C. Bell.

5 Memorandum of Lord Robert Cecil, July 8, 1916, in France, Comité de Restriction, "Accord anglo-danois pour les réexportations en Suède et en Norvège," annexe, *Documents numérotés,* no. 311.

6 Those listed were: the Admiralty, the ministries of War, Munitions, and Agriculture, the Board of Trade, the Customs Administration, the War Trade Department, the Licensing Committee, the Restriction of Enemy Supply Committee, the Commission Internationale de Revitaillement, and the procurator-general.

7 Such a notice constituted what was known as a "statistical embargo." A copy of one such notification, dated September 9, 1916, is reproduced in H. Ritchie, *The "Navicert" System during the World War* (Washington, D. C.: Carnegie Endowment for International Peace, 1938), Annex F, pp. 46–47.

8 See the next section of this chapter for a discussion of letters of assurance.

9 Fayle, *Seaborne Trade,* III, 37.

10 Ritchie, *The "Navicert" System,* pp.5–6.

11 Skinner to Bryan, April 16, 1915, in United States, Department of State, *Papers Relating to the Foreign Relations of the United States, 1915 Supplement* (Washington, D. C.: Government Printing Office, 1928), p. 371. Hereafter cited as *Foreign Relations.* Page to Bryan, April 19, 1915, *ibid.,* pp. 371–372; Skinner to Bryan, April 20, 1915, *ibid.,* pp. 372–373. Skinner had recently been urging that some meeting of representatives of the principal American shipping interests be held in London in order to formulate definite proposals to present to the British. See Skinner to Bryan, April 14, 1915, *ibid.,* pp. 373–374.

12 Skinner to Bryan, April 21, 1915, in *Foreign Relations, 1915 Suppl.,* pp. 382–383.

13 Ritchie, *The "Navicert" System,* p. 6.

14 Circular issued by the British consulate general in New York, March 4, 1916, enclosure in letter of Edwin F. Sweet to Lansing, March 9, 1916, in *Foreign Relations, 1916 Suppl.,* pp. 496–497. The beginning of the navicerting system was announced in the Comité de Restriction, *Bulletin,* no. 52, April 26, 1916, p. 12, where it was stated that for the time being copper, gasoline, and lubricants would benefit from the regime.

15 See the letter addressed to the State Department by Carl S. Stern, July 7, 1916, in *Foreign Relations, 1916 Suppl.,* pp. 498–499; and by H. U. Gade to the American legation in Norway, October 18, 1916, *ibid.,* pp. 500–501.

16 Ritchie, *The "Navicert" System,* p. 14, gives statistics to show that by the autumn of 1916 a preponderant number of items of the cargo on any ship was covered by navicerts, and that as early as June it was unusual to find shipments on Danish vessels that were not so covered. Where the Danish and Norwegian shipowners had already made agreements with the British, it was always possible that the vessels might be permitted to proceed through the patrol lines on condition that suspected cargoes, not covered by a navicert, would be stored until the British were convinced of their innocence. It should be added that the overwhelming part of American-Scandinavian trade was carried in Scandi-

navian bottoms, so that American ships were very little affected by the navicert system.

17 There was nothing particularly new in this claim, for it had been brought to the attention of the British government by Skinner in 1915, and had been refuted by it. See, for example, Skinner to Lansing, June 28, 1915, in *Foreign Relations, 1915 Suppl.*, 466–467, and Page to Lansing, August 16, 1915, enclosing note from Grey of August 3, *ibid.*, pp. 511–515.

18 Marion Letcher to Stern, July 11, 1916, in *Foreign Relations, 1916 Suppl.*, pp. 499–500.

19 Letcher to Crawford, December 9, 1916, in *Foreign Relations, 1916 Suppl.*, p. 501.

20 Secretary of the Admiralty to the under-secretary of state for foreign affairs, July 27, 1916, contained in the minutes of the subcommittee of the War Trade Advisory Committee for September 25, 1916, in France, Comité de Restriction, "Memorandum de l'amirauté britannique relatif au contrôle exercé sur le commerce neutre," *Documents numérotés*, no. 496.

21 France, Comité de Restriction, *Documents numérotés*, no. 496.

22 The decision to appoint the subcommittee was made on September 14, 1916; the following departments were to be represented on it: Foreign Office, Foreign Trade Department, Board of Trade, Admiralty, War Trade Department, and the Contraband Department. France, Comité de Restriction, "Compte-rendu de la séance du War Trade Advisory Committee, 48ème séance, Admiralty House, 14 septembre 1916," *Documents numérotés*, no. 512.

23 France, Comité de Restriction, *Documents numérotés*, no. 496.

24 France, Comité de Restriction, "War Trade Advisory Committee, Rapport du sous-comité sur l'extension du système des garanties pour contrôler le commerce des neutres, 9 octobre 1916," *Documents numérotés*, no. 494.

25 Great Britain, *Public General Statutes*, 5 and 6 George V (London: Eyre and Spottiswoode, 1916), Vol. LIII, ch. 98, pp. 351–352.

26 This idea is well expressed in a note sent to Page on February 16, 1916, by the Foreign Office: "They are careful, therefore, in devising the necessary legislation, not only to avoid any definition which would impose enemy status upon all persons of enemy nationality and associations, but also to take powers of discrimination which would enable them to apply the purely commercial restrictions contemplated only in regard to those persons from whom it was necessary in British interests to withhold the facilities offered by British resources." See *Foreign Relations, 1916 Suppl.*, p. 353.

27 Proclamation Prohibiting Trading with Certain Persons, or Bodies of Persons, of Enemy Nationality or Enemy Associations, in *Foreign Relations, 1916 Suppl.*, pp. 359–360.

28 Information supplied to me by A. C. Bell.

29 The existence of List B was reported by Skinner to Lansing on July 21, 1916, when he cited the case of a London firm that had difficulty in entering into business relations with Messrs. Herskovits and Co. of New York. Skinner inquired at the Foreign Office about this and received the following reply: "With reference to the note which you were good enough to address to me on the 7th instance, I have the honor to inform your excellency that, as Messrs. Herskovits and Son are not regarded at present as suitable consignees for British goods for the reasons stated in my previous note, firms in this country have been advised not to trade with them. His Majesty's Government are unable to contemplate the possibility of such advice being disregarded by any British firms." See *Foreign Relations, 1916 Suppl.*, pp. 423–424.

30 France, Comité de Restriction, *Comptes-rendus*, 62nd meeting, June 7, 1916. Later representatives of the ministries of Finance, Commerce, and Colonies were added; Vice-Admiral Amet was the president.

31 Briand to Cochin, June 20, 1916, in France, Comité de Restriction, "Note sur les listes noires françaises," *Documents numérotés*, no. 204. Annexed to this letter was a memorandum of the Service de la Guerre Economique, a department of the Ministry of Foreign Affairs, which recommended the methods to be used in establishing the French confidential black list. The subject was also considered in the Comité de Restriction, *Comptes-rendus*, 64th and 65th meetings, June 21 and 28,

1916; and *Procès-verbaux*, no. 155 and no. 159.

32 For a discussion of this conference, see Chapter X.

33 France, *Journal officiel* (Paris: Imprimerie Nationale), August 6, 1916, p. 7052. Some difficulties arose, for example, that between the Ministry of Marine and the Customs in the actual execution of the new controls as they affected goods consigned to the N.O.T. and the Société de Surveillance Suisse. See France, Comité de Restriction, *Comptes-rendus*, 76th meeting, September 13, 1916.

34 Skinner to Lansing, July 21, 1916, in *Foreign Relations, 1916 Suppl.*, pp. 423–424. The subject of American reaction to the black lists has been well treated by Thomas A. Bailey, "The United States and the Blacklist during the Great War," *Journal of Modern History*, VI (March 1934), 14–35.

35 Instructions to deliver the enclosed note were sent by Polk to Page on July 26, 1916. See *Foreign Relations, 1916 Suppl.*, pp. 421–422.

36 Page to Lansing, October 12, 1916, in *Foreign Relations, 1916 Suppl.*, pp. 461–465.

37 Memorandum by Polk of a conversation with Spring Rice, July 25, 1916, in *Foreign Relations, 1916 Suppl.*, p. 419.

38 Page to Lansing, November 16, 1916, in *Foreign Relations, 1916 Suppl.*, p. 484. Another report of this conversation is available in a letter from Grey to Colville Barclay, dated Foreign Office, November 14, 1916, in France, Comité de Restriction, "Compte-rendu de la séance du War Trade Advisory Committee, 59ème séance, 30 novembre 1916," *Documents numérotés*, no. 696R, annexe 2, "Effet des listes noires," no. 1.

39 Lansing to Page, November 24, 1916, in *Foreign Relations, 1916 Suppl.*, pp. 485–486; Page to Lansing, November 27, 1916, *ibid.*, pp. 486–487.

40 "Memorandum rédigé par le War Trade Department du Foreign Office. Effet de la liste statuaire sur la conduite de la guerre," in France, Comité de Restriction, *Documents numérotés*, no. 696R, annexe 2, no. 2.

41 On the cruise of the *Moewe* in January-March, 1916, see Fayle, *Seaborne Trade*, II, 253–257.

42 Letters and cables intercepted by the British and French censors showed the anxiety of German branch houses abroad.

Extracts from these cables were frequently printed in France's Comité de Restriction, *Bulletin;* for example, one in no. 73, September 20, 1916, pp. 2–4.

43 On Allied shipping controls see Chapter IX.

44 Great Britain, *British and Foreign State Papers* (London: H.M. Stationery Office), C (1906–1907), 428; the English translation is published in James Brown Scott, ed., *The Hague Conventions and Declarations of 1899 and 1907* (New York: Oxford University Press, 1915), pp. 182–183.

45 Information supplied by A. C. Bell.

46 The types of mail censored by the British were explained in a letter from the Foreign Office to John Scheepers and Co. of New York, June 23, 1916, after this company had taken issue with a statement released by Lord Cecil to the effect that neutral mails taken from neutral ships for examination were forwarded as quickly as possible. See *Foreign Relations, 1916 Suppl.*, pp. 611–612.

47 Great Britain *Parliamentary Debates*, Commons, 5th Series (London: H.M. Stationery Office), LXXIV, 1165–1166.

48 On these cases see the letter of the Foreign Office to Scheepers cited above, note 46. In view of this later admission that these ships had been brought in and the mails seized, the statement made by Grey in the Commons on January 6, 1916, would seem to be a misrepresentation of the existing policy of the government. He said, "Goods otherwise liable to seizure on board neutral vessels do not, under international law, acquire immunity by the mere fact of being sent through the post. The Allied Governments are accordingly applying the same treatment to all such goods, however conveyed. With postal correspondence found on neutral vessels on the high seas the Allied Governments do not at present interfere, but they exercise their undoubted rights to examine and censor such correspondence when ships carrying them enter their territory or territorial waters." Great Britain, *Parliamentary Debates, Commons*, 5th Series, LXXVII, 1077–1078.

49 Lansing to Page, January 4, 1916, in *Foreign Relations, 1916 Suppl.*, pp. 591–592. Page's memorandum is included in Great Britain, *Parliamentary Papers, Miscellaneous No. 5 (1916), Correspondence with the United States Ambas-*

sador *Respecting the Treatment of Mails on Neutral Vessels*, Cd. 8173 (London: H. M. Stationery Office, 1916), no. 1.

50 Jusserand to Lansing, April 3, 1916, in *Foreign Relations, 1916 Suppl.*, pp. 598–602. The same note appears in Great Britain, *Parliamentary Papers, Miscellaneous No. 9 (1916), Memorandum Presented by His Majesty's Government and the French Government to Neutral Governments Regarding the Examination of Parcels and Letter Mails*, Cd. 8223 (London: H.M. Stationery Office, 1916).

51 Lansing to Jusserand, May 24, 1916, in *Foreign Relations, 1916 Suppl.*, pp. 604–608; and in Great Britain, *Parliamentary Papers, Miscellaneous No. 20 (1916), Note from the United States Government Regarding the Examination of Parcels and Letter Mails*, Cd. 8261 (London: H.M. Stationery Office, 1916).

52 This was refuted in a memorandum handed to Page by Crowe on July 20, 1916, which asserted also that many of the delays were caused by the irregularity of the sailing of ships, which was beyond the control of the British government. See *Foreign Relations, 1916 Suppl.*, pp. 613–614; and Great Britain, *Parliamentary Papers, Miscellaneous No. 23 (1916), Note Addressed to the United States Ambassador Regarding the Examination of Parcels and Letter Mails*, Cd. 8294 (London: H.M. Stationery Office, 1916).

53 *Foreign Relations, 1916 Suppl.*, pp. 615–616.

54 Jusserand to Lansing, October 12, 1916, in *Foreign Relations, 1916 Suppl.*, pp. 624–628; Great Britain, *Parliamentary Papers, Miscellaneous No. 2 (1917), Memorandum Addressed by the French and British Governments Regarding the Examination of Parcels and Letter Mails*, Cd. 8438 (London: H.M. Stationery Office, 1917).

55 Wrangel to Grey, December 18, 1915, in Great Britain, *Parliamentary Papers, Miscellaneous No. 28 (1916), Correspondence with the Swedish Minister on the Subject of the Detention by the Swedish Government of the British Transit Mail to Russia as a Reprisal for the Search of Parcels Mail by His Majesty's Government*, Cd. 8322 (London: H.M. Stationery Office, 1916), no. 2. The question of postal difficulties is discussed in Karl Hildebrand, *De svenska statsmakterna och krigstidens folkhushållning* (Stockholm: P. A. Norstedt, 1916–1920), I, 152–153, 205–207; II, 51–52, 124–125.

56 Grey to Wrangel, January 1, 1916, in Great Britain, *Parliamentary Papers, Miscellaneous No. 28 (1916)*, no. 5; Grey to Wrangel, January 19, 1916, *ibid.*, no. 6, Wrangel to Grey, January 21, 1916, *ibid.*, no. 7.

57 Grey to Wrangel, January 31, 1916, in Great Britain, *Parliamentary Papers, Miscellaneous No. 28 (1916)*, no. 8. The French were delighted with this Swedish admission. In a meeting of the Comité de Restriction Gout called attention to it and added, "This neutral country is one which is *le plus à cheval* on international conventions." France, Comité de Restriction, *Comptes-rendus*, 45th meeting, February 5, 1916.

58 The pertinent correspondence, February 11 to August 2, 1916, is printed in Great Britain, *Parliamentary Papers, Miscellaneous No. 28 (1916)*, nos. 9–18.

59 The correspondence was published in a White Book and in two Orange Books issued by The Netherlands, *Diplomatieke Bescheiden betreffende de Inbeslagneming door de Britsche Autoriteiten van over zee vervoerde Brievenpost* (The Hague: Algemeene Landsdrukkerij, 1916); *Overzicht van eenige in het Tijdvak October 1915 tot Juli 1916 door het Ministerie van Buitenlandsche Zaken behandelde Aangelegenheden* (Transmitted to the Dutch Parliament, July 22, 1916) (n.p., n.d.), pp. 8–9; and *Mededeelingen van den Minister van Buitenlandsche Zaken aan de Staten-Generaal, Juli-December 1916* (Transmitted to the Dutch Parliament, December 28, 1916) (n.p., n.d.), pp. 11–12. The most important Dutch notes are reproduced in Paul Fauchille, *La Guerre de 1914, Recueil de documents intéressant le droit international* (Paris: Pedone, 1916–1920), III, nos. 706–710.

CHAPTER IX

1 For a table showing the location of fueling stations and the source of their coal, see C. Ernest Fayle, *Seaborne Trade, History of the Great War Based on Official Documents*, by direction of the Historical Section of the Committee of Imperial Defence (New York: Longmans, Green and Co., Inc., 1920–1924), II, 156.

2 Steam coal used for bunkering should be capable of producing considerable heat, for which purpose it should have a high fixed carbon content with sufficient volatile matter to permit easy ignition and consumption of the fixed carbon. From a consideration of analyses of bituminous coals, one receives the general impression that the average coal produced in the United Kingdom was equal to almost the best quality coal produced in the United States, i.e., that mined in Maryland, Western Pennsylvania, West Virginia, and Ohio. Thus three coal specimens from certain Maryland mines produced respectively 13,432 B.T.U. per lb. as received, 14,087, and 14,031; certain Ohio mines produced coal giving 12,731, 13,025, and 12,722 B.T.U.; and certain Pennsylvania coals gave 13,037, 13,653, 13,813, and 14,063 B.T.U. See Robert T. Haslam and Robert P. Russel, *Fuels and Their Combustion* (New York and London: McGraw-Hill Book Co., 1926), pp. 68–70. On the other hand, British analyses (given in calories where 1 calorie × 1.8 = 1 B.T.U.) show that certain Derbyshire coal gave 8,077 calories, Yorkshire coal, 8,307, Nottinghamshire coal, 8,046, and South Staffordshire coal, 7,720 calories. See *Proceedings of the Third International Conference on Bituminous Coal, November 16–21, 1931* (Pittsburgh: Carnegie Institute of Technology, 1932), II, 852–855.

3 Information supplied to me by A. C. Bell.

4 Order in Council, May 6, 1915. See Great Britain, *Board of Trade Journal*, May 13, 1915, pp. 444–445.

5 Fayle, *Seaborne Trade*, II, 156–157.

6 Great Britain, *Board of Trade Journal*, May 13, 1915, p. 446. These restrictions were noted in the *Bulletin*, no. 10, July 2, 1915, of the Comité de Restriction des Approvisionnements et du Commerce de l'Ennemi (hereafter cited as France, Comité de Restriction). It was stated that the demand on the Continent for American coal had thereby been stimulated.

7 France, Comité de Restriction, *Bulletin*, no. 11, July 10, 1915. The British government had informed the Swedish government that it would authorize coal exports necessary for Swedish industry only after a general agreement, then in the course of negotation, was concluded. See above, Chapter VI.

8 N.O.T. to Johnstone, August 2, 1915, in Charlotte A. van Manen, *De Nederlandsche Overzee Trustmaatschappij, Middelpunt van het Verkeer van onzijdig Nederland met het Buitenland tydens den Wereldoorlog, 1914–1918* (The Hague: Martinus Nijhoff, 1935), VII, bijlage no. 75. Hereafter cited as van Manen, *N.O.T.*

9 Fayle, *Seaborne Trade*, II, 157.

10 Enclosure in Spring Rice to Lansing October 16, 1916, in United States, Department of State, *Papers Relating to the Foreign Relations of the United States, 1916 Supplement* (Washington, D.C.: Government Printing Office, 1929), pp. 458–459. Hereafter cited as *Foreign Relations*.

11 Information supplied to me by A. C. Bell. France's Comité de Restriction, *Bulletin*, no. 33, December 11, 1915, reported that the control over coal exercised by England was as effective an instrument as the Allies had for the restraint of trade with Germany. Formerly navigation between Norway and Germany had accounted for 30 per cent of Norway's total, but during 1915 it had fallen to 0.75 per cent. It was explained that ships in this traffic could only get

coal from Germany, and in consequence there remained in operation only one insignificant line between Christiania, Lübeck, and Stettin. Another line—a Swedish one—ran a service between Christiania and Stettin.

12 British coal exports to Norway in 1913 were 2,227,620,900 kilograms and 2,684,105,800 kilograms in 1915. (Norway, *Norges officielle statistik, Norges handel*, 1913, and 1915 [Christiania: Grøndahl and Sons]), and to Sweden they were 4,614,725 metric tons in 1913 and 2,723,980 in 1915 (Sweden, *Sveriges officiella statistik, Handel berättelse, för ar 1913, and Handel . . . 1915* (Stockholm: P. A. Norstedt, 1915). Consett later wrote a book on the blockade, in Chapter IV of which he discussed coal policy. See Montagu W. W. P. Consett, *The Triumph of Unarmed Forces (1914–1918), An Account of the Transactions by Which Germany during the Great War Was Able to Obtain Supplies Prior to Her Collapse under the Pressure of Economic Forces* (London: Williams and Norgate, 1923).

13 In 1913, Sweden imported 198,669 metric tons of coal from Germany, and in 1915 this amount rose to 813,785 tons, although Sweden's total imports from all sources in 1915 had decreased by more than 1,043,000 tons. See Sweden, *Sveriges officiella statistik, Handel . . . 1913, and Handel . . . 1915.*

14 Fayle, *Seaborne Trade*, II, 274–276.

15 Board of Trade to The Baltic Exchange, January 28, 1916, in van Manen, *N.O.T.*, VII, bijlage no. 271.

16 Fayle, *Seaborne Trade*, II, 276–282.

17 Fayle, *Seaborne Trade*, II, 318, 324–326.

18 At the same time that some neutral ships were required to carry coal to Italy, others were forbidden to call at Italian ports. Thus Dutch ships in the East Indies trade, with their rich cargoes, were required to take on coal on the homeward voyage at Natal and then go around Africa rather than through Suez in order not to risk touching at Italian ports, since the British found Italian regulations against exportations to Germany—with whom Italy was not yet at war—unsatisfactory. See van Manen, *N.O.T.*, II, 119–120. The British also required that other Dutch ships calling at Italian ports on their way to Egypt should ship cargoes of non-Italian origin only if they were covered by a British

consular certificate of origin, an indication of lack of faith in Italian measures to prevent trading with the enemy. See Percy D. Botterell to C. J. K. van Aalst, July 6, 1916, *ibid.*, VII, bijlage no. 199.

19 Wilhelm Keilhau, "Norway and the World War," in *Sweden, Norway, Denmark and Iceland in the World War*, Economic and Social History of the World War, James T. Shotwell, ed. (New Haven: Yale University Press, 1930), pp. 347–349.

20 Van Manen, *N.O.T.*, III, 27–31, 36–48; VII, bijlagen nos. 196 and 197. Dutch press opinion on the demand for 30 per cent of Dutch tonnage was summarized in France, Ministères de la Guerre et des Affaires Étrangères, *Bulletin périodique de la presse hollandaise* (Paris: Imprimerie Nationale, 1916), no. 4, May 16, 1916.

21 See Einar Cohn, "Denmark in the Great War," in *Sweden, Norway, Denmark*, p. 456; Eilert Maegaard and Jens Vestberg, *Dansk Dampskibsrederiforening, 1884—17. Januar 1934* (Copenhagen: Fr. G. Knuedtzon, 1934), pp. 79–84; Denmark, *Samling af Love, Anordningen, offentlige Kundgørelser, ministerielle Cirkulaerer og Skrivelser*, 1915, p. 637; and Denmark, *Rigsdagstidende, Forhandlinger paa Folketinget*, 1915–1916 (Copenhagen: J. H. Schultz, 1916), pp. 721–722, 977–978.

22 See Keilhau, in *Sweden, Norway, Denmark*, p. 351; Norway, *Lover, resolutioner og skrivelser, foranlediget ved krigsforholdene, 1 august 1914—31 december 1916* (Christiania: Grøndahl and Sons, 1917), pp. 112, 178.

23 Van Manen, *N.O.T.*, III, 30–31, and VII, bijlage no. 262. This law was extended by royal ordinances on April 6 and June 19, 1916. See *ibid.*, VII, bijlagen nos. 263 and 264. On Swedish regulations, see Chapter XII below.

24 Lansing to Page, December 28, 1916, in *Foreign Relations, 1917 Suppl. 1*, p. 505; Page to Lansing, January 19, 1917, *ibid.*, pp. 507–508.

25 Some original documents, the gift of the Textile Alliance are in the Hoover Library, Stanford University (hereafter referred to as Textile Alliance file). On the Alliance's agreements with the British see Ethel C. Phillips, "American Participation in Belligerent Commercial Controls, 1914–1917," *American Journal of International Law*, XXVII (October 1933), 674–693; and Page to Bryan,

January 29, 1915, in *Foreign Relations, 1915 Suppl.*, pp. 665–666, which encloses the wool agreement. Something of the way in which Allied control over wool was exercised was shown in France, Comité de Restriction, "Rapport sur les mesures à prendre pour empêcher le ravitaillement des empires centraux en laine, par M. Chaptal, 5 août 1916," *Documents numérotés*, no. 294, and in "Mesures à prendre pour empêcher le ravitaillement des empires centraux en laine. Note du Service Technique du Ministère de Commerce, 12 juillet 1916," *ibid.*, no. 251.

[26] Great Britain, *Board of Trade Journal*, October 8, 1914, pp. 93–94; February 4, 1915, pp. 328, 331; and July 15, 1915, pp. 158–159.

[27] Textile Alliance to Spring Rice, February 24, 1916, and Spring Rice to Textile Alliance, March 23, 1916, in Hoover Library, Textile Alliance file. France's Comité de Restriction *Bulletin*, no. 46, March 18, 1916, p. 11, mentioned the agreement as being made. Phillips, in *American Journal of International Law*, XXVII (October 1933), p. 685, dates the agreement in July 1916, citing the *Textile Alliance Bulletin*, no. 16, July 26, 1916.

[28] France, Comité de Restriction, *Bulletin*, no. 74, September 27, 1916. In the margin of the copy in the Library of Congress is written "Lettre Chévalley du 31 juillet." Chévalley was the French minister to Norway. The text of the agreement is included in Comité de Restriction, "Accords passés entre le gouvernement britannique et certaines associations norvégiennes," *Documents numérotés*, no. 723.

[29] Botterell to van Aalst, December 15, 1916, enclosing "Memorandum respecting Raw Jute and Jute Manufactures to be Imported into the Netherlands, December 8, 1916," in van Manen, *N.O.T.*, VII, bijlage no. 211; van Aalst to Botterell, December 29, 1916, *ibid.*, VII, bijlage no. 212; van Aalst to Botterell, January 5, 1917, *ibid.*, VII, bijlage no. 213A; and van Aalst to Botterell, January 19, 1917, *ibid.*, VII, no. 213B. See *ibid.*, III, 279–280. On the purchasing agreement see Chapter XI.

[30] Van Manen, *N.O.T.*, III, 116–117.

[31] France, Comité de Restriction, "Accords sur le cuir et les matières tannantes conclus entre le gouvernement britannique et les associations privées neutres,"

Documents numérotés, no. 707. The terms of the American tanners' guarantee were communicated to the N.O.T. in a British memorandum, dated February 26, 1916. See van Manen, *N.O.T.*, VII, bijlagen nos. 240 and 244.

[32] France, Comité de Restriction, *Bulletin*, no. 74, September 27, 1916, p. 17.

[33] France, Comité de Restriction, "Accords sur le caoutchouc conclus entre le gouvernement britannique et des associations privées neutres," *Documents numérotés*, no. 709, and in van Manen, *N.O.T.*, VII, bijlage no. 80. The guarantee given by the American manufacturers was transmitted to the Trust. For the text, see *ibid.*, bijlage no. 242. See also Spring Rice to Lansing, February 3, 1915, in *Foreign Relations, 1915 Suppl.*, pp. 663–664. On the Dutch smuggling trade in rubber see van Manen, *N.O.T.*, III, 290–293.

[34] France, Comité de Restriction, "Liste des accords conclus par les gouvernements alliés avec des gouvernements ou des organisations neutres au sujet de la restriction des approvisionnement et du commerce de l'ennemi," *Documents numérotés*, no. 861. The formulas are summarized in van Manen, *N.O.T.*, VII, bijlage no. 243.

[35] France, Comité de Restriction, *Documents numérotés*, no. 861; and *Bulletin*, no. 68, August 16, 1916, p. 13, where in the margin of the Library of Congress copy is written, "Féer, 9 juillet." E. Féer was the French secretary of legation in Christiania.

[36] Botterell to van Aalst, June 28, 1916, in van Manen, *N.O.T.*, VII, bijlage no. 217; Botterell to van Aalst, August 31, 1916, *ibid.*, bijlage no. 218; N.O.T. to Botterell, September 1, 1916, *ibid.*, bijlage no. 219; "Agreement between the British Government and the N.O.T. in regard to Tin, November 16, 1916, *ibid.*, bijlage no. 220. See also *ibid.*, III, 101–102, where it is explained that tin plate has a gloss and black plate has none, and that terneplate is used for light packing, such as for tinned cocoa or biscuits.

[37] France, Comité de Restriction, "Memorandum britannique sur le café de M. A. R. Tendy," *Documents numérotés*, no. 319. The memorandum is undated, but since it contains statistics covering May 1916, it was probably written in June or July of that year.

[38] This statement in the Tendy memorandum in regard to coffee exports to

Russia is not borne out by the statistics published by the British in *Parliamentary Papers, Accounts Relating to the Trade and Navigation for Each Month during the Year 1915*, printed by order of the House of Commons (London: H.M. Stationery Office, 1915), although the decline in exports to the Netherlands is very noticeable. See Appendix H.

[39] German statistics for 1913 showed an importation of 168,250 tons of raw coffee in 1913 and 170,867 tons in 1912. See Germany,*Statistisches Jahrbuch für das deutsche Reich, 1914* (Berlin: Puttkammer and Muhlbrecht, 1914), p. 188.

[40] France, Comité de Restriction, "Compte-rendu de la séance extraordinaire et de la 10ème séance du War Trade Advisory Committee," *Documents numérotés*, no. 312.

[41] See Appendix H.

[42] France, Comité de Restriction, "Memorandum britannique, Importations de café en Hollande et au Danemark," [n.d.], *Documents numérotés*, no. 298. Tendy's memorandum (*Documents numérotés*, no. 319) cites minutes of the Contraband Committee, January 5, 1916, as the source for the information on the N.O.T. arrangement to accept 10,000 sacks monthly from England.

[43] France, Comité de Restriction, *Comptes-rendus*, 43rd meeting, January 22, 1916; and Comité de Restriction, *Procès-verbaux*, no. 61. In the *Procès-verbaux*, the report of Branet was quoted to the effect that in the first seventeen months of the war these northern states had imported 8,543,000 sacks of coffee, although their normal consumption would have been only 2,437,000 sacks. A summary of Branet's report and the subsequent developments of French policy is contained in Comité de Restriction, "Rapport sur l'exportation du café en

Hollande et l'arrangement franco-danois, par M. le Lieutenant-Colonel Ed. Théry, 7 juillet 1916," *Documents numérotés*, no. 229.

[44] France, Comité de Restriction, *Comptes-rendus*, 50th meeting, March 11, 1916, and its *Procès-verbaux*, no. 81. Van Manen, N.O.T., III, 281, explains that coffee prices in the Netherlands had doubled and that therefore the high quality Dutch colonial coffees were not bought in Holland, but were exported, and inferior Brazilian coffees were put on the Dutch market.

[45] Swiss coffee imports were considered in the 56th meeting, April 26, 1916, and in the 59th meeting, May 17, 1916, of France's Comité de Restriction. See *Comptes-rendus* for these dates and *Procès-verbaux*, no. 107.

[46] The Tendy memorandum cites the minutes of the Contraband Committee of April 24, 1916, and also a telegram, no. 1860, to Esmond Ovey, first secretary of the British legation at Christiania, on the restrictions of coffee exports to Norway. Similar information was cited in a note of the secretariat of the Comité de Restriction, "Ravitaillement de l'ennemi en café," *Documents numérotés*, no. 320.

[47] Van Manen, N.O.T., III, 281–285.

[48] Théry's "Rapport," in *Documents numérotés*, no. 229.

[49] The French General Staff had many times called to the attention of the Comité de Restriction the importance of coffee for the German Army. A note on the subject had been transmitted to the British Military Mission through the Fifth Bureau of the French General Staff on January 9, 1916.

[50] France, Comité de Restriction, *Bulletin*, no. 81, November 15, 1916. p. 13.

CHAPTER X

[1] Grey instructed Sir Rennell Rodd, British ambassador in Rome, on May 1, 1915, to ask the Italian government to prevent the exportation of sulfur, used in the manufacture of asphyxiating gases, to Germany, Austria, and Switzerland. France, Comité de Restriction des Approvisionnements et du Commerce de l'Ennemi, *Bulletin*, no. 3, May 14, 1915, p. 1. (Hereafter this committee will be cited as France, Comité de Restriction.) On May 21 Gout reported to the Comité that the counselor of the Italian embassy had already, in anticipation of Italy's intervention, come to speak of questions of Swiss supply. Camille Barrère, the French ambassador, had been instructed to take up the matter in Rome. See France's Comité de Restriction, *Comptes-rendus*, 9th meeting, May 21, 1915. In early August the Comité urged that a *démarche* be made by Barrère to seek Italy's coöperation in the control of Italian exports. *Ibid.*, 20th meeting, August 7, 1915. Late in the year concern of another kind arose when the British learned that the Germans were doing business in Italy under Italian names in an attempt to build up stocks of goods that would be immediately available for German use at the end of the war. *Ibid.*, 37th meeting, December 11, 1915.

[2] Victor, "L'Inghilterra nel conflitto europeo; Di una lega economica degli stati alleati per la guerra vittoriosa e breve," *Nuova antologia*, 5th Series, CLXXVII (June 16, 1915), 513–532.

[3] Friedrich Kahl, *Die Pariser Wirtschaftskonferenz vom 14. bis 17. Juni 1916, und die ihr voraufgegangenen Beratungen der Ententestaaten über den Wirtschaftskrieg gegen die Mittelmächte* (Jena: Gustav Fischer, 1917), pp. 6–12. The French who attended were Stéphen Pichon; Gabriel Honotaux; Louis Barthou; Edouard Herriot; Albert Métin; Rafael Levi; Adolphe Landry, deputy from Corsica; Derville, director of the P.L.M. Railway; and Buchaire, director of the Institute in Florence. Italy was

represented by Senator Luigi Luzzatti; Salmoiraghi, president of the United Italian Chambers of Commerce; Senator Andrea della Torre; Maggiorini, a member of the Italian Chamber of Deputies; and others.

[4] See E. B. Dubern, "Les Projets d'union économique entre les alliés dans l'hiver 1915–1916," *Revue des sciences politiques*, XXXV (June 15, 1916), 363–376. In England the columns of the London *Morning Post* were a favorite place in which to carry on arguments on the subject. See, for instance, the letter written by Senator Maggiorino Ferraris, editor of *Nuova antologia*, which appeared on November 13, 1915, p. 5, and other articles on November 22, 23, and December 4, 7, 11, 27, and 28, 1915. A bulletin of the Franco-Russian Chamber of Commerce in Petrograd was reproduced as "Union douanière contre les Allemands," *Nouvelles de France*, IV (March 2, 1916), 177–178.

[5] For an excellent discussion of German war aims and plans for the reorganization of Europe see Hans W. Gatzke, *Germany's Drive to the West (Drang nach Westen), A Study of Germany's Western War Aims during the First World War* (Baltimore: Johns Hopkins University Press, 1950).

[6] Reports of German purchases were sometimes published in France's Comité de Restriction, *Bulletin*, and in the British *Contraband Herald*, published for intragovernmental use by the British government.

[7] See "Le Comité interparlementaire franco-britannique," *Nouvelles de France*, IV (February 24, 1916), 144–146, and IV (March 2, 1916), 167–168.

[8] Joseph J. C. Joffre, *The Personal Memoirs of Joffre*, tr. Col. T. Bentley Mott (New York and London: Harper and Brothers, 1932) II, 434.

[9] France was represented by Briand, foreign minister and president of the conference; General Pierre Roques, minister of war; Admiral Marie Jean Lucien

Lacaze, minister of marine; Léon Bourgeois, minister of state; Albert Thomas, undersecretary of state for munitions; General Joffre; General de Castelnau, chief of the General Staff; and Jules Cambon, secretary-general of the Ministry of Foreign Affairs. Great Britain was represented by Asquith; Lord Bertie, ambassador in Paris; Grey; Lloyd George; Lord Kitchener, and General Sir William Robertson. The delegation from Italy included Antonio Salandra, Sidney Sonnino, Tommaso Tittoni, General Luigi Cadorna, and General Alfredo Dal'Olio. Alexandre P. Isvolsky and General Gilinsky represented Russia; Matsui represented Japan; Joao Chegas represented Portugal. Nicholas Pasić, Jovanović, Rasić, and Milenko, R. Vesnić were included in the Serbian delegation, and Belgium was represented by Baron Charles de Broqueville, Baron Eugène Beyens, and General Wielemans, chief of the General Staff. See *Nouvelles de France*, IV (March 30, 1916), 245.

10 The Pact of London had been signed originally by Great Britain, France, and Russia. Later in the war Japan and Italy acceded to it. See Howard M. Ehrmann, "The Pact of London, September 5, 1914," *Berliner Monatshefte*, XIII (March 1935), 231–241.

11 The text of the published resolutions is to be found in Georg F. de Martens, *Nouveau Recueil général de traités et autres actes relatifs aux rapports de droit international*, 3e Série, tome X (Leipzig: Theodor Weicher, 1921), no. 179; and in United States, Department of State, *Papers Relating to the Foreign Relations of the United States, 1916 Supplement* (Washington, D.C.: Government Printing Office, 1929), pp. 972–973. Hereafter cited as *Foreign Relations*.

12 Kahl, pp. 27–28, citing *Economista d'Italia*, April 1916, and the *Corriere mercantile*, April 1916.

13 Kahl, pp. 27–28; "La Conférence internationale du commerce," *Nouvelles de France*, IV (April 27, 1916), 337–338, and IV (May 4, 1916) 356–358. More than four hundred delegates were present at the meetings, which were held at the Luxembourg Palace.

14 Étienne Clémentel, *La France et la politique economique interalliée*, Economic and Social History of the World War, French Series (Paris: Dotation Carnegie, 1931), pp. 75–76.

15 Great Britain, *Parliamentary Debates*, Commons, 5th Series (London: H.M. Stationery Office), LXXXI, 503–522; *ibid.*, Lords, 5th Series, XXI, 629–656.

16 Their text was published in France's *Journal officiel* (Paris: Imprimerie Nationale), June 21, 1916, pp. 5435–5437; and also in Great Britain's *Parliamentary Papers, Recommendations of the Economic Conference of the Allies, Held at Paris on June 14, 15, 16, and 17, 1916*, Cd. 8271 (London: H.M. Stationery Office, 1916); Martens, 3e Série, tome X, no. 180.

17 Robert W. Bliss to Lansing, June 23, 1916, in *Foreign Relations, 1916 Suppl.*, pp. 977–981.

18 Sazonov gave the same impression of reluctance in his conversations with David Francis, the American ambassador, in St. Petersburg. See Francis to Lansing, June 26, 1916, in *Foreign Relations, 1916 Suppl.*, pp. 981–982. The Russian Ministry of Commerce and Industry had established by mid-May a Committee of Restriction of Enemy Supply. France, Comité de Restriction, *Comptes–rendus*, 59th meeting, May 17, 1916.

19 The French Council of Ministers hastened to ratify the resolutions of the conference on June 27, 1916. The Italian government ratified the resolutions so far as they concerned the war itself, but reserved its action on the other sections. See Kahl, p. 76, citing a speech of Paolo Boselli in the Italian Chamber of Deputies on December 6, 1916. The British government did not formally ratify the resolutions because of the nature of the document, but they were approved by the cabinet. See Page to Lansing, December 27, 1916, *Foreign Relations, 1916 Suppl.*, p. 983.

20 Information supplied to me by A. C. Bell.

21 "Trade Agreements Abroad, Message from the President of the United States. . . ," United States Congress, 64th Cong., 1st sess., Senate, *Senate Documents*, Vol. XLIII, Document No. 490, and "Trade Agreements Abroad, Articles Relating to the Resolution (S. 220). . . ," *ibid.*, Document No. 491 (for full citations, see Bibliography under United States Congress).

22 France, Comité de Restriction, "Unification des listes des prohibitions de sortie entre les états alliés (Projet du Comité Permanent International d'Action Économique), Note du secrétariat, 8 septem-

bre 1916," *Documents numérotés*, no. 361.

23 At the first meeting on June 20 the Comité Permanent had named Cochin its president. Some of the members were Gout and Amet for France, Lord Granville, counselor of the British embassy in Paris, for Great Britain; Prince Ruspoli, Italian minister in Paris, Commander Antonio Dell'Abbadessa, assistant director of excises, and Colonel Brancaccio, of the General Staff, for Italy; M. Taksuke and M. Sevastopoulo, counselors for the Japanese and the Russian embassies, respectively; as well as other representatives for Serbia, Belgium, and Portugal. Later a Rumanian representative was added. See Denys Cochin, ed., *Les Organisations de blocus en France pendant la Guerre, 1914–1918* (Paris: Plon, 1926), p. 25, note 1.

24 France, Comité de Restriction, *Documents numérotés*, no. 361. The annexed list included abrasives, asbestos, ammonia and its salts, cattle, wood, liquors, carbon, calcium, cellulose, cereals and their flours, cocoa and chocolate, coffee, tea, camphor, rubber, shoes, wax, fuel, cyanide, diamonds, explosives and their raw materials, disinfectants, forage, fruits, ferro-silicate, gas, graphite, oils and fats and oleaginous grains, optical instruments and glasses, wool, hair, milk and its products, vegetables, machines and tools, war materials and munitions, electrical materials susceptible of military uses, tanning materials, metalloids for war uses, metals, minerals, hides, phosphorus, fish, potassium, distilled products of oil and wood, resin, silk, caustic and carbonate of soda, sulfur, sugar, terebenthine, wagons, carriages, and automobiles, and birds and fowls.

25 France, Comité de Restriction, "Rapport sur la suite à donner aux avis formulées par la Commission Internationale des Contingents, par M. le Controleur Chappius, 7 août 1916," *Documents numérotés*, no. 284; *Comptes-rendus*, 71st meeting, August 9, 1916; Cochin, *Organisations de blocus*, pp. 19–20.

26 France, Comité de Restriction, "Compte-rendu de la séance du War Trade

Advisory Committee, 57ème séance, 16 novembre 1916," *Documents numérotés*, no. 657 R.

27 France, Comité de Restriction, *Documents numérotés*, no. 657 R.

28 Order in Council of March 30, 1916, in *Foreign Relations, 1916 Suppl.*, p. 361, where the text is taken from the *London Gazette*, March 31, 1916.

29 Information supplied to me by A. C. Bell.

30 *Lloyd's Reports of Prize Cases, Heard before and Decided by the Right Honourable Sir Samuel Evans, et al., during the European War Which Began in August, 1914* (London: Lloyd's, 1915–1924) IV, 84–116.

31 Information supplied by A. C. Bell.

32 Cochin, *Organisations de blocus*, pp. 21–22.

33 This point was emphasized when Cochin reported on the conferences with Cecil to the Comité de Restriction. Cochin revealed that the reason for the delay in issuing the new order and decree was that they had been communicated to Italy and Russia, and their adherence was being awaited. See France, Comité de Restriction, *Comptes-rendus*, 64th meeting, June 21, 1916.

34 Great Britain, *Parliamentary Debates, Commons*, 5th Series, LXXXIII, 816–817.

35 Maritime Rights Order in Council, July 7, 1916, in Great Britain, *Statutory Rules and Orders, 1916* (London: H.M. Stationery Office, 1917), I, 211–213; *Foreign Relations, 1916 Suppl.*, pp. 413–415 (including the Memorandum). French decree, July 7, 1916, in *Journal officiel*, July 8, 1916, p. 6050; *Foreign Relations, 1916 Suppl.*, pp. 417–418.

36 Identic notes of protest were presented to the British and French governments by the Swedish, Norwegian, and Danish ministers at London and Paris on July 25, 1916. See W. A. F. Ekengren to Lansing, July 25, 1916, in *Foreign Relations, 1916 Suppl.*, p. 427. See also Karl Hildebrand, *De sevenska statsmakterna och krigstidens folkhushållning* (Stockholm: P. A. Norstedt, 1916–1920), II, 125.

CHAPTER XI

[1] See above, Chapter IV, note 41, citing Denys Cochin, ed., *Les Organisations de blocus en France pendant la Guerre, 1914–1918* (Paris: Plon, 1926), pp. 9–11.

[2] France, Comité de Restriction des Approvisionnements et du Commerce de l'Ennemi, *Comptes-rendus*, 3rd meeting, April 9, 1915, and its *Procès-verbaux*, no. 6 (issued at the meeting of April 30, 1915) (hereafter this committee will be cited as France, Comité de Restriction); Cochin, *Organisations de blocus*, pp. 57–58.

[3] France, Comité de Restriction, *Procès-verbaux*, no. 15 (issued at the meeting of June 11, 1915); *Comptes-rendus*, 17th meeting, July 17, 1915. It was reported in January 1916 that Great Britain had purchased 700,000 tons of wheat in the Rumanian market. *Ibid.*, 44th meeting, January 29, 1916.

[4] France, Comité de Restriction, *Comptes-rendus*, 56th meeting, April 26, 1916; 57th meeting, May 3, 1916.

[5] Norman B. Dearle, *Dictionary of Official War-Time Organizations*, Economic and Social History of the World War, British Series (London: Humphrey Milford, 1928), p. 47. See Appendix I for statistics on British importations of agricultural and fish products from the Netherlands, Denmark, and Norway.

[6] Olaf Knudsen, *Dansk Industriberetning 1915–1918* (Copenhagen: Nielsen and Lydiche, 1921) I, 39.

[7] Einar Cohn, "Denmark in the Great War," in *Sweden, Norway, Denmark and Iceland in the World War*, Economic and Social History of the World War, James T. Shotwell, ed. (New Haven: Yale University Press, 1930), pp. 446–449.

[8] France, Comité de Restriction, *Bulletin*, no. 28, November 6, 1915, p. 12; *ibid.*, no. 30, November 20, 1915, p. 12. For further details on the traffic in dairy products to Germany, see *ibid.*, no. 32, December 4, 1915, p. 13.

[9] Cohn, in *Sweden, Norway, Denmark*, p.

450; Memorandum by E. G. Forbes Adam on the sale of Danish agricultural products, July 27, 1916, in France, Comité de Restriction, "Compte-rendu de la séance du War Trade Advisory Committee, 48ème séance, 14 septembre 1916," *Documents numérotés*, no. 512, annexe 4.

[10] Information supplied to me by A. C. Bell; France, Comité de Restriction, *Bulletin*, no. 47, March 25, 1916, pp. 15–16, citing the *Contraband Herald* (n.d.).

[11] The Danes also sought in the spring of 1916 to purchase oil cake in France, but on three occasions the Comité de Restriction disapproved. See France, Comité de Restriction, *Comptes-rendus*, 56th meeting, April 26, 1916; 57th meeting, May 3, 1916; 59th meeting, May 17, 1916; 63rd meeting, June 14, 1916; and *Procès-verbaux*, no. 114 and no. 128.

[12] France, Comité de Restriction, *Documents numérotés*, no. 512, annexe 4.

[13] France, Comité de Restriction, *Bulletin*, no. 89, January 11, 1917, p. 10. In the margin: "Lettre du Consul de France à Esbjerg, 8/12/16."

[14] France, Comité de Restriction, *Bulletin*, no. 106, May 9, 1917, p. 15. In the margin: "Lettre du Ministre de France à Copenhague, 22 mars 17."

[15] France, Comité de Restriction, *Bulletin*, no. 82, November 22, 1916, p. 12.

[16] Cohn, in *Sweden, Norway, Denmark*, pp. 450–451; and information supplied to me by A. C. Bell.

[17] France, Comité de Restriction, *Bulletin*, no. 92, January 31, 1917, p. 13. This report was supplemented by later information appearing in the *Ribe Stifts Tidende*, February 8, 1917. *Ibid.*, no. 102, April 11, 1917, p. 15.

[18] The following Icelandic prices, in krónur, were quoted in France, Comité de Restriction, *Bulletin*, no. 54, May 10, 1916, p. 11:

	July 1915	March 1916
1 horse	100.00	320.00

1 kilo of wool	1.50	2.50
1 bbl. of cod-liver oil	50.00	275.00
1 kilo of mutton	0.45	1.25
1 hectolitre of herring	16.00	87.00
1 kilo of salted cod	0.32	0.91

[19] France, Comité de Restriction, *Bulletin*, no. 51, April 17, 1916, p. 10.

[20] The following purchases were made in Iceland in March and April 1916: by Germany—18,000 tons of coal, some herring, 1,000 bbls. of cod-liver oil; by England—1,850 tons of fish oil, 7,000 tons of herring, 8,300 tons of klipfish, 8,000 tons of salted fish, 900 tons of stockfish, representing in all a value of 61 million krónur; by France—2,500 tons of herring, 3,000 tons of cod, and 300 tons of stockfish, some of these purchases being made on behalf of the Serbian army at Corfu. France, Comité de Restriction, *Bulletin*, no. 54, May 10, 1916, p. 12.

[21] The text of these notes is in France, Comité de Restriction, "Accord anglo-islandais concernant des achats à effectuer en Islande," *Documents numérotés*, no. 313.

[22] The text is given in France, Comité de Restriction, *Documents numérotés*, no. 313, annexe 3, and it was also published in the Comité de Restriction, *Bulletin*, no. 67, August 9, 1916, p. 13, having been communicated by the French consul at Reykjavík on June 29, 1916.

[23] France, Comité de Restriction, *Bulletin*, no. 67, August 9, 1916, p. 13.

[24] Great Britain, *Parliamentary Papers, Annual Statement of the Trade of the United Kingdom with Foreign Countries and British Possessions, 1916, Compared with the Four Preceding Years*, Vol. II, Cd. 8714 (London: H.M. Stationery Office, 1917), p. 169.

[25] A summary of Allizé's early proposals and the consequent action of his government was set forth in a memorandum of the Ministry of Foreign Affairs. France, Comité de Restriction, "Offres de vente de betail et de viande de Hollande," *Documents numérotés*, no. 181.

[26] Gallieni's decision was discussed in the Comité de Restriction on August 7, 1915. *Comptes-rendus*, 20th meeting, August 7, 1915.

[27] France, Comité de Restriction, *Comptes-rendus*, 47th meeting, February 19, 1916; *Procès-verbaux*, no. 73.

[28] Joffre to Briand, February 22, 1916, in France, Comité de Restriction, *Documents numérotés*, no. 181; the note was

discussed by the Comité, *Comptes-rendus*, 49th meeting, March 4, 1916. Joffre pointed out that a comparison of Dutch exports to Germany in December 1915 with those in December 1914 showed an increase of 384 per cent in fresh and canned meat, 77 per cent in fish; 216 per cent in eggs; 275 per cent in butter; 818 per cent in fruits.

[29] France, Comité de Restriction, *Comptes-rendus*, 50th meeting, March 11, 1916.

[30] France, Comité de Restriction, *Comptes-rendus*, 52nd meeting, March 24, 1916.

[31] Charlotte A. van Manen, *De Nederlandsche Overzee Trustmaatschappij, Middelpunt van het Verkeer van onzijdig Nederland met het Buitenland tydens den Wereldoorlog, 1914–1918* (The Hague: Martinus Nijhoff, 1935), III, 21–24. Hereafter cited as van Manen, N.O.T.

[32] Memorandum proposing additions to the rationing agreement of the Netherlands Oversea Trust, with the British government, March 17, 1916, in van Manen, *N.O.T.*, VII, bijlage no. 190. See Chapter XII.

[33] Van Manen, *N.O.T.*, III, 34.

[34] France, Comité de Restriction, "Rapport sur les mesures à adopter pour restreindre le ravitaillement de l'Allemagne en denrées alimentaires par la Hollande, par M. le Controleur Chappuis, 26 juin 1916," *Documents numérotés*, no. 205.

[35] Van Manen, *N.O.T.*, III, 39–53.

[36] Allizé to Briand, May 17, 1916, in France, Comité de Restriction, *Documents numérotés*, no. 181. Allizé wrote a separate letter on May 25 concerning the advantages of French purchases in the Dutch cheese market.

[37] Van Manen, *N.O.T.*, III, 53–54.

[38] The note was communicated by Briand to the Comité de Restriction on June 13, 1916. France, Comité de Restriction, *Documents numérotés*, no. 205.

[39] Basis of agreement between the British government and the Landbouw Export Bureau, in Van Manen, *N.O.T.*, VII, bijlage no. 252; France, Comité de Restriction, "Accord anglo-hollandais concernant l'achat de produits agricoles en Hollande (Allizé à Briand, 21 juin 1916)," *Documents numérotés*, no. 237.

[40] The charter was published in the *Nederlandsche Staatscourant* on August 29, 1916, no. 203. It is reproduced in van Manen, *N.O.T.*, VII, bijlage no. 253.

[41] France, Comité de Restriction, *Comptes-*

rendus, 65th meeting, June 28, 1916; and *Documents numérotés,* no. 205.

42 France, Comité de Restriction, *Comptes-rendus,* 66th meeting, July 5, 1916.

43 France, Comité de Restriction, *Bulletin,* no. 77, October 18, 1916, p. 17, based on a letter from Allizé of September 14, 1916.

44 See Appendix I.

45 Van Manen, *N.O.T.,* III, 201. When a provisional agreement was signed with Germany on December 16, 1916, by the Landbouw Export Bureau, no security was promised for Dutch exports to other countries. See the Netherlands, *Mededeelingen van den Minister van buitenlandsche Zaken aan de Staten-Generaal, Juni 1919—April 1920* (n.p., n.d.), bijlage no. III, pp. 66–72; van Manen, *N.O.T.,* III, 233.

46 Van Manen, *N.O.T.,* III, 205, 213–214.

47 Van Manen, *N.O.T.,* VII, bijlage no. 254; France, Comité de Restriction, "Accord anglo-hollandais pour l'exportation des produits agricoles en Hollande, 1 novembre 1916," *Documents numérotés,* no. 615 R.

48 Van Manen, *N.O.T.,* III, 233–234.

49 Information supplied to me by A. C. Bell.

50 Van Manen, *N.O.T.,* III, 369–371.

51 The texts of these British communications are not available, but they were cited in the Dutch note of protest of July 11, 1916. See note 52 below. For detention statistics see van Manen, *N.O.T.,* III, 371–372, and VII, bijlage no. 313.

52 Loudon to Johnstone, July 11, 1916, in the Netherlands, *Mededeelingen . . . Juli —December 1916* (n.p.,n.d.), pp. 19–20.

53 Loudon to Johnstone, July 26, 1916, in the Netherlands, *Mededeelingen . . . Juli —December 1916,* pp. 20–21, and van Manen, *N.O.T.,* VII, bijlage no. 269; Loudon to Johnstone, August 17, 1916, in the Netherlands, *Mededeelingen . . . Juli—December 1916,* pp. 21–22, and van Manen, *N.O.T.,* VII, bijlage no. 270.

54 Proposal of the Owners Association of the Dutch Herring Fisheries, July 13, 1916, in van Manen, *N.O.T.,* VII, bijlage no. 247.

55 Proposal of the British government, July 27, 1916, in van Manen, *N.O.T.,* VII, bijlage no. 249.

56 Van Manen, *N.O.T.,* III, 373–376.

57 The Dutch calculated that the British proposal would provide one herring per year per German!

58 Van Manen, *N.O.T.,* VII, bijlage no. 313. But see *ibid.,* III, 378, where van Manen says that at a meeting of the fishing interests on August 17 it was asserted that no less than 1,300 fishing boats were detained on which no formal report had been made. This figure is not impossibly high, since in 1914 the Dutch sea-fishing fleet was made up of 5,760 ships, and about three fourths of their catch was herring. See France, Comité de Restriction, "Le Ravitaillement de l'Allemagne en poissons," *Documents numérotés,* no. 897.

59 Van Manen, *N.O.T.,* III, 378–379, and information supplied by A. C. Bell.

60 Van Manen, *N.O.T.,* VII, bijlage no. 250.

61 Notice of the release of the vessels was communicated to Loudon by Johnstone on September 10, 1916. See the Netherlands, *Mededeelingen . . . Juli—December 1916,* p. 21.

62 These statistics are given in France, Comité de Restriction, *Documents numérotés,* no. 897.

63 The first detailed account of negotiations on Norwegian fisheries was published in the Norwegian edition of Wilhelm Keilhau, *Norge og Verdenskrigen, Economic and Social History of the World War,* Scandinavian Series (Oslo: Aschehoug and Co., 1927). It was supplemented later in the same year by Johann Hjort's account, *Utenrikspolitiske oplevelser under Verdenskrigen* (Oslo: Gyldendal Norsk Forlag, 1927). A general account of British fish purchases in Norway was made in the report of the British Board of Agriculture and Fisheries for 1920, *Parliamentary Papers, Fisheries in the Great War, Being the Report on Sea Fisheries for the Years 1915, 1916, 1917, and 1918,* of the Board of Agriculture and Fisheries, Parts I and II, Cmd. 585 (London: H.M. Stationery Office, 1920), pp. 108–110. On the situation in 1915, see Hjort, pp. 9–21.

64 Hjort covers these negotiations, pp. 22–32. Information on British fish purchases in Norway is contained in France, Comité de Restriction, *Bulletin,* no. 49, April 5, 1916, p. 18; no. 59, June 15, 1916, p. 16; and no. 61, June 28, 1916, p. 13.

65 Hjort, pp. 33–50; Wilhelm Keilhau, "Norway and the World War," in *Sweden, Norway, Denmark,* pp. 307–313; Paul G. Vigness, *The Neutrality of*

Norway in the World War (Stanford, California: Stanford University Press, 1932), pp. 70–80, which is based primarily on Keilhau and Hjort.

[66] Hjort, p. 45, note 1, reproduces a private letter from Maurice dated April 19, 1916, in which Maurice expresses discontent.

[67] Hjort, pp. 51–66.

[68] Hjort, p. 61, note 1, reproduces the memorandum in which he presented, at Cecil's request, his views of the future problems of the Norwegian fishing and whaling industries. He pointed out, for instance, that the least for which the Icelandic fish could be sold to cover the costs, was 45 kroner per barrel of 75 kilos, and that the fishermen would regard a price of 40 kroner per 100 kilos as an outright prohibition of the Icelandic fishing.

[69] Foreign Office to Hjort, May 27, 1916, in Hjort, p. 64, note 1.

[70] The text of this scheme is printed in Hjort, p. 72, note 1. On the negotiations, see *ibid.*, pp. 72–92; Keilhau, in *Sweden, Norway, Denmark,* pp. 317–324; Vigness, pp. 80–84.

[71] The Norwegian cabinet decided to refuse permission on July 20, 1916. See Hjort, p. 80.

[72] Leverton Harris to Hjort, August 3, 1916, in France, Comité de Restriction, "Accords et correspondance relatifs aux pecheries norvégiennes et à un prêt de la Norges Bank à M. M. C. J. Hambro et Fils," *Documents numérotés,* no. 375 R.

[73] These notes and the text of the agreement are included in France, Comité de Restriction, *Documents numérotés,* no. 375 R. Keilhau, in *Sweden, Norway, Denmark,* pp. 319–320, summarizes the more important articles of the agreement, but gives the text of only three of them; he omits from article 1 the phrase concerning canned fish without indicating that he has done so. The Norwegian edition, p. 125, gives the whole article.

[74] The British arranged through Hambro and Sons a loan of 140 million kroner from the Norges Bank.

[75] Hjort, pp. 95–96, gives a table showing the prices originally recommended by the Fisheries Committee, and those that were actually set up under the agreement, and which were in every instance considerably lower.

[76] Hjort, pp. 102–111 and pp. 134–141, discusses some of these difficulties.

[77] Keilhau, in *Sweden, Norway, Denmark,* pp. 325–333.

[78] France, Comité de Restriction, *Bulletin,* no. 82, November 22, 1916, pp. 12–13.

[79] Norway, Storting *Forhandlinger,* (Christiania: Centraltrykkeriet, 1917), pp. 138–231. Hjort, p. 156, gives the following figures on tonnage and value of fish exports:

Year	Tonnage	Value in kroner
1913	582,229	53,768,000
1914	598,588	61,849,000
1915	557,494	87,294,000
1916	580,213	187,646,000
1917	557,096	138,898,000

CHAPTER XII

[1] Sweden, *Riksdagens protokoll,* Second Chamber, 1916 (Stockholm: P. A. Norstedt, 1916), no. 6, pp. 3–68, and no. 7, pp. 1–89 (January 24, 1916); Eli F. Heckscher and Kurt Bergendal, "Sweden in the World War," *Sweden, Norway, Denmark and Iceland in the World War, Economic and Social History of the World War,* James T. Shotwell, ed. (New Haven: Yale University Press, 1930), p. 92.

[2] Karl Hildebrand, *De svenska statsmakterna och krigstidens folkhushållning* (Stockholm: P. A. Norstedt, 1916–1920), II, 55–57, quoting C. L. Schönmeyr's speech at the 18th meeting of the Nordiska Inter-parliament Forbundet, held in Stockholm in 1916.

[3] Sweden, *Svensk författningssamling,* 1916 (Stockholm: P. A. Norstedt, 1916), no. 102, pp. 261–262; *Riksdag protokoll,* Second Chamber, 1916, no. 37, pp. 13–23; *ibid.,* First Chamber, no. 56, p. 43. The bill was passed without debate in the First Chamber.

[4] Hildebrand, II, 4–9.

5 Sweden, *Svensk författningssamling,* 1916, no. 109, p. 275.

6 Hildebrand, II, 146–147.

7 Sweden, *Riksdagens protokoll,* Second Chamber, 1916, no. 37, p. 15.

8 Sweden, *Svensk författningssamling,* 1916, no. 47, pp. 91–92; a royal proclamation dealing with details was issued the same day. See *ibid.,* no. 48, pp. 92–93; *Riksdagens protokoll,* Second Chamber, 1916, no. 33, p. 1 (March 6, 1916); *ibid.,* First Chamber, 1916, no. 30, pp. 53–56 (March 4, 1916). See also, Hildebrand, II, 12–13, 146–147.

9 Sweden, *Svensk författningssamling,* 1916, no. 272, p. 700. A royal letter to the State Commerce Commission gave it authority to execute this law and to grant exceptions to it. See *ibid.,* no. 274, p. 702.

10 Hildebrand, II, 73, and bilaga no. 8, containing the texts of the guarantee forms. They are also included in France, Comité de Restriction des Approvisionnements et du Commerce de l'Ennemi, "Note complementaire sur la Handelskommission, 25 octobre 1916," *Documents numérotés,* no. 465. Hereafter this committee will be cited as France, Comité de Restriction.

11 Heckscher and Bergendal in *Sweden, Norway, Denmark,* p. 84; Hildebrand, II, 70, 140–141.

12 Statistics provided by A. C. Bell.

13 Heckscher and Bergendal in *Sweden, Norway, Denmark,* p. 85; letter of R. V. Carlstrom of the Svenska Bomullsspinnereiforeningen to me, August 9, 1939. The agreement is listed in France, Comité de Restriction, "Liste des accords conclus par les gouvernements alliés avec des gouvernements ou des organisations neutres au sujet de la restriction des approvisionnement et du commerce de l'ennemi," *Documents numérotés,* no. 861.

14 The text is included in France, Comité de Restriction, "Accords anglo-suédois," *Documents numérotés,* no. 860.

15 These agreements are listed in France, Comité de Restriction, *Documents numérotés,* no. 861; for the text of the Vacuum Oil Company agreement, see *ibid.,* no. 860; and for the text of the notes exchanged between the two governments, "Echange de notes entre la grande Bretagne et la Suède au sujet de l'importation en Suède de lubrifiants," *ibid.,* no. 441 R.

16 The text is included in France, Comité

de Restriction, "Pays scandinaves, Accords et arrangements passés par le gouvernement britannique avec des maisons de commerce neutre," *Documents numérotés,* no. 889.

17 Sweden, *Svensk författningssamling,* 1916, no. 6, pp. 9–10; Hildebrand, II, 61, gives the date as January 21, but this was the date the decree was to come into effect.

18 France, Comité de Restriction, "Ravitaillement des pays neutres voisins de l'ennemi; Consignations à l'ordre des gouvernements," *Documents numérotés,* no. 597 R.

19 Note of the Swedish legation to the British Foreign Office, June 2, 1916, quoted in France, Comité de Restriction, "Organismes officiels suédois pour l'exportation et l'importation; Note du secrétariat, 12 septembre, 1916," *Documents numérotés,* no. 371.

20 France, Comité de Restriction, "Régime des importations de corps gras en Suède; . . . Rapport de M. Carrier, directeur au Ministère de l'Agriculture," *Documents numérotés,* no. 325.

21 France, Comité de Restriction, *Comptes-rendus,* 73rd meeting, August 23, 1916; *ibid.,* 74th meeting, August 30, 1916; and *Procès-verbaux,* no. 226, August 30, 1916. *Procès-verbaux,* no. 219, contains proposals drawn up by Carrier for Swedish rations of oils and fats.

22 Hildebrand, II, 132–133, 272–274.

23 Hildebrand, II, 126–127; France, Comité de Restriction, *Comptes-rendus,* 75th meeting, September 6, 1916. The text is printed in Charlotte A. van Manen, *De Nederlandsche Overzee Trustmaatschappij, Middelpunt van het Verkeer van onzijdig Nederland met het Buitenland tydens den Wereldoorlog, 1914–1918* (The Hague: Martinus Nijhoff, 1935), VII, bijlage no. 297. Hereafter cited as van Manen, *N.O.T.*

24 Wallenberg to Howard, October 6, 1916, in France, Comité de Restriction, *Documents numérotés,* no. 860. See Hildebrand, II, 128–129, on the difficulties encountered over cargoes carried by Danish lines.

25 Hildebrand, II, 127–128.

26 Hildebrand, II, 129–130. The Comité de Restriction urged in late September that the French government should associate itself directly with the British in these negotiations (France, Comité de Restriction, *Comptes-rendus,* 77th meeting, September 27, 1916), and the

British minister in Stockholm suggested to his Russian, Italian, and Portuguese colleagues that their governments should do likewise. See "Rapport sur les garanties à obtenir pour les marchandises françaises importées en Suède, directement ou à travers le Danemark," *Documents numérotés*, no. 358.

27 Great Britain, *Daily Review of the Foreign Press, Neutral Press Supplement,* issued by the General Staff, War Office (hereafter cited as *Neutral Press Supplement*), November 17, 1916.

28 *Neutral Press Supplement*, November 24, 1916.

29 *Neutral Press Supplement*, December 15, 1916, and December 22, 1916.

30 *Neutral Press Supplement*, January 5, 1917.

31 Sweden, *Riksdagens protokoll*, Second Chamber, 1917, no. 6, January 22, 1917, pp. 2–72, and no. 7, January 22, 1917, pp. 1–105.

32 The question of reorganization of relations between the Riksdag and the government on foreign affairs had been raised in a series of motions introduced by Palmstierna, Hjalmar Branting, and Sandler on May 13, 1916. Some felt that secret sessions of the Riksdag might be held as in Norway; others suggested that the Secret Committee should be made a permanent institution. See Sweden, *Riksdagens protokoll*, Second Chamber, 1916, no. 71, May 13, 1916, pp. 2–63; *ibid.*, First Chamber, 1916, no. 68, May 13, 1916, pp. 3–43.

33 *Neutral Press Supplement*, February 9, 1917.

34 Ira Morris, American minister to Sweden, states in his memoirs, *From an American Legation* (New York: Alfred A. Knopf, Inc., 1923, p. 104) that Sweden insisted on the right to refuse transit of all articles of military value, including automobiles. This had, of course, been its policy since January 9, 1915.

35 Hildebrand, III, 76.

36 This question will be more thoroughly discussed in a later volume of this study. Hammarskjöld's resignation was not accepted by Gustav V until March 30.

37 Heckscher and Bergendal, in *Sweden, Norway, Denmark*, p. 93.

38 See Chapter V above.

39 France, Comité de Restriction, *Bulletin*, no. 46, March 18, 1916, p. 16.

40 France, Comité de Restriction, "Liste des accords conclus par les gouvernements alliés avec des gouvernements ou des organisations neutres au sujet de la restriction des approvisionnement et du commerce de l'ennemi," *Documents numérotés*, no. 861. Apparently the ration for the Mustad Company was included as a part of that set for the Christiania association, for it is mentioned in a special accord between Mustad and the British of July 26–27, 1916. In spite of their 1915 agreement some of Mustad's cargoes had been taken before a British prize court and their release was made conditional upon acceptance of new terms offered them on July 6, 1916, which, among other things, required that in the future Mustad's Swedish factory must import its raw materials directly on ships that were bound to call at a British port. However, no such imports would be permitted until the British made a satisfactory arrangement with the Swedish government. The correspondence is included in France, Comité de Restriction, "Accords anglo-norvégiens," *Documents numérotés*, no. 880, V.

41 Text transmitted to Sir Mansfeldt Findlay, November 8, 1916, in France, Comité de Restriction, *Documents numérotés*, no. 880, IX.

42 Wilhelm Keilhau, *Norge og Verdenskrigen*, Economic and Social History of the World War, Scandinavian Series (Oslo: Aschehoug and Co., 1927), pp. 103–105. This entire section is omitted from the English edition.

43 Keilhau, *Norge og Verdenskrigen*, p. 106.

44 Norway, *Lover, resolutioner og skrivelser, foranlediget ved krigsforholdene, 1 august 1914—31 december 1916* (Christiania: Grøndahl and Sons, 1917), p. 156. In the debate on the Speech from the Throne in the Storting on March 15, 1916, Knudsen revealed that Norwegian shipping companies had made agreements not to deliver cargoes that the British wished to be sent no farther, and that they would land such goods in Norwegian ports to be returned later to England if necessary. See Norway, Storting, *Forhandlinger*, 1916 (Christiania: Centraltrykkeriet, 1916), p. 400.

45 Keilhau, *Norge og Verdenskrigen*, p. 107.

46 Norway, *Lover*, pp. 164–165.

47 Keilhau, *Norge og Verdenskrigen*, p. 110.

48 Text in France, Comité de Restriction, "Accord passé le 18 septembre 1916 entre le gouvernement britannique et l'association . . . ," *Documents num-*

érotés, no. 478.

49 Text in France, Comité de Restriction, "Accords passés entre le gouvernement britannique et certaines associations norvégiennes," *Documents numérotés,* no. 723, V.

50 Text in France, Comité de Restriction, *Documents numérotés,* no. 723, VII.

51 Text in France, Comité de Restriction, *Documents numérotés,* no. 723, VI.

52 Text in France, Comité de Restriction, *Documents numérotés,* no. 723, VIII.

53 Texts in France, Comité de Restriction, *Documents numérotés,* no. 723, I–IV.

54 Letter of the British Foreign Office to various British government departments, January 25, 1917, in France, Comité de Restriction, "Accords anglo-norvégiens," *Documents numérotés,* no. 756, III.

55 Text in France, Comité de Restriction, *Documents numérotés,* no. 880, VIII.

56 Keilhau, *Norge og Verdenskrigen,* pp. 112–113.

57 Text in France, Comité de Restriction, *Documents numérotés,* no. 723, X.

58 Text in France, Comité de Restriction, "Nouveaux Accords anglo-norvégiens," *Documents numérotés,* no. 779, I–V.

59 An agreement had already been signed with the Stavanger group on January 26, 1916. Once it was reached the British asked the French government to permit exports of olive oil to Norway only to the Stavanger Union, but objection was raised that the French legation had very certain evidence of the trustworthiness of some of the other houses with whom French sellers were dealing and that, therefore, so strict an embargo ought not to be enforced. France, Comité de Restriction, *Comptes-rendus,* 52nd meeting, March 24, 1916.

60 France, Comité de Restriction, *Comptes-rendus,* 81st meeting, November 3, 1916; *Procès-verbaux,* no. 259, December 21, 1916; *ibid.,* no. 306, January 10, 1917; "Rapport sur les accords passés entre le gouvernement britannique et certaines associations norvégiennes, 10 janvier 1917," *Documents numérotés,* no. 674; "Accords franco-norvégiens," *Documents numérotés,* no. 819.

61 Letters of Mair to Chandler Anderson, December 11, 1916, December 29, 1916, and April 4, 1917, in Veeder Papers. See also my article, "British Negotiations with American Meat Packers, 1915–1917: A Study of Belligerent Trade Controls," *Journal of Modern History,* XXIII (December 1951), 343–353.

62 Keilhau, *Norge og Verdenskrigen,* pp. 116–117.

63 Norway, Storting, *Forhandlinger,* 1917 (Christiania: Centraltrykkeriet, 1917), pp. 152–153.

64 On the American copper agreement see Chapter III above. It was not until December 1915 that the adverse effects of this control were felt by the Norwegian importers who placed orders with American companies not included in the agreement. The Norwegian ministers in London and Washington got nowhere with their protests, the latter reporting that no copper could be exported from the United States except with the approval of the British consul in New York. See Keilhau, *Norge og Verdenskrigen,* pp. 154–155. The English edition, *Sweden, Norway, Denmark,* pp. 334–345, has an abridged discussion of these copper negotiations.

65 France, Comité de Restriction, *Procès-verbaux,* nos. 6, 7, and 11.

66 France, Comité de Restriction, *Comptes-rendus,* 9th meeting, May 21, 1916.

67 The texts of these agreements are in France, Comité de Restriction, "Accords franco-norvégiens," *Documents numérotés,* no. 819, I.

68 Keilhau, *Norge og Verdenskrigen,* pp. 155–157.

69 France, Comité de Restriction, *Comptes-rendus,* 58th meeting, May 10, 1916; *Procès-verbaux,* no. 122.

70 France, Comité de Restriction, *Comptes-rendus,* 66th meeting, July 5, 1916.

71 France, Comité de Restriction, *Comptes-rendus,* 67th meeting, July 12, 1916; *Procès-verbaux,* no. 171.

72 France, Comité de Restriction, *Comptes-rendus,* 70th meeting, August 2, 1916; Keilhau, *Norge og Verdenskrigen,* pp. 157–158.

73 The text in French translation is included in France, Comité de Restriction, "Accord sur le cuivre, conclu entre le gouvernement britannique et la norvège, 28 août 1916," *Documents numérotés,* no. 411. A summary is given in Keilhau, *Norge og Verdenskrigen,* pp. 158–160.

74 Norway, *Lover,* pp. 195–196.

75 Keilhau, *Norge og Verdenskrigen,* pp. 160–169. Part of the difficulty in the negotiations arose from the fact that since Ihlen spoke no English, and Findlay no Norwegian, their conversations had been carried on in French.

76 Considerable discussion of the copper agreement and difficulties encountered

in its execution took place in the Storting on February 21, 1917, during the debate on the Speech from the Throne. Apparently even more had been said by Ihlen in a secret session of the Storting on January 17. See Norway, Storting, *Forhandlinger*, 1917, pp. 140–142, 153–155.

77 Keilhau, *Norge og Verdenskrigen*, p. 141; Paul G. Vigness, *The Neutrality of Norway in the World War* (Stanford, California: Stanford University Press, 1932), Chapter VII.

78 Norway, *Lover*, pp. 205–206.

79 Keilhau, *Norge og Verdenskrigen*, p. 167, and information supplied to me by A. C. Bell.

80 Keilhau, *Norge og Verdenskrigen*, pp. 145–146, 151. In March 1916 there had been some criticism of the Norwegian government in the Storting for its failure to arrange a compensation trade as Sweden had done. In addition there was the usual complaint against the secrecy with which foreign affairs were conducted, a charge which was partially answered with the publication by the government of its colored book, *Oversigt over de vigtigste av utenriksdepartmentet under Krigen indtil mai 1916, Behandlede saker som egner sig for offentliggjørelse* (Christiania: Grøndahl and Sons, 1916), but only after the Norwegian government's attention was called to the publication of Hildebrand's book in Sweden as well as the presentation to the Riksdag of the correspondence on neutral mails. See Norway, Storting, *Forhandlinger*, 1916, pp. 371–378, 389.

81 A royal ordinance to this effect was published on January 30, 1917, in Norway, *Norske lovtidende, Samling av love, resolutioner og skrivelser*, 1917 (Christiania: Grøndahl and Sons, 1917), I, 37. Submarines were permitted to enter Norwegian waters "when necessary on account of rough weather, damage or in order to save human life." See also Vigness, pp. 103–104.

82 France, Comité de Restriction, "Compterendu de la séance du War Trade Advisory Committee, 59ème séance, 30 novembre 1916," *Documents numérotés*, no. 696 R.

83 Olaf Knudsen, *Dansk Industriberetning 1915–1918* (Copenhagen: Nielsen and Lydiche, 1921), I, 60.

84 France, Comité de Restriction, *Comptesrendus*, 52nd meeting, March 24, 1916.

85 Foreign Office to Rottbøll, July [23],

1916, in France, Comité de Restriction, "Accord anglo-danois pour les réexportations en Suède et en Norvège," *Documents numérotés*, no. 311.

86 France, Comité de Restriction, "Rapport sur les garanties à obtenir pour les marchandises françaises importées en Suède, directement ou à travers le Danemark," *Documents numérotés*, no. 358.

87 Rottbøll to Foreign Office, November 2, 1916, and Foreign Office to Rottbøll, November 11, 1916, in France, Comité de Restriction, "Accord anglo-danois pour les réexportations en Suède et en Norvège," *Documents numérotés*, no. 594.

88 France, Comité de Restriction, *Documents numérotés*, no. 597.

89 Knudsen, I, 83–84.

90 Denmark, *Rigsdagstidende, Forhandlinger paa Folketinget, 1915–1916* (Copenhagen: J. H. Schultz, 1916), p. 4297.

91 Denmark, *Rigsdagstidende, Forhandlinger paa Folketinget, 1915–1916*, p. 4351.

92 Denmark, *Lovtidende for Kongeriget Danmark for Aaret 1916* (Copenhagen: J. H. Schultz, 1917), p. 416; Knudsen, I, 63–64.

93 Denmark, *Rigsdagstidende, Forhandlinger paa Folketinget, 1915–1916*, pp. 2653–2850, 3578–3622, 3633–3670, 4710–4719, 4775–4787; *Rigsdagstidende Forhandlinger paa Landstinget, 1915–1916*, pp. 1386–1422, 1431–1434, 1462–1465. The text of the law is given in Denmark, *Samling af Love, Anordningen, offentlige Kundgørelser, ministerielle Cirkulaerer og Skrivelser, 1916* (Copenhagen: J. H. Schultz, 1916), pp. 878–880. An ordinance of July 3, 1916, laid down as the basis for the assessment of the special payment, taxes paid in two of the tax years 1913–1914, 1914–1915, or 1915–1916, whichever two were the highest. See *ibid.*, pp. 1064–1065.

94 The members of the Committee, named by royal ordinance on May 27, 1916, were C. M. T. Cold, chairman, A. O. Andersen, P. de Nully Brown, Johan Hansen, Niels Johan Høst, D. Lauritzen, K. Reinhard, and Chr. Schmiegelow, with E. Maegaard as secretary. See Eilert Maegaard and Jens Vestberg, *Dansk Dampskibsrederiforening, 1884—17. Januar 1934* (Copenhagen: Fr. G. Knuedtzon, 1934), pp. 115–118, and Johannes Hansen, *Hovedtraek af Industriraadets Historie* (Copenhagen: Nielsen and Lydiche, 1935), p. 145.

⁹⁵ Maegaard and Vestberg, p. 120; Denmark, *Love*, 1917, p. 2.

⁹⁶ Denmark, *Love*, 1916, p. 1338; *Rigsdagstidende, Forhandlinger paa Folketinget*, 1916–1917, pp. 1311–1333.

⁹⁷ Denmark, *Rigsdagstidende, Forhandlinger paa Folketinget*, 1916–1917, pp. 136–150. Knudsen, I, 73, cites figures showing great increases in Denmark's exports, which, in spite of the general rise of the price level, are indicative of Denmark's relative prosperity. Thus in 1913 the value of Danish exports was 66 million kroner, in 1914—85 million kroner, in 1915—150 million kroner, and in 1916—168 million kroner.

⁹⁸ Van Manen, *N.O.T.*, III, 25–26.

⁹⁹ The text of the memorandum is printed in van Manen, *N.O.T.*, VII, bijlage no. 190.

¹⁰⁰ British "Proposal for Additions to the Relationing Agreement," June 28, 1916, in van Manen, *N.O.T.*, VII, bijlage no. 191; *ibid.*, III, 64–65.

¹⁰¹ N.O.T. to the British commercial attaché, June 30, 1916, in van Manen, *N.O.T.*, VII, bijlage no. 192.

¹⁰² Henri Allizé to the N.O.T., July 20, 1916, in van Manen, *N.O.T.*, VII, bijlage no. 193; N.O.T. to Allizé, July 21, 1916, *ibid.*, VII, bijlage no. 194. Also in France, Comité de Restriction, "Accords avec le N.O.T. sur le contingentenment de la Hollande, 21 juillet 1916," *Documents numérotés*, no. 282.

¹⁰³ Van Manen, *N.O.T.*, III, 502–552; France, Comité de Restriction, "Ravitaillement des pays neutres voisins de l'ennemi; Consignations à l'ordre des gouvernements," *Documents numérotés*, no. 597 R.

¹⁰⁴ Oppenheimer to Snouck, July 27, 1916, in van Manen, *N.O.T.*, VII, bijlage no. 205.

¹⁰⁵ Van Manen, *N.O.T.*, III, 57–60, 68, 81–82. A question concerning Oppen-

heimer's place of birth and the whereabouts of members of his family in Germany was asked in the House of Commons on July 12, 1916. Sir Francis' father became a naturalized British subject in 1864, and Sir Francis was a natural-born subject himself. See Great Britain, *Parliamentary Debates, Commons*, 5th Series (London: H.M. Stationery Office), LXXXIV 304.

¹⁰⁶ Oppenheimer to the N.O.T., July 29, 1916, in van Manen, *N.O.T.*, VII, bijlage no. 206; van Aalst to Oppenheimer, August 7, 1916, *ibid.*, VII, bijlage no. 207; Oppenheimer to van Aalst, August 17, 1916, *ibid.*, VII, bijlage no. 208; van Aalst to Oppenheimer, August 19, 1916, *ibid.*, VII, bijlage no. 209. See also *ibid.*, III, 72–81.

¹⁰⁷ Oppenheimer to van Aalst, October 16, 1916, in van Manen, *N.O.T.*, VII, bijlage no. 210; *ibid.*, III, 206–207.

¹⁰⁸ Text in van Manen, *N.O.T.*, VII, bijlage no. 261.

¹⁰⁹ Van Manen, *N.O.T.*, III, 239.

¹¹⁰ Van Manen, *N.O.T.*, III, 222–225, 230–231.

¹¹¹ Van Manen, *N.O.T.*, III, 179, 211–212, 221.

¹¹² Van Manen, *N.O.T.*, III, 166–167, 172, 290–295, 429–432, 444–445.

¹¹³ The Netherlands, Staten-Generaal, *Handelingen*, First Chamber (The Hague: Algemeene Landsdrukkerij, 1916), December 22, 1915.

¹¹⁴ France, Comité de Restriction, "Mesures prises en Holland pour combattre la fraude et la contrebande," *Documents numérotés*, no. 838. This document is undated, but was probably written in the spring of 1917.

¹¹⁵ Van Manen, *N.O.T.*, III, 486–487.

¹¹⁶ The Netherlands, Staten-Generaal, *Handelingen*, Second Chamber, June 15 and 16, 1916.

CHAPTER XIII

¹ Great Britain, *Parliamentary Debates, Commons*, 5th Series (London: H.M. Stationery Office), LXXX, 557, 784, 1168, 2225–2226; LXXXI, 8–9, 1319–1320.

² Great Britain, *Parliamentary Debates, Commons*, 5th Series, LXXXI, 550.

³ Great Britain, *Parliamentary Debates, Lords*, 5th Series, XXII, 231–232.

⁴ Great Britain, *Parliamentary Debates,*

Commons, 5th Series, LXXXIII, 1496–1497.

[5] Great Britain, *Parliamentary Debates*, 5th Series, LXXX, 258.

[6] Great Britain, *Parliamentary Debates*, Commons, 5th Series, LXXXI, 166–167, 1482.

[7] Great Britain, *Parliamentary Debates*, Commons, 5th Series, LXXXII, 2271–2273; LXXXVII, 55, 240.

[8] Great Britain, *Parliamentary Debates*, Commons, 5th Series, LXXXI, 27, 503–522, 1482–1483, 1778–1779; LXXXV, 332–398, 648.

[9] Great Britain, *Parliamentary Debates*, Commons, 5th Series, LXXXII, 449; LXXXVI, 227.

[10] Great Britain, *Parliamentary Debates*, Commons, 5th Series, LXXXIV, 559. See Chapter XI above on the Dutch purchasing agreement.

[11] Great Britain, *Parliamentary Debates*, Commons, 5th Series, LXXXIV, 2037; LXXXVI, 349–351; 1099–1100.

[12] Great Britain, *Parliamentary Debates*, Lords, 5th Series, XXI, 388–393.

[13] Great Britain, *Parliamentary Debates*, Commons, 5th Series, LXXXV, 2748–2755. In December Cecil gave another general expression of confidence in the N.O.T., when he explained the procedure by which a Dutch importer secured overseas goods through the Trust. See *ibid.*, LXXXVIII, 622–623.

[14] United States, *Congressional Record*, 64th Cong., 1st Sess. (Washington, D.C.: Government Printing Office, 1916), Vol. LIII, Part XIII (Sept. 5, 1916–Sept. 8, 1916), pp. 13,938–13,942, 14,124, 14,156.

[15] United States, Department of State, *Papers Relating to the Foreign Relations of the United States, 1916 Supplement* (Washington, D.C.: Government Printing Office, 1928), pp. 466–477.

[16] See various communications in *Foreign Relations, 1916 Suppl.*, pp. 688–697.

[17] These general remarks are based chiefly on information which appeared in various numbers of the *Bulletin* of the French Comité de Restriction des Approvisionnements et du Commerce de l'Ennemi, late in 1916.

Index

Aalst, C. J. K. van, 37, 41, 84, 294
Adrian, P. C., 294
Allied economic conferences, 75, 80–81, 146, 173–81, 251, 254–55, 321–22
Allied purchasing agreements, 88–89, 127, 187–212, 249; with Denmark, 189–93; with Iceland, 193–94; with the Netherlands, 187, 195–205; with Norway, 205–12, 231–36; with Rumania, 188
Allizé, Henri, 187–88, 195, 197–99, 324
American Civil War, 4
Amet, Vice-Admiral, 313, 322
Andersen, A. O., 330
Andersen, H. N., 45, 48, 100, 190
Anderson, Chandler, 57
Asquith, Herbert H., 14, 64, 68, 302, 311, 321
Augagneur, Jean V., 299
Austria-Hungary, 18, 96, 256

Bachmann, 299
Bagge, Algot, 216
Balfour, Arthur J., 11, 251
Balkan Wars, 1912–1913, 31
Ballin, Max, 96
Banbury, Frederick, 250
Barbosa, Ruy, 7
Barkley, Alben W., 253
Barrère, Camille, 320
Barthou, Louis, 320
Bathurst, Charles, 302
Bauer, Captain, 62
Bekker, H. L., 294
Belgium—Commission for the Relief of, 199, 241; neutrality of, 15–16
Bell, Archibald C., 129
Benckendorff, Count, 115
Benn, Shirley, 131, 311
Beresford, Charles, 64, 130, 311
Bergendal, Kurt, 224
Bertie, Lord, 321
Bethell, Alexander, 14
Bethmann-Hollweg, T. von, 299
Beyens, Eugene, 321
Bildt, Axel R., 119–20, 309

Björnsson, Svein, 193–94
Black Lists, 135, 137, 144–48, 178, 184, 242, 247, 251–52; of ships, 160–61
Blockade—Law and practice, pre-1914, 1–6, 8–9, 11–16, 290; during World War I, 67–70, 111, 131–32, 246; effects of long-distance blockade on Germany, 125–26, 256–57; machinery, 30–32, 70–73, 124–25, 131–32, 136–37, 179–81
Bonar Law, Andrew, 177
Boone, Jules, 72
Boothius, G., 106
Boselli, Paolo, 321
Bourgeois, Leon, 183, 321
Bowles, Thomas Gibson, 5, 10, 13, 311
Brally, 170
Bramson, M. L., 103–104
Brancaccio, Colonel, 322
Brandstrom, P. H. E., 220
Branet, Jean, 72, 170, 319
Branting, Hjalmar, 114, 328
Bratlie, 211
Briand, Aristide, 145, 171, 195–96, 320
Bright, John, 289
Brisman, Sven, 216
Brockdorff-Rantzau, Ulrich von, 96
Broqueville, Charles de, 321
Brun, Constantin, 296
Bryan, William J., 57–58, 127
Bryce, Lord, 177
Buchaire, 320
Buchner, 251
Butcher, J. G., 311
Byrns, Joseph M., 253

Cables, transatlantic. See Censorship
Cadorna, Luigi, 321
Call in British ports, 46, 85, 124–26, 153, 160, 193. See also Shipping agreements, and Coal, bunker controls
Calthorp, Clayton, 144
Cambon, Jules, 177, 321
Cambon, Paul, 19, 111, 150, 170–71, 232, 302, 309
Castelnau, General de, 321

Cave, George, 143
Cecil, Robert, 101–2, 128, 130–31, 136, 138, 147, 168–69, 182–84, 201, 207, 234, 250–52, 255, 310–11, 314, 322, 326, 332
Censorship of mails and cables, 29, 70–71, 81, 87, 115, 135, 145, 148–55, 246–47, 300, 314
Certificates of Origin, 71, 84–86, 99, 236–37
Chair, Dudley R. S. de, 143
Chappuis, 199
Chaptal, 72
Chegas, Joao, 321
Chilton, H. G., 84
Christensen, L. Brahe, 305
Christian X of Denmark, 45
Churchill, W. A., 14
Churchill, Winston, 15, 30, 64, 292
Clan, J. C. T., 47–48, 94, 296
Clarendon, Lord, 3
Claringbould, J. E., 37
Clausen, C. C., 98, 190, 305–6
Clemenceau, Georges, 176
Clémentel, Étienne, 177, 195
Cleminson, H. M., 116
Coal—Bunker control, 133, 158–64, 215–16, 235, 247, 316; see also country headings
Coates, A. G., 193
Cochin, Denys, 137, 145, 183, 232, 322
Cold, C. M. T., 47, 49, 97, 140, 296, 330
Comité Permanent Internationale d'Action Économique, 180, 322
Commission for the Relief of Belgium. See Belgium
Commission Internationale des Contingents, 181
Compensation Trade. See Germany, Trade negotiations with neutrals, and Sweden, Transit trade to Russia
Consett, Montagu W. W. P., 161, 249
Continuous Voyage, 4–5, 7, 22–23, 67–68, 131–32, 182, 184, 246
Contraband of War, 3–7, 9–11, 21–23, 25–28, 30, 40, 49, 51–55, 62, 66–68, 81, 85, 117, 182–84, 245–46, 251; cotton as contraband, 126–29, 310–11
Cooper, R., 311
Cosnier, Henri, 195
Craigie, 183
Crawford, Richard, 129, 140, 142
Crewe, Marquess of, 101, 103, 133, 136–37, 177, 250
Crowe, Eyre, 10, 16, 30, 48, 58, 81, 98–100, 115, 119, 136, 149, 189, 225, 229, 235–36, 297, 315
Cuthbertson, Clive, 226

Dal'Olio, Alfredo, 321
Dalziel, Henry, 101, 177, 252, 302

Daneo, E., 177
Days of Grace, 292
Declaration of London, 1909, 7, 8–14, 21–28 (American attempt to secure its recognition), 42, 62, 65, 67, 132, 154, 181–85 (abrogation of), 245–46, 290
Declaration of Paris, 1856, 2–5, 8, 10, 67, 289
Delcasse, Theophile, 64, 72, 187
Dell'Abbadessa, Antonio, 322
Denmark—Allied negotiations, 44–49 (1914), 94–104 (1915), 166, 189–93 (purchasing), 236–40, 248, 250, 252; coal, 162–63; coffee controls, 171–72; consignments to Danish government, 238; cotton agreement, 97–99, 129; embargoes, 45–49, 96, 192, 296; exports to Germany, 190–93; fish, 192–93, Fragtnaevn (Shipping Committee), 239; Industriraadet (Raad), 45, 94–104, 123, 129, 237–39, 305; Merchant Guild (Grosserer Societat), 94–104, 123, 148, 227, 238–39, 305; Rigsdag debates, 238–40; rubber control, 166; shipping agreements, 47, 49, 97, 140, 296, 330; Textilfabricant-foreningen, 305; war risk insurance, 45–46
Derby, Lord, 289
Derville, 320
Desart, Lord, 290
Devonport, Lord, 102
Dillner, Gustav, 116
Doumergue, Gaston, 177

Eden, Nils, 214, 223
Embargoes—Allied co-ordination of, 57, 180–81, 322; Denmark, 45–47, 48–49, 96, 192, 296; France, 31, 80, 111, 251; Great Britain, 31, 57, 100, 111, 141, 165, 168, 220–21, 247, 251, 294; Italy, 170, 320; Netherlands, 26, 35–36, 39, 63, 89, 243–44; Norway, 53–55, 165, 208, 227, 229, 329; Sweden, 50–52, 109–10, 112, 117, 121, 219, 307
Emmott, Lord, 71, 100, 103, 133
Enemy character, 2, 22. See also Trading with the enemy legislation
Evans, Samuel, 68, 82, 246, 299

Fabre, 190
Faringdon, Lord, 133
Farup, Erik, 121
Fayle, C. Ernest, 139, 159
Federspiel, Holger, 97
Findlay, Mansfeldt, 54, 55, 104–5, 121, 158, 161, 206, 229, 233, 329
Finlay, Robert, 311
Forbes Adam, E. G., 190–91

Foss, Alex, 96–100, 189, 305, 306
Foster, George, 177
Fountain, J., 193
France—Comité de Restriction des Approvisionnement et du Commerce de l'Ennemi, 72–73, 81, 86, 89, 90, 137, 145, 170–71, 179–80, 188–91, 193, 195–96, 199, 219, 230–32, 255, 302, 308–10, 318, 322, 327; Comité des Contingents, 136; Commission des Derogations, 31, 80, 145; Criticisms of British policy, 77–78, 80–81; decrees on maritime warfare, 22, 32, 66–70, 181–85; prewar plans for economic warfare, 31; trade with neutrals, 145–46, 187–89, 195–99, 231, 238
Franco-Prussian War, 4–5
Fredholm, John, 221
Friis-Petersen, K., 206–7
Frissell, E., 221
Fromageot, Henri, 31, 81
Fryxell, Karl A., 113
Furness, Withy and Company, 161

Gallieni, Joseph S., 195
Germany—Declarations of submarine warfare, 61–63, 224; Naval Prize Code, 21, 28; overseas trade in World War I, 20, 85–88, 125, 147–48; trade with northern neutrals, 77, 123, 125–26, 132–33, 175; with Denmark, 95–99, 101–2, 190–93, 238; with Iceland, 193–94; with the Netherlands, 36, 37, 84–85, 89–91, 195–205, 252; with Norway, 205–12, 231–36, 316–17; with Sweden, 51, 110–12, 116–17, 125–26, 215, 222; Zentraleinkaufsgesellschaft, 192, 202, 205, 208, 223, 256.
Gevers, W. A. F., 85
Gilinsky, General, 321
Goeben, The and The Breslau, 147
Gout, Jean, 31, 64, 72, 81, 129, 302, 309, 315, 320, 322
Granville, Earl, 5
Granville, Lord, 322
Great Britain—Government departments and committees: Admiralty, Trade Division, 30, 159; Board of Trade, 25, 30, 38, 76, 80–81, 128, 131, 162, 164, 168, 193, 206; British Purchasing Agency (later the British and General Trading Association), 197–200; Coal Exports Committee, 159, 161; Committee of Imperial Defence, 5, 13, 14, 18, 70, 76; Contraband Committee, 30, 51, 55, 71, 125, 131, 136, 138–39, 141, 143, 145, 250; Contraband Department of the Foreign Office, 30, 136, 138, 141, 143; Cornhill Committee, 168; Cotton Licensing Committee (War Trade Department), 128; Diverted Cargoes Committee, 30; Enemy Exports Committee, 71–72; Foreign Trade Department, 137, 139, 141, 145; Licensing Committee (War Trade Department), 30–31, 71; Ministry of Blockade, 135–37; Port and Transit Executive Committee, 162; Rationing Committee (War Trade Department), 136, 138; Release of Prize Cargoes Committee, 30; Restriction of Enemy Supply Committee, 25, 30, 46, 47, 54, 139, 168, 189; War Trade Advisory Committee (War Trade Department), 136, 140, 143, 168–69, 181, 197, 237; War Trade Department, 71, 99, 100, 125, 128, 136, 139, 141, 147, 148, 302; War Trade Intelligence Department (War Trade Department), 71, 125, 136; War Trade Statistical Department (War Trade Department), 125, 136, 138, 141, 171. Subject references: Controls over goods produced in the Empire, 58, 142–44, 157–72, 215–16, 247; criticism of blockade policy in Parliament and press, 101–4, 121–22, 126–33, 150–51, 249–52, 302, 310–11; export trade to northern neutrals, 83–86, 97–98, 128, 130–31, 167–72, 302; naval plans, pre-1914, 13–18; Naval Prize Bill, 1911, 10–12; Orders in Council (Maritime), August 20, 1914, 21–26, 246; October 29, 1914, 26–29, 39, 42, 46–49, 67, 181, 246; March 11, 1915, 61–73, 80, 84–85, 95, 101–2, 110, 117, 127, 128, 131, 150, 155, 181, 184, 246, 303; March 30, 1916, 182; July 7, 1916, 181–85
Greene, Graham, 14
Grevenkop-Castenskiold, H. de, 47, 190
Grey, Edward, 8, 10, 11, 24–25, 36, 47–48, 55, 64–65, 69, 100, 106, 110–11, 114, 116, 119, 126, 128–29, 131, 137, 138, 146–47, 150, 171, 179, 203–4, 314, 321
Guichard, Louis, 81
Gustav V, King of Sweden, 114–15, 308–9, 328

Hague Conference and Conventions, 1907, 5–9, 29, 35, 149, 151–52, 154–55, 183, 290–91
Haldane, Viscount, 15
Hambro, C. J., and Son, 206, 326
Hambro, E., 116
Hamilton, Alexander, 215
Hammarskjöld, Hjalmar, 50, 114, 116–17, 214–17, 222–24, 308, 328

Hankey, Maurice P. A., 12–13, 65, 144
Hanotaux, Gabriel, 320
Hansen, Johan, 330
Haren Noman, Th. J. van, 41
Hargreaves, 159
Harwood, Kurt, 224
Hedin, Sven, 214
Heldring, Ernest, 295, 304
Hellner, J., 221
Herriot, Edouard, 174, 320
Hertslet, Cecil, 14
Hewins, W. A. S., 133, 183
Highmore, Nathaniel, 71
Hildebrand, Karl, 214, 297, 330
Hintzen, G. H., 41, 294
Hjort, Johann, 205–11, 326
Hopwood, Francis, 30, 95, 169
Horsfall, Thomas B., 289
Høst, Niels Johan, 330
House, Edward M., 25, 127
Howard, Esme, 51–52, 110, 114, 116, 158–59, 308–9
Hughes, W. M., 177, 179
Hunt, R., 250, 311
Hurst, Cecil, 15–16, 80, 138, 143, 201, 290

Iceland—Allied purchasing agreements, 193–94, 321–22, 326; trade with Germany, 193–94, 322
Ihlen, Nils C., 50, 54–55, 120, 206–11, 226, 229, 232, 234, 329
Ingenohl, Admiral von, 62
Insurance. See War Risk Insurance and Lloyd's of London
International Harvester Company, 218
International Prize Court, 1907, 8, 10, 291
Isaacs, Rufus, 11
Isvolsky, Alexandre P., 321
Italy—Agreements with northern neutrals, 87, 100; participation in the economic war, 139, 174–79, 317, 320–21, 328

Jagow, Gottlieb von, 299
Janushkevich, General, 115
Jellicoe, Admiral, 250
Joffre, Joseph J. C., 175, 196, 321, 324
Johnstone, Alan 39, 159, 202, 242, 294
Jovanović, 321
Jutland, Battle of, 1916, 202

Kahl, Friedrich, 174, 176
Keilhau, William, 53, 226
Kim, The, 82, 246, 311
King, Joseph, 150, 310
Kitchener, Lord, 321
Knudsen, Gunnar, 54
Kriege, Johannes, 149
Krogius, Lars, 119–20
Kröller, A. G., 36, 40, 198, 295, 304

Lacaze, Marie J. L., 184, 320–21
Landry, Adolphe, 320
Laneuville, M., 170
Langley, W., 104
Lansdowne, Marquess of, 102, 252
Lansing, Robert, 25–28, 127, 129, 151–52, 162
Lauritzen, D., 330
Leith, Lord, 250
Leonora, The, 69
Letters of Assurance. See Navicerting
Leverton Harris, Frederick, 71, 131–33, 189, 197, 200–203, 207–9
Levi, Rafael, 320
Liguria, The, 219
Lindman, Arvid, 116–17, 214
Linthorst, Homan, J. T., 197, 304
Lloyd George, David, 234, 255, 321
Lloyd's of London, 139, 301
London Naval Conference, 1908–1909, 8–10
Longden, 80
Lonsdale, John, 311
Loudon, J., 39, 40, 42–43, 294
Lusitania, The, 127
Luzzatti, Luigi, 320

Madsen-Mygdal, Th., 190
Maegaard, Eilert, 330
Maggiorini, 174, 320
Manen, Charlotte A. van, 198, 204
Mannheim Convention, 1868, 35
Marcus, Moritz, 221
Marcy, William L., 3
Markham, Arthur, 101, 177, 251, 311
Martens, Albert, 206
Maseng, Einar, 121, 226
Matsui, 321
Maurice, Henry J., 206–7
McKinnon Wood, Thomas, 10–11
Meat packers—See United States, meat packers
Meline, 195
Mellor, John, 138
Metin, Albert, 177, 320
Mine fields, 29, 45
Moeller, 92–93, 303–4
Mörch, Ole, 104
Moewe, The, 147
Moltke, Carl, 190
Moreau, Frederic P., 31, 64, 72, 81
Morris, Ira, 309
Mowinckel, Johan, 53
Mustad, O. and Son, 105, 225
Mygind, K., 95, 99, 100, 305

Nail, L., 177
Napoleonic Wars, 2, 76
Naval operations, World War I, 19–20, 124, 147. See also Submarine warfare

Navicerting, 135, 139–44, 229, 249, 312
Nekludov, Anatoli, 113, 115, 117–18
Netherlands, The—Allied Negotiations, 34–44 (1914), 83–94 (1915), 165, 195–205 (purchasing), 240–44 (1916), 247, 252; coal, 159, Committee for Dutch Overseas Interests, 84–85, 86, 90; Committee on Trade with Foreign Countries, 90–91; consignments to the Dutch government, 36, 90, 240–42; cotton, 88, 129; declarations of State of Siege, 294; Dutch Commerce Commission, 37–38, 40–43; embargoes, 26, 35–36, 39, 63, 89, 243–44; fish, 201–5, 252; Landbouw Export Bureau, 165, 197, 199–200, 325; Netherlands Oversea Trust (Nederlandsche Overzee Trustmaatschappij), 37, 40–44, 48, 56, 71, 83–94, 112, 116, 123–24, 129, 148, 159, 163, 165, 167, 169, 196, 201, 213, 227, 231, 233, 240–44, 247, 314, 333; N.O.T. controls over jute, 165–66, 318; over margarine, 91–94, 303; over rubber, 166–67; over tea and coffee, 91, 169–71, 319; over tin, 167; over tobacco, 90–91; protests against mail censorship, 155; Rhine transit trade, 34–35, 39; seizure of Dutch fishing vessels, 202–4, 325; shipping agreements, 36–38; smuggling, 88, 166–67, 243–44, 318
Neutral flags, misuse of, 29, 63, 299
Neutrality, declarations of—Denmark, 45; the Netherlands, 35; Norway, 54; Sweden, 50
Neutral mails, interception of. See Censorship
Nierop, F. S. van, 41
Nierstrasz, 304
Norges Bank, 53, 206, 326
North Sea, military zone, 29, 51, 54–55, 62
Norway—Allied negotiations, 52–56 (1914), 104–6 (1915), 120–22, 166–67, 205–12 (purchasing), 225–36; Canners Union, 167, 230, 329; chocolate manufacturers, 229; coal, 161, 317; coffee, 170, 319; copper, 55, 158, 231–36, 329–30; cotton, 104–5, 120, 129; embargoes, 53–55, 165, 208, 227, 229, 329; Federation of Norwegian Manufacturing and Industry, 120–21; fish, 205–12, 326; jute, 229–30; lubricating oil, 225–26; margarine, 105, 225, 328; Norwegian Trade Association, 120–21; oil and paint, 228, paper and pulp, 227–28; shipping, 106, 140, 161–62; soap, 228–29; State Committee on Trade, Industry and Shipping, 120–21; State Food Commission, 207, 229–30;

Storting debates, 54, 211, 328–30; sulfuric acid, 105, 231–32; tanners and leather manufacturers, 105, 166; tires, 105–6, 166, 229; war risk insurance, 53–54; wholesale provision merchants, 170, 230
Nully Brown, P. de, 330

Oberndorff, Alfred, 211
Olsen, H. A. N., 121
Olsen, Hjalmar, 305–6
Oppenheimer, Francis, 14, 40, 43, 196, 242, 294, 331
op ten Noort, L. P. D., 37, 41, 84, 294–95

Pact of London, September 5, 1914, 175
Page, Walter H., 24–28, 57, 65, 69, 129, 146–47, 151, 163–64, 313, 315
Palmerston, Lord, 3
Palmstierna, Erik, 214, 216–17, 223, 328
Parker, Alwyn, 30, 119, 136
Pašić, Nicholas, 321
Paus, 226
Pedersen, Harald, 229
Persson, 215
Peto, Basil E., 311
Pichon, Stephen, 320
Pohl, Admiral von, 62
Pokrovsky, N., 177
Polk, Frank, 140, 147
Pollock, E. M., 100, 131
Pont, A. Maclaine, 41
Portsmouth, Earl of, 102, 252
Postal Convention, Universal, 1878, 150–51
Posthuma, F. E., 90, 197
Postwar trade controls, plans for, 174–79, 320
Pretyman, E. G., 206
Prilejaiev, B., 177
Prior, H. P., 95
Produits similaires, 49, 220, 223
Progresso, The, 299

Ramel, Baron, 50
Rasić, 321
Rasmussen, L., 240
Rationing, forcible, 135, 137–39, 142, 224, 248–49
Rationing of Neutrals—General, 81–83, 123, 125, 131–33, 137–39, 247–48, 302; of Denmark, 97, 99–100, 238, 305; of the Netherlands, 87–88, 90, 240–43; of Norway, 104–6, 121, 225; of Sweden, 106–7, 112–13, 118, 218, 221, 223
Reay, Lord, 6
Redfield, William C., 253–54
Rees, J. D., 126, 302
Rehbein, Paul, 208, 210–11

Reinhard, K., 330
Reitsma, O., 198
Renault, Louis, 7, 9, 290
Reprisals, British Order in Council and French Decree, March, 1915, 64–73, 84, 111, 132, 181–82, 246, 299, 300
Reventlow, Ernst, 299
Rew, Henry, 197, 202
Rhine transit trade, 34–35, 39
Ribot, Alexandre, 171, 196, 199
Rijn, C. M. van, 295
Rio Tinto Company, 234
Robertson, William, 321
Roelvink, Adam, 41, 294
Roques, Pierre, 320
Rottbøll, Christian, 100, 237
Rumania—Oil and wheat, 192–93, 323
Runciman, Walter, 95, 128, 177
Ruspoli, Prince, 322
Russia—Agreements with northern neutrals, 87, 100; Committee on Restriction of Enemy Supply, 321; participation in economic warfare, 22, 177–79, 191, 193, 328; see also Sweden, transit trade to Russia
Russo-Japanese War, 5
Ruys, B. E., 294
Ryden, 215, 223

Salandra, Antonio, 321
Salmoiraghi, 320
Sandler, 328
Satow, Ernest, 7
Sazonov, Sergei, 115, 220, 321
Scandinavian co-operation, 48, 50–55, 70, 297
Scavenius, E. J. C., 46
Scheel, Arne, 208–9, 226
Schmedemann, A. G., 254
Schmiegelow, Chr., 330
Schönmeyr, C. L., 106, 116, 221
Schotte, 214
Schou, Rudolph, 97
Scott, Leslie, 11, 132
Sembat, Marcel, 177
Serjeant, O., 98
Sevastopoulo, 322
Shipping—Allied agreements with neutral shipowners, 36–38, 47, 49, 91, 97, 106, 140, 160–61, 306, 312. Controls over: British, 86, 250–51, 317; Danish, 45–46, 163, 239–40; Dutch, 36–37, 38, 84–85, 91, 163; Norwegian, 163; Swedish, 163, 217; United States, 57–59, 163. Detentions of ships and cargoes in British ports, 23, 48, 50–51, 58, 88–89, 92, 99, 107, 110, 116, 118, 138, 140–41, 171, 202–4, 216–17, 241–42, 248–49, 300, 307

Simpson, James H., 207
Sir Ernest Cassel, The, 110–11
Skinner, Robert, 140, 312, 313
Slade, Edmond, 14, 80, 140, 183
Smith, Hoke, 129
Smith, M. Lancelot, 116
Sonne, Christian, 190
Sonnino, Sidney, 321
Sperry, Charles S., 7
Spicer, G. S., 136
Springbok, The, 4
Spring Rice, Cecil, 22, 25, 26, 29, 57, 58, 126, 128, 129, 146, 150, 166, 297
Statistical evidence, 81–82, 137, 246
Statutory List—See Black Lists
Stigstad, The, 68
Stone, William J., 179
Strachie, Lord, 102
Submarine warfare, 61, 65, 85, 123, 127–28, 224, 235, 330
Sumner, Lord, 69
Sweden—Allied negotiations with, 49–52 (1914), 106–7, 109–20 (1915), 214–24 (1916), 247–48, 255; coal, 119, 159, 161, 316, 317; coffee, 170; cotton agreement, 106–7, 115, 123, 216, 218, 222; embargoes, 50–52, 109–10, 112, 117, 121, 219, 307; Food Commission, 50, 219–21; Industrikommission, 50; iron ore, 107, 110–11, 159; oil, 107, 218–19; press criticisms, 115, 120, 214, 221–23, 309; protests over mail censorship, 154–55; Riksdag debates, 114, 214–17, 222–23, 328; State Commerce Commission (Statens Handelskommission), 113, 216–18, 220, 237; tires and rubber, 166; transit trade to Russia, 50, 52, 110, 113, 115–17, 119–20, 132, 171, 220, 224, 248, 328, 330; war risk insurance, 50, 217; War Trade Law, 1916, 216, 218, 226, 237; wood pulp and pit props, 159, 162, 219
Swinderen, R. de Marees van, 36
Switzerland—Coffee, 319; rationing, 181, 314, 320; Société de Surveillance Suisse, 314

Taksuke, M., 322
Tendy, A. R., 168, 170
Tennant, H. J., 127
Tex, Cornelis A. den, 294
Théry, Eduard, 31, 72, 126, 171, 199
Thierry, J., 177, 195
Thomas, Albert, 321
Thomson, Gaston, 78
Tirpitz, Alfred von, 62, 299
Tittoni, Tommaso, 177, 321
Toepffer, D., 96
Tønder, 211
Torre, Andrea della, 320

Trading with the enemy legislation, 30–31, 75–78, 131, 135, 137, 144–48, 168, 178, 184, 313
Transito Aktiebolaget, 119–20, 217–18, 309
Treub, M. W. F., 40
Trolle, E. B., 113, 116
Turner, R. M. A. E., 98, 191

United States—Allied relations with United States businessmen; copper, 57–58, 231, 296, 329; Corn Products Refining Company, 219; cotton, 126, 128–29; International Harvester Company, 218; meat packers, 23, 47, 82, 91–93, 99, 128, 296, 303–4, 311, 316; oil, 107, 219; rubber, 166, 318; steel, 58; tanners, 166; Textile Alliance, 58, 164–65; tin, 167. Attempt to secure recognition of the Declaration of London, 21–28, 293; proposal for working arrangement on mines, neutral flags, and submarines, 64–66; protests against: black lists, 146–47, 252–53; against censorship, 151–54; against Reprisals Order in Council, 69–70; reaction to Paris Economic Conference, 1916, 179; retaliation proposals, 252–55; Working Arrangement, December 5, 1914, 57, 298

Van Alstyne, Richard W., 28, 293
Vansittart, Robert, 31, 116
Verzijl, Jan H. W., 69
Vesnić, Milenko R., 321
Vogt, Benjamin, 234
Vollenhoven, Cornelius van, 37
Vollenhoven, Joost van, 37, 41, 43, 84, 86, 88, 196–98, 201, 304

Wahlberg, Axel, 116
Walewski, Alexandre, 3
Wallenberg, Kurt, 50–51, 113, 115–16, 118–19, 220, 222
Wallenberg, Marcus, 221–22, 224
Walton, John L., 290
Ward, William, 14
Wardrop, O., 206
War risk insurance—Danish, 45–46; Norwegian, 53–54; Swedish, 50, 217
Westerman, William, 294, 304
Westman, C. G., 116, 221
Wetten, Folke P., 216
Wielemans, General, 321
Wierdsma, J. R., 295
Wilmink, Jan, 295
Wilson, Arthur, 13, 15
Wilson, Woodrow, 25, 127–28
Wrangel, A. M. H., 111

Zahle, Carl T., 238, 295
Zamora, The, 68